CATHOLICS AND NUCLEAR WAR

A Commentary on
The Challenge of Peace
The U.S. Catholic Bishops'
Pastoral Letter on War and Peace

A National Pastoral Life Center
Publication
Edited by Philip J. Murnion
Foreword by Theodore M. Hesburgh

CROSSROAD • NEW YORK

1983
The Crossroad Publishing Company
370 Lexington Avenue, New York, N.Y. 10017

Printed in the United States of America

Library of Congress Cataloging in Publication Data
Main entry under title:
Catholics and nuclear war.
    1. Catholic Church. National Conference of Catholic
Bishops. Challenge of peace—Addresses, essays, lectures.
    2. Peace (Theology)—Addresses, essays, lectures.
    3. Atomic warfare—Religious aspects—Catholic Church—
Addresses, essays, lectures.
    4. Catholic Church—Doctrines—Addresses, essays,
lectures.   I. Murnion, Philip J. (Philip Joseph)
II. Catholic Church. National Conference of Catholic Bishops.
Challenge of peace. 1983.

BX1795.A85C39   1983 Suppl.   261.8'73   83–15388
ISBN 0–8245–0600–6 (pbk.)

Catholics and Nuclear War

Contents

Foreword

When Father Philip Murnion asked me to write the Foreword to this book, I readily agreed, even though I had four other writing tasks which demanded rather immediate attention. The reason is quite simple. Of all the problems that demand priority today, the nuclear threat to humanity is, by all odds, the greatest. The fact that the American Catholic bishops have just completed their magistral pastoral letter on the subject highlights the necessity of further discussion, which they anticipated, invited, and welcomed. This book is one of the first reasoned reactions to their statement and I am delighted to be even a small part of it.

The subject is highly emotional, as evidenced by the fireworks on all sides following the publication of the bishops' pastoral. I have the uneasy feeling that many of those who criticize *The Challenge of Peace* have yet to read it in its entirety. Possibly the same may be said of those who praise it. Anyway, my advice to all who wish to engage seriously in this discussion is: Read the bishops' pastoral first—the full text is included here—and read it with an open mind, prayerfully and thoughtfully.

Now may I declare myself on the pastoral. I believe it is the finest document that the American Catholic hierarchy has ever produced, and I say this for several reasons. First, they have had the courage to address the greatest moral problem that has ever faced humanity, knowing full well that whatever they said would be open to serious criticism on all sides, especially if they seemed to disagree with our own national defense policy. They knew they would be accused of being unpatriotic, naive, meddling in something beyond their competence, further complicating an already too complicated problem.

No matter. The bishops do not cease to be citizens by becoming bishops. But, what is more important, by becoming bishops they become the spiritual and moral leaders and teachers of fifty million Catholics in the United States, one of the two great super powers in deadly conflict with the other, the Soviet Union, and the possessor of roughly half of the awesome fifty thousand nuclear warheads on earth. They knew that the nuclear threat to humanity was embedded in the history of this conflict, which was characterized by President Eisenhower, thirty years ago, as "two colossi, glaring at each other, across a nuclear abyss."

That abyss has widened, deepened, and become increasingly more dangerous over the past thirty years. Obviously, the nuclear problem is political, military, and diplomatic. But it is also inherently a moral problem of unprecedented dimensions and a spiritual problem relating not only to the well-being but to the survival of the human race.

If our spiritual and moral leaders were silent on this problem, how could they possibly speak out on all the lesser problems—important though they are—in our times? As the leader of the bishops' drafting group for the pastoral, Joseph Cardinal Bernardin, said at Notre Dame last May, "A purely political definition does not adequately identify the threat posed by modern warfare. Today, the stakes involved in the nuclear issue make it a moral issue of compelling urgency. The church must be involved in the process of protecting the world and its people from the specter of nuclear destruction. *Silence in this instance would be a betrayal of its mission.* . . . The premise of the letter is that *nuclear weapons and nuclear strategy constitute a qualitatively new moral problem.*" If this be so, and it is, how could the bishops be silent, even though they were walking into a moral mine field?

Second, the letter has another unusual challenge. Not only are the bishops facing the quintessential moral problem of our times, but in their field of reference there are practically no theological moral precedents. It is like the Supreme Court's hearing a case unlike any ever heard, anywhere, before. They used the only two possible theological precedents available, the theology of pacifism and the theology of a just war. Both were admittedly weak reeds. First, pacifism is a theological current going back to pre-Constantinian times, but it refers more to a highly idealistic, individual Christian stance than to a moral imperative of a nation state committed to the effective defense of its people. Even Gandhi had doubts about the efficacy of passive nonviolent resistance against the Nazis, and today the USSR is a much greater threat.

As to the Augustinian theology of a just war, it was elaborated in the days of bows and arrows and spears—hardly comparable to ICBMs, MXs, cruise missiles, SS-20s, and all its numerical Russian cousins. Augustine lived in a day of hand-to-hand combat, not one with the potential for the total annihilation of hundreds of millions of people in a few minutes.

Even so, the bishops used what they had in the matter of moral principles and came as close as possible to admitting that the key just-war principles of discrimination (not killing innocent civilians) and proportionality (not using force of greater magnitude than the good to be achieved in justifiable defense) are practically meaningless as applied to nuclear warfare.

Their conclusions are blunt and clear and courageous:

1. Initiation of nuclear war at any level cannot be morally justified in any perceivable situation. Nations should adhere to a "no first use" policy.
2. Limited nuclear exchanges must also be questioned, since they may not be controllable (may escalate).
3. No nuclear weapons may ever be used to destroy population centers or civilian targets. Even if the target is military or industrial, the principle of proportionality would rule out targeting if the civilian casualty toll would be too great (i.e., millions in fact).
4. Deterrence policies are morally acceptable only on a strictly conditioned basis. They must not be an end in themselves, but be a step toward realistic and progressive nuclear disarmament.
5. Immediate *bilateral and verifiable* agreements to halt the testing, production, and deployment of new nuclear weapons are supported, followed by deep cuts in the nuclear arsenals of both super powers.

Third, I admire this document because of the process that produced it. That process was almost as important, for both bishops and laity, as the document produced. The process was open, something unusual in the production of church documents. It involved experts of every possible kind: scientists, theologians, military and government officials, political and social scientists, specialists in nuclear theory and strategy, and, above all, those who both agreed and disagreed with the general direction that the document traversed. Even the bishops' drafting committee of five had opinions ranging from A to Z. There were three quite different versions, each discussed publicly by both concerned experts (including government officials) and the bishops, in anything but secret sessions. The press had its own field day which was open to all, including some bishops who definitely thought otherwise.

There were even discussions with European bishops, who tend generally to think otherwise, and with the Vatican, which was hardly unconcerned in a matter of such global importance, the subject of many papal statements from those of Pius XII through those of John Paul II, especially the latter's remarks at Hiroshima and, before that, at the United Nations Disarmament Conference.

By the end of the process, which was last May in Chicago, the document had become better and better in its precision and balance. Everyone who wanted to become involved was involved, including the pickets during the final session.

When it came to the finale, the approval of the total episcopate was practically unanimous, something almost unimaginable for a document of such monumental importance and difficulty. The few who did not agree were given full time to propose amendments and to express their disagreement before the matter came to a final vote. All of this I find remarkable and good.

The final and fourth reason I find this document so remarkable is its modesty, a quality not true of all church documents. What it asserts as binding on Catholics is fairly minimal, given the sweep of the letter. Rather than a final word on a perplexing matter, it is clearly and expressly a first word. It is a call to discussion by Christians *and others*, and it modestly attempts to place the ongoing public discussion in a framework of reason and faith. It is a call for the ultimate formation of a "Community of Conscience," as Cardinal Bernardin so well described it to our graduating seniors.

If war is too important to be left to generals, this problem is too important to be left solely to the governments involved, without serious discussion by all citizens, because in this matter we are all, willy-nilly, involved. Our survival is involved; our total future and that of the whole human race is involved. This book is an attempt to insure and facilitate such involvement in parishes, colleges, and universities, yes even in homes where mothers and fathers discuss this problem intelligently with their children. The book is also following the bishops' intent to have a discussion with a wider public that is not Catholic, but concerned, as we are.

It has often been said, by Cardinal Bernardin and others, that this is an open moment in the history of the church and of the world in which we live. Einstein said, after the discovery of atomic energy of which he was a pioneer, that from now on we must think differently about everything in this world. We did, except in that most important matter concerning our own survival as the only intelligent species we yet know of in our universe. (I except angels, in whom I believe, since they are not affected by this nuclear threat. Their crisis came earlier and they may not be uninvolved in our current crisis which at heart is a magnified version of the struggle of good and evil.)

Some scientists, like Carl Sagan with whom I am presently involved in a search for extraterrestrial intelligence, have an interesting first question to put to whatever intelligent beings we may, in the future, encounter: How were you able to develop your advanced technological civilization without destroying yourselves by nuclear warfare? Not a silly question, especially in our current situation.

One last observation on the bishops' pastoral. The bishops have been accused of thwarting the First Amendment on separation of church and state. While Thomas Jefferson coined the phrase, that is not exactly what the First Amendment said. It did say that the state should not interfere with religion, but did not say that religion should not become involved with some matters of state. In any issue of great moral concern, religion should become involved because that is its role.

* * *

Now I would ask you to allow me a personal comment, since it does affect the reaction to the bishops' pastoral that I have just given. Some have wondered why the burning concern of the past two years when for the thirty-eight years since Hiroshima and Nagasaki the deterrence of mutually assured destruction (MAD) has apparently prevented nuclear war. What finally gave birth to all the counter-nuclear forces? Is it all a Soviet plot to have us disarm unilaterally while they proceed to take over the world? This is not an idle question, but one that each one of us must answer for himself or herself. May I answer for myself? We all have our own story.

Almost two years ago, there was a November 11th "Nuclear Day" at Notre Dame and at 250 other colleges and universities. I offered Mass and preached a homily about the nuclear problem. Then one of our alumni, Dr. James Muller of Harvard and Physicians for Social Responsibility, spoke to our students on the effect of a one megaton bomb exploding over South Bend. Suddenly, the dire facts became clear in a local context.

As I walked alone back to my office, it suddenly occurred to me that all the good things I had been working on during the past thirty years were irrelevant if we did not solve this problem. Civil Rights, world hunger, development in the Third World, education, immigration and refugees, illiteracy, housing, health—all of these would be irrelevant if there were no more human beings left to have problems. All the progress I had worked so hard for could be obliterated in a few minutes if the nuclear weapons, now existing, were unleashed.

This was not just a vague possibility. They existed, fifty thousand of them, a million times the power that had obliterated Hiroshima and Nagasaki. They were positioned on delivery systems, they were hair-triggered and targeted, they could be launched, most likely by accident and computer error. If it happened, and it could, any day or night, all would be over. We would, in the span of a few moments, reverse God's good creation and our own, by wiping out for all time all that is good and beautiful on Planet Earth.

Others have their own stories. This is mine. I decided to eliminate all my other human campaigns and concentrate on this one. With some reluctance, I left the chairmanship of the Rockefeller Foundation, the Overseas Development Council, the Select Commission on Immigration and Refugee Policy, the board of the Chase Manhattan Bank, and some other positions as well.

What could one person do? The perennial question. I decided that I might bring together two groups who have not made common cause since Galileo—the religious and scientific leaders of the world. There was good reason for this. When scientific leaders speak against nuclear war, they are accused of acting with poor grace, since they created the science that produced nuclear weapons. When religious leaders speak, they are accused of being naive, not knowing what they speak of. But together? The scientists could clearly elaborate the nuclear situation and then the religious leaders could pass moral judgment on the real facts.

I will spare you the odyssey that followed, beginning a week later, after Jim Muller's talk. It has involved the important collaboration of Franz Cardinal Koenig of Vienna, several meetings in Vienna and at the Royal Society in London, two at the Pontifical Academy of Sciences at the Vatican, with Pope John Paul II present at the second meeting on September 23–24, 1982.

What happened simply is that scientists worldwide agreed to make common cause with religious leaders, even saying that there was no scientific solution to the nuclear threat; it required moral judgment that was beyond them. The first moral judgment took place in Vienna in January 14–15 of this year.

Additional meetings are planned in Kyoto with Buddhists, in Bangalore with Hindus, and in Cairo with Jews and Muslims. I am commending the two documents already elaborated to the Appendix of this book. It is noteworthy that over sixty distinguished scientists from over thirty National Academies of Sciences worldwide (more than half represented by their presidents) signed the Vatican scientific document. Six of the Academies were from Iron Curtain countries (USSR, East Germany, Bulgaria, Hungary, Poland, Czechoslovakia, Yugoslavia). Vice Chairman Velikov of the USSR attended every meeting and saw that three million copies of the scientific statement were distributed in the Soviet Union. I was asked to address an international scientific meeting of the Soviet Academy of Sciences on the subject of peace in May of this year, but, unfortunately, it was the same day as our commencement exercises at Notre Dame.

This is not a Soviet or an American problem. It is a human problem. We may continue creation or utterly destroy it. What sin could be greater? To reverse creation must be the worst blasphemy imaginable.

So we do what we can to avert disaster. The bishops have made a beginning. The authors of this book have made their contribution to what must be a continuing dialogue. We are not assured of success. Some of my fundamentalist friends have accused me of interfering with God's plan for the end of the world soon, by nuclear disaster. I disagree with them. Much as the Old and New Testament prophesies seem to track the ultimate results of nuclear disaster, it is my firm conviction that we must strive mightily to avert it. I truly believe that, like those difficult devils that resisted the disciples of Christ who tried to cast them out, this worst of all evils will ultimately be exorcized by prayer and penance. Discussion alone won't do it. But, even with prayer and penance, we must discuss, too, and try to understand the full dimensions of this evil. That is the purpose of this book.

THEODORE M. HESBURGH, c.s.c.
President
University of Notre Dame

Introduction

On May 3, 1983, 247 bishops of the United States, assembled in a Chicago hotel for a rare special meeting devoted to a single subject, voted on the final text of a pastoral letter on war and peace. Fully aware of the historic character of their action, the bishops had gone through hundreds of proposed amendments and this final step in a thirty-month process had made clear that the vast majority of them wanted their statement to offer a clear and specific moral critique of prevailing policy regarding nuclear weapons. At the same time, in an unusual move in which the body of bishops voted, then reconsidered, and finally reversed their vote on an amendment that would have left no room for any policy of nuclear deterrence, it had become equally clear that the bishops were reluctant to place themselves outside the political realities of public policy. They wanted to make a strong, moral statement that left the Catholic community within the range of practical policy alternatives.

Assured that they had achieved such a position and having disposed of all the proposed amendments, the bishops finally voted on the complete text: 238 voted to accept it and only 9 demurred.

That vote marked the end of the first stage in the history of the pastoral letter *The Challenge of Peace: God's Promise and Our Response*. Since the November 1980 annual meeting of the bishops, where a handful of bishops electrified the normally businesslike proceedings with a passionate call for moral leadership on the uniquely apocalyptic issue of nuclear arms, the bishops had gone through an extraordinary process of consultation and collegiality. The process had captured the attention of citizens and political leaders, parishioners and national hierarchies, Catholics and non-Catholics, technical and theological experts, the world over. Here was an issue and a process that transcended the boundaries that typically separate disciplines of thought, professions, churches, nations, and the religious and secular realms. Now that the process of fashioning a position is complete, the second stage of church teaching begins: disseminating the teaching throughout the U.S. Catholic community in such a way as to encourage Catholics to form their consciences and to act in light of their moral commitments. To be sure, this second stage had overlapped the first stage, as Catholics for the past two and half years discussed and debated the emerging pastoral in reaction to the published drafts and the reports in church and secular media. Yet the ultimate impact of the pastoral letter on the U.S. Catholic community and on public policy will largely depend on the extent to which it becomes the object of careful study and reflection in parishes, educational institutions, and discussion groups throughout the church.

This book is intended as an aid in this second stage. It is designed as a tool for all who wish to consider the many issues involved in the pastoral letter, and there are indeed many issues. Just as the bishops consulted experts in many disciplines, so we have assembled here for the wider public essays by experts regarding many of the specific questions that arise in the pastoral letter.

First, there are three background papers concerning: where the pastoral fits in the development of the church's teaching on nuclear weapons (David Hollenbach); the history of Catholic involvement in public policy in the United States (David O'Brien); and developments in recent U.S. foreign policy that are the context of the current debate (Peter Steinfels).

Then there are three essays on how the church forms moral judgments and relates to public policy: the sources and methods of moral judgment (Charles Curran); the relationship between church community and civil community and between principles and specific questions and policies (William Murnion); and the nature and content of this pastoral (J. Bryan Hehir).

Next, Sandra Schneiders discusses the use of scripture as a guide to moral action and Joseph Komonchak analyzes the relationship between the church and the reign of God in history.

Two competing frameworks for analysis of the Christian position on war and peace are those of pacifism and the just-war tradition. Representing alternative views on these claims are the essays by Gordon Zahn and James Finn.

The essays that follow deal with: the doctrine of deterrence which stands at the center of the current moral and policy debates (Bruce Martin Russett); and current views on the morality of the declared or implied intention to use nuclear weapons which is involved in deterrence (Richard McCormick). The relationship between the United States and the Soviet Union is the subject of the essay by George Kennan, and the relationship between the arms race and economic development within the United States and in the Third World is the subject of the paper by Lester Thurow.

Finally, the last two essays relate to the specifically religious call of the pastoral (John Haughey) and the steps toward use of the letter in the pastoral life of the church (Harry Fagan).

The essays follow the order of the pastoral, and each group of essays is introduced by a synopsis of the section of the letter to which they refer. They are not meant simply to be a commentary on what the bishops stated, and indeed the authors neither all agree with everything in the pastoral nor all agree with each other. Nor does this editor agree with all that is contained in these essays. Rather the essays are by competent authors who can illuminate the issues involved whether by explaining them or by disputing the positions taken in the letter. As such the book serves to continue the debate and build on the pastoral letter which itself, as Father Hesburgh has noted, does not claim to be the final word on the subject. The majority of the writers are themselves Catholic, though George Kennan and Lester Thurow are not. And the majority of the essays were written expressly for this collection, though those by Sandra Schneiders, George Kennan, and Richard McCormick are reprints or adaptations of earlier papers.

As context for these essays and for consideration of the pastoral, I would like to discuss briefly the significance of the pastoral letter in terms of ecclesiology, ecumenism, and evangelization.

Ecclesiology
Many of the essays examine various ingredients in the understanding of the church illustrated or asserted in the pastoral. I will not repeat what these authors have written. Rather, I would like to underscore some of the qualities of the church implicit or explicit in both the process of developing the pastoral and the positions taken by the pastoral. As Father Hesburgh has noted in the Foreword, the process used by the bishops with its extensive consultation sets a new standard for the

articulation of church teaching, undoubtedly a standard to which appeal will be made by people in the church regarding many other issues.

Furthermore, as the process developed, it became clear that the Committee on War and Peace was trying to steer a course between what might be called a "prophetic" approach and an "accommodationist" approach. Bishops and others who adopt the "prophetic" approach were inclined to move directly from biblical injunctions against use of the sword to either pacifism or at least a kind of nuclear pacifism that allowed for no compromises in matters of policy. The "accommodationist" approach was inclined to limit episcopal teaching to general statements about the work for peace and to leave to the political or military experts judgments about details in weapons policy. The former approach placed emphasis on the universal family of humanity while the latter emphasized the moral precedence of Western democracy over Soviet Communism. The committee and ultimately the pastoral diligently tried to avoid the fundamentalism of the former and the chauvinism of the latter. For the letter refuses to simplify the issues and insists on relating the teaching of the church both to specific details of weapons and policy development and to the practical steps of policy formation. As such, the pastoral is a classic of the characteristically Catholic approach to moral judgment and the exercise of moral responsibility.

In the consultation process, therefore, the committee drew on the tradition of Gospel and church, the contributions of experts—technical, political, and theological—and the views of the members of the church. This approach reflects the current attempt so to bring together these three elements of authority as to avoid the distortions that are: traditionalism (simply preserving and rehearsing the past without allowing for development in understanding), professionalism (simply handing over to experts the judgments that are never simply technical or theological), and populism (simply appealing to prevailing currents of opinion). Some have lamented, as a result, that the pastoral is insufficiently prophetic. Leaving aside, however, the Catholic style of forming moral teaching which I have already noted, there is also some tension between prophecy and consultation. Prophets are not known to consult; nor are consultative processes notoriously prophetic. To choose to consult thereby means that the outcome will not be strictly prophetic.

If the pastoral reflects such an explicitly Catholic style of teaching, it raises other questions which will be with us for some time. Thus the pastoral raises questions about the teaching authority of a national conference of bishops. Catholic tradition provides for the teaching authority of the pope, an ecumenical council, and an individual ordinary of a diocese. Discussion has already begun on the relationship of an episcopal conference to these centers of teaching authority. Secondly, the mode of teaching, with its clear distinctions among principles, the teaching of popes and councils, and specific applications of principles to policies and practices—distinctions made to allow for differences of judgment and opinion regarding applications of principles—will surely be cited by others regarding other issues in the church. Further discussion along these lines will surely affect Catholic understanding of the nature of church teaching.

It is undoubtedly this latter distinction that accounts in part for the final vote, with so few bishops remaining opposed to the pastoral. For the fact that the pastoral does not claim the weight of episcopal authority for all of its specific judgments (e.g., regarding the "no-first-use" policy or a bilateral "freeze") not only leaves to individual Catholics the right to make their own judgments of conscience but also allowed bishops who harbored doubts and disagreements about some of the pastoral's conclusions to support the publication of the pastoral in its present form. One unfortunate result of this distinction is that some bishops and others have used it to allay fears of those who oppose the pastoral and to minimize the impact of the pastoral's judgments. In fact, such a distinction places a burden on the individual Catholic to go through a process of forming his or her own conscience, making his or her own prudential judgments, attentive, however, to the same principles and processes of judgment exemplified in the letter as well as to the fact that the bishops had an extraordinarily rich opportunity to examine all the issues most carefully.

The pastoral is of great significance, therefore, for its illumination of elements in Catholic style and questions about church structure.

Ecumenism

It is perhaps the essay by my brother, William Murnion, that most illuminates the ecumenical nature of this exercise in teaching, though he never uses the word "ecumenical," for that essay challenges even the pastoral's restricted distinction between the Catholic community and the wider human community, both of which the bishops hope to address. But the evidence of the ecumenical impact of the document is already abundant. Many bishops have reported that, during the process of the pastoral, a considerable portion of their mail (in some instances, the majority) came from non-Catholics expressing support for what the bishops were doing. Since the completion of the pastoral, there have been many votes of support by assemblies of various denominations and the newly united Presbyterian Church has voted to send a copy of the pastoral to all of its over 13,000 congregations. The pastoral seems to have offered a concrete possibility for bringing together a moral community in support of a common commitment.

A caution needs to be registered, however, regarding the appeal of the pastoral to a community far broader than that within the boundaries of Catholic church membership. And it is this. Concern about the threat of nuclear catastrophe brings together people with very diverse grounds for concern. Some are concerned, naturally enough, because they fear the prospect that deliberate or accidental use of the weapons will destroy all they have, their possessions, society as we know it, and their very lives. It is perhaps because such fear requires investment in present conditions of life that the anti-nuclear movement has been largely middle-class. The pastoral, however, and the position of others opposing the possession and use of nuclear arms on moral grounds, places priority not on the risk to our lives, possessions, and culture, but on our moral commitment. The issue at stake in the pastoral and moral posture is (as stated in the report of the Church of England cited by Richard McCormick below) not "whether we will die for our beliefs but whether we will kill for them." The elements of the dilemma are not those assumed in the statement "Better Red than dead," but those involved in the choice "Better Red than an indiscriminate killer." Thus, while there may be common cause among those trying to turn back the race to extinction, there may not be common grounds.

Evangelization

Finally, and paradoxically in light of what I have said about the ecumenical significance of the pastoral, the letter could be of great significance regarding the evangelizing mission of the church. For just as the Acts of the Apostles records that people became curious about the early followers of Jesus because of their way of life, so in our own time people may become curious about the kind of church that would produce such a document. What kind of faith and view of life lies behind a position like this? What kind of church takes such an approach to the relations between faith and world? What kind of people is it that sees the relationship between complex political strategies of shaping a just and humane policy and the simple religious actions of fasting and prayer? What kind of church is it that insists on the universal fellowship of all people as the ultimately necessary context for the policies of sovereign states? It may well be that, in pursuit of such curiosity, people will be led to think again about the relationships between the Gospel and modern life, between conscience and citizenship, between the church and modern society. It would be tragic, therefore, if church leadership were to backpedal from this pastoral or were to do little to further local discussion or to encourage public action, thus raising suspicions about the sincerity of the undertaking.

The positions any of us adopt regarding the matter of nuclear policy will depend heavily on profound questions of our deepest convictions and sentiments. This has become clearer and clearer to me as I talk with people who take contrary positions. The intellectual instruments offered here are just that, instruments for elaborating the intimations of our hearts and for exercizing the responsibilities of our convictions. They cannot substitute for our taking stock of where our treasure and security lie or make sense if we do not believe that we already share the imperishable life of the Spirit. Thus, one hope I have for this volume is that by clearing away some of the intellectual underbrush the authors may bring us ever closer to the ground of our positions and the roots of our stances.

In closing, I dedicate this volume to those whose leadership brought the pastoral to completion. Among them are the bishops who first called their brothers to exercise moral leadership on this issue, the bishops and especially Bishop Thomas Gumbleton who appealed for a new statement on war and peace at the bishops' meeting in 1980. Included also are all the bishops of the National Conference of Catholic Bishops, particularly the ad hoc Committee on War and Peace and its consultants. Most especially I dedicate this volume to Joseph Cardinal Bernardin whose leadership as chairman of the committee has been widely recognized as having been crucial at every stage of the process.

My personal thanks also go: to all the authors who contributed so readily and generously to this effort; to Father Theodore Hesburgh for both his Foreword and the scientific and religious statements that have resulted from his global efforts and which are included in the Appendix; to James Jennings for the synopses of the pastoral; and to Richard Payne who first conceived this volume and invited my editorship of it. The National Pastoral Life Center, devoted to serving the pastoral ministry of the church, is pleased to collaborate with The Crossroad Publishing Company on the project.

PHILIP J. MURNION
Director
National Pastoral Life Center

I

The Background of the Pastoral Letter on War and Peace

DAVID HOLLENBACH

The Challenge of Peace in the Context of Recent Church Teachings

In their pastoral letter on war and peace the American Catholic bishops seek to address the urgent moral questions posed by the threat of nuclear war from the vantage point of Christian faith and the church's long tradition of ethical reflection. The two and a half years devoted to the preparation of the letter involved the bishops in a host of religious, philosophical, historical, political, and military issues of great complexity. The significance and success of the outcome can therefore be evaluated from a number of perspectives. This essay will analyze and assess the letter from a single, somewhat limited point of view. It will situate the letter in the context of the official teachings of the Catholic church on war and peace since World War II and outline the distinctive contributions of the letter to developing Catholic thought. This limited task can provide a first step in the larger project of determining the overall contribution of the letter.

Though the question of the relation between the views expressed in the letter and the official teachings of the church since 1945 is a limited one, it seems to have been very much on the minds of its drafters and the bishops' conference as a whole. Several explicit discussions of this relation are contained in the document itself. For example, in outlining the basis on which the pastoral letter proposes guidance for Christian conscience and public policy, the bishops state that they draw heavily on Vatican II's Pastoral Constitution on the Church in the Modern World. They add that "for similar reasons we draw heavily upon the popes of the nuclear age, from Pope Pius XII through Pope John Paul II."[1]

They go on to add, however, that they intend to bring their own distinctive contribution to the debate rather than simply to reaffirm the conclusions of the council and recent popes.

> The teaching of popes and councils must be incarnated by each local church in a manner understandable to its culture. This allows each local church to bring its unique insights and experience to bear on the issues shaping our world. From 1966 to the present American bishops, individually and collectively, have issued numerous statements on the issues of peace and war, ranging from the Vietnam War to conscientious objection and the use of nuclear weapons. These statements reflect not only the concerns of the hierarchy, but also the voices of our people who have increasingly expressed to us their alarm over the threat of war. In this letter we wish to continue and develop the teaching on peace and war which we have previously made, and which reflects both the teaching of the universal church and the insights and experience of the Catholic community of the United States.[2]

The pastoral letter, then, sets out to interpret the recent teachings of councils and popes in light of American experience and insight.

That the bishops' decision to do more than reiterate conciliar and papal teaching was quite self-conscious is evident from a comparison of the above quoted paragraph from the final version of the document with the paragraph from the third draft which it replaced. The third draft had described the relation between the bishops' teaching and that of recent Roman statements this way:

> We make our own their [the popes'] teaching and that of the council, while in consonance with such teaching we add observations born of the experience of the church in the United States.[3]

The differences between these two paragraphs is significant. They show that the final version of the pastoral letter acknowledges that it intends not only "to continue" but also "to develop" the recent teachings of the church on war and peace. The final document goes beyond "adding observations" related to the American experience to making a distinctive American contribution to the understanding of the church as a whole.

The contribution of the letter to such ecclesial understanding can be made more explicit by comparing it with conciliar and papal teaching since World War II on three points: its basic perspective toward the morality of war, the moral norms proposed concerning the use of nuclear weapons, and the complex question of the morality of deterrence policy.

Basic Perspective on the Morality of War and Peace

Pius XII was the first pope of the nuclear age and therefore the first to address the problem of warfare in light of the nuclear threat. Pius XII stood firmly in the just-war tradition which for centuries has been linked with the Catholic moral tradition. The advent of the new dangers posed by modern total warfare, including atomic, biological, and chemical warfare, did not lead Pius XII to question the just-war tradition's argument that the use of force could sometimes be a tragic necessity. Pius XII argued forcefully that Christians are called by both faith and reason to the pursuit of peace. But this peace must be firmly based on justice. Therefore, the Christian commitment to peace does not imply an acquiescence in the perpetration of injustice by an aggressive nation. Governments have an obligation to protect their citizens against injustice by resisting such aggression, even by the use of force. The pastoral letter cites Pius XII's unambiguous words on this issue:

> A people threatened with an unjust aggression, or already its victim, may not remain passively indifferent, if it would think and act as befits a Christian. . . . Among (the) goods (of humanity) some are of such importance for society that it is perfectly lawful to defend them against unjust aggression. Their defense is even an obligation for the nations as a whole, who have a duty not to abandon a nation that is attacked.[4]

This right of self-defense was reiterated by the Second Vatican Council and was recently strongly reaffirmed by Pope John Paul II in his 1982 World Day of Peace Message. The most notable point in the citation of Pius XII, however, is the insistence on the *duty* of states to resist aggression and the violation of basic human rights. The existence of such a duty was the basis of Pius XII's rejection of the legitimacy of conscientious objection to all war as a position open to Catholics.[5] For if states have a duty to resist aggression, and citizens have a duty to serve the common good of their country, then it is difficult to see how one can affirm a right to conscientious objection to all participation in warfare.

It is interesting, therefore, that the pastoral letter has drawn on this aspect of the teaching of Pius XII while, at the same time, affirming that conscientious objection is a legitimate position within the framework of Catholic teaching. The legitimacy of conscientious objection was affirmed by the Second Vatican Council and again by the American bishops' own 1968 pastoral letter, *Human Life in Our Day*. These earlier affirmations are cited with approval by *The Challenge of Peace*.[6] The bishops affirm both the duty to resist aggression and the right not to so resist.

One way to deal with this apparent contradiction is to note that the pastoral letter assigns the duty to resist evil to governments and the right to conscientious objection to individuals.[7] Also it is clearly and forcefully argued by the pastoral letter that armed force may be used to resist injustice only under the stringent conditions of the just-war norms and that non-violent means must first have been exhausted. However, the pastoral letter has developed a perspective on the relation between just-war theory and non-violence which goes beyond these distinctions between governmental duties and individual rights on the one hand and the last resort of force and the preferable option of non-violent resistance on the other.

The most significant development contained in the letter's basic perspective on the morality of war and peace is its argument that the just-war ethic and the ethic of non-violence are interrelated approaches and are not simply to be juxtaposed as contradictory alternatives. In affirming this the bishops state that they are putting forward "Catholic teaching":

> Catholic teaching sees these two distinct moral responses as having a complementary relationship, in the sense that they both seek to serve the common good. They differ in their perception of how the common good is to be defended most effectively, but both responses testify to the Christian conviction that peace must be pursued and rights defended within moral restraints and in the context of defining other basic human values.[8]

It is certainly true that the Catholic social tradition, which the pastoral letter sees as "a mix of biblical, theological and philosophical elements which are brought to bear upon the concrete problems of the day," will sustain this conclusion.[9] However, it is clear that the pastoral's position on the complementarity of the just-war ethic and the ethic of non-violence had not been affirmed previously in these explicit terms in the conciliar and papal teaching since World War II.

The United States bishops are aware that they are breaking new ground in affirming this interdependence of just-war and pacifist perspectives in the contemporary situation. The impetus for such development comes from the conditions of the "new moment" in which we are located—a moment characterized by the massive destructive potential of nuclear weapons and by the new public perception of the dangers of these weapons.[10] In the face of both the threats and possibilities of the present situation the pastoral letter states:

> The task before us is not simply to repeat what we have said before; it is first to consider anew whether and how our religious-moral tradition can assess, direct, contain, and, we hope, help to eliminate the threat posed to the human family by the nuclear arsenals of the world.[11]

Here the bishops explicitly echo the call of the Second Vatican Council "to undertake a completely fresh reappraisal of war."[12] They go beyond the council, however, in proposing their own understanding of the basic moral perspectives to which such a fresh reappraisal should lead:

> While the just-war teaching has clearly been in possession for the past 1,500 years of Catholic thought, the "new moment" in which we find ourselves sees the just-war teaching and non-violence as distinct but interdependent methods of evaluating warfare. They diverge on some specific conclusions, but they share a common presumption against the use of force as a means of settling disputes.
>
> Both find their roots in the Christian theological tradition; each contributes to the full moral vision we need in pursuit of a human peace. We believe the two perspectives support and complement one another, each preserving the other from distortion.[13]

It seems clear that the bishops have been led to this conclusion by the particular form that the nuclear debate has taken in the United States in recent years. Their letter argues the case for the mutual complementarity of just-war theory and pacifism within the church on both biblical and theological grounds. The need for both positions to be present within the church is the result of the tension between justice and peace in a world in which the kingdom of God has not yet been fully established.[14] But the American debate on the nuclear question has been the occasion of the emergence of an articulate pacifist movement within the Catholic church in the United States. The bishops' involvement in this debate has convinced them that the pacifist commitment to the non-violent defense of justice should be granted new status as an expression of the deepest concerns of Catholic tradition.

The pastoral letter does limit the absolute rejection of the use of force to individuals and leaves open the limited right of governments to resort to arms. Nevertheless, the complementarity of the two moral perspectives has had a significant impact on how the United States bishops formulate their understanding of the just-war theory itself. The link which binds the two perspectives together and prevents them from being simply contradictory is the presumption they share against the use of force. This strong presumption against war is the central thread of the Christian tradition on the morality of warfare *both* for individuals *and* for governments. The bishops affirm that "the moral theory of the 'just-war' or 'limited-war' doctrine begins with the presumption which binds all Christians: We should do no harm to our neighbors; how we treat our enemy is the key test of whether we love our neighbor; and the possibility of taking even one human life is a prospect we should consider in fear and trembling."[15] The suggestion that non-violence is the norm and that the legitimacy of the resort to force must be seen as an exception to be justified in every case is an important new emphasis of a perspective which is at the heart of Catholic tradition. The "new moment" brought about by public understanding of the nuclear threat has led the bishops to make a significant contribution to the clarification and understanding of this tradition for the church as a whole.

Moral Norms Regarding the Use of Nuclear Weapons

In the papal and conciliar discussions of war and peace since World War II the catastrophic effects of the massive use of nuclear weapons have been a constant matter of deep concern. Denunciation of the arms race and appeals to turn back from the precipice of destruction is a central theme of this recent teaching. However, the post-Hiroshima teachings have been less detailed than one might expect in addressing the question of whether nuclear weapons might ever be legitimate means in the conduct of warfare.

Pius XII, for example, frequently referred to the grave dangers attendant on the use of these weapons. In 1953 he reaffirmed the just-war position that a nation would be called upon to "suffer injustice" if the only effective means of resistance would violate just-war norms.[16] In the same address, however, he left unresolved the question of whether all uses of nuclear weapons would come under this judgment.

> What we have just discussed applies especially to ABC warfare— atomic, biological and chemical. As to the question of knowing whether it (ABC warfare) can become clearly necessary in self-defense against ABC warfare, let it suffice for Us to have posed it here.[17]

A year later Pius XII was somewhat more specific. He affirmed that the use of nuclear weapons without just cause is a "crime." This statement implies that there might possibly be circumstances in which such a just cause would justify use. However, the pope recognized that any use of nuclear weapons involving "such an extension of evil that it entirely escapes the control of man" must be rejected as immoral. Any use of these weapons which produces "the pure and simple annihilation of all human life within the radius of action . . . is not permitted for any reason whatsoever."[18]

In the writings of Pius XII we see foreshadowed an uncertainty about the morality of the use of nuclear weapons which has resurfaced in the debate leading up to and following the American bishops' pastoral. Relying on just-war norms, Pius XII condemned all forms of unlimited warfare, especially the indiscriminate use of nuclear, bacteriological, and chemical warfare. At the same time, the pope was hesitant to conclude that *every* use of nuclear weapons must be indiscriminate. This argument has become more heated and pointed with the development of a variety of tactical, intermediate range, and precision-guided strategic nuclear weapons which are alleged to be discriminate enough to destroy military forces without falling under the condemnation of those uses of force which "entirely escape the control of man." The issue which Pius XII faced and was unable to answer was debated at length by the American bishops: can *any* use of nuclear weapons be reasonably expected to remain discriminate and limited?

Pope John XXIII approached this issue also, though with a similarly ambiguous result. In *Pacem in Terris* he stated:

> In an age such as ours, which prides itself on its atomic energy, it is contrary to reason to hold that war is now a suitable way to restore rights which have been violated.[19]

This statement, taken literally, suggests that no use of force, let alone the use of nuclear weapons, could ever be justified in the nuclear age. From the body of John XXIII's writings, however, it is clear that this conclusion was not meant by him as an apodictic one. Nor did John XXIII enter into a detailed analysis of the morality of the use of nuclear weapons, the circumstances of such use, or the different kinds of nuclear weapons available for use in the arsenals of the world.

The most clear-cut statement on this question of use is that contained in the pastoral constitution of Vatican II. The council affirmed one of the strongest norms of the just-war theory—that of discrimination or non-combatant immunity from direct attack—in a way clearly relevant to the issue of the use of nuclear weapons.

> Any act of war aimed indiscriminately at the destruction of entire cities or of extensive areas along with their population is a crime against God and humanity itself. It merits unequivocal and unhesitating condemnation.[20]

This pronouncement was one of the few clear condemnations made by the council. It is a direct application of the just-war norm of discrimination. However, it does not settle the hard cases about nuclear war fighting. Can there be a discriminate and proportionate use of nuclear weapons? Can there be a use of nuclear weapons which will succeed in achieving justice? Can there be a use of nuclear weapons which remains within human control and therefore satisfies the just-war demand that any marginally justifiable war must be limited and conducted by legitimate authority?

The pastoral letter makes its own the council's clear conclusion when it states that any use of nuclear weapons directly targeted against population centers—even in retaliation—must be condemned. The bishops personalize this position when they affirm, "No Christian can rightfully carry out orders or policies deliberately aimed at killing non-combatants."[21] The reference here to carrying out both "orders" and "policies" suggests that the bishops intend this conclusion to be carefully considered not only by soldiers and military personnel but also by Christians in governmental service at whatever level.

The recent teachings of popes and council, therefore, do not provide either comprehensive analysis or detailed moral guidance on the key debate today about the use of nuclear weapons: can use be discriminate and proportionate? John Paul II, in his sermon at Coventry Cathedral, stated:

> Today, the scale and horror of modern warfare—whether nuclear or not—makes it totally unacceptable as a means of settling differences between nations.[22]

Despite the ringing quality of this statement, it is clear from John Paul II's support of the right of self-defense that he did not mean it to be taken literally. John Paul's eloquent statements on these questions are more valuable for their homiletic than for their analytic quality.

The American bishops' letter is, in fact, the first official Catholic church analysis of the issue of the morality of the use of nuclear weapons that seeks to make careful distinctions between different ways these weapons might be used and to draw appropriate conclusions for public policy. *The Challenge of Peace* engages the public debate on three crucial points.

First, it resoundingly rejects the use of nuclear weapons against population centers. Here it is in continuity with the modern just-war theory, with Pius XII and Vatican II. *Second*, it strongly rejects any first use of nuclear weapons, no matter how just the cause or how careful the intent that such first use be kept limited within just-war norms. The bishops reach this conclusion on the basis of their judgment that "the danger of escalation is so great that it would be morally unjustifiable to initiate nuclear war in any form."[23] *Third*, they express their extreme skepticism about the possibility that *any* use of nuclear weapons can be kept limited.[24] Therefore, though they do not apodictically condemn all possible uses of nuclear weapons, they do state that the risk entailed by any such use is so great that there is "no moral justification for submitting the human community to this risk."[25] The pastoral letter, then, is a more nuanced and careful treatment of the issue of the use of nuclear weapons than can be found in other church teachings since World War II.

The American bishops' conclusions are not all of equal weight. In pre–Vatican II theology it was common to assign so-called "theological notes" to various positions contained within church teachings. Some positions were judged to be at the core of Christian belief, others to be important expressions of Christian faith in a particular social or cultural context. The "notes" attributed to different conclusions were an indication of their place on this scale of importance. I read the American bishops' letter as assigning the following notes to their conclusions on the various possible uses of nuclear weapons:

> Use against population centers, even in retaliation: *resoundingly rejected*;
> First use, even in a just cause: *strongly rejected*;
> Any use, even in defense of justice and human rights: rejected as an *unacceptable risk*.

In situating *The Challenge of Peace* in the context of recent church teaching, one thing becomes clear about its discussion of the use of nuclear weapons. It is at once more forceful and more nuanced than any of the documents produced by the popes or the council in the years since World War II. The care with which the actual dilemmas about the use of nuclear weapons have been approached is one of the most important results of the bishops' serious engagement in the current American debate.

The Morality of Deterrence Policy

There are two key statements which set the larger church context for the American bishops' discussion of the morality of deterrence: the pastoral constitution of the Second Vatican Council and the message of John Paul II to the Second Special Session of the United Nations General Assembly on Disarmament. The council acknowledged the dangers inherent in the possession of nuclear weapons for purposes of deterrence and appealed for a reversal of the arms race. It did not, however, reach a specific conclusion on the morality of deterrence as such.

> This accumulation of arms, which increases every year, also serves, in a way heretofore unknown, as a deterrent to possible enemy attack. Many regard this state of affairs as the most effective way by which peace of a sort can be maintained at the present time. Whatever be the case with this method of deterrence, all people should be convinced that the arms race in which so many countries are engaged is not a safe way to preserve a steady peace.[26]

John Paul II also spoke forcefully of the dangers of the arms race. Like the council he stopped short of condemning the possession of nuclear weapons for purposes of deterrence. Indeed, his message to the United Nations Special Session went beyond the council in explicitly accepting the legitimacy of deterrence, provided such possession was in the context of serious efforts at disarmament.

> In current conditions "deterrence" based on balance, certainly not as an end in itself but as a step on the way toward a progressive disarmament, may still be judged morally acceptable. Nonetheless in order to ensure peace, it is indispensable not to be satisfied with this minimum which is always susceptible to the real danger of explosion.[27]

The difficulty faced by both the council and the pope in addressing deterrence can be stated simply. Nuclear deterrence strategies rest on a threat to do something which is itself immoral or which runs an unreasonable risk of violating moral norms, i.e., a threat to use nuclear weapons. Catholic moral thought has always maintained that to intend an immoral act is itself immoral, even if the act is not in fact carried out. This would seem to imply that nuclear deterrence strategies should be condemned. However, if one were to condemn deterrence and follow through with the implications of this condemnation, then one should also call for immediate nuclear disarmament, even unilateral nuclear disarmament. The fear that unilateral disarmament could occasion either the outbreak of war or the loss of freedom and human rights led both the council and John Paul II to stop short of such a condemnation. John Paul II went beyond Vatican II, however, in subjecting his "acceptance" of deterrence to a significant moral condition: it must be "a step on the way toward progressive disarmament."

The United States bishops faced this same dilemma. They accepted the basic structure of John Paul II's position. But they faced a further problem which has arisen in the context of the United States policy debate. A number of new weapons systems are currently being developed and deployed for the alleged purpose of encouraging the Soviet Union to make concessions in arms-control negotiations. Thus the bishops were concerned that John Paul II's position, left as it stands, could provide legitimacy for an escalating arms race. This they clearly did not want to do, for some of these new weapons threaten to destabilize the nuclear balance and thus to increase the likelihood of nuclear war.

The pastoral letter goes beyond the position of John Paul II by entering into an analysis of different types of deterrence policies, together with the weapons systems and targeting doctrines associated with these policies. Like the pope, the United States bishops are willing conditionally to accept the legitimacy of deterrence. But the conditions they set are considerably more detailed and stringent than are the pope's. The bishops state that "any claim by any government that it is pursuing a morally acceptable policy of deterrence must be scrutinized with the greatest care."[28] They enter into such a process of careful scrutiny of United States policy and apply John Paul II's basic position through their "own prudential judgments." The conditions they set down exclude so-called "war-fighting" strategies, the quest for superiority, and all weapons systems which make disarmament more difficult to achieve. This leads them to oppose first-strike weapons and strategies which lower the nuclear threshold.[29] These conditions provide considerably more guidance for the evaluation of the morality of deterrence than previous conciliar or papal statements. They represent another major contribution of the letter. They show just how marginal a Christian "acceptance" of deterrence must be.

Conclusion

One can conclude that the deepest significance of the way the American bishops have related Catholic teaching since World War II to the nuclear challenge is that they have in fact proposed a clear development in this tradition. They believe that this development is needed if Christians are to "assess, direct, contain and, we hope, help to eliminate the threat to the human family."[30] The pastoral letter is therefore a genuinely prophetic document. And as in all prophetic speech which is rooted in concern for God's people rather than in self-righteousness, it is an appeal made both in humility and with the courage to present the reasons which support its challenging message. It is clear that not everyone, not even all Christians, are in agreement with all the conclusions of the pastoral letter. Some would like to see a greater willingness to accept present governmental strategies, while others would urge a complete rejection of all warfare and the entire system of nuclear deterrence. The American bishops state their openness to ongoing dialogue with these views. But their letter is no middle of the road document that seeks to split the difference between the views found within the church today. It is a prophetic advance and a call to the whole church to a significant new development in its centuries-old tradition of moral-religious reflection and action.

NOTES

1. *The Challenge of Peace: God's Promise and Our Response*, # 64.
2. Ibid.
3. *The Challenge of Peace*, Third Draft, *Origins* 12 (April 14, 1983), p. 704, col. 3.
4. Pius XII, Christmas Message 1948, cited in *The Challenge of Peace*, # 76.
5. Pius XII, Christmas Message 1956, in Vincent A. Yzermans, ed., *The Major Addresses of Pope Pius XII*, vol. II (St. Paul: North Central Publishing Co., 1961), p. 225. For an analysis of this papal message see John Courtney Murray, *Morality and Modern War* (New York: Council on Religion and International Affairs, 1959).
6. *The Challenge of Peace*, # 118.
7. See ibid., # 75.
8. Ibid., # 74.
9. Ibid., # 14.
10. Ibid., #s 124–25.
11. Ibid., # 122.
12. Ibid.
13. Ibid., #s 120–21.
14. See ibid., # 60.
15. Ibid., # 80.
16. Pius XII, Address to the International Office of Documentation for Military Medicine, 19 October 1953, in *Peace and Disarmament: Documents of the World Council of Churches and the Roman Catholic Church* (Vatican City: Tipographica Poliglotta Vaticana, 1982), p. 128.
17. Ibid.
18. Pius Xii, Address to the Eighth Congress of the World Medical Association, 30 September 1954, in *Peace and Disarmament*, p. 131. This passage is cited in *The Challenge of Peace*, # 147.
19. John XXIII, *Pacem in Terris*, no. 127, in David J. O'Brien and Thomas A. Shannon, eds., *Renewing the Earth: Catholic Documents on Peace, Justice and Liberation* (Garden City: Doubleday, 1977), p. 154.
20. *Gaudium et Spes*, no. 80.
21. *The Challenge of Peace*, # 148.
22. John Paul II, Homily at Coventry Cathedral, 30 May 1982, no. 2, in *Origins* 12 (1982), p. 55.
23. *The Challenge of Peace*, # 152.
24. Ibid., # 159.
25. Ibid.
26. *Gaudium et Spes*, no. 80.
27. John Paul II, Message to the Second Special Session of the United Nations General Assembly Devoted to Disarmament (June 1982), 8.
28. *The Challenge of Peace*, # 195.
29. Ibid., # 190.
30. Ibid., # 122.

DAVID J. O'BRIEN
American Catholics and American Society

"Congress shall make no law respecting the establishment of religion or prohibiting the free exercise thereof." Disestablishment and free exercise, separation of church and state and religious liberty, enshrined in the First Amendment to the American Constitution, seem to lie at the very heart of the American experiment. During the revolutionary bicentennial, historian Henry Steele Commager noted that religious liberty, freedom of conscience, was the first and most essential of all rights, for from it flow freedoms of speech, of press, of assembly, and all the rest. At the same time, Lutheran sociologist Peter Berger told a Catholic audience that its church stood as the foremost defender of the idea that men and women have rights independent of the state. In the decade that will witness the two hundredth anniversary of the Constitution, it appears that liberty in matters of religion and the separation of church and state stand forth as central tenets of the American way of life requiring the support of all churches and all citizens.

Yet the opposite seems to be the case as religious antagonists battle over such "moral issues" as abortion and school textbooks, churches contend for public support for education and charity, and religious groups from the Moral Majority to the Roman Catholic bishops offer vigorous, usually critical, comments on public policies. Religious liberty remains an experiment and church-state separation, far from settling the question, structures a continuing conversation about religion and public life. Many strong supporters of separation, nevertheless, believe that society requires some common values, if not common beliefs, to be shaped by voluntary action. Many also believe, with equal conviction, that churches have a right and obligation to offer judgments on public policy. Most important of all, American churches have long recognized that politics flows from the beliefs, values, perceptions, and attitudes of the people; if religion can influence these through private and voluntary action, its influence will permeate the political culture and direct the course of public policy. This is what the nineteenth-century European commentator Alexis de Tocqueville meant when he wrote that "religion in America takes no direct part in the government of society, but nevertheless it must be regarded as the foremost of the political institutions of that country."

Few Americans have ever been comfortable with the prospect of religious establishment, but neither have they been sympathetic to the idea that public policies are beyond criticism, or exempt from opposition from churches or church members. Indeed, many have held the more positive view that Christian churches of their very nature are required not simply to oppose un-Christian policies but to participate in shaping policies and institutions which reflect the beliefs and ideals of the American people, beliefs and ideals they regard as gounded in the Christian inheritance. And all believe that by worshiping God, expressing their beliefs in public, educating their children, seeking converts, and inspiring their members to share in the responsibilities of public life, in short by being the church, they make an authentic contribution to the well-being of the nation.

The Catholic Problem

In this context, it is not hard to understand why Catholicism seemed to pose a special problem. Disestablishment and free exercise required vigorous voluntary effort to develop and maintain a Christian consensus, and that seemed plausible only within a broad Christian, even evangelical, understanding of faith and church. Like the American of recent times who wondered whether the United States could tolerate the presence of subversives bent on the overthrow of free institutions, Protestants in the nineteenth century wondered whether the experiment in self-government could survive the presence of a massive Catholic population organized under hierarchical control, in separate churches and schools, upholding an intolerant view of religious liberty, making exclusive claims for their denomination, and recognizing the authority of a foreign, supposedly infallible, pope, who taught that all the modern liberties, including freedom of conscience and church-state separation, were violations of the law of God. Anti-Catholics were hardly crazy and anti-Catholicism could easily appear as one of those reform movements seeking to insure the success of the American republic.

As long as Catholics were a tiny minority, long subject to religious persecution and therefore deeply grateful for the freedom made possible by separation, the problem was not critical. But when large numbers of Catholic immigrants flooded the country after 1830, the Catholic problem became very real. Decades of mutually reenforcing anti-Catholicism and Catholic separatism then highlighted a complex history through which the church adjusted Catholic claims to the requirements of American democracy, but also forced American democracy to include Catholics in the framework established by the Constitution and shaped by an ever-changing pluralism.

With remarkable skill, the American bishops developed a three-part strategy for affirming American religious arrangements while insuring the possibility of a Catholic presence in American life. First, they distinguished carefully between spiritual and temporal matters, between religion and politics, and they upheld that distinction even when European Catholicism moved away from it in the ultramontane movement which climaxed at Vatican I. On the basis of this distinction they defended the spiritual supremacy of the pope and encouraged a warm devotion of American Catholics to the Holy See, but they denied with equal fervor that the pope had any political power or influence over American Catholics. Similarly, they defined their own leadership in terms of spiritual and moral instruction, insisting that their people remained free in their political affairs. Bishop John England, for example, told Congress in 1826 that American Catholics wished to be indistinguishable from their fellow citizens in all things save their religious affiliation.

Bishops were therefore vociferously non-partisan. Some even refused to vote, and the occasional bishop who expressed a partisan loyalty risked correction by his ecclesiastical superiors and isolation from his brother bishops. They regularly instructed their people to place the public good above group interests and partisan considerations. Indeed, they shared with many other national leaders a profound suspicion of political parties or "factions," regularly warning against the machinations of selfish and unscrupulous politicians.

At the same time, the bishops argued that by confining themselves to religious matters, bringing people into an organized relationship with the church, instructing them in the doctrines of their faith, providing them with moral guidance, and encouraging them to associate with one another for mutual assistance, they were making a valuable contribution to American life. Far from jeopardizing community consensus, Catholicism actively contributed to it by imposing on its members, with the authority of Christ himself, the very values and attitudes required for the success of the American experiment in self-government in a setting of religious and cultural pluralism.

The second element in the Catholic strategy was the defense of the rights of the church, a requirement that seemed to outsiders to conflict with the claim to disinterested non-partisanship and respect for church-state separation. To Catholics it appeared otherwise, for in the name of that separation they insisted on their right and responsibility to defend their church against any effort to impose alien values or to exclude them from public life. They fought for what they took to be their rights as guaranteed by the Constitution, demanding the removal of Protestant Bibles and anti-Catholic texts from the schools, access for Catholic clergy to prisons, public hospitals, and asylums, a fair share of public moneys available to Protestant-sponsored charity schools or Indian missions, and, later, school reform that would enable all denominations to exercise their right to teach their children. Few went as far as Archbishop John Hughes, who sponsored his own slate of candidates in the 1842 state assembly elections in New York, in order to defend what he took to be the rights of Catholics to a fair educational system. Most confined themselves to less objectionable means, speaking strongly of these issues, lobbying state legislatures, and using what influence they could muster to insure their rights, all in the name of church-state separation and religious liberty. Sometimes such efforts had unexpected benefits, for by sharpening intergroup tensions, they drew together as Catholics the diverse and often contentious national groups who composed the church. But such efforts could also backfire by fueling nativist and anti-Catholic sentiment, forcing the state toward more neutral and necessarily secular policies. What is important, however, is that these efforts were always justified in terms of the First Amendment and religious liberty; they almost never led Catholics to any serious criticism of American constitutional arrangements.

Finally, the bishops combined non-partisanship and self-defense with public-spiritedness. At moments of crisis they would rally to the cause of public order or the defense of the government, even putting aside private doubts about the wisdom or morality of a particular policy, as

Hughes did during the draft riots of 1863 and John Carroll had done during the war of 1812. Hughes traveled to Europe at the request of the Lincoln administration during the Civil War, while the bishop of Charleston made a similar trip on behalf of the Confederacy. Bishops on both sides avoided discussion of constitutional problems and of slavery, instead instructing their flock in the responsibilities of citizenship. When the United States went to war with Spain, Archbishop John Ireland enthusiastically supported the government; later Bishop John Lancaster Spaulding actively opposed the taking of the Philippines, but, again, most bishops simply accepted government decisions, and tried to avoid division among their people and conflict with public opinion. When the United States entered World War I, President Wilson was deeply concerned about national unity. The bishops rallied to the nation's cause, organizing programs of support for Catholic troops, marketing bonds, and quietly suppressing the more militant opposition. Of course such decisions reflected the self-interest of a minority church, but more frequently they expressed the widely held conviction that bishops were moral leaders who shared a responsibility to modify legitimate diversity and help shape a common consensus required by public institutions in a free society. In a nation without an established church or a dominant religious group, the leaders of every church had a responsibility to provide moral leadership, including mobilizing the conscience of the nation to accept the sacrifices required when its existence or its ideals were at stake.

This tripartite strategy worked well throughout the nineteenth century. Indeed, if the standard of Americanism is the clear determination of the church to avoid partisanship, to judiciously defend its religious freedom against the government and against aggressive outsiders, and to provide moral support of the Constitution, including the First Amendment, the bishops of the immigrant church were at least as American as any other group of denominational leaders.

Catholics and Social Policy
In the twentieth century a maturing industrial economy brought dramatic increase in governmental responsibility and posed new problems for the church. The detached non-partisanship, public-spiritedness, and militant defense of group rights characteristic of the nineteenth century depended in part on the limited role of government in national life. Catholics had a stake in limited government, for a Protestant ma-

jority, perceived as at least residually anti-Catholic, could use government power to violate Catholic rights or impose policies in conflict with church teaching. A deep suspicion of federal authority has therefore always characterized American Catholicism, even when the administration was in apparently friendly hands.

Yet, Catholics helped build the very federal establishment they so often fear and criticize. Many laws enlarging the role of government arose from real problems which beset the Catholic population. For example, the bishops had wisely avoided placing any barriers in the way of Catholic membership in non-confessional unions. As more and more Catholics looked to the unions for help in achieving better incomes and job security, church leaders could hardly avoid supporting legislation to protect union rights. Similarly, the corporate order of industry made moral exhortation alone inadequate to overcome unsafe and unhealthy working conditions, insecure employment, sickness, accident, and old age. As pastors with responsibility for a vast array of charitable and social service agencies and institutions, the bishops were personally aware of these problems. To deal with them they lent their support to social reform legislation, first in the states and later, during the New Deal, at the national level. Indeed, as heirs to a tradition of social and political thought which emphasized the positive role of government, the American bishops found it easier to justify positive government intervention than did many of their Protestant counterparts. In 1919 the bishops adopted a "program of social reconstruction" which called for a federal employment office, equal wages for women, and social insurance against sickness, disability, old age, and unemployment. During the 1930s the hierarchy endorsed and defended the basic reforms of the New Deal, including the National Labor Relations Act, social security, minimum wage legislation, and government regulation of banks and securities.

This clear Catholic support for social legislation has coexisted uneasily with suspicion of federal power and authority. The bishops who issued the social reconstruction program of 1919 wrote a pastoral letter the same year which warned against the dangers of bureaucracy and big government. When nativism and anti-Catholicism surged in the 1920s, Catholic leaders reaffirmed their opposition to a strong federal role, many actively opposing the child labor amendment to the Constitution. Even in the thirties, the bishops grew increasingly suspicious after the court-packing plan of 1937. In the postwar years, Catholic bishops continued to defend unions and social legislation while sharing the widespread concern about the dangers of government bureaucracy and centralized power.

This ambivalence was reflected in the arguments Catholics made in support of social reform. Drawing upon Catholic teaching, they argued that each person possessed basic rights, including the right to life and the means to maintain life in dignity. On this basis, they argued for a living wage, for a just distribution of the benefits and rewards of economic activity, for the right of labor to organize and bargain collectively, for the responsibility of government to exercise a general supervision of the economy in order to ensure that rights were respected and justice was achieved.

This positive understanding of the role of government was balanced by an insistence on personal liberty, including religious freedom and private property. By means of the principle of subsidiarity Catholics argued that the provision of social goods should always take place at the level closest to the people concerned. This meant less an emphasis on local government than on unions, trade associations, and other such bodies which should engage in self-determination, subject only to general government supervision. This Catholic progressivism balanced individual rights with social obligations; the church recognized the need not only to defend rights, such as the right to a living wage, but to address the question of how such rights could be met in the concrete conditions of American life. Catholic teaching, then, was not explicitly confessional or religious; rather, it professed to offer arguments not only compatible with American democracy but arising from the very values of liberty and justice on which that democracy rested.

Thus the original tripartite strategy held firm. Catholics still distinguished sharply between religious and political affairs, now believing even more strongly that the liturgical, educational, and moral work of the church made a valuable contribution to American democracy without intruding the church in any way into politics. Education, voluntary action through unions and trade associations, self-help programs and community organization were all non-governmental means of fulfilling the obligations of social justice, defending human rights, and contributing to the common good. At the same time, the bishops defended what they took to be Catholic rights, resisting proposals to nationalize education, fighting in the states for school aid and against laws to permit the dissemination of birth control information. Finally, the bishops continued to exemplify public-spiritedness. They rallied to the New Deal in 1933 because they felt that partisanship should be put aside to support emergency measures to deal with the crisis. They defended unions while combating Communism within them because they believed unions, properly organized and conducted, would stabilize national institutions and lessen the dangers of class conflict. And, once again, when the nation faced external dangers, Catholics differed among themselves until the war began and then rallied to the national cause. In doing so, they simply continued to act as moral leaders with public responsibilities, which was, in fact, what they were.

Maintaining the Balance

It is this historical experience which provides the foundation for understanding recent Catholic response to public issues. In the years following World War II, theologian John Courtney Murray put a theoretical framework on the Catholic experience in the United States. On the one hand he argued that church-state separation and religious liberty as practiced in the United States were civil and temporal, not religious, arrangements; they implied a political theory, they grounded a constitutional structure, they did not constitute a theological position and did not threaten the right of the church to be the church. Like his American Catholic predecessors, Murray distinguished sharply between spiritual and temporal affairs, and he argued that far from making Catholics bad citizens, Catholicism taught as true those doctrines of human dignity, justice, and freedom which were central to the American experiment. The Catholic entered civil society with the heritage of a long wisdom of political and social thought which affirmed human reason and provided a basis for pluralism, civic order, and harmony. In the future as in the past, the church could and should defend its right to be the church. It should contribute to civic well-being by upholding the American consensus, and its people should share in public life with others on the basis not of distinctive Catholic tenets of political morality but on the basis of commonly shared values and principles, which for Catholics were solidly grounded in faith. Catholics spontaneously and honestly supported the "American proposition" of equality and inalienable rights, and the constitutional system based on them, because that proposition was true.

Murray's argument was given authority by the Second Vatican Council in its Declaration on Religious Liberty and in the Pastoral Constitution on the Church and the Modern World. While the church has no political agenda of its own, the council fathers taught, it has a responsibility to share in public life and in particular to defend and promote human rights. On this basis the bishops have continued their long practice of collectively addressing public issues. Since Vatican II they have regularly spoken strongly on abortion, racism, economic justice, education, and a host of other domestic issues. They have been even more active in dealing with issues of foreign policy, the arms race, and war and peace. In 1976 and again in 1980 the hierarchy issued statements on political responsibility notable for their moderation and their continuity with long-standing positions. Public policy decisions necessarily involve moral judgments, the bishops argue, so that the church has a clear responsibility to share in the development of a public moral consensus on the basis of which such decisions must be made. Citizens have a responsibility to consider the moral dimensions of issues when deciding among parties and candidates. The moral principles to be considered include the catalogue of human rights developed in church teaching since John XXIII's "Peace on Earth" (1963), including both political and civil rights like free speech, freedom of the press, freedom of religion and the right and duty of political participation, and the social and economic rights flowing from the right to life and to those things necessary for living in dignity. Clearly, the bishops continue to believe, as Murray did, that Catholics share with other Americans a commitment to these rights, so that moral judgments based on such criteria constitute no unconstitutional intrusion into politics and no violation of church-state separation. Rather, the church by addressing such problems on the basis of human rights fulfills a long standing requirement of American political culture: the church must help shape a moral consensus, and a people, which alone will allow the American experiment in free government and freedom of religion to work.

Thus the three-part strategy of the past holds firm. Distinguishing between spiritual and temporal matters, the bishops insist on the duty of Catholics to be good citizens, to participate in public life with a concern for human rights and for the common good. The church thus contributes to the vitality of democracy and the stability of American institutions, both by instructing its own members in their moral obligations and by sharing in the wider public dialogue. Second, with no violation of that distinction, the church has the right and responsibility within the pluralistic framework of American religion to defend its own freedom, its right to be the church, to worship, to govern itself, to educate, and to comment freely on public affairs. And finally, the church has the responsibility to share with others in upholding the institutions of American society, rallying to their support when they are in danger, calling for their reform when that is needed, working with others to insure that they correspond to the requirements of the common life and the values which inform that life, always in a way which affirms and strengthens the community and the nation.

Commentary

Despite this continuity, several problems have arisen in recent years as a result of changes in the church and in American society. First, the bishops have gradually adopted human rights as their foundational criteria for evaluating public policy and making suggestions for change. In the encyclicals of Leo XIII and Pius XI concern for human rights was placed in the context of a Christian social order in which rights and responsibilities were balanced and the state's positive role was limited both by the principle of subsidiarity and by the requirements of the common good. The Catholic commentator on public policy stood both with the persons whose rights had been violated and with the sovereign who had responsibility for maintaining order and coherence in the community. Thus, at one and the same time the church could advocate reforms designed to make decent life possible for the poor, counsel the poor to be patient, encourage non-governmental approaches to achieving relative justice, and support moderate legislation to achieve a minimum of justice.

Since Vatican II, the church has more or less accepted a minority situation in the world, and neither expects nor advocates the replacement of the present society by one explicitly based on the natural law and on a position long consensual among American Catholics. Yet, in many countries which have been historically Catholic, the church remains a powerful social and cultural force. There, church leaders understandably often see themselves both as the protectors of the poor and as the moral guides for society as a whole. They feel a responsibility both to promote greater justice, and even to advocate fairly drastic changes to achieve it, and an equal responsibility for the well-being of the whole society, for all classes, and for the maintenance of existing institutions. They desire to be neither revolutionary nor reactionary but rather to integrate their commitment to human rights within an ethic of responsibility for national well-being.

In the United States, however, the Catholic church has always been somewhat on the margins of the larger society and culture. Its bishops have shared with other Americans a confidence that political and civil rights are guaranteed, and a belief that American abundance makes the achievement of social and economic rights proper and possible. If the public can simply be made aware of the existence of specific injustices, and be persuaded that those injustices violate accepted standards of equality and justice, then means will be found to correct those problems. Accordingly, when the bishops have focused their attention on social and economic injustice, they have attempted to educate the larger public that these injustices exist and to persuade them that they violate such American values as equality of opportunity. The task of solving the problem, of reform through legislation and government action, is left to public determination.

A second problem arises from within the church. Changes taking place since Vatican II have combined with the social changes in the American Catholic population and currents in the culture generally to weaken the traditional understanding of the church as the body of Christ. Episcopal and papal authority is weaker, the church has become more voluntary, and few Catholics are familiar with church teaching on social justice and world peace, even fewer with the natural-law tradition on which so many of those teachings are based. Sectarian currents have appeared in American Catholicism, calling the church to be smaller and more committed to the Gospel, adopting a more prophetic stance regarding the society at large. More broadly, evangelical styles of ministry involving reliance on scripture and emphasizing personal conversion and commitment have led to a moral language based on the words and spirit of Jesus, using his teaching directly as the standard by which to judge personal and sometimes public problems. Powerful and understandable as this may be, it encourages an individualistic, highly personal understanding of social morality and makes dialogue with wider publics, and even civil conversation, increasingly difficult. Equally important, it places pressure on the hierarchy to focus exclusive attention on the faith and witness of the church and deprives their public role of authority, even legitimacy.

Critics of the bishops are quite right to point out that they appear as advocates on behalf of the poor, and thus as moral critics of the society. Church leaders recognize that they have, as bishops, no real answer to the question of how the goal of a better life and greater equality for poor are to be achieved. While they frequently endorse specific reforms to overcome specific problems, they rarely examine the costs of such changes. The bishops' critique, based almost exclusively on human rights, is powerful and convincing but, without a systematic concept of the common good, as embodied previously in the notion of a Christian social order, they are weak on positive alternatives and thus vulnerable to the criticism that they are irresponsible, imposing unrealistic moral demands on the political order. The development of Part Three of the pastoral letter on war and peace, offering suggestions for alternatives to war, based on the notion of "the universal common good" demonstrates the bishops' effort to deal with this problem. It is worth noting that almost all of this section was added after the publication of the first draft of the pastoral.

The bishops are thus caught in a classic bind. If they ground themselves exclusively in the scriptural imperative of love and withdraw from the effort to influence the public consensus and public policy, they may indeed mobilize considerable support for a critical, prophetic witness within the church, even it if costs the church many members and opens the community to charges of public irresponsibility. At the other extreme, they may stand too closely to the prevailing framework of responsibility, looking at issues through the lense of decision makers, become sympathetic to their dilemmas, and accept only the limited alternatives that seem to be presently available. If they move one way they seem utopian, unrealistic, and irresponsible. If they move the other they appear to have lost their integrity as Christian leaders by acquiescing in situations they themselves have defined as unjust and immoral.

The debate over the pastoral letter on nuclear weapons reflects this dilemma quite clearly. So far, while individual bishops have adopted one or another of these conflicting positions, the hierarchy as a whole has continued to insist that they can be both responsible participants in the public debate and faithful custodians of the Gospel. In this they reflect the experience of many Catholics, who also are torn between the apparent demands of Christian love and their responsibilities in daily life. The process has highlighted the fact that perfectionism based on exclusive Christian standards and a realism which all but exempts the policy process from moral evaluation are equally dangerous for the church, the nation, and the world. The bishops have placed themselves on the edge, at the boundaries between faith and politics, where they have always tried to be, but now at a time and on an issue when faith and politics seem to be moving from tension to contradiction.

The bishops continue to believe that integration is possible, that Christian citizenship in a free and pluralistic society need not become a contradiction in terms. They search for positive theology of peace and constructive policy options which can enable the nation to be true to its professions while fulfilling its reponsibilities and enable citizens to participate in American society in ways which are just and make some contribution to peace. The task before them is doubly difficult. They must encourage the church to renew its traditional wisdom about public life in ways appropriate to the new world it confronts. And they must find a pastoral style which enables their people to share the task with them. In the past bishops might have attempted to carry out these tasks alone. Today they will be able to do so only to the extent they learn to stand within their community of faith, so that when they speak they will speak on behalf of their church, and their words will carry the credibility and authenticity of a living witness in the lives of its members.

To accomplish all this, they might return to the wisdom embodied in the experience we have described. First, the church distinguished between its spiritual role and the temporal concerns of its members, so that it affirmed the freedom of the political community without surrendering its own responsibility to speak the truth by publicly stating its view of the moral dimensions of public life. The bishops insisted that, in its specifically religious work, the church empowers men and women to bear the responsibilities of public life informed by a faith which affirms the values and ideals of a free society. Thus, in addition to emphasizing the moral basis of its commentary on public affairs the bishops should recognize that the quality of church life—its worship, community life, and the living faith of its members—constitutes its major contribution to shaping the political culture and alone gives weight to its moral commentary. Second, the church should continue to defend its right to be the church, including its right to speak strongly on public affairs, to affirm those of its members who are compelled by conscience to refuse to endorse or participate in public activities they consider immoral, and its right if necessary to collectively withdraw from those forms of work and political participation which violate its integrity as a church. And finally, the church should affirm always its acceptance of its role as a supporter of American ideals and institutions, not only when they are threatened by foreign adversaries but even more when they are threatened by an internal loss of confidence. Almost a quarter of a century ago John Courtney Murray argued that Catholics had become almost the last Americans who really believed that the truths we have held as self-evident were in fact true. In ways he never suspected, it may well be that on the Catholic ability to structure a constructive public role for the church and its members rests the integrity of the American proposition and the future of the experiment in religious liberty and the separation of the church and state.

PETER STEINFELS

The Foreign Policy Context of the Nuclear Debate

On or about June 13, 1971, the American foreign policy consensus of the postwar years dissolved. Of course one might select another date than the morning on which the leading newspaper of the American establishment published the Pentagon Papers, a mass of classified documents exposing the flimsy underpinnings of the nation's policy in Vietnam. And one might also concede that there had never been any want of acrimonious disputes over foreign policy in the years since the 1947 declaration of the Truman Doctrine and the commitment of the United States to a strategy of "containing" Soviet power.

There had been the frustrations of "losing" China and facing stalemate in Korea. There were the bitter battles associated with the names McCarthy and MacArthur. Yet containment was a bipartisan policy and an establishment one. Parts of the establishment may have connived in the attacks of McCarthy and McCarthyites on both the principles and personnel of containment, but there were limits—as McCarthy swiftly learned when he took on the army and Republican presidency. Besides, McCarthyism seemed more concerned with setting upon scapegoats for past failures than with offering alternative policies for the future. The right wing argued that mere containment was a half-hearted and morally debilitating way to confront a global and nearly satanic challenge to the Christian West. But a Republican administration, no less than a Democratic one, was willing to settle the war in Korea pretty much where it had started, with the land still divided and the Communists still in power in the North. It was John Foster Dulles himself who in 1956 could offer the Hungarian Freedom Fighters nothing but moral support. Notions of rolling back Communism in Eastern Europe or of unleashing Chiang Kai-shek from his Taiwanese citadel to liberate mainland China from the "Reds" were relegated to the periphery of foreign policy debate where, practically speaking, most of their advocates had already been exiled.

The division brought on by Vietnam was different. Yes, the polls had registered public opposition to the Korean War—it was, after all, a very disappointing war—but that opposition had been far less vocal, far less rooted in the ranks of the foreign-policy elite itself, than was the case with Vietnam. In the "News of the Week" section of the *New York Times*, one of the choice places where the political establishment communicates with itself, one *early* year of the Vietnam War saw twenty-seven political advertisements, containing almost ten thousand signatures, commenting on the government's policy. Almost all were opposed. The entire Korean War saw two such war-related ads, one seeking contributions to clothe Korean children, the other proposing a single citizen's peace scheme. Korea had provoked no campus demonstrations, no marches on Washington, no widespread draft resistance, no anti-war presidential candidacies. Korea was followed by soul-searching over the possibility that American prisoners of war had violated their military code. Vietnam, on the other hand, stirred debate over the possibility that American troops were extensively engaged in war crimes and that American leaders had violated the principles established after World War II at Nuremberg. Korea left few traces in the national conscience. A dozen years after Vietnam had brought to an end the presidential career of Lyndon Johnson, former anti-war activists were still publicly reexamining their roles and a monument to Vietnam veterans became the center of extended controversy and reflection.

The prolonged agitation over the war in Vietnam led to a thorough-going questioning of America's international role; indeed, coming as it did after the civil rights struggles and the urban disturbances of the early and middle sixties, the war inspired sweeping criticisms of American society and culture. A few anti-war activists detected in Vietnam a kind of American pact with death, a point they would later repeat in reference to U.S. reliance on nuclear weaponry. Others saw Vietnam as an exercise in economic imperialism. Neither explanation found much echo in the public at large, or even among intellectuals. Far more persuasive was the idea, compatible with ecological concerns and critiques of technology, that the nation had lost its sense of limits. Extraordinary power had mated with crusading idealism to beget a dangerous arrogance. We could combat any insurgency, channel any nationalism, remake any society. . . . The result was Vietnam where not even a massive effort involving the deaths of 58,000 American servicepeople and over a million Vietnamese, expending more fire-power than employed in all theaters of World War II, could establish a regime capable of withstanding the Vietnamese forces. What the United States had done seemed increasingly, indeed blindly, out of all proportion to the stakes, at least the stakes for the United States. Later, observing the outcome for the Vietnamese, as well as parallel events in Cambodia, some Americans insisted that even a highly uncertain victory should have been pursued longer. At the time, however, the outcome for the Vietnamese had never played as determinative a role in U.S. policy as had a shifting set of geopolitical concerns, from containing China to maintaining American credibility in other parts of the world.

It was in response to the new awareness of limits that between 1968 and 1980 two new models of American foreign policy were developed, first by Henry Kissinger, under the Nixon and Ford presidencies, and then by the Carter administration. Both were fiercely debated. Both were eventually rejected. Intertwined with those debates, however, was a continuing controversy over what came to be known as the "Vietnam syndrome."

Vietnam Syndrome
If there were lessons to be learned from Vietnam, if indeed three presidential administrations insisted that they *had* learned lessons from Vietnam, that raised another possibility. Perhaps the lessons had been *over*learned. Or perhaps they were even the wrong lessons. Such was the contention of those who complained of the "Vietnam syndrome."

Diagnosis of the "Vietnam syndrome" had its roots early in the national debate over the war. President Johnson had called war critics "nervous Nellies." Spiro Agnew called them worse. Demonstrators were charged with being unpatriotic. "Love it or leave it" was the popular response to the impression that war opponents despised America, as indeed some among the more radical clearly did. Moderate critics of the war were said to be suffering from a "new isolationism."

Perhaps the brief but intense debate in 1975 over further U.S. involvement in Angola finally crystallized the idea of a "Vietnam syndrome" as applying not to Vietnam itself but to U.S. foreign policy generally. The idea was that the crucial foreign policymaking elites had been traumatized by the unhappy outcome in Southeast Asia. They were paralyzed, particularly in regard to the exercise of American power. Not only were they overly fearful about the entangling dangers of such use of power; they had lost all faith in the cause for which it might be used. Failure of nerve, crisis of confidence—these were the terms that were bandied about—or just plain "guilt." The left and the Third-World left, in particular, were supposed to be expert at manipulating the guilt of America's elites. But the guilt might spring from something else— self-hatred, rejection of America's middle-class values, a dismissal of liberal democracy itself.

From 1975 on, whether the topic was OPEC, Iran, Central Intelligence Agency covert operations, the Panama Canal, SALT, or Central America, one could expect to hear evocations of the "Vietnam syndrome." It was certainly a damning psychological—and moral—portrait. It could be played in various keys; it could be played *fortissimo* or *pianissimo*. It could be sounded heavily or with a light, ironic touch. But was it true?

Unfortunately, there was, and is, no way to know. "Elites" cover a lot of ground, and among those taking public stands on foreign policy one could find examples that might correspond to this or that aspect of the "Vietnam syndrome." How representative were they—the radical student editors at Harvard who dismayed Daniel Patrick Moynihan, or the foundation officials who jousted with him and Kissinger?

Virtually no one in positions of any responsibility avowed the outlook constituting the "Vietnam syndrome." It always had to be detected and deduced by their critics. Caution could be a "failure of nerve." Self-criticism could be "self-hatred." Resistance to the use of American military power in a series of specific situations could be interpreted as a traumatic rejection of military power altogether. A possibly realistic belief that the United States should be much more modest in its hopes to influence societies of a very different historical and cultural cast could be alternatively interpreted as a "crisis of confidence." Obviously "Vietnam syndrome" may exist largely in the eye of the beholder; one need only recall the chain of denunciations: while a Kissinger was detecting "failure of nerve" in his critics to the left, those to Kissinger's right were detecting the same illness in his own policies of detente.

In fact, it would have been surprising if events so dramatic and painful as the national division over Vietnam and the eventual defeat of American purposes there did not, in some measure, provoke an overreaction. But one that thoroughly penetrated and paralyzed policy-making elites and immured them to pragmatic considerations? The public, of course, was typically contrasted with the elites: it retained a healthy patriotism, showed no symptoms of decadence or self-hatred, and so on. Yet the public, both in 1978 and 1982, registered itself far more likely than opinion leaders to agree with the statement "The war in Vietnam was more than a mistake; it was fundamentally wrong and immoral" (public: 72 percent agreement; opinion leaders, 45 percent). One study showed that even the elite which produced the most sweeping denunciations of America in its role in Vietnam—the intellectuals—had tended, when queried, to eschew "moral" grounds for "pragmatic" ones in opposing the war.

Perhaps, then, the lesson American elites took from Vietnam—rightly or wrongly—was of a far more pragmatic and limited nature than the moral-psychological outline the "Vietnam syndrome" suggests. Two very representative foreign policy "opinion leaders"—Charles William Maynes and Richard H. Ullman—once insisted that the "lasting legacy of Vietnam" was quite specific: "It is a greater skepticism about the ability of outsiders, even those willing to employ a large-scale military intervention, to control the politics of Third World states over the long haul. This skepticism is combined with a view of U.S. interests that attaches less importance to the political alignment of individual Third World governments and with a more realistic recognition of the high costs of using military force against even guerrilla troops that are armed with sophisticated modern weapons."[1] Such a skepticism does explain a great deal about post-Vietnam foreign policy—Congress's and the Carter administration's reluctance, for example, to consider military measures in Angola, Iran, and Nicaragua—but it does not lend itself to the polemical uses of the "Vietnam syndrome."

Polemical labels are not a monopoly of one side in recent debates on foreign policy, however. If advocates of a ready projection of American power frequently discredited their opponents as victims of "Vietnam syndrome," the opponents frequently replied with sweeping references to "cold warriors." The implication was that the cold war constituted an unnecessary and destructive reaction to an exaggerated Soviet threat; certainly it was an outdated policy. Furthermore, any assertions that the Soviet Union posed real dangers to the United States, or that Communism was a menacing ideology, or that greater American military strength might be appropriate were rather summarily dismissed as ritualistic, if not self-serving, expressions of a "cold-war mentality."

All political debate involves strong feelings, and rightly so. Strong feelings, in turn, produce polemics. But the case for keeping polemics to a minimum is the case against distraction. The post-Vietnam search for a new foreign policy has given Americans plenty of hard questions to face, even without distracting caricatures of contending positions.

Kissinger and Detente

Henry Kissinger and Richard Nixon proposed an alternative to the alleged overextension that had led to Vietnam.[2] The United States had persisted in expecting some decisive victory over its adversary. Now it would have to live with simply maintaining a balance of power. The United States had been ideological in foreign policy. Now it would have to recognize that Soviet power challenged the United States, not Communist ideology per se; agreement with a Communist nation like China, when it served to balance Soviet power, was entirely thinkable. The United States had reacted to challenges indiscriminately. Now it would have to distinguish between the essential interests it had in the security of Europe, Japan, and the Persian Gulf, and the peripheral interests that, under the "Nixon Doctrine," it might leave to the care of surrogate powers like Iran or Saudi Arabia. The United States had relied single-mindedly on power in dealing with the Soviets. Now it would have to combine power with diplomacy, the stick with the carrot, to so channel Soviet self-interest that containment became self-containment and the USSR a stable element in the existing international order: this was detente. The United States had conceived of power almost exclusively in military terms. Now it would have to recognize the other dimensions of power, especially psychological; power existed where it was *perceived* to exist—credibility was essential. The United States had confronted one foreign policy problem after another, or an array of them at any moment, without understanding their interconnectedness and without subordinating them to any overall design. Now it would have to see the *linkage* between issues: everything might affect everything else; nothing ought to be compartmentalized. The United States had been steered by emotion, ideology, wishful thinking. Now it would have to follow a foreign policy stripped of all sentimentality.

It is now generally conceded, even by Kissinger himself, that although this conception led to some notable successes, in its grand outline it failed. The reasons why are disputed. Domestic opposition to the war in Vietnam, congressional recalcitrance, and finally Watergate—these are Kissinger's explanations for the disintegration of his model. Others felt that the problems were more fundamental, the flaws within the scheme itself.

Kissinger's conception was attacked both for departing from the nation's previous approach to containment and for not departing from it, both for abandoning America's single-minded, across-the-board confrontation with Communism and for not abandoning it. Curiously enough, both criticisms could be simultaneously true. In principle, Kissinger and Nixon announced a new policy; in practice, the old one seemed to creep in through the back door under an altered identity. Some people worried more about the change in principle; others were disturbed by the persistence in practice.

The linking of so many international issues to the constant search for "balance" with the Soviet Union, an ambitious definition of balance that approximated house-breaking Moscow to Washington's set of international rules, an acute sensitivity to subtle shifts in psychological advantage ("credibility")—all this seemed to produce a foreign policy that was as globally entangled as ever. We could banquet with a Communist China but had to subvert Chile's democratic processes simply out of *anticipation* of a Communist government. The fact that credibility, in Kissinger's and Nixon's eyes, required a prolongation of the war in Vietnam for four (?) years made it extremely difficult for them to address issues that, on the face of their own theory, should have been much more central, namely the increasing military strength of the Soviet Union and the growing disaffection of America's NATO partners. These were the issues which would ultimately transform detente into a point for contention rather than consensus. And ironically, despite the focus on U.S.-Soviet relations, it may have been relatively independent events in the rest of the world that had the most lasting impact on the shape of international relations—above all, the coalescing of OPEC's power in the wake of the Egyptian-Israeli war of 1973.

The interconnectedness and insistence on swift maneuver implicit in the Kissinger-Nixon model of American foreign policy had other ramifications. A premium was put on secrecy, on freedom from congressional restraints, on circumvention when necessary even of the foreign policy bureaucracy itself. The quest for stability had to be seen as having moral precedence over various ideological claims, whether those of anti-Communism or the liberal principles of individual rights and national self-determination.

It was not surprising that a reaction set in to the Kissinger-Nixon approach. Conservatives complained that detente had been a cover for resigned acquiescence in ascending Soviet power, formalized in SALT I. Liberals complained that treating conflicts all over the world in terms of their relationship, often only psychological, with the Washington-Moscow contest returned the United States to the role of global policeman. Both sides complained of secrecy and disregard for fundamental values.

That reaction helped form the Carter administration's alternative.

The Carter Model
The Carter model differed from Kissinger's in a number of respects. First, U.S.-Soviet relations would no longer occupy such a dominant place in Washington's attentions. Instead of a largely bipolar world (or occasionally triangular one, when Kissinger was playing the "China card" or celebrating the "Year of Europe"), North-South questions, that is, rich-poor ones, and other issues would come into their own.

Second, regional conflicts would be approached in their own terms and not primarily in relationship to the rivalry between the two superpowers. Linkage, in other words, would no longer be a dominant concept.

Third, American foreign policy would be guided, in some fundamental (but never very precise) sense, by a commitment to human rights. This did not mean conducting international politics, Carter insisted, according to "rigid moral maxims," nor expecting prompt responses to high-sounding declarations. It did propose, however, to promote the cause of human rights whenever possible. Kissinger had tried to remove unqualified anti-Communism as the presiding rationale of U.S. foreign policy and replace it with a *realpolitik* concern for stability. Many Americans perceived the result as sheer amorality. Now Carter hoped that a positive ideology of human rights would connect the nation's conduct overseas to the principles it valued at home.

Fourth, the Carter administration would make a sustained effort to reduce the growth of armaments. It sought a treaty with Moscow to limit strategic arms. It declared its determination to restrain the sales of conventional weapons. It sought to strengthen the barriers against nuclear proliferation.

The Carter model, like Kissinger's, could claim notable successes—the Camp David accords; the end of guerrilla war and successful transition from white to black rule in Zimbabwe; reinforced inhibitions on nuclear proliferation; the emphatic establishment of human rights as a touchstone in international politics; the setting of an open and moral tone in foreign policy that, if nothing else, held out the promise of building a new American consensus on the basis of popular ideals. Defenders of the Carter administration's approach might also argue that it enjoyed much less time than Kissinger's had to prove itself. Critics would reply that it had required much less time to discredit itself. For the Carter model, too, seemed to end in self-contradiction and disarray—and certainly in rejection by the public.

Part of the trouble was a matter of style. If Kissinger had appeared secretive and duplicitous, the Carter team simply appeared erratic. But part was also substantive. It was certainly defensible to want to reduce America's preoccupation with the Soviet Union (although the Carterites may have been unduly complacent about the possibility that status-conscious Soviet leaders might perceive this as diminishing their world role rather than relieving them of American attentions). But beyond that, what was the Carter administration's view of the Soviets and the U.S. policy that should follow from this view? Carter declared the United States "now free of that inordinate fear of Communism which once led us to embrace any dictator who joined us in that fear," a declaration for which he has been roundly criticized but which, read carefully, is merely a sensible judgment on past policy. The reason, however, that it was so easily misread was that he failed to indicate what might be a reasonable fear of Communism or of Soviet power, instead leaving this central question unexamined. According to Stanley Hoffman, this was the "hole in the doughnut." The Carter administration "failed to define what it wanted out of U.S.-Soviet relations. It failed to decide and communicate, through deeds as well as words, which Soviet activities were intolerable, and which were compatible with Washington's concept." The administration was challenged on the continued Soviet arms buildup and on continued American support for detente—by the same critics who had challenged Kissinger. When the Soviets invaded Afghanistan, there was no administration position which might have accounted for that action—or related it to other foreign policy issues. The field was left open to the "worst case" reasoning of the critics. Revolutions against U.S. clients in Nicaragua and

Iran, which the Carter model could have otherwise accommodated, were consequently seen as part of the drift and deterioration in America's position vis-a-vis Moscow.

The Carter administration appeared to end headed in exactly the direction it had originally rejected: preoccupied with the Soviet threat (Afghanistan, Persian Gulf, Soviet brigade in Cuba), advancing armaments (MX, Presidential Directive 59, Rapid Deployment Force, Euromissiles) rather than disarmament (SALT II not only blocked in the Senate but debated by the administration largely on its critics' terms), resorting almost wildly to linkage (ratification of SALT II, economic sanctions, and boycott of the Olympic games all tied to Soviet behavior in Afghanistan), and pursuing a foreign policy that the public neither understood nor backed (confusions and reversals on Iran and the hostage crisis, contradictions over El Salvador, growing impatience with the United States being "pushed around").

The Reagan Administration
Ronald Reagan did not win the 1980 election because of his foreign policy. It was enough that he did not lose it because of his foreign policy. Not a few political analysts, including some in the camp of the incumbent administration, thought that he might. It turned out that Reagan's reputation as a hardliner did not frighten away an electorate that, for several years, had supported higher defense spending and chafed under the United States's apparent inability to set things right with OPEC, Afghanistan, Iran, and a host of other international irritants.

Behind Reagan was a whole party of Kissinger and Carter critics who thought that the search for a post-Vietnam model of foreign policy had become the problem rather than the solution. They hearkened back to what they considered the heroic years of containment, from Truman to JFK. They believed that since Vietnam Washington had naively deemphasized power in its world politics—power in the sense specifically of military might and evident willingness to use it. Their view of the world was even more bipolar than Kissinger's. The contest with the Soviet Union and the totalitarianism it sponsored overshadowed all other issues. The United States, they said, had fallen behind Russia in strategic power. The Soviets might be able to achieve the nuclear equivalent of a Pearl Harbor, or less dramatically, they might intimidate Europe into a craven accommodation. And the Soviets' new ability to project military power beyond their borders, directly or through surrogates like the Cubans, threatened a totalitarian sweep of the Third World.

The first priority, obviously, was to build up American military strength; all the rest was commentary. Premature negotiations on arms control would only undercut the national determination to redress the military situation. A firm will was essential. Our allies had grown uneasy because they questioned American steadfastness. Now their doubts would give way before American clarity of purpose.

That clarity, it turned out, was less than it first appeared. The new Reagan model of foreign policy was ideological as well as bipolar. The conviction that ideology determined nations' behavior reinforced opposition to Third-World revolutions but created uncertainty about the "China card." More important, it posed the question of whether military pressure could alter Soviet conduct without altering the Soviet regime. Was the administration's aim to train the Soviets gradually, as Kissinger had hoped to do, with incentives and threats, except that now Washington had confidence only in the threats? Or was its aim actually to induce a crisis in the Kremlin after, say, putting Russia under the severe economic strain of a full-scale arms race? The administration never announced such a design, but both Americans and allies began to wonder whether it wasn't implicit in the Reagan model. They doubted whether such a goal, resting on a low estimate of Soviet capacities, could be achieved, and whether, in view of the uncertainties involved, it ought to be achieved.

Clarity was also lacking on another crucial point, nuclear strategy. Strategists, and not only those in the Reagan administration, had become preoccupied with the unlikely but still nightmarish possibility of a Soviet first-strike that eliminated all of the United States's most accurate missiles. For some time Washington had also faced complex problems of "extended deterrence"—maintaining a believable nuclear umbrella over allies or countering the advantages of Soviet conventional force in Central Europe and the Persian Gulf even when our own cities were at risk. With the breakdown of the SALT process, and the relentless pressure of new weapons technology, it seemed that problems like these might inevitably set off an ever accelerating arms race. Was the logical conclusion that the United States had to regain, perhaps surreptitiously, its former nuclear superiority? But was that even a possibility? In fact, would not the effort simply to maintain nuclear parity or "crisis stability" in the absence of arms-control agreements involve repeated risks of destabilization? With its unblinking approach to military power, had the administration adopted extreme doctrines about the plausibility of prolonged nuclear wars or complacent scenarios of nuclear survival and "victory"?

Nor was there clarity about the administration's revived application of "linkage." Its rhetoric at first held Moscow responsible for terrorist activities throughout the world. New sanctions were declared after the Jaruzelski coup in Poland. Europe and Washington were soon at odds over trade and energy dealings with the USSR. At the same time, no firm policy emerged on Polish debts. Carter's post-Afghanistan institution of draft registration was not followed by reinstitution of conscription. The grain embargo was lifted.

Linkage with revolutionary turbulence in Central America, on the other hand, was virtually unqualified. The administration did not believe that successful left-wing revolutions anywhere could be isolated from the central East-West struggle. Not even the remnants of the Carter human-rights policy, which enjoyed considerable public support but had been severely criticized by Reagan supporters for undermining pro-American but authoritarian regimes, was allowed to interfere with military assistance to right-wing allies in Central America.

After two years in office, the Reagan administration had encountered a changed public mood. Support for defense spending declined sharply, perhaps in recognition of the difficulty in reconciling it with economic recession, cuts in social services, and looming federal deficits. A wave of anti-nuclear feeling in the United States and Europe compelled the administration to make arms-control negotiations a highly visible part of its public stance, but doubts about the administration's sincerity and seriousness were widespread. War in Lebanon, with little prospect of a postwar settlement, reminded both the administration and the public of the limits of American diplomacy. Congressional and public resistance to escalation in Central America seemed to be bringing the foreign policy debate full circle to the days of Vietnam.

* * *

None of these models of foreign policy—two responses to the trauma of Vietnam and one response to those responses—has yet achieved a public consensus. They have all featured different evaluations of the Soviet Union and how to deal with it, of the relationship between the superpowers' rivalry and other international issues, of the role of armaments and military measures, of the place of ideology in international calculations. They have also justified their efforts in terms that were sufficiently broad to overlap and yet sufficiently distinct to shade policy in different ways.

Each of these models was animated by a different spirit. Kissinger's reflected a pessimism about the possibilities of order and agreement in international affairs and hence the need to balance power against power with extraordinary vigilance and, if necessary, tragic ruthlessness. Carter's reflected an optimistic faith that America could best master the currents of world change by cutting its foreign policy to fit the democratic principles that ruled in its domestic life; there was no essential discontinuity between national and international politics. Reagan's reflected an almost unqualified confidence in the beneficence of American intentions and power; there was no essential discontinuity between American interests and the interests of other peoples.

Each of these models also demanded a different national disposition. Kissinger asked for a shedding of "sentimentality" and a deference to the delicate maneuverings of the statesman. Carter asked for a patient belief that the force of America's historical vision counted for more than the observable flux of power relationships. Reagan asked for a hearty assertion of American strength and the faith that American purposes will eventually justify temporary resort to painful or risky or unpalatable measures.

Citizens do not usually become galvanized, morally and politically, by foreign policy in general, but by particular issues—U.S. aid or intervention decisions, world hunger and economic development, or, most recently, the nuclear arms race. Of course, policies in each of these areas are determined by special factors, but they are also shaped by the broad sets of convictions about international politics espoused by different American administrations. These distinct models of foreign policy are not only the context in which Americans can understand recent developments, for example, the nuclear policy. The models also should be the object of analysis and judgment.

NOTES

1. *Foreign Policy*, Fall 1980, p. 10.
2. For much of what follows, I have leaned heavily on the interpretations of U.S. foreign policy by Stanley Hoffmann, collected in *Dead Ends: American Foreign Policy in the New Cold War* (Cambridge, Mass.: Ballinger, 1983); and by John Lewis Gaddis, in *Strategies of Containment* (New York: Oxford, 1982).

II

Taking Up the Question: The Role and Tradition of the Church

The Challenge of Peace

(Introduction and Part I, #s 1-26)

A major theme of Vatican II that shaped the substance of the peace pastoral is the council's call for bishops to examine "the signs of the times" and to interpret them in the light of the Gospel. Three contemporary signs, the bishops said, influenced the writing of the pastoral.

For the first sign, they repeated Pope John Paul II's observation: "The world wants peace, the world needs peace." The second sign reflects the council's condemnation of the arms race, because "the harm it inflicts upon the poor is more than can be endured." The third sign, the major focus of the pastoral, is the judgment that the current dangers of the arms race pose problems that challenge traditional applications of moral principles.

As a prelude to the pastoral's examination of the church's teaching on war and peace, readers are offered a series of qualifications about the text.

First, persons seeking simple answers to complex questions on war and peace will be disappointed, because the Catholic tradition is "long and complex" and it defies easy categorizations.

A second caution: each of the pastoral's statements do not carry the same moral authority. Interspersed are statements of binding moral principles and specific applications of these principles based on contingent circumstances.

Related to this caveat is the need to recognize that judgments based on specific circumstances can be interpreted differently by people of good will. The preparation of the pastoral, in fact, disclosed "the range of strongly held opinion" among Catholics on questions of war-peace.

Regarding Vatican II's challenge "to undertake a completely fresh reappraisal of war," the pastoral is modest about its contents. It does not claim to be *the* reappraisal. Rather, the letter, directed especially to the members of the church, is "an invitation to continue the new appraisal."

CHARLES E. CURRAN

The Moral Methodology of the Bishops' Pastoral

The bishops' pastoral letter on war and peace obviously develops its positions within the context of Catholic moral theology. In the beginning of Part I the pastoral letter itself briefly describes some aspects of the moral methodology which will be used in the document. The purpose of this essay is to discuss the pastoral letter from the viewpoint of moral methodology as discussed in the beginning of the letter and as used throughout the pastoral. This discussion will consider two different questions. The first section will discuss what has traditionally been called the *sources* of moral theology, that is, where both the discipline of moral theology and the individual Christian or the church find ethical wisdom and knowledge. The second section will develop the various *aspects* of moral theology especially insofar as they are mentioned in the pastoral letter in relation to the questions of war and peace.

Sources of Moral Theology

In presenting their teaching on peace and war the American bishops explicitly mention that they have found profound inspiration and guidance in the Pastoral Constitution on the Church in the Modern World of the Second Vatican Council. Frequent citations from the Vatican II document prove that the American bishops have relied very heavily upon it. However, not only the content of the pastoral constitution but also its moral method have been followed by the pastoral letter of the American bishops.

The most characteristic methodological feature of the document from the Vatican Council is its insistence on attention to the signs of the times. The second part of the constitution considers in depth five specific areas of concern: marriage and family, culture, socio-economic life, political life, peace, and the international community. Each of these considerations begins with a discussion of the signs of the times. This marks the first time in official Catholic teaching that such a methodological approach was used at the beginning of the consideration of social issues. In addition, the pastoral constitution places strong emphasis on the role of the scriptures in moral theology—an emphasis which before that time had been lacking in Catholic moral method. As might be expected in the Catholic tradition, the Vatican II document also underscores the role of human reason and employs a generic natural-law approach even though there are only three explicit references to natural law in the pastoral constitution. These three sources of ethical wisdom and knowledge—the signs of the times, scripture, and human reason—are explicitly mentioned and often employed in the pastoral letter on war and peace.

Signs of the Times
In the pastoral's short discussion of method, three signs of the times are explicitly mentioned as having greatly influenced the letter: the need for peace, the curse of the arms race for humanity, and the unique dangers brought about by nuclear arms. In my judgment the most significant sign of the times influencing the position taken by the bishops is the existence of enough nuclear weapons to destroy humanity and perhaps the world itself many times over. It is precisely this reality that makes the present situation qualitatively different from all that has gone before. The terrifying effects of nuclear war form the basis for the primary moral imperative found in the letter—the need to say no to nuclear war. In this context of possible global destruction, the American bishops maintain it is wrong even to think about fighting a limited nuclear war. The proximate danger of escalation seems to defy any hope of limitation. For this reason the bishops do not perceive any situation in which the first use of nuclear weapons can be morally justified. The letter does not absolutely exclude the limited use of nuclear weapons in response to a nuclear attack, but the bishops remain highly skeptical about a limited war. (In my opinion their argument logically and rightly leads to saying no to any use of nuclear weapons even in retaliation.)

Use of Scripture
A second source of ethical wisdom and knowledge which has come to the fore in recent Catholic moral theology, especially since Vatican II,

is scripture. The pastoral letter in its different drafts has considerably modified its approach to the scriptures. The final document develops understandings from both the Old and New Testaments. In addition, the bishops call attention to three factors that must condition any methodological use of the Bible in this area. First, peace has been understood in different texts and contexts to mean many different things, such as the interior peace of the individual or the peace of the final kingdom. Second, the scriptures were written over a long period of time and in many different situations, all of which differ from our own time and circumstances. Finally, the scriptures deal primarily with God's intervention in human history and contain no specific treatise on war and peace.

There is a continuing discussion in ecumenical Christian ethics about the use and role of the scriptures in moral theology.[1] This important methodological question will continue to be with us, but for the present it is sufficient to point out three very important questions that are involved in this discussion. First, what does the Bible or the particular scriptural text mean in terms of the time and place it was written? The answer to this question is given primarily by exegetes using all the tools of contemporary biblical and historical study. In the light of the answer to this first question one can proceed to a second and even more difficult one: what does the text mean for us in our very different historical situation? Hermeneutics deals with this problem of interpretation. In addition, much New Testament moral teaching is influenced by the eschatological coloring of the times; that is, many thought that the end of history was coming quickly, and such an understanding obviously colored their approach to moral questions. However, our understanding of eschatology is quite different. It is our understanding that the end-time has begun in Christ Jesus but will be completed only in his second coming.

A third step in the use of the scriptures in moral theology concerns primarily the way in which the Bible is integrated into moral theology. Here much depends on the various ways in which moral theology is construed. If moral theology is primarily concerned with norms and rules, how is the biblical data incorporated into these norms or laws? If moral theology is primarily interested in the character of the self, what information do the scriptures furnish about the virtues and attitudes that should characterize the Christian who takes responsibility for his or her actions?

In its brief explanation of moral theory the letter explicitly recognizes the importance and the limitations of the scriptures for method in Christian ethics. The bishops point out that one cannot find a specific treatise on war and peace in the Bible. An analysis of the text reveals that the contents of the letter are consistent with the methodological statement that the scriptures do not supply us with detailed answers to the specific questions we face today but only give a clear, urgent direction when we look at today's concrete problems. In the actual development of their teaching on peace and the specific questions we face, the letter appeals to the scriptures to give us a certain vision. The Bible also tells us something about the values of peace and justice for which we strive. Above all, the letter refers to the sacred texts in describing the characteristics that should mark the person as a responsible moral actor. Although the letter often refers to principles and makes particular judgments, none of these principles or judgments appeals primarily to the scriptures for support. The actual use of the Bible throughout the document is thus basically consistent with what is briefly said in theory about the role and use of the scriptures in moral method.

The methodological description and the actual use of the scriptures are also consistent with the substantive conclusions reached in the letter. The document recognizes pacifism as a legitimate personal vocation within the church, but this is not an acceptable position for governments. It is obvious that most pacifist positions would tend to find in the scriptures much more concrete and specific guidance than the bishops find in the Bible. Pacifists often rest their very particular conclusions about the use of force on the biblical witness.[2] But, as we have said, it is difficult to find in scripture specific answers to today's questions.

Human Reason

In the opening section which briefly discusses moral methodology, the pastoral letter merely mentions that there are philosophical elements contained in its approach. A reading of the full document reveals that quite frequently the letter appeals to what human reason can discern about what must be done. Such an approach is very much in keeping with the Roman Catholic theological tradition, which has accepted the goodness and importance of human reason as a source of ethical wisdom and knowledge for the Christian. Historically, Roman Catholicism has been associated with the natural-law tradition which, from the theological perspective of the question, claims that human reason and human experience furnish true ethical wisdom and knowledge for the Christian. Many in the Protestant tradition, because of an emphasis on scripture alone or the primacy of grace or the all-pervading presence of sin, have downplayed or even denied the use of human reason as a source of ethical wisdom and knowledge for the Christian person and the church. The pastoral letter frequently appeals to human reason to determine exactly how human beings should act in this world.

The bishops address the specific moral questions of the use and threat of nuclear weapons in the light of the just-war theory. Historically, this just-war tradition has been associated with Catholic moral theology. In its development, especially from the time of Thomas Aquinas, the natural law has served as the ultimate grounding of the theory. The discussion here has centered on the general question of the use of reason in moral theology, but the next section will briefly treat the more philosophical question of exactly how reason functions in the moral life.

Thus, the bishops' pastoral letter is in general continuity with contemporary Catholic moral theology with its emphasis on the signs of the times, the use of the scriptures, and the guidance obtained from human reason for the moral life of Christians. The document in its very brief description of its own methodological presuppositions does not go into the very difficult question of how these various aspects are related to each other. Throughout the entire letter there is the impression that all three are harmoniously related and no real contradictions can exist among them. There are very significant questions that moral theology must explore on the exact relationship among all these three. However, one cannot fault the letter for not doing what is an important task for the discipline of moral theology but which obviously lies beyond the scope and purpose of such a document.

Aspects of Moral Theology
The second section will now discuss the understanding and structuring of moral theology as found implicitly and explicitly in the bishops' pastoral. There can be no doubt that principles and norms are a very important part of the approach to moral theology used in this document. The document also recognizes the need to make even quite specific and concrete moral judgments, but it acknowledges that there are important considerations in moral method in addition to principles

and judgments about the morality of specific acts. These other aspects of moral theology have a meaning in themselves and also are related to a proper understanding of principles and specific judgments. The important considerations in moral theology actually used in the development of the letter include: the general vision one brings to all human reality, the understanding of human history (eschatology) and of human beings in general (anthropology), the virtues and values that must be present in human society, the need for structures in human society to safeguard and promote these values, the importance of the person as agent and subject with the call to continual conversion and to the virtues that characterize the Christian agent and subject, the principles and norms that govern human conduct, and the application of these principles to the concrete problems at hand.

In general, I applaud the understanding of moral theology found in this document precisely because of its recognition of the many aspects of moral theology. I have pointed out these aspects of moral theology in a particular order—from general (the vision) to more specific (the principles and their application in particular judgments). Each of these aspects will now be briefly discussed.

Christian Vision in an Imperfect World
The brief theoretical description of method near the beginning of the letter explicitly mentions the biblical vision of reality which is at the heart of our religious heritage. This vision sees all reality as created and sustained by God, scarred by sin, redeemed in Christ, and destined for the kingdom. Such a vision constitutes the first logical step in moral theology and grounds much of what is found in the document. The acceptance of the goodness of creation sustained by a gracious God grounds the insistence that human reason can be a source of ethical wisdom and knowledge for the Christian. Such a basic vision with its recognition that the world is scarred by sin also argues strongly against a perfectionist ethic which would call for separation from the inevitably imperfect world. The fullness of the kingdom will never be here in this world. In the meantime the Christian lives in a world marked by incompletion and sin but redeemed by Christ Jesus.

In Part I.B under the heading "Kingdom and History," the letter develops an eschatology consistent with its basic theological vision. Christians will always live in the tension of "the already but not yet" characteristic of our existence. In a world marked by conflict and in-justice, we are pilgrim people, participating in the pull of the future kingdom. Peace must be built on the basis of justice in a world where the personal and social consequences of sin are both evident. The bishops thus believe that peace is possible but a permanently and perfectly peaceful society is unrealistic and utopian. The anthropology or understanding of the human person implied throughout the doc-ument is in keeping with this eschatological view. Such an eschatology and anthropology cannot support a totally pacifist position but rather ground the just-war theory which is developed and applied in the letter. It should be noted that the bishops rightly recognize the pos-sibility of pacifism and non-violence as a legitimate option for individ-uals but not for governments at the present time, precisely because of their eschatology.

The Just War

The just-war theory has a twofold purpose: to limit war but at the same time to justify war reluctantly in the one case of defense against unjust aggression, and then only when such violent defense is a last resort. Even in the course of a just war there are limits on what can be done. The principles of discrimination (distinguishing combatants from non-combatants) and proportionality (that the good to be attained outweigh the destruction caused) are developed to explain these limits on the conduct of the one type of war which is accepted as a last resort. In a generic way, such a theory and its applications are coherent with the vision, the eschatology, and the anthropology found in the pastoral letter. The theory objects to much of the violence and force which exist in the world and tries to limit such violence. However, in this imperfect world a limited right of nations to self-defense still exists. Likewise, the bishops' unwillingness to call for immediate unilateral nuclear dis-armament, together with their condemnation of anything more than a sufficient deterrent while working for mutual total nuclear disarma-ment, is consistent with the vision and theology found in the letter.

Catholic moral theology traditionally has understood human civil society and the state in the light of the obligation to work for the common good which redounds to the good of all persons in society.[3] The short theoretical explanation given in the first part of the letter itself maintains that the dignity of the human person is at the center of all Catholic social teaching. This statement is correct, but even in such a very brief introductory paragraph it would have been helpful to add that the Catholic tradition has insisted that human persons are by nature social and are called to work together in human and political communities to achieve the common good and ultimately their own good.

There are many values that comprise the common good. In addition to the dignity of the human person and human rights which flow from that dignity, the letter explicitly mentions justice and peace and almost invariably links these two together. Such a linking of the two prevents one from absolutizing either justice or peace. Especially in the eschatological perspective accepted here, at times in the name of justice one might have to violate an existing but very imperfect and unjust peace. There is a position in contemporary Catholic theology known as proportionalism which argues that certain "premoral" evils might be accepted for a proportionate reason. In the light of this particular theory, violence is considered as "premoral" and therefore might be proportionately justified because of the concerns of justice.[4] However, it is not only such a theory that allows for violence; the traditional Catholic theory is also unwilling to absolutize peace.

International Order
Catholic social ethics in general, as illustrated in the papal encyclicals dealing with social justice from the time of Pope Leo XIII (1878–1903), has consistently recognized the need for structural change to insure and bring about justice and peace.[5] Government intervention to help the needy and poor and labor unions as a way of achieving justice for workers were some of the types of structural change suggested by Leo XIII. Pope Pius XI in his encyclical *Quadragesimo Anno* (1931) even called for the reconstruction of the social order along a solidarist or corporatist model. In *Pacem in Terris* (1963), Pope John XXIII discussed the structural aspects of the present international problems. There will never be true peace in this world until there is some international structure or ultimate authority which can insure peace. The American bishops explicitly quote *Pacem in Terris* and recognize the need for a properly constituted political authority with the capacity to shape the world's material interdependence in the framework of our moral interdependence. Today the absence of adequate international structures places an

even greater responsibility on the policies of the individual states. Thus, the letter recognizes the importance of structural change to bring about and insure peace and justice in our world.

Conscience and Conversion

A very important aspect of moral theology is the individual person as subject or agent who is called by God to continual conversion and growth—especially recognized in Part IV of the bishops' pastoral. The Christian community calls itself and its individual members to an ever more intense life of discipleship. Christians are to be doers of the word, witnesses to Jesus. The bishops eloquently call for the disarmament of the human heart and the conversion of the human spirit. Christians working for peace should be people of prayer, penance, and reverence for life. The consciences of all Christians must be educated to carry out their commitment to work for peace in our age.

Roman Catholic moral theology has traditionally emphasized the role of principles and their application to particular cases as of paramount importance. Secondary principles of the natural law are derived by deductive reasoning from the primary principles. The actual judgment of conscience was also understood traditionally to be based on a deductive reasoning process or an application of universal moral principles. There can be no doubt that the framers of the pastoral letter continue to think and operate within such a context. In the beginning of Part I the letter devotes a number of paragraphs to the distinction between the universally binding moral principles of Catholic moral teaching and their application to contemporary issues. The impression is definitely given that morality is seen primarily in terms of moral principles and their application to specific cases.

A good number of contemporary Catholic moral theologians would not see the model of the moral life primarily as a matter of deducing from moral principles or norms the guidance for specific questions. Most moral decisions in our lives are not the result of an application of a moral norm or principle to a specific question. In my theory the primary ethical model for the moral life is one of relationships and responsibility rather than of obedience to norms and principles. There is always a place for principles and norms in moral theology, but such a model is not the primary way of understanding the moral life. In addition, principles and norms themselves are not always arrived at on the basis of a deductive reasoning process. Many moral judgments are not based on deductive syllogistic reasoning but derive from experience and reflection. Even neo-Thomists such as Jacques Maritain have rejected an understanding of moral judgments based on deductive reasoning. According to Maritain, our knowledge of the natural law occurs through a kind of natural inclination and not through concepts and a deductive reasoning process.[6] There is a greater affective aspect to our moral judgments than an older Catholic theology was willing to admit. I have theoretical difficulties with the apparent view of the document which sees the moral life primarily in terms of universally binding principles derived deductively from first principles of the natural law and then applied to particular questions. However, in practice these theoretical and conceptual differences do not necessarily result in any practical differences on the specific principles and judgments proposed in the bishops' pastoral.

There can be no doubt that the final document stresses the distinction between universal moral principles and their application much more than did the earlier drafts. Why? The distinction allows the letter to differentiate the levels of teaching authority found in the document. Statements of universally binding principles carry a greater authoritative weight than the application of these principles. The document implies that the principles are certain and admit of no other possible interpretation. However, the application of these principles involves prudential judgments based on specific circumstances which can change or be interpreted differently by people of good will (e.g., no first use of nuclear weapons). The distinction thus serves the important purpose of showing where and why there can be legitimate diversity and different positions among members of the church. This emphasis in the final document on the distinction between universally binding principles and their prudential applications which admit of different interpretations results from comments made by a number of sources on the second draft of the pastoral, but especially from a meeting held in Rome in January 1983.[7]

The approach taken by the pastoral tries to avoid two extreme positions. Some claim that the bishops as official church teachers have no right or competence to speak on such complex issues as military and political strategy. These are questions that must be left to the experts who have the necessary expertise and learning. Others claim that church teachers or believers can have great certitude on these questions. Against these positions the bishops assert their right and obligation to speak out on such specific issues but admit their lack of absolute certitude. Such questions are not just political or military matters; they are truly moral questions which involve a knowledge of many complex political realities as well as prudential assumptions. Specific moral judgments made in these areas require some knowledge and expertise involving the complex questions under discussion. In the hearings, study, and meetings of the bishops' committee, bishops tried to assimilate the necessary data. However, such specific judgments are truly moral judgments even though they involve much political science data and many prudential interpretations. Considering how understanding is achieved, one cannot claim a certitude that excludes the possibility of error on such complex questions.

Such an approach to understanding is consistent with an understanding of the church which recognizes what might be properly called "a big church." One should never attempt to find the unity of the church or to eject people from the church on issues which by their very nature are so complex and specific that one cannot achieve a certitude that excludes the possibility of error. The bishops as teachers have the right and the responsibility to make their specific moral judgments known to the church, but individuals who respectfully disagree and dissent from such teaching remain members of the church.

Logically this understanding must also be present in other areas of Christian morality. Precisely because questions such as contraception and divorce are very complex issues one cannot here achieve a certitude that excludes the possibility of error. These issues too must be open to diversity and possible dissent within the church. An older Catholic theology tended to say that in these areas we are dealing with universally valid principles which are deduced with certitude from the primary principles of the natural law. This is precisely where a good number of contemporary Catholic moral theologians differ with the older approach. Moral methodology is not primarily deductive with the resulting certitude that is attached to deduction. As a result, such principles cannot claim to have certitude that excludes the possibility of error. It seems likely that recognition in the pastoral letter that dissent in the Roman Catholic church is possible on complex, specific issues is bound to have some repercussions in other areas of moral teaching and church life.

NOTES

1. Bruce C. Birch and Larry L. Rasmussen, *Bible and Ethics in the Christian Life* (Minneapolis: Augsburg Publishing House, 1976).

2. For two frequently cited titles in the pacifist tradition, see G. H. C. Macgregor, *The New Testament Basis of Pacifism and the Relevance of an Impossible Ideal* (Nyack, New York: Fellowship Publications, 1954); John Howard Yoder, *The Politics of Jesus* (Grand Rapids, Michigan: Eerdmanns Publishing Co., 1972).

3. Heinrich A. Rommen, *The State in Catholic Thought* (St. Louis: B. Herder, 1945); Jacques Maritain, *The Person and the Common Good* (Notre Dame, Indiana: University of Notre Dame Press, 1966).

4. Charles E. Curran and Richard A. McCormick, eds., *Readings in Moral Theology No. 1: Moral Norms and Catholic Tradition*, (New York: Paulist Press, 1979).

5. For commentaries on this papal social teaching, see Jean-Yves Calvez and Jacques Perrin, *The Church and Social Justice: The Social Teaching of the Popes from Leo XIII to Pius XII, 1878–1958* (Chicago: Henry Regnery Co., 1961); Jean-Yves Calvez, *The Social Thought of John XXIII* (Chicago: Henry Regnery Co., 1964); John F. Cronin, *Social Principles and Economic Life*, rev. ed. (Milwaukee: Bruce Publishing Co., 1964).

6. Jacques Maritain, *Man and the State* (Chicago: University of Chicago Press, 1952), pp. 89–94.

7. "January Meeting in Rome on the War and Peace Pastoral," *Origins* 12 (7 April 1983):690–695.

WILLIAM E. MURNION

The Role and Language of the Church in Relation to Public Policy

The rhetoric of *The Challenge of Peace* is binary, but the logic of the argument in the letter is at once too subtle and too fluid to be trapped within the simple matrix of this dualistic structure.

The binary nature of the rhetoric is conspicuous and pervasive. The body of the document consists of two parts—an analysis of the problems of nuclear warfare and a set of proposals for the promotion of lasting peace—and this policy statement is bounded by a doctrinal introduction and a pastoral conclusion. The bishops profess to speak from faith but rely upon reason. They act both as bishops of the universal church, in communion with the pope and the rest of the bishops throughout the world, and also as American citizens with a share in the responsibility for the foreign policy of the first of the nuclear superpowers. While their minds are informed by an eschatological vision of peace among peoples and nations, their topic is the political problems of realizing this vision in a world fraught with sin and divided among bellicose sovereign states. The basis for their teaching is the classical Christian doctrine of just war, but they have adapted it to the need nuclear weaponry has created for "a completely fresh reappraisal of war." This reappraisal remains at heart a matter of principle, and yet it must necessarily descend to matters of opinion. In either case it embraces both a specifically Catholic and a naturalistic ethic in order to respond to the concerns of both the Catholic and the wider civil community. And the bishops' purposes in doing this are to contribute to the wider public debate as well as to form individual consciences.

The trouble with these neat dichotomies, though, is that they obscure as much as they clarify. Some of them are logically dubious to begin with, and even those that are valid the bishops often fail to follow through on. The result is that the language of the document tends to conceal the innovation that the argument in it represents for the role of the church in the formation of public policy.

At three points in particular the gap between the rhetoric and the logic becomes especially perplexing: on the distinction between faith and reason, on the differences between matters of principle and matters of opinion, and on the division between the two audiences of the Catholic faithful and the wider political community.

Faith and Reason

The distinction between faith and reason concerns the basis for the bishops' authority to speak on issues of public policy in general and, in particular, on the morality of nuclear warfare. If these are issues for which the contribution of reason and experience is crucial, then what right or competence do the bishops have to pronounce upon them since, as they are free to admit, they "write this letter from the perspective of Catholic faith," and, as everyone knows, they have no professional expertise in any of these areas?

In the recent past, when the American hierarchy has spoken on public policy about the right to life, questions about their authority have come mostly from non-Catholics—though occasionally from liberals and leftists within the Catholic·community—whose opposition to the bishops' stand on abortion led them to object to their right to have any stand at all. In this case, though, the situation has been reversed. Support for the letter has been widespread from liberals and leftists outside as well as within the church, while the opposition to it has come mainly from conservatives, and more vigorously from those within the church than from those outside it.[1] Now too, though, the support as well as the opposition has been fueled more by the nature of the respondents' reactions to what the bishops have had to say than by any cogent position about their right to say it.

The bishops may be partly responsible for this confusion. Within the letter they make no theoretical defense of their right to pronounce authoritatively on public policy, either to the Catholic or to the wider civil community. They do allude to "the nature of Catholic moral teaching, the principles of Catholic ecclesiology, and the demands of our pastoral ministry"(# 19) to explain their motives for appealing to both audiences. And they cite the four-decade history of the church's teaching on the morality of nuclear war, especially Vatican II's Pastoral

Constitution on the Church in the Modern World and Pope John Paul II's addresses, as precedents for their action. But the main warrant they allege for issuing their letter is pragmatic: a conscience-stricken need to respond to the "supreme crisis" which the whole human race faces of having to save the existence of the planet from nuclear annihilation (#s 3–4).

It is important, therefore, to realize that there is a traditional theological basis, previously articulated in the modern papal social encyclicals and repeated in earlier statements by the American hierarchy on social issues, for the right of the church to pronounce on public policy. There is good reason to say this tradition has been implicit in the practice of the church from its beginnings, and certainly St. Thomas Aquinas gave it a classical formulation in the Middle Ages. But the official statement upon which the papacy and the hierarchy have relied in modern times is to be found in the Dogmatic Constitution on Catholic Faith from the First Vatican Council. In it is stated the Catholic belief that divine revelation comprises all of the truths necessary for salvation: not just supernatural truths, completely beyond the reach of human reason and purely a matter of faith, but also natural truths, which are, strictly speaking, rationally intelligible but in our present state of sin difficult for us to comprehend without the help of revelation. In the content of these natural truths divine law is supposed to coincide with natural law, and the church interprets them exclusively from the perspective of faith. Hence, the church has understood its competence in public policy to extend essentially only to the degree it affects the unchanging moral conditions for salvation, not to technical questions or to changing institutions as such. Yet this has not meant that the church's social teaching has remained unchanged or that concrete circumstances have not affected it. For technological breakthroughs and social crises have created new exigencies for the church to interpret the application of the unchanging elements of its moral teaching to the facts and judge whether under the circumstances their demands have been fulfilled.[2]

In *The Challenge of Peace* the American bishops have undertaken the task of reinterpreting the application of the unchanging elements of the Catholic doctrine on peace and war to the qualitatively changed circumstances created by nuclear warfare in order to judge whether the moral demands of these unchanging elements can be fulfilled under the circumstances. The novel conclusions they may have reached should not be allowed to eclipse what is by now the conventional nature of their work. True, they have drawn upon their own experience to assess the likelihood of peace (# 59) and upon "the experience and insights of members of the church"(# 24) and, it must be added, of political and military and medical experts outside the church to get a grasp of the issues and the alternatives. But their incorporation of reason and experience does not belie the fact that *The Challenge to Peace* is, as the bishops say, from first to last a sketch for a theology of peace written exclusively from a faith perspective (Summary).

Thus the distinction between faith and reason should not be allowed, especially outside the church, to blur the realization that the letter is, in its entirety, essentially a theological, not a philosophical or political, tract. The bishops are relying upon their belief in the coincidence of faith and reason in moral issues to assure that what they urge from the perspective of faith will also be convincing from the perspective of reason. Nor should this distinction be utilized, on the other hand, especially within Catholic circles, to impugn the bishops' right to pronounce upon concrete questions of public policy. They are drawing upon the traditional Catholic position that the unchanging elements of Christian moral teaching must be applied concretely to the impact of technological and social changes upon the conditions for salvation. If the bishops cannot speak pointedly from faith without using reason, it is also true that the authority they invoke is strictly that of faith.

Principles and Practice
From a clear understanding of the functions of faith and reason in the letter, it becomes easier to understand the interrelationship between the distinctions the bishops make about the levels of teaching they employ in it and the two communities to which they are addressing it. A diagram will give an initial *aperçu*:

LEVELS OF TEACHING	KINDS OF COMMUNITY	
	Catholic/Religious	Civil/Political
Moral Principles	Formal church teaching	Universal moral principles
Concrete questions	Pastoral responses	Policy choices

Let us examine both of these distinctions and then the resultant categories to assess the fit between rhetorical form and logical substance.

Levels of Teaching

The distinction the bishops make between moral principles and concrete questions (or specific applications) seems to be grounded on the degree of certitude and, consequently, of moral authority to be found in either case. The principles may come from "formal church teaching" or be "key moral rules formulated on the basis of reason and experience," but in either case they are expected to be universally (and, it seems, necessarily) binding on those to whom they apply. By contrast, the specific applications or concrete questions derive from prudential judgments "based on specific circumstances which can change or which can be interpreted differently by people of good will"(# 10).

But it is not at all certain such a distinction is valid in theory, and, in any case, the bishops do not follow it in practice.

For this distinction to be valid in theory, there would have to be a structural difference between theory and practice, value and fact, principle and application. But no such distinction can logically be validated, for it would have to be grounded ultimately upon a distinction between analytic truths—those that are self-evidently true or true by the very meaning of the words in which they are expressed—and synthetic truths—those that are true only as a matter of fact or by virtue of direct observation. And no such distinction can be maintained, for we gain even the meanings of the words in putatively analytic truths from experience, and any synthesis we may make of facts is contingent upon the perspective we bring to our obervations. Therefore, all that we can validly maintain is a functional differentiation between what we take as unquestioned background and what we regard as questionable issues.[3]

And whatever validity there might be for a structural differentiation between principles and facts in speculative or theoretical matters, there can be none in practical or moral issues.[4] For in any crucial moral issue we have always to decide both the meaning of the principle in question and whether it holds in a particular case. Take euthanasia, for example, in the case of withdrawing a life-support system from someone terminally ill. This is certainly the deliberate taking of an innocent life. Is it then murder, which we usually define as the deliberate taking of an innocent life, or must we redefine murder or else decide there are exceptions to the principle it is always evil? No matter how we decide the case, there will be no structural differentiation between principle and fact.

Since we get no information and develop no capacity for judgment apart from experience, we cannot understand the meaning of moral terms or grasp the validity of moral principles except from experience. Until we develop practice in handling a certain kind of case and gain an insight into the nature of the issues involved in it, we can be more certain about our intuitions and judgments in particular cases than we can be about the definitions of the terms we must use or the validity of the principles we invoke. Even when we become clear about our terms and certain about our principles, we show what we really mean by them and demonstrate whether we really believe in them by how we decide upon and act in particular cases.

And the practice of the bishops in this letter confirms the difficulty of trying to put into practice what is impossible to maintain in theory. From the start they show no doubt about the fact that, to quote Vatican II, " 'The whole human race faces a moment of supreme crisis' " because "nuclear weaponry has changed the nature of warfare, and the arms race poses a threat to human life and human civilization which is without precedent"(Summary). In the Summary they include under "Principles of Catholic Teaching" concrete questions about nuclear weaponry, deterrence, the arms race and disarmament, and even cases of conscience. Any separation between these matters and what they then list under "Moral Principles and Policy Choices" would seem to be the proverbial distinction without a difference. More importantly, the multitude of revisions and counter-revisions that the bishops made in the four drafts of the letter show that they were certain from the start that they had to condemn nuclear war but found it difficult both to formulate the principles of Catholic teaching and natural morality from which to draw a conclusive argument for their position and to define the precise terms in which to couch their condemnation.

Evidently they believed that in dealing with the threat of nuclear warfare they had encountered the kind of paradigmatic case which requires a reinterpretation of moral terminology and a reevaluation of moral principles. If war now means nuclear war with its threat of global annihilation, can there still be in principle any such thing as a just war, at least without a revision of the meaning of just war? It was doubtless this interlocking uncertainty of principle and fact that prompted the bishops to regard their letter more as the beginning than the end of a discussion of the issue.

The same uncertainty is reflected in the obscurity of whether they regard the elimination of war as practicable. Although they recite more than once Pope John Paul II's precaution that "Christians know that in this world a totally and permanently peaceful society is unfortunately a utopia"(# 78), they also cite a much more apodictic statement of his to the contrary:

> Today, the scale and the horror of modern warfare—whether nu-
> clear or not—makes it totally unacceptable as a means of settling
> differences between nations. War should belong to the tragic past,
> to history; it should find no place on humanity's agenda for the
> future. (# 219)

They also cite both him and Pope Paul VI to support their conviction "that 'peace is possible' " (# 59) and Vatican II to argue for the need " 'to strain every muscle as we work for the time when all war can be completely outlawed by international consent' " (# 72). If there is a coherent teaching to be derived from these contrasting statements, it would seem to be that, although perfect peace may be an eschatological gift of God, there is a practical political possibility of eliminating warfare as a legitimate means of settling international disputes and a moral imperative to prevent the outbreak of nuclear warfare or of total war of any kind.

It is difficult to see, therefore, how the way the bishops have decided the concrete question of the morality of nuclear warfare has not altered their conception of the matter of principle concerning the morality of warfare and the meaning of just war.

Kinds of Community

The distinction the bishops make between the Catholic community and the wider civil community is in a sense clear and unexceptionable. They define the Catholic community by the fact that it is "formed by the premises of the Gospel and the principles of Catholic moral teaching" (# 16), leaving the wider civil community to become the residual category for all those who "do not share the same vision of faith" (# 17).

But the bishops not only recognize explicitly "that Catholics are also members of the wider political community" (# 16), but maintain as well that "the church, as a community of faith and social institution, has a proper, necessary and distinctive part to play in the pursuit of peace"(# 21), presumably as an integral part of the same "wider political community." There is every sign, in fact, that the bishops phrased even the sections on Catholic doctrine and pastoral responses to make them intelligible and even appealing to non-Catholics, and, conversely, in the sections on public policy they give no sign of limiting any of their prescriptions for moral obligations to Catholics. In other words, the bishops seem to have acted on the assumption that the "supreme crisis" of our time has at least begun to dissolve the modern separation between church and state but not so as to lead to any restoration of the medieval hegemony of the church over the state.

Just as the bishops treat the Catholic faithful as an integral part of the wider political community, so also do they seem to consider this community implicitly part of the Catholic community. They describe the Catholic community more broadly as "the religious community [sharing] a specific perspective of faith" (# 17), while they speak of the political or civil community more specifically as "a more pluralistic audience, in which our brothers and sisters with whom we share the name Christian, Jews, Moslems, other religious communities, and all people of good will *also make up our polity*" (# 16; emphasis added). Certainly all of the religious groups they mention share at least partially in the same "specific perspective of faith" as Catholics. And clearly the bishops are tacitly categorizing good-willed non-Catholics under Tertullian's rubric of souls that are naturally Christian, within the membership of Augustine's city of God, and among Rahner's anonymous Christians. For all the overt diffidence in how they assert their authority, they are acting as if they believe their mission, and indeed their authority, as bishops of the church extends to this wider non-Catholic community, whether or not this community is ready to recognize their authority or appreciate their mission.

It becomes difficult, therefore, to believe that the bishops' interpretation of the Catholic teaching on war really has two *separate* purposes: "to help Catholics form their consciences and to contribute to the public policy debate about the morality of war," or that "these two purposes have led Catholic teaching to address [the] two distinct but overlapping audiences [already described]," or, finally, that the need to address these two communities "on war and peace has produced two complementary but distinct styles of teaching" (# 17).

If the bishops acknowledge that Catholics as individuals and the church as an institution both belong to the wider civil community and suggest, conversely, that the members of this wider civil community also belong within the church as the eschatological community of God's good will, they have really only one purpose in mind with two facets— forming consciences and shaping the public debate—and one style of teaching with two warrants—faith and reason. What would be the purpose of forming the consciences of Catholics except to get them to shape public opinion and how could they expect to contribute to the public debate except by also forming the consciences of the wider political community?

It may be that the American Catholic bishops have devised in this letter a kind of moral discourse that begins to fulfill Jonathan Schell's desire for "the full-scale reexamination of the foundations of political thought which must be undertaken if the world's political institutions are to be made consonant with the global reality in which they operate."[5] By doing that they also seem to have convoked a homogeneous audience, without distinction of religion and perhaps not of nationality, to hear what they have to advise about the response we should make to this moment of supreme crisis for the species and the planet.

Having analyzed the basic distinctions which the bishops make in their teaching, we can turn to the analysis of the four categories which result from these distinctions.

Formal Catholic Teaching vs. Pastoral Responses
The application of the distinction between formal Catholic teaching and pastoral responses is clear enough in the differentiation between the doctrinal statements of the Introduction in Part I and the operational implications outlined in Part IV: "The Pastoral Challenge and Response."[6] But the bishops also want this distinction to apply to the differentiation between the doctrine in Part I and the problems and the policies they address in Parts II and III although they have spun between these parts a cat's cradle of interrelationships between theory and practice.

We have already analyzed the logical difficulty of distinguishing in ethics between principles and applications. Here is the more substantive difficulty (which the bishops mention in a footnote [n. 4] cited from the Pastoral Constitution on the Church in the Modern World) of making the analogous distinction between doctrinal and pastoral teaching when the doctrine has intentionally been defined to apply to a specific pastoral need and the pastoral response is deliberately framed in explicitly doctrinal terms. In these circumstances, for the bishops to advise that "consequently, the constitution must be interpreted according to the general norms of theological interpretation"(# 8) has all the deadpan irony and enigmatic lucidity of "Round up the usual suspects" or "Audit the books according to standard accounting practices."

The greatest difficulty in interpreting the distinction between doctrinal and pastoral teaching or between formal church teaching and pastoral response arises over the central issue of the doctrine of the just war. This doctrine the bishops clearly treat as the heart of Catholic teaching on peace and war (# 82). In the third and the final drafts of the letter they gave it the pride of place that in the second draft they had accorded to the tradition of non-violence, to the extent of treating non-violence as obviously a secondary and very dubious option (I.C.4). Yet the just-war doctrine is not clearly a matter of principle, nor is it merely a concrete application.

The basic principle of the Catholic teaching on peace and war is that only peace is basically moral and war is basically immoral.

> The moral theory of "just-war" or "limited-war" doctrine begins with the presumption which binds all Christians: we should do no harm to our neighbors; how we treat our enemy is the key test of whether we love our neighbor; and the possibility of taking even one human life is a prospect we should consider in fear and trembling. How is it possible to move from these presumptions to the idea of a justifiable use of lethal force? (# 80)

But if the just war must satisfy the higher presumption of the necessity for peace, it is not, for all that, a mere option.

> The council and the popes have clearly stated that governments threatened by armed, unjust aggression *must* defend their people. This includes defense by armed force if necessary as a last resort. (# 75)

And the duty of seeing that this social obligation of governments is fulfilled devolves upon the individual Christian:

> The Christian has no choice but to defend peace, properly understood, against aggression. This is an inalienable obligation. It is the *how* of defending peace which offers moral options. (# 73)

The bishops interpret these obligations of self-defense to allow for the use of non-violent resistance and diplomatic negotiation to avert the violence of war only to the extent that their use does not amount to an abrogation of the right of self-defense or a renunciation of the obligation to defend the innocent from unjust aggression (I.C.2 and 3).

In one sense, therefore, the bishops treat the theory of just war as an immutable principle uniquely appropriate to the Catholic interpretation of Christian eschatology, an interpretation according to which the kingdom of God stretches from the resurrection to the Second Coming. In this "already but not yet" comprising the remainder of history, the church has always assumed "that peace is possible but never assured and that its possibility must be continually protected and preserved in the face of obstacles and attacks upon it"(# 60). This middle-of-the-road eschatology does not suppose the feasibility of millennial pacifism, but neither does it countenance the possibility of a chiliastic holy war or crusade, although warrants for both of these alternatives could have been found in sacred scripture and tradition.[7] In this sense of a moral principle the just-war theory means simply that "faced with the fact of attack on the innocent, the presumption that we do no harm, even to our enemy, [yields] to the command of love understood as the need to restrain an enemy who would injure the innocent"(# 81).

In another sense, though, the bishops treat the just-war theory as a concrete application of principle. The right and the obligation of a nation to defend itself against unjust aggression pertains to the period of modern history; that is, the period between the Peace of Westphalia in 1648, when the international community dissolved into a regime of sovereign nation-states, and the time when an effective central authority can be established to enforce international peace (#s 20, 81, 237). During this period the just-war theory means, as was stated in Vatican II: "As long as the danger of war persists and there is no international authority with the necessary competence and power, governments cannot be denied the right of lawful self-defense, once all peace efforts have failed"(# 82). The effective institution of such an international authority would eliminate the morality of the just war in this sense.

It is not clear from the document whether the bishops have clearly understood that they are using the just-war doctrine in the two senses of moral principle and concrete application—or, more properly, in neither of these two senses. Nor is it clear in light of the way they analyze the morality of nuclear war whether they can any longer properly refer to the innocent's right to self-defense against aggression in terms of the moral principle of just war. And if they can imagine no legitimate use of nuclear weaponry and believe besides that "the presumption of the nation-state system that sovereignty implies an ability to protect a nation's territory and population is precisely the presumption denied by the nuclear capacities of both superpowers" (# 136), then they leave themselves no basis for continuing to employ the just-war doctrine as a concrete application of moral principle. They have so emptied the doctrine of significance that it survives only as a vague afterglow of a past age.

Universal Moral Principles vs. Policy Choices

Much the same fate occurs to the doctrine of deterrence in the gap between universal moral principles and policy choices in the section of the letter concerned with nuclear policy and explicitly addressed to the wider political community. The distinctions implied in these categories affect equally the bishops' statements on the prosecution of nuclear war, the promotion of peace, and the development of international interdependence. But the central interest of the entire document is the bishops' analysis of deterrence.

In the Summary and in the body of the document they make clear verbal distinctions between "moral principles" and "policy choices" regarding deterrence. They adopt as a statement of principle Pope John Paul's judgment: " 'In current conditions "deterrence" based on balance, certainly not as an end in itself but as a step on the way toward a progressive disarmament, may still be judged morally acceptable. Nonetheless in order to ensure peace, it is indispensable not to be satisfied with this minimum, which is always susceptible to the real danger of explosion' "(# 173). Their policy choice seems, at first glance, simply to be a straightforward application of this principle: "These considerations of concrete elements of deterrence policy [that is, targeting doctrine and war-fighting strategies], made in light of John Paul II's evaluation, but applying it through our own prudential judgments, lead us to a strictly conditioned moral acceptance of deterrence. We cannot consider it adequate as a long-term basis for peace"(# 186).

Yet the way they distinguish between action policy and declaratory policy in nuclear deterrence evinces a profound skepticism about the ability of any form of nuclear deterrence to preclude the threat of indiscriminate and disproportionate retaliation against an aggressor. They clearly rule out deterrence as a sufficient strategy in itself. They so tightly proscribe any imaginable form of nuclear retaliation that it becomes inconceivable how a nation that accepted these proscriptions could maintain a realistic posture of deterrence. And they mention—without adopting but without refuting—the position of those who deny that nuclear deterrence is a policy at all, who warn that even as a fact it has not facilitated disarmament, and who caution "that even the conditional acceptance of deterrence as laid out in a letter such as this might be inappropriately used by some to reinforce the policy of arms buildup"(# 198).

It is indeed hard to see how any positive acceptance of deterrence, in principle or in policy, survives these reservations. Evidently what the bishops have done is to treat deterrence as an unforeseen consequence of nuclear weaponry, neither moral nor immoral in itself, but moral in effect if it facilitates disarmament and immoral in effect if it simply perpetuates a balance of terror.

What the bishops have not done about this issue is perhaps almost as important as what they did do. They have abandoned without comment the argument for deterrence that John Courtney Murray developed in a much reprinted and very influential article, originally entitled "Theology and Modern War."[8] Writing in the context of the Cold War, Murray may not have actually advocated the adaptation of the just-war doctrine to the justification of a crusade against Communism, but he did advise refining Pope Pius XII's interpretation of the doctrine into "an over-all political moral doctrine with regard to the uses of force" in a limited nuclear war. Murray even went so far as to urge the "need for a thorough moral re-examination of the basic American policy that 'we will never shoot first.'" He asked "Under contemporary circumstances, viewed in their entirety, is this really a *dictamen rationis?*"[9] At Vatican II, flushed with his triumph in shaping the Declaration on Religious Liberty, Murray helped steel the American bishops in their opposition to any criticism of nuclear deterrence.

In abandoning his position, which inspired a generation of Catholic cold warriors, the American bishops have left in their wake a few of their own colleagues, the German and the Italian Catholic hierarchies, and many American political theorists, Catholic and non-Catholic alike. They have come a long way, even since Vatican II.

In *The Challenge of Peace*, therefore, the American church has begun to develop a new role for itself in the formation of public policy. Surprisingly, almost despite itself, the hierarchy seems to have moved into the avant-garde, a prophetic band, leading not by an assertion of bureaucratic authority but by demonstrating a charismatic rational authority. The language of the document strains and occasionally breaks under the pressure. But the thought it embodies verges upon a new conception of international political morality. The realism the bishops advocate may suit neither pragmatists nor idealists, but it may help to assure a less apocalyptic and more peaceable future.

NOTES

1. See, for example, Michael Novak, "Moral Clarity in the Nuclear Age," *National Review* XXXV/6 (1 April 1983).

2. See J.-Y. Calvez and J. Perrin, *The Church and Social Justice* (Chicago, 1961), pp. 1–74.

3. W. V. O. Quine, "Two Dogmas of Empiricism," *From a Logical Point of View* (New York, 1983), chap. 2.

4. See A. MacIntyre, *After Virtue* (Notre Dame, Ind., 1981), pp. 49–59, 70.

5. J. Schell, *The Fate of the Earth* (New York, 1982), p. 219.

6. The precedent the bishops give for the distinction of "doctrinal" from "pastoral" teaching is Vatican II's Pastoral Constitution on the Church in the Modern World (I). The author of this distinction, though, was probably Pope Paul VI (in 1957, when he was still Archbishop Montini), who characterized Pope Pius XII's teaching in his later addresses to professional audiences as "pastoral," to distinguish it from the "doctrinal" teaching of his earlier encyclicals, insofar as it was "suggested not so much by the intrinsic requirements of doctrine—although that matters, too—as by the extrinsic needs of the groups of people" (see the citation in Calvez and Perrin, p. 74).

7. See Roland H. Bainton, *Christian Attitudes Toward War and Peace* (New York, 1960).

8. See *Theological Studies* 20 (1959):40–61; also John Courtney Murray, *We Hold These Truths* (New York, 1960), pp. 249–74.

9. Ibid., p. 255.

J. BRYAN HEHIR

From the Pastoral Constitution of Vatican II to *The Challenge of Peace*

This essay examines the pastoral letter as a theological document. Since the pastoral is an exercise of the teaching ministry of the bishops of the United States, it should be understood in light of the broader framework of Catholic social teaching.

The key to locating the pastoral letter in the wider tradition is found in the Introduction where the bishops explicitly state their dependence upon the Second Vatican Council's Pastoral Constitution on the Church in the Modern World.[1] This essay will examine *The Challenge of Peace* as both a product of and a response to the pastoral constitution. Specifically, the case argued here is that the American pastoral letter stands *theologically* on the ecclesiological foundation of the conciliar text, while *morally* it develops the arguments of the pastoral constitution beyond the point reached at Vatican II.

The Challenge of Peace: A Product of the Pastoral Constitution

There are two ways in which the pastoral constitution establishes a framework for understanding the letter of the American bishops. First, the ecclesiology of the pastoral constitution, its description of "the presence and function of the Church in the world of today,"[2] laid the theological and pastoral foundation on which the U.S. bishops stood in writing their letter. Second, the moral argument of the pastoral constitution on modern warfare defined the starting point from which the U.S. bishops proceeded to address concrete aspects of the nuclear age. Both of these contributions of the pastoral constitution need to be explicated.

The Church in the World: The Conciliar Vision

In the secular media the specific positions which the pastoral letter took on contemporary questions of strategy and politics dominated all commentaries. In the church, it is necessary also to see the place of the pastoral letter in the wider ministry of the church.

The pastoral constitution of Vatican II has proven to be one of the most influential of the conciliar documents.[3] It is difficult to imagine the bishops of the United States issuing their pastoral letter in 1983 if they had not been schooled in the ecclesiology of the pastoral constitution for the last eighteen years. There are three aspects of the theology of the pastoral constitution which prepared for the pastoral letter: (1) its definition of the *place* of the church in the world; (2) its description of the church's *presence* in the world; and (3) its *perspective* on the church's teaching style.

The pastoral constitution provides the most comprehensive statement in modern times of the church's *place* in the world. The conciliar document is not content either with homiletic statements that the church should be active in the affairs of the world or even with a repetition of previous moral teaching on specific social questions. Rather, the distinctive contribution of the conciliar text is that it provides a theological rationale for the entire social ministry of the church. The significance of this contribution can be grasped by showing what the pastoral constitution adds to the social teaching of the last hundred years. Embodied in a succession of papal encyclicals from Leo XIII through John Paul II, that social teaching has been principally devoted to an articulation of the dignity of the person and the defense of the spectrum of human rights and duties which flow from and protect that dignity. These twin themes of human dignity and human rights have been incorporated in a developing moral vision which has assessed the conditions of the industrial revolution, the postwar interdependence of the globe, and today's postindustrial society.

Noticeably absent, even in the best of the social encyclicals, has been an explicit discussion of how the social vision is related to a theological understanding of the church's nature and mission. The gap has been an ecclesiological one, a failure to join the activity of the church in the world to the inner nature of the church. The lack of such a statement has the effect of leaving the valuable social tradition at the edge of the church's life; it resides there as an aspect of the church's ministry but not as a central focus of its life.

The pastoral constitution establishes an explicit theological relationship between the moral vision of Catholic social teaching and its ecclesiological significance. The linkage is made in two steps.

First, the pastoral constitution takes the key concept from the social teaching and describes the church's role in society in light of it. The church, says the conciliar text, "is at once the sign and the safeguard of the transcendental dimension of the human person."[4] In this passage the tasks of protecting human dignity and promoting human rights takes on ecclesial significance. They are not purely "secular" functions toward which the church is benignly but distantly disposed. Rather, the pastoral constitution calls the church to place itself in support of these tasks in every political system. The engagement of the Catholic church, as an institution and a community, in defense of human rights in political cultures as diverse as Poland, Brazil, South Africa, and South Korea testifies to the impact of this linkage of moral teaching on human rights and of ecclesial teaching on the ministry of the church.

Second, the authors of the conciliar text recognized that it was insufficient to leave the theological argument at the point of linking the moral and the ecclesial themes. For as soon as the church takes this linkage seriously and engages in a consistent pursuit of human rights the question which inevitably arises is whether such activity is beyond the scope of its competence or involves a politicization of religion. The deeper issue which needed to be addressed, therefore, was how the church influences the socio-political order without itself becoming politicized.

The response of the pastoral constitution, found in paragraphs 40–42, is clear and basic. The place of the church in the socio-political order is shaped by the following principles: (a) The ministry of the church is religious in nature; it has no specifically political charism. (b) The religious ministry has as its primary object the achievement of the kingdom of God; the church is in a unique way the "instrument" of the kingdom in history. (c) The power of the kingdom is intended to permeate every dimension of life. (d) As the church pursues its properly religious ministry, it contributes to four areas of life which have direct social and political consequences. (e) These four religiously rooted but politically significant goals are: (i) the defense of human dignity; (ii) the promotion of human rights; (iii) the cultivation of the unity of the human family; and (iv) the provision of meaning to every aspect of human activity.[5]

In the theology of the pastoral constitution the *place* of the church in the world is set by two principles: transcendence and compenetration. On the one hand, the church, because of its religious ministry, transcends every political system; it cannot be identified with or contained within any one political system. On the other hand, the church, precisely in pursuit of its religious ministry, adequately defined, should be engaged in the daily life of every socio-political entity. The engagement is "indirect," that is, through the pursuit of the four goals outlined above. This form of witnessing to the life of the kingdom in history is what the late John Courtney Murray called the principle of "compenetration."[6]

Examination of the place of the church in the world led the pastoral constitution to discuss the mode of the church's *presence* in the world. The church must contribute to each and every political system in a manner which preserves its identity and still makes an effective contribution to a just and peaceful society. The style of presence outlined in the pastoral constitution is the method of dialogue: "And so the Council, as witness and guide to the faith of the whole people of God, gathered together by Christ, can find no more eloquent expression of its solidarity and respectful affection for the whole human family to which it belongs, than to enter into dialogue with it about all these different problems."[7]

The pastoral constitution describes the attitude which the church brings to this dialogue with the world: the church has something to learn and something to teach. In a spirit strikingly different from that of the eighteenth and nineteenth centuries, the church acknowledges its need for and its desire to draw upon the various disciplines and areas of expertise which contribute to the building of contemporary society. In a major teaching document of the council, the bishops committed themselves to a teaching style which seeks a precise understanding of contemporary problems in all their complexity prior to making moral judgments or providing religious guidance about these questions.

The willingness to learn from the world is partly motivated by the desire of the church to contribute to a deeper sense of the human and religious significance of contemporary life. While the pastoral constitution exhibits an attractive modesty in the face of secular complexity, the council was not paralyzed by the data of the empirical sciences. The pastoral desire to dialogue moves beyond listening to that of interpreting: "The Church likewise believes that the key, the center and the purpose of the whole of man's history is to be found in its Lord and Master. . . . And that is why the Council, relying on the inspiration of Christ, . . . proposes to speak to all men in order to unfold the mystery that is man and cooperate in tackling the main problems facing the world today."[8] At the heart of the dense technical complexity of the age lie problems of meaning, purpose, and moral direction.

The method of dialogue was a central theme in the preparation of *The Challenge of Peace*. The Bernardin committee, charged with the drafting of the letter, followed the style of the pastoral constitution: it first listened, then it spoke. The first year of the committee's work was largely given over to a series of "hearings" in which a number of people were invited before the committee to share their expertise and experiences.

The "witnesses" included a panel of biblical scholars, a dozen moralists of differing persuasions, a spectrum of arms control experts, two former secretaries of defense, a physician, two retired military officers, a panel of peace activists, and specialists in non-violent defense and conflict resolution. The hearing process closed with a full day of discussion with representatives of the Reagan administration: the secretary of defense, the under secretary of state for political affairs, and the director of the Arms Control and Disarmament Agency. Through these hearings the bishops were immersed in the problems of nuclear strategy, arms control, and the likely consequences of a nuclear war.

The process of dialogue extended to the whole bishops' conference when the various drafts of the pastoral letter were published for analysis and debate. The scope of the dialogue and the degree of detail the committee addressed went beyond that used in the pastoral constitution, but the method of dialogue was drawn from the conciliar experience.

The dialogue was carried on within the *perspective* of the pastoral constitution. That perspective is expressed in the following passage from the document: "At all times the Church carries the responsibility of reading the signs of the times and of interpreting them in the light of the Gospel. . . ." The biblical phrase "signs of the times" points toward a methodological principle of the pastoral constitution. It means beginning the process of theological analysis with a concrete examination of the nature of the questions to be addressed, then moving to a theological reflection on the major characteristics of the problem.

The American pastoral letter began with an assessment of the "new moment" in the nuclear age. The bishops sought first to understand the content and dynamics of this "new moment" prior to making their contribution to it. They went on in the letter to assess the *nature* of deterrence as a predominant sign of the times before they tried to make a *moral* judgment on the policy of deterrence.

On all three of these ecclesiological themes—the place of the church in the world, its style of presence, and its perspective—the contributions of the pastoral constitution directly shaped how the American bishops pursued their task.

The Morality of Modern Warfare: The Conciliar View

The pastoral constitution was approved at Vatican II twenty years after the atomic bombing at Hiroshima and Nagasaki. The U.S. bishops' letter was published almost twenty years after the council, but its point of departure was the assessment of modern war found in the pastoral constitution.

The American pastoral letter said, "The Catholic tradition on war and peace is a long and complex one, reaching from the Sermon on the Mount to the statements of Pope John Paul II."[9] The pastoral constitution is one chapter in this long narrative, but it was a crucial chapter. It has determined the state of the question of Catholic teaching on warfare for the post-conciliar church. The contribution of the pastoral constitution lay in its synthesis of major elements of the classical Catholic tradition and in its statement of a contemporary theology of peace for the nuclear age.

The classical character of the pastoral constitution is evident in the way it proposes a positive vision of peace (an idea rooted in the scriptures and Augustine) and joins it with an ethic of limits on war (a concept found in Augustine, Aquinas, Vitoria, and recent papal teaching). Positively, the pastoral constitution defines peace as "more than the absence of war"; peace is "the fruit of that right ordering of things with which the divine founder has invested human society and which must be actualized by man thirsting after an ever more perfect reign of justice."[10] The building of peace at every level of society, shaping it through the values of justice, truth, freedom, and love, is the primary way to prevent war.

The pastoral constitution reaffirms this ancient idea, but it does so in conjunction with an equally venerable part of the classical Catholic tradition: "Insofar as men are sinners, the threat of war hangs over them and will so continue until the coming of Christ. . . . As long as the danger of war persists and there is no international authority with the necessary competence and power, governments cannot be denied the right of lawful self-defense once all peace efforts have failed."[11]

These two dimensions of the classical case, mediated by the pastoral constitution, flow directly into the U.S. bishops' letter. Other elements of the classical tradition are highly visible: the categories of non-combatant immunity and proportionality as key ideas of an ethic of force, a sober realism about the difficulty of building peace in a world of sovereign states, and healthy skepticism about claims that force can be both used and precisely limited.

The pastoral constitution mediated more than a restatement of the classical concepts for the pastoral letter. The conciliar text was acutely conscious of the different circumstances posed for any moral doctrine by the nuclear age. Its assessment of the signs of the times gave the Vatican II document a distinctively contemporary tone. The pastoral constitution shaped the state of the question for the American letter in three ways: its description of facts, its development of the tradition, and its definition of the moral problem of deterrence.

The contemporary tenor of the pastoral constitution is found in its description of the qualitatively new danger of the nuclear age and in the theological response evoked by such new dangers. The opening sentence of the conciliar text asserts that "the whole human race faces a moment of supreme crisis in its advance toward maturity."[12] The moment of supreme crisis is formed by the destructive capabilities of "the kind of weapons now stocked in the arsenals of the great powers"[13] and by the complexity of international relations today. In the face of this moment of supreme crisis the council states a theological imperative which leads directly toward the American bishops' letter twenty years later: "All these factors force us to undertake a completely fresh reappraisal of war. Men of this generation should realize that they will have to render an account of their warlike behaviour; the destiny of generations to come depends largely on the decisions they make today."[14]

The pastoral constitution not only called for a "fresh reappraisal," it began the task itself. Key developments in the moral analysis of warfare are present in the conciliar text; the American letter is shaped by these concepts. An example of this is the stress on individual conscience found in the pastoral constitution. Precisely because the destiny of future generations depends upon present choices, the council sharpens the responsibility of conscience which each person bears regarding decisions of war and peace. The classical formulation, which held that on questions of this magnitude the "presumption of the laws" meant that the burden of proof rested upon the citizen who dissented on moral grounds, is not found in this document. Instead there is a reaffirmation of binding principles of natural law and an instruction that "any action which deliberately violates these principles, and any order which commands such actions is criminal and blind obedience cannot excuse those who carry them out."[15]

This stress on conscience is then extended to include praise for those who "forgo the use of violence to vindicate their rights . . . provided it can be done without harm to the rights and duties of others and of the community."[16] This position in turn is complemented by a statement to governments that "it seems just that laws should make humane provision for the case of conscientious objectors who refuse to carry arms, provided they accept some form of community service."[17]

All this development on the doctrine of conscience and warfare is articulated within the context of a reaffirmation of the just-war ethic of the classical tradition. But the new weight given to the protection of the rights of conscience illustrates the strain placed on the classical vision by the conditions of modern warfare. The classical case holds, but with modifications. Both the lines of continuity and of change will be evident in the American pastoral.

Finally, the contemporary character of the pastoral constitution is manifested by its willingness to grapple, however tentatively, with the dominant ethical question of the nuclear age, the policy of deterrence. The direct linkage between the pastoral constitution and *The Challenge of Peace* is more visible here than on any other topic. The council opened the question of deterrence but did not move very far in the direction of providing guidance about it. The conciliar text admirably grasped the political and moral paradox of the problem in the following sentence: "Since the defensive strength of any nation is thought to depend on its capacity for immediate retaliation, the stockpiling of arms which grows from year to year serves, in a way hitherto unthought of, as a deterrent to potential attackers. Many people look upon this as the most effective way known at the present time for maintaining some sort of peace among nations."[18] This lucid statement of the problem was not followed by an equally clear assessment. In the next two decades leading to the American pastoral, many would struggle with the question whether deterrence is the "most effective way" or even a morally acceptable way to maintain the peace. By the time the bishops came to write their letter, the specifics of the issue could not be avoided.

In a sense the deterrence issue symbolized the challenge faced by the American bishops. Forty years into the nuclear age, twenty years after the council and faced with increasing political tension, galloping technology, and dim prospects for effective arms control, what should a "fresh reappraisal of war" look like? The pastoral constitution had provided the framework of a response, but there was need for a specific address to the "moment of supreme crisis."

The Challenge of Peace:
A Response to the Pastoral Constitution

The purpose of this section is not to provide a detailed commentary on *The Challenge of Peace*, but to select three themes which illustrate both continuity with and development beyond the pastoral constitution. Each topic is rooted in the conciliar document, but each is given its own distinctive character in the U.S. bishops' letter.

Dimensions of the Dialogue with the World

In the opening section of the pastoral letter the bishops establish their objectives as teachers: "Catholic teaching on peace and war has had two purposes: to help Catholics form their consciences and to contribute to the public policy debate about the morality of war. . . . As bishops we believe that the nature of Catholic moral teaching, the principles of Catholic ecclesiology, and the demands of our pastoral ministry require that this letter speak both to Catholics in a specific way and to the wider political community regarding public policy."[19]

An explicit choice of which audiences they would address was one of the early decisions the bishops had to make. Both the pastoral constitution and the encyclical "Peace on Earth" of John XXIII had explicitly stated that they were written for consumption beyond the community of the church. Both had been examples of the church speaking to the world, but they had used different means for the dialogue.

The encyclical "Peace on Earth" exemplified the natural-law ethic which has been such a major part of Catholic social teaching.[20] Its mode of discourse is philosophical not theological; it makes extensive use of secular categories and minimal use of biblical imagery; it engages complex public issues in a detailed and sophisticated fashion. The conciliar document, written only two years after the encyclical, is distinctively different in style. The role of natural law is minimal; the categories of analysis are explicitly biblical, theological, ecclesial, and christological. The document, while addressed to all people in terms of the topics analyzed, uses an analysis which presumes some identification with the Christian faith.

The two documents, both products of Catholic teaching in the 1960s, exemplify two quite distinct ways for the church to engage in dialogue with the world.

The differences between them are not confined to questions of language (philosophy versus theology); in deciding *how* the church is to conduct its dialogue with the world, we move from issues of language to ecclesiology and theology. One purpose of the natural-law ethic, exemplified in the concepts and terminology of the just-war ethic, has been to allow a community of faith to address its concerns to the wider civil community. The natural-law ethic is designed to provide a mediating instrument which allows an ethic rooted in a faith perspective to be explained and expressed in a way which others could grasp and support.

The issue of *language* is related, therefore, to which *audiences* the church seeks to address in a given document. The choice of audience in turn depends upon how the church conceives its pastoral responsibility.

The choices made by the Bernardin committee and then affirmed by the bishops in the final document took a "traditionally" Catholic position. They decided to speak to both the church *and* the wider society. This decision shaped not only the language of the pastoral but the logic of its moral reasoning. If appeal was to be made to the society as a whole, then mediating language, in this case just-war ethics, would be needed. If the church sought to shape not only Christian witness but public policy, then engagement in highly technical issues (the nature of the deterrent, targeting doctrine, negotiating positions) would be necessary. The letter uses both mediating language and detailed analysis of intricate policy issues.

At the same time the style of the pastoral constitution is evident. The sharp distinction between an ethic of reason versus an evangelical ethic is not clearly drawn. The appeal to the witness of the scriptures and specifically to the way of life of Jesus is a major focus in the pastoral. The extreme choices posed for Christians by the nuclear age run through the pastoral.

The trade-offs made in shaping this letter are similar to those which have been debated for centuries in the Christian church. To choose to speak to *both* the church and world is to lose some of the "prophetic edge" of the scriptures. To attempt to shape public policy leads inevitably to consensus positions which are not a clear witness against the evil threatened by nuclear war.

The pastoral letter at times speaks directly and clearly to the community of the church, particularly in Parts I and IV. For many these sections constitute the real message of the letter. Others, particularly in the media and the policy community, focus on Part II and Part III. Here the consensus choices—which should not imply that consensus is possible on every choice—are hammered out. For some in policy circles the choices made by the bishops are beyond what can be followed. For some in the church the choices give away too much to the prevailing presumptions of policy.

There is a tension in the way the bishops chose to shape their dialogue with the world, but they found the method of speaking to both the ecclesial and civil communities closest to their sense of pastoral responsibility.

From Principles to Cases:
The Issue of Specificity

The effective role played by the pastoral constitution in setting the state of the question on issues of war and peace is demonstrated by the dependence of the pastoral letter on it. At the same time, it is clear from reading the two documents that the eighteen year interval had been a time of significant development in Catholic theological thought on the ethics of war in the nuclear age. The best way to illustrate both themes—dependence by the pastoral on the council and development beyond the conciliar analysis—is to examine the principles of the pastoral constitution and the conclusions of *The Challenge of Peace.*

To examine both principles and conclusions is to highlight a fundamental decision made by the bishops in the preparation of their pastoral. It involved the willingness to draw specific conclusions in a teaching document. The pastoral constitution is strong on the articulation of basic principles, but not very expansive about the consequences of applying these principles to policy choices and personal decisions. Such caution is very understandable both in terms of the *kind* of document the council produced (a document for the whole church) and the *time* when it was written (twenty, not forty, years into the nuclear age).

When the U.S. bishops chose to address issues similar to those faced by Vatican II, they did so as pastors in one of two major nuclear nations. This meant that the pastoral responsibilities they exercised were more specifically defined than those of a general council of the church. The specific choices they had to address were more concretely articulated by the widespread public debate going on in the United States about nuclear policy, and the need to indicate the role of moral principles in policy choices was more urgent. The risk of maintaining the same level of generality as the conciliar text was that the meaning of the moral principles would be blunted, the opportunity to place the voice of the church decisively in the midst of the public debate would be lost, and the developments which had occurred theologically since the council would not be well utilized by the episcopal magisterium of the local church.

At the same time the willingness to be specific needed to be balanced by principles of interpretation which made clear that increasing specificity on the part of the bishops meant declining moral authority. This is a general principle of moral analysis; as one moves from statements of clear principle to the application of such principles to complex and concrete situations, the mixture of principle and fact means that a number of contingent judgments must be made which are open to debate by others.[21] The acknowledgment of this general principle was particularly necessary in the pastoral letter not only because of the intricacy of the nuclear issues, but also because other episcopal conferences in other parts of the world were also addressing many of these same issues and could quite legitimately differ from judgments made in the U.S. pastoral letter. The decision, therefore, to be specific in judgment and flexible in interpretation was an attempt to reconcile several legitimate concerns of the bishops as teachers in the Catholic church. They desired to use the wisdom of the universal church, to fulfill their responsibilities as pastors of a local church, to open a process of serious examination of these issues in their congregations, and to be fair to their brother bishops in other parts of the world.

The issues of the *use* of nuclear weapons and the strategy of *deterrence*, both found in Part II of *The Challenge of Peace*, illustrate how the American bishops sought both to use the classical moral teaching and to extend its contemporary application.

Three cases of use were considered. The pastoral constitution had performed a significant service by restating with great clarity the just-war principle of non-combatant immunity.[22] The American letter not only reaffirmed the binding force of this principle but applied it to one of the key questions in the strategic debate when they ruled out retaliatory strikes against civilian centers, even if our cities had been hit first. Such a judgment stands as a moral barrier against a tactic which has been proposed more than once in the nuclear age.[23]

The clarity of the principle of non-combatant immunity and its very special role in Catholic ethics made the step between principle and application very short. This was not the case when the bishops addressed two other cases of use: "first use" and limited nuclear war. On both questions the pastoral letter entered an arena of intense controversy. On both questions one finds the debate among strategists yielding very different views.

The bishops examined both issues from the perspective of moral principles, but they were aware that in neither case could they escape the task of reading the signs of the times, of understanding why the technical authors divide over the empirical data. Both "Peace on Earth" and the pastoral constitution had questioned whether the criterion of proportionality could be observed in a nuclear exchange. The American letter, using proportionality as its principal but not exclusive criterion, made a specific judgment against the moral acceptability of first use of nuclear weapons and expressed radical skepticism about the possibility of containing a "limited" nuclear exchange.[24]

In both instances the U.S. bishops took specific positions not previously found in either the papal literature nor, to my knowledge, in any statement of another episcopal conference. On both questions the bishops staked out a position for themselves in the public debate, and they openly acknowledged that the very strength and specificity of their moral judgments invited debate about them within the church and in the society.

The complexity of first use and limited war pales when the topic of deterrence arises. This has been the key political and moral issue of the nuclear age. It does not yield easily to the resources of reason or faith. We have already seen how the pastoral constitution opened the topic for consideration in 1965. In the period from 1965 to 1980 the debate about deterrence in the church intensified in theological writing and in the community of peace activists. In the United States Cardinal Krol's congressional testimony in 1979 served as a catalyst in the discussion. The Cardinal had rendered a judgment of "toleration" of the deterrent on the condition it be used to move the superpowers toward effective arms control and disarmament.[25]

A qualitatively new impetus was given to the debate when Pope John Paul II addressed the deterrence question in a message sent to the United Nations Special Session on Disarmament (1982): "In current conditions 'deterrence' based on balance, certainly not as an end in itself but as a step on the way toward a progressive disarmament, may still be judged morally acceptable."[26]

The bishops were already deeply into the deterrence debate when John Paul II spoke to it. They continued to struggle with the question for the next year. The final version of the pastoral letter illustrates the dynamic of development which had occurred since Vatican II. The essential judgment of the U.S. bishops on deterrence is that of "strictly conditioned moral acceptance."[27]

Shorn of all modifiers, the verdict is "acceptance" rather than "condemnation." Clearly the Holy Father's statement plus the bishops' own struggle with the various elements of deterrence were the moving forces in this final judgment. But it is not their intent to give a blank check to every form of deterrence or to every proposal made in the name of deterrence.

Hence the meaning of "strictly conditioned" must be precisely understood. The phrase is designed to place two kinds of limits on deterrence. The first is temporal: the argument of the pastoral is that the marginal justification accorded deterrence means it is acceptable *only* if it is used as a step toward a different kind of basis for national and international security. We are not to be complacent, politically or morally, about deterrence.

The second limit is analytical: deterrence is such a faulty and dangerous way to keep the peace that it must be restricted to its most limited function. The bishops enumerate a series of nine conditions designed to limit the role and function of deterrence. Here again they must be specific to be effective: they oppose: (1) "hard-target kill" weapons, (2) blurring the difference between nuclear and conventional forces, (3) the quest for superiority in the arms race, and (4) the extension of deterrence into war-fighting strategies.[28]

All of these specific judgments on use and deterrence go beyond the analysis of previous Catholic teaching. But each judgment is rooted in the principles and perspective of the prior teaching. In this way the pastoral letter seeks to preserve what has been received and to use it creatively and constructively.

From "Presence in the World" to Issues of Identity

The pastoral constitution called the church to be present in the midst of the drama of history, to be visible and vocal at all the key places where decisions are made which shape the fabric of human life. The pastoral letter is an attempt by one local hierarchy to respond to the conciliar call, to be present in the midst of the nuclear debate.

But "presence" is not a static category. To be present in the style of the pastoral constitution is to face questions about our identity as a church and our vocations as Christians. These are the questions which the church in the United States struggles with in virtue of its response to the pastoral constitution.

The questions of identity arise from the dialogue to which the church is called by Vatican II. As the pastoral letter was being prepared and the successive drafts were published for public scrutiny, four different forms of dialogue became evident.

The first, perhaps the most dramatic, was a classical church-state dialogue. The ethic of war and peace touches upon issues of "national security." No state can be indifferent when a major institution in society questions the legitimacy or morality of the means proposed to guarantee the security of the nation. But the pastoral letter raises precisely these questions. One commentator wrote of the pastoral: "The Catholic bishops' logic and passion have taken them to the very foundation of American security policy."[29] In brief, neither church nor state can be neutral when a serious examination of "national security" occurs. The issues of politics and morality are so closely linked that each will feel its identity is at stake. But to enter this argument the church needs a clear sense of its role in society, of its teaching obligation, of the limits and the scope of its pastoral responsibility. All of these themes surround the concrete questions of war and peace.

A second dialogue which has been a by-product of the pastoral involves religion and science. This topic has not been a happy one since the Enlightenment and it has touched upon the identity of religious faith and its meaning in a scientific age. Many times the church appears on the defensive. The experience of the pastoral has been one of positive engagement of religion and science, an opportunity to illustrate that at the heart of scientific power, as embodied in the nuclear age, there stands moral questions which must be addressed and do not yield simply to more technical data. But the dialogue also is an opportunity for the church to use the resources of science to probe the very problem it seeks to assess in moral terms.

A third dialogue involves the church and the university. The terms of the nuclear debate have been set in the academic world. The very complexity and dynamism of the nuclear age forces the government to rely upon research to define the questions it must decide. Shaping the intellectual debate means helping to shape political decision making. The pastoral has become a much discussed resource in university communities. This too provides an opportunity for the church to define its identity as a major contribution to one of the intractable intellectual and political problems of the day.

Finally the dialogue between church and state and the church and other major institutions in society moves back inside the community of the church itself. The bishops have conducted the dialogue which led to the pastoral letter. Now they put their finished product into the hands of the people of the church. The attention which the other levels of dialogue with the world have attracted means that our dialogue in the church will be watched carefully. As we discuss war and peace, the Catholic moral tradition and the American political tradition, we will be forging an image of the church in our culture. The discussion will cut across the proper role of the church on public issues, the questions of personal and professional choice in the nuclear age and the cooperation of the church with other institutions. How we decide these issues will project an identity for the Catholic church in American society.

The council called us to be present in the world. The pastoral has given us a very visible presence. The quality of our presence is now going to be tested.

NOTES

1. *The Challenge of Peace: God's Promise and Our Response*, #8.
2. Vatican Council II, The Pastoral Constitution on the Church in the Modern World, #2, in A. Flannery, O.P., ed., *Vatican Council II: The Conciliar and Post-Conciliar Documents* (Collegeville: The Liturgical Press, 1975).
3. For commentary cf. J. C. Murray, "The Issue of Church and State at Vatican II," *Theological Studies* 27 (1966): 580–606.
4. Pastoral Constitution, #76.
5. Ibid., #40.

6. Murray, p. 600.
7. Pastoral Constitution, #3.
8. Ibid., #10.
9. *The Challenge of Peace*, #7.
10. Pastoral Constitution, #78; the same theme is found in John XXIII, "Peace on Earth," in J. Gremillion, *The Gospel of Peace and Justice* (New York: Orbis Books, 1979).
11. Pastoral Constitution, #78.
12. Ibid., #77.
13. Ibid., #80.
14. Ibid., #80.
15. Ibid., #79.
16. Ibid., #78.
17. Ibid., #79.
18. Ibid., #81.
19. *The Challenge of Peace*, #s 16 and 19.
20. "Peace on Earth," in Gremillion, cited.
21. For comments on this theme cf. J. C. Murray, *We Hold These Truths* (New York: Sheed and Ward, 1960), p. 272; R. B. Potter, *War and Moral Discourse* (Richmond, Va.: John Knox Press, 1969); J. Gustafson, "Context Versus Principles: A Misplaced Debate in Christian Ethics," *Harvard Theological Review* 58 (1965): 171–202.
22. Pastoral Constitution, #80.
23. "Under no circumstances may nuclear weapons or other instruments of mass slaughter be used for the purpose of destroying population centers or other predominantly civilian targets. . . . Retaliatory action whether nuclear or conventional which would indiscriminately take many wholly innocent lives . . . must also be condemned" (*The Challenge of Peace*, #s 147 and 148).
24. *The Challenge of Peace*, #s 150–61.
25. Cardinal John Krol, Testimony on SALT II, *Origins* (1979), p. 197.
26. John Paul II, Message to the Second Special Session of the United Nations General Assembly Devoted to Disarmament (June 1982).
27. "These considerations of concrete elements of nuclear deterrence policy, made in light of John Paul II's evaluation, but applying it through our own prudential judgments, lead us to a strictly conditioned moral acceptance of nuclear deterrence. We cannot consider it adequate as a long term basis for peace" (*The Challenge of Peace*, #186).
28. Ibid., #s 188–91.
29. Stephen S. Rosenfield, "The Bishops and the Bomb," *The Washington Post*, 29 October 1982, Op-Ed page.

III

Peace and the Kingdom of God

The Challenge of Peace

Part I.A-B, #s 27–65

The pastoral positions sacred scripture as the foundation for confronting issues of war and peace. In its overture, therefore, it offers "a sketch of the biblical concepts for peace."

From the Hebrew scriptures is drawn the development of the relationship of the people to the creator. The initial dominant metaphor of the warrior God, who is the main actor providing security for the people against their enemies, gradually emerged into a more complex imagery, marked by a covenantal relationship of mutual promises to be kept.

On God's part, the commitment was to be present with his people in a protective way. For the people, the promises included constructing a society characterized by justice, especially for those who are needy and helpless.

However, experiences convinced the people that while they frequently failed in their fidelity, they clung tenaciously to God's promise that ultimately a messiah would bring justice and peace.

For Christians, Jesus is the messiah. In the New Testament, gone are all facets of a warrior God. In its place, Jesus poses a new way, the path of forgiveness reflecting the tender mercy of an ever-loving God, and the pursuit of justice which is the foundation of peace. In his intervention into history, Jesus announced that the reign of God is near. For his followers, to live in history is to accept the tension of "already but not yet," a kingdom of justice and peace, but a kingdom not yet in its fullness.

Willingness to accept this tension, the pastoral notes, accounts for much of the complexity of Catholic teaching on warfare. While the expectation that peace is possible is valid, its possibility must be continually protected in the face of obstacles and attacks.

SANDRA M. SCHNEIDERS

New Testament Reflections on Peace and Nuclear Arms

With so many others, Catholics and non-Catholics alike, I rejoiced at the prophetic witness the bishops gave to the possibility of peace and the moral leadership they provided for those who are working to bring it about.[1] The pastoral is a major contribution to reflection and incentive to action on the most pressing issue of our time. Nevertheless, I have to conclude that the weakest element of the letter is the section on scripture. The biblical section in the final document is a major improvement over the corresponding sections in the first and second drafts. It evokes the biblical message with greater fullness and shows better the relationship between the Old and New Testaments. However, the major weakness, namely, the failure to integrate the biblical material into the central reasoning of the document, remains.

This weakness is not peculiar to this pastoral. The pastoral merely exemplifies a problem which is becoming more evident as Catholics try to make their relatively recently recovered sense of the centrality of scripture function in their reflection on contemporary issues. The problem is that we lack an adequate hermeneutical theory to ground our use of biblical material in relationship to contemporary problems. As a result, we tend to "invoke" scripture at the outset of a reasoning process whose real dynamics are derived from moral theology, papal social teaching, theology, or elsewhere. What I will try to do in this essay is to demonstrate a more integral use of biblical material, not as an introduction to other kinds of reasoning but as the substance of the argument. First, I will outline briefly the theoretical framework for the biblical reflection; second, I will briefly summarize the theological-ecclesial context of the reflections; third, I will discuss at some length five aspects of the New Testament vision of Christian discipleship which bear upon the questions of peace and nuclear arms.

Theoretical Framework

To begin, I want to mention, in order to repudiate them, two approaches to New Testament material which are unreliable as contributions to pastoral reflection. Then I will examine two legitimate approaches to New Testament material and the kinds of contributions each can make to the effort to find Christian responses to questions and problems which could not have occurred to the first-century authors who composed the New Testament texts.

The first illegitimate approach, biblical fundamentalism, is not historically characteristic of Roman Catholics but has recently achieved a disturbing prominence in certain conservative Catholic circles. Fundamentalism might be defined as literalism in interpretation based on an untenable theological doctrine that each word of the Bible is divinely dictated and thus must be regarded as not subject to error. Its basic theological error is its rejection of the incarnational character of divine revelation which entails that God's word is mediated through historical human understanding and speech.[2]

This theological error leads directly to the methodological position of rejecting the methods and conclusions of historical criticism[3] and treating the biblical texts as timeless formulations, in an unchanging language, of eternal truths. Although often motivated by a genuine desire to hear God's word without guile, that is, without possible distortion by human scientific interventions in the interpretative process, fundamentalism results in a type of reading which is sometimes merely simplistic but often enough completely erroneous. This type of interpretation becomes particularly dangerous when used to deal with issues of such extraordinary complexity as nuclear war.

The second illegitimate approach is closely related to fundamentalism and is historically much more characteristic of Roman Catholic theology. It is still sometimes operative even in official documents and is descriptively referred to as "prooftexting." Prooftexting could be defined as the use of isolated texts out of context to substantiate conclusions derived from extrabiblical premises, for example, from moral theology or papal teaching. Although the positions finally taken may be quite valid, the use of scripture to support it is not, because the text in question has been read outside the literary context which controls its meaning.

The faulty theological position which underlies prooftexting involves a misunderstanding of the complex nature of the biblical witness to divine revelation. Scripture is understood as a kind of collection of aphorisms or detachable citations which have meaning independently of their literary and canonical context and which can be applied, like proverbs, as universal truths unaffected by the historical conditions in which they were written.

What fundamentalism and prooftexting have in common is their reading of scripture out of context. A valid approach to the sacred text demands that it be read and used as a canonical whole, a theologically complex and pluriform unity in which time-conditioned human understanding and expression is the medium of divine, ever-actual revelation. The final pastoral, in its reading of scripture, is happily free of both fundamentalism (which is a frequent trap of both "hawks" and "doves") and prooftexting (which is a frequent weakness in official ecclesiastical documents).

Let us turn now to two legitimate approaches to biblical material which, although both useful, make different kinds of contributions in the pastoral sphere. The first, classical historical criticism, is the approach of the majority of recognized Roman Catholic and non-fundamentalist Protestant scholars. It seems to be the underlying approach of the pastoral.

Historical criticism assigns to the biblical scholar as his or her primary (although not necessarily exclusive) task the critical exegesis of specific passages such as the Sermon on the Mount as a whole (Mt. 5–7) or a subsection such as the Beatitudes (Mt. 5:3–11), in order to discern the literal sense of the text, that is, the sense intended by the sacred author.[4] Such exegesis, carried out by rigorously critical methods, provides both historical and theological data. This material can then, in a subsequent and independent operation, be applied to pastoral or theological problems.[5]

A growing number of biblical scholars, while fully accepting the methodological soundness and the absolute indispensability of historical critical exegesis as the basis of any valid interpretation, are finding themselves increasingly uncomfortable with the separation of what the Bible meant in its own time (which inevitably appears to be its only *real* meaning) from what the Bible means today (which inevitably appears to be a kind of extraneous and non-necessary "application" rather than a real meaning) and are seeking a more integrated approach to the meaning of texts based on a more dynamic understanding of the reality of "meaning."[6]

Basic to this hermeneutical approach, or approach to the meaning of texts, is an understanding of the text not as a collection of words that can have but one meaning, which can be stated in a finite number of correct propositions and which is imbedded in the text in a permanent and unchanging way,[7] but as an experience which has the power to transform us in the encounter between the text and the interpreter. Thus every experience of genuine understanding, although subject to the controls and norms of historical and literary analysis, is potentially new and always somewhat different from its predecessors because the mind which encounters the ancient text is a contemporary mind bringing to the text new questions and a new context of understanding.[8] In other words, rather than applying an ancient meaning which, in itself, is limited by its first-century context, to a contemporary question such as the nuclear arms race, the scholar who adopts this approach interprets the text as always speaking to and in the present because of the transcendent and ever-active power which can be found in all classical texts and a fortiori in the scriptures which are our primary witness to divine revelation.[9]

It is within the framework of a contemporary hermeneutical theory of biblical interpretation that I will attempt to draw from the New Testament some light on the issue of nuclear arms.

Theological-Ecclesial Context

The theological-ecclesial context within which the following reflections will be situated is woven of four theological strands articulated, though not originated, by Vatican Council II.

The first strand is the understanding, especially evident in the Pastoral Constitution on the Church in the Modern World,[10] of how Christian ideals operate in our theological efforts to make moral judgments. There seems to be a move away from moral reasoning based on a somewhat static theology that uses God's creation as the framework. In such a theology Christ is seen primarily as eternal Logos, or wisdom of God, who expresses an unchanging natural law from which we can deduce what is acceptable human behavior. The transition is toward a more dynamic approach to moral reasoning rooted in a theology of salvation in which Jesus, the resurrected Lord, is seen as the primary expression of a new humanity, drawing individuals and the race toward the fullness of human existence, according to a developing understanding of natural law.[11]

The prophetic ministry of the historical Jesus, comprised of his authoritative teaching and his martyr's death, has come to play a much larger role than abstract moral principles in our efforts to understand the meaning of discipleship in the contemporary world. This is largely responsible for the post-conciliar tendency to view discipleship as self-transcending love of God and neighbor defined by the dynamic model of divine love embodied in the crucified and risen Jesus rather than in terms of minimal requirements for salvation. Thus, the Christian vocation emerges clearly not as the minimum required of a human being by nature but as the maximum made possible by our sharing in divine life. It is on this basis that I will argue below that it is not a theory of just war, however morally sound, but the gospel imperative to make peace even at the cost of ultimate self-sacrifice that must guide our response to the question of nuclear arms.

The second strand in the theological-ecclesial context is the conciliar reemphasis on the integral role that reading the "signs of the times" must play in our discerning what Christian discipleship means in our day. We are not called merely to apply timeless and unchanging norms to changed conditions but to allow our own hearts and consciences to be the theater in which occurs the encounter between the unsearchable riches of divine revelation and the arresting realities of our contemporary human experience. In fact, only in this encounter do we experience the potentiality of sacred scripture to be divine revelation for us.

It seems to have been, at least in part, such an encounter between the word of God and the realities of twentieth-century existence which led the participants at Vatican II, contemplating the incredibly destructive capacity of nuclear weapons, to declare that they felt compelled not to refurbish old views or doctrines but to "undertake an evaluation of war with an entirely new attitude."[12]

The third strand in the theological-ecclesial context is the renewed theology of the church. As we see in the council's Dogmatic Constitution on the Church[13] there is a discernible tendency away from a static understanding of the church as a perfect and superior society which proposes the minimal demands of natural morality to the state which is considered as a perfect but inferior society, and toward a dynamic conception of the church as the people of God called to be in the world as sign, herald, and agent of the reign of God.[14] It is from this perspective that I will argue that violence, prepared for, threatened, intended, or used can never function as a Christian option, can never be given a place, however grudging, within our preaching as a church even though it might, at times, be the justifiable option of an individual Christian.

Finally, and as a consequence of the preceding three developments, there has emerged a powerful sense of the Christian vocation not as a second and/or private identity nor simply as a religious motive for ordinary good citizenship, but as a prophetic responsibility to transform the world in liberty, justice, and peace.

My own work on the New Testament leads me to affirm, and to operate within, this understanding of the Christian vocation as a distinctive call, not contrary to our human vocation but only clear to us in the light of the self-transcending act of reconciliation on Calvary. In short, the context of theology and church within which we should draw on the scriptures is one that sees the human encounter with Christ as a continually developing reality. It is one that sees discipleship as a demanding conversion of heart and the church as a people calling the world to the quality of God's reign. It is a context which calls the Christian to transform the world.

The New Testament Contribution to the Question of Peace and Nuclear Arms

There are numerous possible approaches to the New Testament data which bear upon the questions with which we are concerned. I will explore five aspects of the New Testament message which seem to me particularly important for reflection on peace and nuclear arms. In line with the observations in the preceding section I will try to show not what could conceivably be justified as consonant with New Testament demands, but what the Christian vocation as presented in the Gospels seems to call us to in the face of the incessant build-up of nuclear arms in our country and abroad. In other words, I will attempt to bring the inner dynamics of Christian discipleship into dialogue with the inner dynamics of the current situation in order to expose the challenge that the former addresses to the latter. In what follows I shall, first, look briefly at the Christian mandate to make peace; second, and in somewhat greater detail, explore the radicality of the Christian love commandment; third, examine the ministry of reconciliation as the concrete locus of peacemaking and Christian love; fourth, look at Jesus' preferential option for the poor in relation to military spending. Finally, I shall make some suggestions about the bearing of the Gospel's "reversal dynamic" on the practical question of political realism in the present situation.

The Christian Vocation to Peace

The Sermon on the Mount (Mt. 5–7; cf. Lk. 6:17–49), and especially the Beatitudes, is recognized by most scholars as a kind of Christian *Magna Carta*, an aphoristic description of the Christian vocation. Only one of the beatitudes has as its reward the ultimate gift of becoming a child of God. "Blessed are the peacemakers, for they shall be called children of God" (Mt. 5:9).

The New Testament notion of peace is rooted in that marvelously comprehensive Old Testament conception of *shalom*. Peace, in the biblical perspective, is not simply the absence of conflict but is that plenitude of life which involves length of days in fullness of strength, covenantal unity within the community and with God, freedom from fear of enemies or calamity, and the immortality achieved through one's descendents when one is finally gathered to one's ancestors.[15]

In John's Gospel the essential gift flowing from the resurrection of Jesus is that peace which the world cannot give (Jn. 14:27 and 20:19). And as John Donahue shows in great detail,[16] it is particularly Luke's Gospel and the Acts of the Apostles which present both the vocation of Jesus and that of the New Testament community as a vocation to preach the "good news of peace" (Acts 10:36). The letters of Paul contain frequent exhortations to the new Christian communities to build, foster, protect, and cherish peace among themselves and with their neighbors (e.g., 2 Cor. 12:11–12 and elsewhere).

We are called by the Gospel not merely to avoid aggression or conflict but to actively announce and bring about peace. If this peace is fullness of life as God's community living together in freedom from fear, and if the condition of both the possibility and realization of justice is such peace (cf. Jas. 3:18), it seems that we must raise serious questions about preparation for war even when such preparation is undertaken as a way of preventing war. The philosophy which regards preparedness for and willingness to engage in war as the best safeguard of peace is radically opposed to the Gospel of Christ. This opposition must create a dilemma for the Christian in regard to deterrence policies based on a balance of terror.

Probably, the most difficult question with which the bishops wrestled in the writing of the pastoral was the question of deterrence, the possession of massive arsenals of nuclear weapons as an incentive to the enemy not to declare war. It seems to me that there are two aspects of the gospel vocation to be peacemakers which challenge the possession of nuclear weapons, even for purposes of deterrence. The first has to do with fear and the second with intention.

Biblical *shalom* involves, in an integral way, freedom from fear. Fear, widespread and constant, is one of the most devastating direct results of the stockpiling of nuclear weapons. We are holding ourselves and all of our sisters and brothers in a web of terror. It is difficult not to raise the question of whether the manufacture and stockpiling of this lethal potential is not so contrary to our Christian vocation to make peace, to establish the conditions of fullness of life in freedom from fear, as to be intolerable as a Christian option for any reason whatsoever.

The second perspective from which deterrence seems questionable in the light of the gospel vocation to make peace has to do with intention. Since the atomic explosion at Hiroshima in 1945 the popes and the episcopal magisterium have insisted repeatedly that the use of nuclear weapons and even the threat or intention to use them are strictly immoral. The pastoral takes the same position. But it is extremely difficult to see what real deterrent force the mere possession of nuclear weapons, if one is publicly committed not to use them under any circumstances, really has. The possession of nuclear weapons as a deterrent seems to imply the willingness to use them if provoked. The United States government has made it perfectly clear that it rules out neither retaliation nor first strike. There is a terrible logic in this position if one intends to be realistic about deterrence. But this only raises again the question of whether the moral acceptability of possession of nuclear weapons is not more academic than morally realistic.

The Christian Love Commandment
All four Gospels, but particularly the Gospel of John, present the command to love one's fellow human beings as the very heart of the lifestyle

Jesus sought to establish among his disciples. This commandment is rooted in the second great commandment of the Mosaic law (cf. Dt. 6:5 and Lv. 19:18): to love one's neighbor as oneself. But Jesus' presentation of it goes well beyond the Old Testament injunction in two important ways.

First, Jesus *universalized* the command which bound the Israelites to love the members of their own people with whom they were united by ethnic and religious bonds and who had not forfeited their right to that love by infidelity to the covenant obligations. Jesus commands his disciples to love even those who are not members of their own community: "If you love those who love you, what reward have you? . . . And if you salute only your brothers and sisters, what more are you doing than others?" (Mt. 5:46–47; cf. also Lk. 6:32–34) He even commands them to love their enemies, not just the anonymous collective enemy such as the Samaritans (cf. Lk. 10:29–37) but the personal enemy who was actually persecuting them (Mt. 5:44; cf. Lk. 6:27). The specific motive of this astounding love, like that of making peace, is "so that you may be children of your Father who is in heaven" (Mt. 5:45; cf. Lk. 6:35). Our vocation to become children of God is intimately bound up with our capacity and obligation to seek unity among ourselves.

Second, Jesus *intensified* the love command. Not only are his disciples to love universally; they are actually to refrain even from resisting evil done against them and positively to return good for evil, praying for their persecutors, and willingly accepting further harm rather than do harm to protect or avenge themselves (cf. Mt. 5:38–42; Lk. 6:27–31). In John's Gospel this love of the enemy is given its final development as the command of universal love in imitation of Jesus' love for us. Furthermore, the Christian's love of others implies the willingness to lay down one's life for those one loves, even as Jesus laid down his life for us (Jn. 15:12–13). No one may remain "enemy" for those who have accepted the love of God in Jesus.

It is in the Gospel of John, in the last discourses, especially chapters 13 and 15, that we have the fullest and most original presentation of the Christian love command. According to the Fourth Gospel the relations among Christians are rooted in the fact that they are all God's children. Jesus came to give power to become children of God to those who believed in him (Jn. 1:12). By sharing in Jesus' own filiation through the gift of the Spirit his disciples become his brothers and sisters (Jn.

20:17) and brothers and sisters of one another. But Jesus, at the Last Supper, both by word and gesture, indicated that the full development of this sibling relationship is friendship. He no longer calls his disciples servants but friends because he has chosen them and because he has, in a certain real way, abolished their natural inferiority to him, made them his equals, by sharing with them everything he had received from his Father (cf. Jn. 15:12–17).

The relationship of friendship, a relationship of equality, mutuality, complete sharing of material and spiritual goods, which Jesus establishes between himself and his disciples must, he says, be the model of their relationships among themselves. They are to love one another as he has loved them (Jn. 15:12). Indeed, this is, in the Fourth Gospel, the single identifying mark of the Christian (Jn. 13:34–35) and the means by which they will draw all other people to participate in the saving revelation of Jesus: "That they may be one even as we [Jesus and the Father] are one, I in them and thou in me, that they may become perfectly one, so that the world may know that thou hast sent me" (Jn. 17:22–23).

The ultimate expression of this love of friendship is the willingness to lay down one's life for one's friends. To love as Jesus has loved us is not only not to injure the other but actually to choose the other's life over our own if the choice comes to that. Jesus chose to die rather than to kill (cf. Jn. 18:36), and he made his death not an unwilling submission to violence but the free preference to suffer violence rather than to inflict it (cf. Jn. 19:11) in order to validate beyond any possibility of doubt his offer of divine friendship.

Of all the conclusions we might draw from these reflections on the nature of the Christian love command I would suggest only two at this point. First, if the distinctive character of Christian love is friendship and the very essence of friendship is equality and mutual total self-gift, then all relations of superiority/inferiority are out of place among Christians. How can we, as Christians, cooperate in building a national defense policy whose intention is to establish and maintain not only superiority over our adversaries but dominance carried to the point of absolute world supremacy?

My second conclusion has to do with the universality of the love command in the Gospel. As Christians we cannot regard others as our enemies because we must love our enemies, thus making them our friends. We are actually called to prefer the life of our friend to our own. How, then, can we support a defense policy which generates and aggravates mistrust between nations and relies on felt hostility toward the "enemy" to keep the "national will" strong? It is precisely the conflict in the Christian conscience between the call to take up arms against enemy regimes and the obligation that such action implies of killing real people whom one must, as a Christian, love as Jesus has loved us that has made Christian conscientious objection an increasingly frequent phenomenon among people whose devotion to the values of democracy cannot be doubted.

The Ministry of Reconciliation
We are called to make peace in a world enmeshed in animosity, to love universally in a world structured by mutual fear and hatred. It is this conflicting reality which, it seems to me, establishes the ministry of reconciliation as the primary practical expression of a Christian stance in a violent world.

Paul presents Jesus as the expression of God's reconciling action among us. "God was in Christ reconciling the world to himself" (2 Cor. 5:19) and the one "who through Christ reconciled us to himself . . . gave us the ministry of reconciliation" (2 Cor. 5:18).

In the Gospels Jesus is presented as giving numerous concrete injunctions concerning the task of overcoming division between ourselves and others. We are to bless those who curse us, pray for those who abuse us, offer the other cheek to the one who strikes us, give our coat to the one who steals our cloak, and refrain from reclaiming the goods that have been taken from us (Lk. 6:27–30). Virtually all reputable scripture scholars recognize that these injunctions cannot be made a literal code for the handling of interpersonal conflicts. They represent, in the form of concrete examples, the real ideal of Christian reconciliation. Yet, the Christian's attitude and desire is not to "even the score" but to dissolve enmity, to soften hatred with love, and to make it possible for the one who is doing the evil to stop doing it without fear of being destroyed. The cycle of violence cannot be broken by retaliation but only by forgiveness.

Jesus' demand that his disciples renounce retaliation as a means of achieving justice has historically been one of the most unrealizable of ideals, whether at the individual or at the societal level. He consistently struggled against injustice toward himself and others. He did not stand idly by wishing for the conversion of those who constituted themselves his enemies. He defended himself against those who sought to entrap him, escaped physically when he could, and protected his outcast friends against the cleverness of the self-righteous defenders of morality. Nevertheless, what we see very clearly in Jesus' own behavior is his refusal, even under the most unjust attack and extreme provocation, to resort to retaliation or the threat of retaliation. Because Jesus would not use violence he could not threaten violence.

One of the most encouraging and original sections of the pastoral is Part III, "The Promotion of Peace: Proposals and Policies." It clearly points out the numerous possibilities open to us for the pursuit of peace without recourse to war or the threat of war. At the heart of these proposals is a constant concern with reconciliation. Peoples must come to know each other so that they can trust one another. Nations must commit themselves to the building and honoring of international institutions and procedures for the resolution of conflicts. The art of peacemaking must be studied and taught. Retaliation and the threat of retaliation can never achieve peace and must finally be renounced in favor of the constant effort at reconciliation to which the Gospel calls us.

Preferential Option for the Poor
Throughout the Gospel we are confronted with Jesus' self-definition as the physician sent to the sick (cf. Mt. 9:12), the savior sent to sinners (Mt. 9:12–13), the divine shepherd of God sent to the lost sheep (cf. Lk. 15:3–7), the long-awaited messiah anointed to preach good news to the poor (Lk. 4:18). Jesus is born in poverty to a mother who celebrates Yahweh's historical choice of the lowly, the hungry, and the downtrodden (cf. Lk. 1:47–55). He chooses to associate with the poor and the sinners (Mt. 9:11; Lk. 7:34 and elsewhere), and finally dies, stripped even of his clothes (Jn. 19:23–24), in utter destitution. Jesus' choice of solidarity with the poor is perhaps the most unmistakable characteristic of his life among us.

As the Statement of the Holy See to the United Nations in 1976 so graphically stated, the overproduction of military devices is an act of aggression against the poor "for even when they are not used, by their cost alone, armaments kill the poor by causing them to starve." If, as bearers of the name of Christ, we must embody Jesus' own preferential option for the poor, it is hard to see how we can tolerate, much less endorse, our government's clear preferential option for military spending at the cost of daily increasing unemployment, hunger, disease, and social unrest here and abroad.

Although the pastoral devotes less space to this issue than one might wish, stressing the need for a more equitable world order if peace is to be established rather than the gospel imperative of solidarity with the poor, it is nonetheless strong and insistent on our obligation to order our economic priorities according to the Gospel.

The "Reversal Dynamic" of the Gospel
Surely anyone reading the above arguments, and especially the questioning of the possession of nuclear weapons for purposes of deterrence, will raise the issue of political realism, the issue raised repeatedly by the Reagan administration as the process surrounding the pastoral developed.

The question comes down to the rather simple dilemma: as long as the Soviet Union is armed with nuclear weapons do we have any choice but to maintain a superior arsenal for defense and deterrence? On the basis of the Gospel I would answer: yes, we do have a choice. The mystery of Jesus' resurrection is the grounds for the Christian defiance of death. For us, death is not the ultimate tragedy (cf. Mt. 10:28) and thus not something which must be avoided at any cost. Security, much less invulnerability, is therefore not the ultimate value for us who are challenged to be willing to lose our life in order to find it (Mt. 10:39), to fall to the ground and die in order to bear fruit (Jn. 12:24–25). Our Judeo-Christian heritage says nothing if not that power is made perfect in infirmity (2 Cor. 12:5–10), that God can and does use the weak to confound the strong (1 Cor. 1:26–31). Like the Israelites who had to learn not to trust in horses or chariots (cf. Ps. 20:7–8) and Jesus who refused to summon the legions of heaven (Mt. 26:53) or the forces of earth (Lk. 22:51) to his defense, can we not, in faith, lay down our arms?

To some this is undoubtedly a counsel of madness if not despair. But even from a human point of view it might be possible to argue the Christian position. Even the current administration has admitted that a nuclear war would mean disaster for victors and vanquished alike. The medical and scientific communities are in agreement that there will be no victors in a nuclear exchange. Our weapons, as defense, are useless, and their stockpiling daily increases the chance of their accidental or deliberate use.

But, as the pastoral points out so well, to say that we have no military defense is not to say that we have no defense at all. It does say that we must rechannel our efforts from military build-up into the building of international agencies of conflict resolution, engagement in mutually respectful and honest negotiations, and the solution of the problem of unjust distribution of resources which underlies so much of the world's tension. To lay down our arms is not to abandon defense, but to abandon useless and, quite possibly, immoral posturing. And it would place all the burden of world opinion on any nation which remained armed or threatened to use arms. I would want to argue that no use of nuclear weapons, either by firing or by threat, and thus probably also by possession, is moral or effective. We have nothing to gain by keeping them and everything, literally, to lose.

Yet, the basic issue is not whether this is a reasonable strategy. The Gospel's peacemaking mandate, its love command, the ministry of reconciliation which it entrusts to the Christian community, the preferential option for the poor to which it calls us, and the reversal dynamic inaugurated by the resurrection of Jesus which it proclaims are not just the requirements of human nature or the conclusions of enlightened rationality. They are a new wine which must burst the wineskins of the ancient dynamics of competition and conflict, aggression and hatred, retaliation, the oppression of the poor and the weak by the rich and powerful, and the search for unlimited human security and national supremacy upon which our current defense policy is based. In other words, the Gospel's contribution to our reflection on war and peace is neither accidental nor purely exhortatory. It is substantive and structural. The question is whether the dynamics of Christian discipleship are reconcilable with the dynamics of national policy in the area of defense. If the answer is no, then those who call themselves Christians have hard choices to make. One of the most encouraging signs of the maturity and commitment of Christians in our time is that increasing numbers of Christians are making those choices and making it clear that the source of their convictions and their actions is the Gospel they profess.

NOTES

1. In January of 1982 I gave the substance of this essay as testimony before the bishops' committee which drafted *The Challenge of Peace*. In the present version I have tried to place my original reflections on this subject in relation to the final document.

2. See R. E. Brown, "The Human Word of the Almighty God," *The Critical Meaning of the Bible* (New York/Ramsey: Paulist, 1981), pp. 1–22.

3. Cf. A. Richardson, "The Rise of Modern Biblical Scholarship and Recent Discussion of the Authority of the Bible," *The Cambridge History of the Bible*, vol. 3, ed. S. L. Greeslade (Cambridge: At the University Press, 1963), pp. 294–338, esp. pp. 306–11, on this point.

4. Pope Pius XII, *Divino Afflante Spiritu*, in H. Denziger and C. Bannwart, eds., *Enchiridion Symbolorum*, rev. A. Schonmetzer, 32nd ed. (Freiburg: Herder, 1963), no. 3826.

5. For a good example of this approach, see R. E. Brown, "What the Biblical Word Meant and What It Means," *The Critical Meaning of the Bible*, pp. 23–44, and "An Example: Rethinking the Episcopate of the New Testament Churches," ibid., pp. 124–46.

6. For a fuller explanation of this position see my articles "From Exegesis to Hermeneutics: The Problem of the Contemporary Meaning of Scripture," *Horizons* 8 (Spring 1981): 23–39; "The Paschal Imagination: Objectivity and Subjectivity in New Testament Interpretation," *Theological Studies* 43 (March 1982): 52–68.

7. J. L. McKenzie gave classic expression to this more static conception of meaning in 1958 in "Problems of Hermeneutics in Roman Catholic Exegesis," *Journal of Biblical Literature* 77 (1958): 199. The position he expressed then is still operative in much of the exegetical work being done today.

8. This position takes much more seriously the role of preunderstanding and effective historical consciousness in the hermeneutical process than does the more classical historical-critical approach which has more faith in the ability of the interpreter to step out of his or her own historical setting and enter the ancient world which was the context of the text. See H.-G. Gadamer, *Truth and Method* (New York: Crossroad, 1975), pp. 235–74.

9. This notion of the surplus of meaning in classical texts is supported by the philosophical work of Gadamer, *Truth and Method*, esp. pp. 258–67, and P. Ricoeur, *Interpretation Theory: Discourse and the Surplus of Meaning* (Fort Worth: Texas Christian University Press, 1976), esp. pp. 43–44 and chap. 3, "Metaphor and Symbol," pp. 45–60. D. Tracy (*The Analogical Imagination: Christian Imagination and the Culture of Pluralism* [New York: Crossroad, 1981]) has explored extensively the notion of "classic text" as a theological category.

10. Available in *Renewing the Earth: Catholic Documents on Peace, Justice and Liberation*, ed. D. J. O'Brien and T. A. Shannon (Garden City: Image, 1977), pp. 171–284.

11. I am indebted to my colleague Drew Christiansen, S.J., for his help on this section.

12. *Gaudium et Spes*, no. 80.

13. Available in *The Documents of Vatican II*, ed. and trans. W. M. Abbott and J. Gallagher (New York: Guild, 1966), pp. 14–101.

14. This ecclesiology is lucidly developed by R. P. McBrien in *Church: The Continuing Quest* (Paramus/New York: Newman, 1970), esp. chap. 4, pp. 67–85, and in *Catholicism* (Minneapolis: Winston, 1981), Part IV, esp. pp. 691–729.

15. See J. Pedersen, *Israel: Its Life and Culture*, vol. 1 (Copenhagen: Brannen Og Korch, 1926), pp. 311–17.

16. J. Donahue, "The Good News of Peace," *The Way* 22 (April 1982):88–99.

JOSEPH A. KOMONCHAK

Kingdom, History, and Church

The Catholic bishops of the United States propose their pastoral letter as a response to the challenge of the Second Vatican Council "to undertake a completely fresh reappraisal of war"(# 24). Such a reappraisal, they argue, must include a "theology of peace," which is not yet available in systematic form, but whose elements or characteristics are sufficiently well known to be outlined:

> A theology of peace should ground the task of peacemaking solidly in the biblical vision of the kingdom of God, then place it centrally in the ministry of the church. It should specify the obstacles in the way of peace, as these are understood theologically and in the social and political sciences. It should both identify the specific contributions a community of faith can make to the work of peace and relate these to the wider work of peace pursued by other groups and institutions in society. Finally, a theology of peace must include a message of hope. The vision of hope must be available to all, but one source of its content should be found in a church at the service of peace. (# 25)

It is clear, if only from the considerable controversy aroused by the early drafts of the letter, that the fresh reappraisal of war required today has led the bishops also to a reappraisal of their own responsibilities, and thus has in fact struck many a reader, inside and outside the church, as itself "fresh" or even illegitimate. What is perhaps most startling is the way in which they have conceived the role of the church in human history this side of the final coming of the kingdom of God. This essay is an attempt to clarify the bishops' effort to relate kingdom, church, and human history. The primary focus will be on the section of the letter entitled "Kingdom and History"(I.B), but it will also be necessary to draw upon other sections to fill out the indications given there.

The Kingdom of God

The chief description of the kingdom of God appears in section I.A, "Peace and the Kingdom." There the kingdom is first intimated in the description of the Old Testament's "hope for eschatological peace"(I.A.d), Israel's expectation of a messianic age of justice and peace. The kingdom is then presented as the central theme of the preaching and ministry of Jesus in whom the reign of God is said to have been both proclaimed and inaugurated. It is "a new reality in which God's power is manifested and the longing of the people is fulfilled"(# 45). It is a reign "in which love is an active, life-giving, inclusive force," demonstrated in the actions of Jesus, especially in his resurrection, the sign that "God indeed does reign," and in his gift of a peace which the world cannot give (#s 50–51). Finally, the kingdom is operative through the gift of the Spirit to the followers of Jesus, bearing with it a knowledge of "the power of the One who creates from nothing"; and, in a world in which reconciliation and peace are "not yet fully operative," the Spirit gives Christians the ability "to look forward with unshakable confidence to the time when the fullness of God's reign would make itself known in the world"(# 53). In their conviction that in the risen Christ the promised covenant of peace has been established, Christians must undertake the continual conversion needed "to act in ways which are consonant with the justice, forgiveness, and love of God's reign" (# 54). "Because we have been gifted with God's peace in the reconciliation effected in Jesus Christ," the bishops conclude, "we are called not only to experience our own peace but to make peace in our world" (# 55).

History

In the section on "Kingdom and History," the theological analysis is carried forward into a brief discussion of the Christian life between the first Easter and the full establishment of the kingdom. This life is lived in "the tension between the vision of the reign of God and its concrete realization in history. The tension is often described in terms of 'already but not yet'; that is, we already live in the grace of the kingdom, but it is not yet the completed kingdom"(# 58). The chief obstacle to the realization of the kingdom is the continued power of sin in history.

The "not yet" of the kingdom is strongly emphasized and used as a warning to Christians, several times repeated, to be "sober and realistic," not to deceive themselves "about their ability to cause peace to triumph nor about the effect of their efforts to this end," to regard the issue with "realism and humility," and not to indulge in the "utopia" of expecting "a totally and permanently peaceful society," or in "ideologies that hold up that prospect as easily attainable"(# 59).

The purpose of this section thus seems to be to make the transition from the confident assertions of the previous section to the sobering complexities of concrete historical existence until the kingdom of God comes. "In the kingdom of God, peace and justice will be fully realized. In history, efforts to pursue both peace and justice are at times in tension, and the struggle for justice may threaten certain forms of peace"(# 60).

The Church
In the two sections so far reviewed, the church is at best described only implicitly; explicit statements must be looked for elsewhere. Earlier there is the simple statement: "The church is called to be in a unique way the instrument of the kingdom of God in history. Since peace is one of the signs of that kingdom present in the world, the church fulfills part of her essential mission by making the peace of the kingdom more visible in our time"(# 22). Much later, a separate section is entitled "The Church: A Community of Conscience, Prayer and Penance." Here the bishops present the church as a community of committed disciples of Jesus Christ. The description emphasizes their distinctiveness: "convinced Christians" are acknowledged to be a minority even in "nominally Christian and Catholic nations"; they are said to live in a world that is becoming "increasingly estranged from Christian values." Obliged to be not only believers but also doers of the word, they must "regard as normal even the path of persecution and the possibility of martyrdom." To be able "to profess the full faith of the church in an increasingly secularized society," they "must develop a sense of solidarity, cemented by affective relationships with mature and exemplary Christians who represent Christ and his way of life"(# 277).

The kingdom, the church, and history constitute three of the central elements of the letter's "theology of peace." The discussions are necessarily brief and selective, but the principle of selection is not always clear. Some theologians may question whether it was wise to make the kingdom of God the central notion and wonder why the bishops do not make more of the redemptive role of Christ and of the church as an instrument in history of his word and grace. The latter, of course, is not denied, but it certainly does not occupy a major role. If it had, it might have been possible to stress more than is now done the "already" aspect of Christian faith. That is, what has already been accomplished by Christ and given to the church as the basis for the Christian community's responsibilities in history until the kingdom comes. The "not yet" is beyond our knowledge and our control; the "already" is the life, light, and power by which the church now lives and teaches.

Besides the kingdom, human history, and the church, a theology of peace must also include, according to the bishops' description, the church's relationship to "the wider work of peace pursued by other groups and institutions in society"(# 25). The bishops do not make this relationship the topic of a single section, and one must uncover what they believe it to be by attending to several different statements throughout the document. What they are doing is, of course, a practical exercise in those areas of concern traditionally treated under the headings "Church and World" and "Church and State." But their exercise differs in important ways from classic discussions of those topics; and it is worth trying to identify the differences.

Church and World

Classically, this topic concerned the relationship between Christianity and the world of human construction or, in H. Richard Niebuhr's terms, between "Christ and culture." In his famous book of that title,[1] Niebuhr identified five typical descriptions of this relationship: (1) an either-or opposition; (2) an agreement or identification; (3) a synthesis of the two in a higher unity presided over by, or even identified with, the church; (4) a distinction of the two into independent realms; and (5) the effort at a Christian transformation of culture. Niebuhr identified the typical Roman Catholic attitude with the third of these types, whose model was medieval Christendom's cultural and political unity which, Niebuhr believed, modern Catholic social teaching sought to restore. While he had some sympathy with the ideal, Niebuhr believed it to be impossible to restore in modern pluralistic, secular, and historically conscious cultures, and so he himself opted, it seems, for the fifth type.

In his remarks on the emergence of historical consciousness, Niebuhr put his finger on the most significant development in the discussion of the church-world relationship. Too often in the older discussion, the "world" was simply the given world, the natural and human context in which Christians must lead their lives. This world was good as created by God, but corrupted by human sin and so a threat to Christian integrity. In its main lines, the world was and always will be what the world is now; and in this world the church must make do as best it can. For example, it must be resigned to the structures of human society, and so, right into the twentieth century, many church leaders opposed movements for genuine social reform on the grounds that they opposed God-given or "natural" differentiations.

But things change if the "world" is seen historically, that is, if the world is seen now as what human beings have made of it. This is obviously true of the world of human society; but it can also apply to the natural world as tamed, transformed, and exploited by human work. What is primary now is not the "natural" but the "historical." And history itself is seen not simply as the number of years God allows between Easter and Parousia, to be lived out within the given framework, but rather as the concrete project of human self-construction. Human history is what we have done and are doing with our intelligence, reason, and freedom.

This development has at least two consequences for the church-world discussion. First, the church itself is seen as an historical event or achievement, an exercise of human self-responsibility under God and in response to his word and grace. Individuals and communities make themselves to be what they are through exercises of intelligence and freedom. Among those individuals are those who decide to become Christians; among those communities there is the one which constructs itself as the church. The decision to become a Christian and the construction of the church are thus instances of the exercise of historical self-responsibility, responses to the challenge of concrete history, whose meaning and distinctiveness really emerge only when understood against the background of the general historical challenge and when compared to other individual and communal attempts to meet the same challenge.

Second, the world itself, as a human construction, becomes the object of Christian moral and religious judgment. As any other human achievement, so also the construction of the social world shows the effects of sin and therefore needs the criticism, challenge, and healing of Christ's word and grace. The world is not "secular," if by that is meant some realm to which religious insights and values are irrelevant.

Although it is not explicitly discussed in the pastoral letter, this move from "world" to "history" is at the basis of the bishops' effort. This is perhaps clearest in the very first paragraphs of the document. Here the bishops describe what Vatican II called "a moment of supreme crisis" in human history. They quote the present pope: "From now on it is only through a conscious choice and through a deliberate policy that humanity can survive." And, on the basis of this recognition of the critical nature of the hour, they acknowledge their own "grave human, moral and political responsibilities to see that a 'conscious choice' is made to save humanity." Later the bishops again quote Vatican II on the task of "constructing for all men everywhere a world more genuinely human" (# 65); and they use that quote to urge a challenge upon every thinking person: "What contributes to and what impedes the construction of a more genuinely human world?"(# 66) And they concretely apply their concern when later, in a discussion of U.S.-Soviet relations, they warn "against that 'hardness of heart' which can close us or others to the changes needed to make the future different from the past"(# 258).

Throughout, the "world" is something humanly constructed, something now being constructed. And it is a project of human self-realization to which they believe the work of Christ and the mission of the church to be directly related as offering criticism, encouragement and even healing, and the hope of a better future even in human history.

Church and State
Classically, this heading has concerned institutional relationships between the church and the civil power: for example, whether a church may or may not be established, whether the state should embody the church's moral and disciplinary rules in its own legal code, whether the state may restrict or infringe upon the activity of the church, etc.

Of these and other typical questions, there is hardly a trace in the bishops' pastoral letter. Their reflections presume the legitimacy of the American constitutional separation of church and state; and in this they are the heirs of the great majority of American bishops throughout our history. The bishops do not claim to speak from a favored political position. If they appeal to political and military leaders and claim a right to be heard by their fellow citizens, they do so with apparently complete confidence in the American resolution of the classical church-state questions.

The bishops are primarily interested in the question of church and *society*. They make use of a right granted to all citizens in a democratic society to participate in the public debate by which it is decided what that society shall be. They confess both their loyalty to the country and its ideals and their adherence to "the universal principles proclaimed by the church"(# 326). They speak because they believe that the "gospel vision of peace" is both "a way of life for believers" and "a leaven in society"(# 303). They wish to help "to create a community of conscience in the wider civil community" by sharing "the moral wisdom of the Catholic tradition within the larger society"(# 328). They are concerned, they say, "for the nation's soul"(# 304), words which evoke not only the Gospel but also central themes of classical political theories that included normative ethical criteria, such as justice, love, and freedom, in their definitions of a truly human society.

There is another respect in which the bishops' pastoral letter differs from the classic terms of the church-state discussion. At least in recent centuries, this debate has taken for granted the legitimacy and the adequacy of the nation-state. The bishops, of course, do not deny that we live in "a world of sovereign states devoid of any central authority and divided by ideology, geography, and competing claims"(# 20). And, as long as the world is so divided, they acknowledge a nation's right to self-defense, even by the violence of a just war. But they also distinguish national loyalty from adherence to their church's universal principles; they call for "a foreign policy which recognizes and respects the claims of citizens of every nation to the same inalienable rights we treasure, and seeks to ensure an international security based on the awareness that the creator has provided this world and all its resources for the sustenance and benefit of the entire human family" (# 202). They regard an absence of war that is based simply on a balance of terror to fall far short of genuine peace. They make their own Pope John XXIII's call for a supranational world order based on "the unity of the human family—rooted in common creation, destined for the kingdom, and united by moral bonds of rights and duties" (# 236). Constructing such a world order, which transcends, even if it does not negate, the nation-states, they see as an essential element in the construction of a genuine peace.

In this respect the American bishops are simply echoing the last three popes who have often insisted that the social question today has become worldwide. This is most obviously true of the question of nuclear arms. The bishops quote Pope John Paul II: "In the past it was possible to destroy a village, a town, a region, even a country. Now it is the whole planet that has come under threat"(# 122). The fate of every nation is thus bound up with that of every other. The historical self-determinations of any nation, or at least of the great superpowers, affect or determine the life of every other nation. The issue now is not whether a particular nation shall have a particular future; it is whether humanity itself shall have any future at all. In this light, the bishops are inescapably acting not only as American bishops but also as bishops within the univeral church which at Vatican II declared itself to be the sign and instrument not only of mankind's union with God but also of the unity of the whole human race.

The Redemption of History

Bernard Lonergan, a Canadian theologian, has described well the fundamental challenge which the bishops' pastoral letter may be considered to be addressing in particularly critical form: "The challenge of history is for man progressively to restrict the realm of chance or fate or destiny and progressively to enlarge the realm of conscious grasp and deliberate choice." It is this fundamental challenge that the Christian church proposes to interpret and to address in its faith and in its activity. It is the failure to act intelligently, reasonably, and responsibly that Christians mean by the word "sin." It is the recovery of the ability to act as human beings ought to act that they mean by the word "redemption."

It is as arbitrary as it is common to restrict the relevance of the central Christian doctrines of sin and redemptive grace to the realm of individual responsibility. In fact, human beings construct their societies and their histories also by the exercise of their intelligence and freedom; and the products of that exercise are no less an amalgam of genuine achievement, sin, and redemptive recovery than what an individual makes of himself. It is not only in the individual's heart but also "at the heart of the world" that, in the words of Pope Paul VI, "there dwells the mystery of man discovering himself to be God's son in the course of a historical and psychological process in which constraint and freedom as well as the weight of sin and the breath of the Spirit alternate and struggle for the upper hand"(*Octagesima adveniens*, 37).

Only this view of the issues of the historical self-responsibility of individuals and societies is adequate to an understanding of the role of the church as a redemptive community and of the concrete exercise of that role which is represented by the bishops' letter. The word which the church proclaims, the grace which it mediates, and the community it tries to achieve are for the sake of the great historical task to be achieved between Easter and kingdom come. The church, of course, is not the only body that undertakes the great historical challenge. Every individual, every community, and every society, whether they know it or not, are engaged in that task. But the church also, precisely in what is most distinctive about it as a community of faith, hope, and love, is a participant.

In an age in which it has surrendered or lost any direct political power, the church can participate in that task only by invitation and dialogue. The church invites others to consider its understanding of the world and of human history; in doing so, it must make every effort to communicate to them why it believes its understanding to state the truth about the world and history. That task involves it in a necessary dialogue with competing interpretations, from which it can learn even while it articulates its vision. The issue in the end is where true historical "realism" lies, an issue that has never before been posed with the stakes as high as they are today.

The choice between chance, fate, or destiny, on the one hand, or intelligence and responsibility on the other, is what is finally at stake in the debate about nuclear war. Fundamentally, the bishops are urging us to refuse to rely upon chance, fate, or destiny, whether on pragmatic, technological, or simplistically religious grounds, and to turn rather to that intelligence, reason, and responsibility with which God endowed us, which has not been corrupted utterly by sin and which has been healed, restored, and elevated in Christ. It is not only faith that one day there will be a kingdom of justice and peace that grounds the bishops' hope; it is also their conviction in faith that Christ has already won the decisive victory and has made possible a new and better human history than the long record of sin has created. In the end, the bishops are saying, the issue is whether we believe what Christian faith says about God, the world, and ourselves:

> It is our belief in the risen Christ which sustains us in confronting the awesome challenge of the nuclear arms race. Present in the beginning as the word of the Father, present in history as the word incarnate, and with us today in his word, sacraments, and spirit, he is the reason for our hope and faith. Respecting our freedom, he does not solve our problems but sustains us as we take responsibility for his work of creation and try to shape it in the ways of the kingdom. We believe his grace will never fail us. We offer this letter to the church and to all who can draw strength and wisdom from it in the conviction that we cannot fail him. We must subordinate the power of the nuclear age to human control and direct it to human benefit. As we do this we are conscious of God's continuing work among us. . . . (# 339)

This paragraph in the conclusion of the pastoral letter is the finest single demonstration that in this document, so far from departing from their proper tasks in order to intrude upon an alien realm, the bishops are in fact addressing their religious and most Christian responsibilities.

NOTES

1. H. Richard Niebuhr, *Christ and Culture* (New York: Harper & Row, 1975; originally published 1951).
2. Bernard J. F. Lonergan, *Insight: A Study of Human Understanding* (New York: Longmans, Green & Co., 1958), p. 228.

IV

Pacifism and Just War

The Challenge of Peace

Part I.C, #s 66–121

The impact of the January 1983 consultation convened by the Vatican with participants of European bishops' conferences is especially evident in this section.* A comparison of the second draft, available at the time of the consultation, with the final text is instructive.

The final version reflects the non-U.S. participants' insistence on two points. First, governments' right and obligation to national defense must be given top priority. Second, the just-war theory has been the church's dominant teaching.

In the second draft this section opened with an exposition of Christian pacifism; in the final version the development of the principle of nations' right to self-defense was substituted. A series of conciliar and papal quotes were added to support this principle. A treatment of pacifism appears in the conclusion of this section.

Furthermore, a description of the just-war criteria, which in the second draft came after the treatment of pacifism, follows the presentation of national defense in the final text. The extent of the revisions can be seen in a review of the word count given to just war and pacifism in each of the texts. In the second draft, the relative word count was less than two to one, just war versus pacifism; in the approved text, the count increased to almost five to one. Five papal quotes appear in the final version's treatment of just war; none appeared in the second draft.

While the pastoral is explicit about a nation's right to defend itself and gives primary position to just-war theory over pacifism, a point of potential significance is the letter's disclaimer that "armed force is the only defense against unjust aggression." It calls for serious study of methods for "individuals and nations to defend [themselves] without using violence."

---

*For a summary of the meeting, see "A Vatican Synthesis," prepared by the Pontifical Commission on Justice and Peace, *Origins* 12, p. 691.

GORDON C. ZAHN

Pacifism and the Just War

When one has dealt with a given topic over and over for a period of several decades, the temptation is to begin with a note of apology for covering the same ground yet once again. The fear of leaving the impression of a mind frozen into a pattern of rigid repetition is heightened by the awareness that others have compiled a dazzling record of almost comprehensive coverage of virtually every possible position on the issues of war and peace. In 1968, for instance, Michael Novak and I contributed to the same volume and shared a strikingly similar negative view of a foreign policy keyed to the fear that the Soviet Union represented an immediate threat to the United States and the cause of freedom. I still believe he was right in declaring that this nation "cherishes the myth of anti-Communism more than it cherishes justice and peace" and that we "have duped ourselves into being warriors and crusaders."[1] Novak, who has emerged as a leading opponent of the pastoral, no longer believes what he so ardently professed then if one is to judge from his widely circulated "counter-pastoral." A pity.

As for me, though there may have been shifts of emphasis from time to time as a given situation provided a slightly different variation on the basic theme, my position remains essentially the same. Now, as then, I am convinced that war and violence are incompatible with the teachings and example given us in the life of Jesus Christ and that all who would claim to follow him must reject both in their personal and social behavior. That earlier Novak did well to protest "the mangled bodies of young men" as the price for our "blindness." Today that same blindness leads him and far too many others to accept the possible incineration not just of a single human being, but of millions. It is to be hoped, therefore, that the bishops' pastoral letter—its ambiguities, equivocations, and evasions notwithstanding—will provide the occasion and the incentive for a thorough reassessment of the church's position concerning war and peace, one in which evangelical pacifism and its critique of the more traditional just-war teachings will receive a fair hearing and serious consideration.

It is a propitious moment for such a review if one is to judge by the growing number of responsible Catholics participating in anti-war demonstrations here and abroad and engaged in active civil disobedience directed against the instruments designed to unleash the final holocaust. In this fiftieth anniversary year of *The Catholic Worker*, that once solitary voice of pacifism within the American Catholic community, one can take satisfaction in hearing the bishops reaffirm their support for the legitimacy of conscientious objection and repeat their call for recognition of selective conscientious objection. The pacifism that once earned the *Worker* a reputation for being "extreme" or even "heretical" is now accorded almost equal status with the just-war theory.

All of this is somewhat late in coming if one considers that twenty years have passed since John XXIII issued *Pacem in Terris* and almost that many since Vatican II called for "an entirely new attitude" toward war. In the intervening years we have witnessed the dramatic pilgrimages for peace undertaken by Paul VI and now John Paul II. Too little it may be and almost too late, but the pastoral is to be welcomed both as an important advance in its own right and, even more, as the foundation for the continued efforts it will take to fulfill its promise.

That "new attitude," I would insist, is really the "old" attitude, the commitment to pacifism and non-violence that characterized the beliefs and behavior of the earliest Christians. This claim to authenticity does not rest solely upon the pacifist practices of those pre-Constantinian centuries. True, the refusal to return violence for violence or to seek or accept military service is persuasive and finds consistent support in the writings of the church fathers as well as confirmation in the martyrs honored in the liturgical calendar. What deserves more attention than it has received is what we might call the spirituality which gave rise to and maintained those honored, even romanticized, patterns of behavior. This spirituality has been all but smothered by centuries of adherence to just-war thinking and the contrary patterns of compliance, compromise, and collaboration with non-Christian and often anti-Christian secular powers.

The Spirituality of Pacifism

From the perspective of the sociology of religion, this spirituality of pacifism can be seen as a complex of perceptions leading to, or derived from, belief (or, as the believer would probably prefer, faith). The core perceptions from which the pacifist commitment draws its strength and validity are: first, the perception of God; second, the perception of the relationship between the believer and God; and, third, the perception of what might best be described as the ultimate purpose or objective of that relationship. These do not exhaust the perceptions that contribute to the structure of the believer's faith, but they are the most crucial to pacifist commitment and behavior.

These perceptions, it should be added, will be influenced and in some cases determined by the believer's early formation, especially that encountered in the family setting and through formal religious instruction. In later years they will be modified or extended by the normal processes of emotional and psychological maturation and sharpened (though possibly more often *weakened*) by education and experience. Members of the same religious community may be expected to share similar perceptions and express them in similar patterns of behavior, but allowance must always be made for individual variations. How dissimilar or widespread those variations may be, especially in matters touching upon these core perceptions, is a problem of ecclesiology. Pacifism and just war represent such a problem. For this reason alone they deserve periodic—even if repetitious—discussion and debate.

1. All perceptions of God include the attribution of omnipotence and authority, but there can be significant differences in how these are assumed to be made manifest. The pacifist perception puts them in the context of God's benign and loving concern for his creation and the infinite willingness to forgive. Seen thusly, he is not likely to be the vindictive being in the manner attributed by more militant types to their wrathful Lord of righteousness. This implies no denial that his is the power and the sole right to judge and even punish, but these will always be exercised in a fashion which assures the repentant sinner an early and relatively easy return to the circle of the beloved.

The pacifist finds it impossible to reconcile this infinity of compassion with the popular notion of a vengeful God visiting his people with the scourge of war as punishment for sin. That wars do come about as a result of human failure and vice is true enough, but the God of the pacifist's perception would never choose to make a point or display his anger by exposing multitudes of innocent men, women, and children—his creatures all—to the suffering and devastation of war. Homer's Greeks and Trojans may have been pawns in a cosmic game played by jealous divinities on Mount Olympus, but that is not the way the God of the Christians is likely to operate. Certainly not the God of the pacifist Christians!

How, then, are we to explain the wars, including wars of extermination, authorized or commanded by the God of the Old Testament to which the pastoral devotes so much attention? The sociologist, dancing along the edges of heresy perhaps, finds part of the explanation for the emphasis placed upon vengeance and the often unrestrained exultation over the excesses of violence reported in these accounts to be related to the perceptions and motives of the human instruments chosen to record the bloody history. Please note, to make allowance for the possibility that a tribalistic gloss may have been added in the course of the presentation (to say nothing of subsequent translations and commentaries) would not necessarily bring the essential truths of revelation into question.

Quite apart from such debatable empirical projections, however, is the question that might be raised as to whether the violence recorded in the Old Testament, divinely initiated or not, should be as relevant to the beliefs and behavior of Christians as some hold it to be. One need not deny what had gone before and the lessons to be drawn from it to insist that Christ's triumph over sin through the cross closed the door on the violent past and opened the future to his all-redeeming, all-forgiving love. After all, the Old Testament accounts are filled with instances where God, pleased by some belated sacrifice or some other display of sincere reparation, "changed his mind" and spared his people from punishments already pronounced. There is every reason to conclude, then, that the sacrifice of his only Son would be more than enough to confirm and ratify the new dispensation under which violence and war are no longer instruments of divine intervention in human affairs.

The efforts that have been made to draw implications of similarly retributive wrath and vengeance from the New Testament are forced and unconvincing. It is remarkable that obviously sincere and devoted Christians are so ready to justify the horrors of modern war by references to the highly ambiguous account of Jesus driving the money-changers from the Temple—even as they ignore the lesson of absolute commitment to non-violence in his more direct instructions and in the behavior of St. Stephen and other of his disciples as recorded in Acts. Content analysis might not carry much weight in theological disputation, but if one were to measure scriptural references to forgiveness, mercy, and the other "soft" virtues against those which even remotely suggest approval of violence or retaliation, there would be little room for doubt as to which is the more appropriate mode of behavior for those who would be followers of Christ.

2. The second perception carries this forward in considering the relationship between the weak and sin-prone believer and this loving and forgiving God. The familiar and much loved Prayer of St. Francis provides a good summary of what the pacifist holds this to be. One pleads to be made an instrument of peace, to learn to replace hatred with love, injury with pardon, despair with hope—and so on. Not an "instrument" in the mechanistic sense, however. Instead of a kind of voluntary depersonalization such as that could imply, what is called for is a fully reasoned and freely willed surrender, a total commitment in the deepest meaning of that often lightly used word. Once such commitment is made, it carries with it the admission of full dependence—even more, complete abandonment—to the will of God such as one finds expressed so beautifully in the less well-known prayer of Brother Charles of Jesus.[2]

This awareness of dependency and the spirit of abandonment reflect the believer's acceptance of the fact that whatever degree of success or well-being one may achieve or whatever setbacks one must suffer lie in God's power to decide. Here again, this is not the abject fatalism some might think it to be, for when one considers the kind of God the pacifist perceives, abandonment is always tempered by the equally thorough confidence that good will prevail. In God's time and in God's way.

This is the key to the pacifist's alternative to war and preparation for war, namely, the theory and practice of non-violence. Both the abandonment and the confidence are grounded in the scriptural promises that God's power will be made perfect in our infirmity, that no matter how hopeless and threatening the situation may appear, the gates of hell will not prevail. This, the pacifist would insist, offers greater security than reliance, permanent or temporary, on nuclear deterrence. This is not naiveté or ignorance of human history. The pacifist knows as well as any, perhaps better than most, about pogroms and massacres of helpless and non-resisting innocents. Monsignor Paul Hanly Furfey, one of the pioneers of Catholic pacifist thought in the United States, saw in this fact and in all the other evidences of social evil he studied that, once we have eliminated all the human causes, we will find that "the mystery of iniquity" will still be at work in the world. To accept this fact is not to be indifferent to the evil itself. Instead the pacifist's insistence upon non-violent resistance is a refusal to succumb to the delusion that it is somehow possible to overcome evil by adding to it.

3. Again by logical progression we come to the remaining dimension of pacifist spirituality. In the eschatological context, the commitment to non-violence develops these themes in more profound intensity. Though Thomas Merton persistently (and, I would insist, mistakenly) rejected the pacifist label for himself, he provides the clearest statement of this intensity in his identification of ours as a "post-Christian era." As he uses the term it has a double meaning. In the most obvious sense it asserts that Christians can no longer act (as if they ever could!) in the confidence that princes and principalities are guided in their acts and policies by Christian principles of moral behavior, most specifically by the conditions of the just war. However much the rhetoric used to justify behavior might exploit religious themes and symbols, there is no reason to believe that "blessed" cannon (or Trident submarines for that matter) will not be used as "military necessity" seems to require, quite irrespective of how immoral that use might be.

But it is Merton's second meaning that bears most directly upon pacifism and its non-violent alternative. To speak of this as the post-Christian era is to affirm that since Christ has come and has conquered sin we have nothing more to fear other than the temptations and sins which could turn us away from him and the loving protection he provides. *These* are "the last days" and, to Merton and his pacifist admirers, they are days of hope, of confident expectation, of anticipation here and now of the promised eternal rewards.

Once we accept this, the insane rush for security through new weapons of ever-increasing destructiveness becomes a threat to the Christian's true security. It is in effect a denial of that hope and expectation and, given the possible outcome of the continued escalation of the propensity for evil, may put salvation itself in serious jeopardy. Consider how far we have come already. From thinking the unthinkable about doing the undoable our nation and its leaders have progressed to the point where the war Merton warned would be a crime "second only to the Crucifixion" is being discussed as a rational option. The bishops do well to be skeptical about the morality of "limited" nuclear war, but a less ambiguous response to a concept which incorporates the "acceptable" lost of 20 to 30 million American lives would be more appropriate. If this is security, the pacifist will have none of it. Skepticism is not enough.

Non-violence, Merton admits, does not always "work" as a means for achieving desired political results but that is because "non-violence is not for power but for truth. It is not pragmatic but prophetic. It is not aimed at immediate political results, but at the manifestation of fundamental and crucially important truth. . . . It does not say 'We shall overcome' so much as 'This is the day of the Lord, and whatever may happen to *us*, *He* shall overcome.' "[3] The pastoral, unfortunately, stops short of making the same precise application, but the possibility that success as the world measures it cannot be the ultimate Christian objective can be inferred from its reminder that "we must regard as normal even the path of persecution and the possibility of martyrdom" if we seek to be "a wayfarer with and a witness to Jesus" (# 276).

Principles and Policies

It would be a mistake to conclude from this heavy concentration upon perceptions and spirituality, culminating in Merton's dismissal of non-violence as an appropriate instrument for seeking power and political change, that the pacifist is ignorant of or indifferent to policy issues. Nor should one assume, as just-war theoreticians often do, that pacifism is too "visionary" and "unrealistic" to contribute anything to public debate on questions of foreign policy and military strategy.

Unfortunately, what it does have to offer is usually not welcomed or given serious consideration. The overriding principle which should govern all policy decisions of this order, the pacifist would hold, is the primacy of religious commitment over national identities and loyalties. In our discussions of these issues they should be approached from the perspective of a Catholic (or, in the broader sense, Christian) *who just happens to be an American*, not, as is too often the case, the other way around. An obvious corollary of this ruling principle would be that the universality of humankind as God's family and creation takes precedence over more limited nationalistic concerns and values. Already in the period between the two world wars this was recognized by an international gathering of theologians in their designation of nationalism as "the characteristic heresy" of the day. There is nothing to suggest that this has become any less true over the intervening years.

Given the priority of religious commitment and the universality it implies, this should mean that war or any violent exchanges between categories of humankind—national, ethnic, religious, racial, etc.—cannot be condoned and that Christians have a special obligation to refrain from taking part. In a more positive vein, it means that Christians are obligated to work for the speedy correction of the inequalities and rivalries which create the tensions out of which wars arise. Pacifists, like those who accept the possibility of justifiable war, are agreed on the importance of diplomacy and negotiation leading to effective multilateral disarmament and peaceful solutions of the conflicts that do occur, but the pacifist is likely to put more emphasis on the need for the contending parties to begin by confessing their own failures and shortcomings and to strive toward an atmosphere of mutual interest and reconciliation.

A second principle of policy and action derives more directly from the pacifist spirituality outlined above. It calls for an expanded definition of the concept of the common good that would include and give priority to the spiritual health and well-being of the members of the commonality. Predictably it rejects any suggestion that the state (or government) is somehow above or not bound by the limitations morality imposes upon the individual citizen. More specifically, it rejects the notion present by implication in the pastoral that what the Christian is forbidden to do as an individual can become permissible (even *obligatory*?) when it is required by public authority under the guise of national defense.

Other inferences to be drawn from this principle: policies which incorporate immoral threats made credible by proclamations of immoral intent must be resisted; citizens must consider whether it is permitted for them to contribute to, or pay for, the manufacture of instruments by which Merton's "crime second only to the Crucifixion" would be committed; all of us must give serious thought to the moral guilt we may bear for exposing young people, mentally and physically, to military training which prepares them to commit these forbidden acts. These positions are all familiar parts of the pacifist program, but the point is not always made that they are tied to the service of the common good. Those who accept a philosophical orientation which sees the state as an institution whose function is to make it possible for its members to meet their needs and fulfill their capacities should have no difficulty in accepting the argument that any policies which constitute or maintain what in former days was referred to as "a proximate occasion of grave sin" is actually destructive of that common good.

The pacifist's rejection of nuclear deterrence, including possession, production, *and preparation to use,* stems from this. While every possible encouragement is to be given to efforts aimed at achieving multilateral disarmament, unilateralism cannot be dismissed as a morally required policy option should those efforts fail. The unilateral initiatives called for in the bishops' pastoral are to be welcomed and endorsed as introductory stages, but the implication that the absence of a suitably complementary response might bring a termination or reversal of the process tends to negate the proposal's impact.

The issue of "preparation" may be the most critical moral problem associated with current deterrence policies, but it is passed over in the pastoral. Though it applies to the murderous potential of "conventional" arms as well, we cannot ignore the fact that men and women in the armed forces, many of them Catholic, are being trained under command to be ready to unleash the kind of area warfare condemned by Vatican II. Thus while one welcomes the reaffirmation of the legitimacy of conscientious objection, what is really needed is a more active promotion of that option for Catholics. At the very least, more attention must be given to assuring conscientious participation on the part of Catholics in the military and to providing them with explicit instructions as to the limits they must respect, the orders they are morally forbidden to give or to obey. It is not altogether inconceivable that, assuming the seemingly irreversible trends in weapons development and strategy continue, the point may be reached where certain forms of military service (on those Tridents, for example) should be placed under formal interdict.

Origen's familar refutation of the charge that Christians by their unwillingness to fight were aiding the cause of the barbarians pointed to their offerings of prayer and penance as a higher form of service to the empire. Now that the means of violence have broken through the moral limits set forth under traditional just-war teachings, the modern Christian may be left with no choice but to return to the weapons in their spiritual armory. This does not mean they are to retire from the world in "angelistic" detachment. Turning away from the works of death and destruction forbidden to them will enable them to dedicate their efforts more fully to works of reparation, relief, and the rehabilitation of a threatened world and its inhabitants. In the process they

will discover, as those earliest Christians did, that through persever-
ance in their witness of sacrifice and love they can overcome the forces
of tyranny and oppression. After all, things have been worse. The
policies and objectives of the Soviet Union may be "reprehensible," to
use the bishops' term, but there have been no reports of helpless
Christians being fed to ravenous bears in the Lenin Stadium. Followers
of Christ might consider adopting the rallying cry that was so popular
among patriots during World War II: we did it before, and we *can* do
it again. *If* we believe as those earliest Christians believed.

The "mutual trust" which the beloved John XXIII identified as the
only sure basis for peace on earth cannot come forth from repeated
threats of mutual destruction. In a very real sense there is nothing less
realistic than deterrence policies based on such threats and accompanied by the constant development and production of new and ever
more sophisticated weapons designed to make those threats credible.
If there is to be any hope that mutual trust can become a reality,
someone must take the first step. To take a risk for peace one must
contemplate the possibility of national defeat, the loss of freedom, and
a host of other sacrifices and hardships. Even so, it would be preferable
to the risk we are taking now with its promise of the final holocaust.
To continue as we are is to enmesh ourselves and the world ever deeper
in the arms race which the Holy See has already condemned unre-
servedly as a "folly," a "crime," and an "act of aggression against the
poor."

Should the risk be taken and the gamble lost, the Christian might
be faced with a return to the catacombs and suffer the persecution,
even martyrdom which, the bishops remind us, we must be prepared
to regard as "normal." Through its centuries-long history the church
has been there many times and has always endured, its witness out-
lasting the tyrannies which have repeatedly sought to eradicate Christ
and his message.

There is no need to seek or resign ourselves to that grim fate. If we
reach out to potential enemies in a spirit of sincere reconciliation and
give as much attention to our own faults and shortcomings as we do
to theirs, we can at least hope for a response in kind. But confessing
and rectifying our failures will require more than the pastoral's belated
and weak admission of "sorrow" over our first use of nuclear weapons—what Paul VI described as "butchery of untold magnitude." If
nothing else, a display of remorse, coupled with suitable acts of pen-

ance and reparation, might lend a touch of credibility to diplomatic negotiations between the major powers which until now have gotten nowhere because they so seldom rise above exchanges of self-righteous rhetoric and mutual recrimination. All too often our negotiating stance seems to reverse the view of Clausewitz, who regarded war as an instrument of diplomacy, and makes of diplomacy a continuation of war by other means.

Unrealistic? Utopian? Perhaps, yet the argument can be made that such an approach is more realistic than present policies which lock us and the world into fixed antagonisms that are almost certain to lead to the very results they professedly are designed to forestall. To the Christian it should be much more realistic than any theory which would defend the slaughter of uncounted millions and the as yet unmeasurable collateral consequences as a possible rectification of injustice. And it is certainly more realistic than the tortured reasoning which would weave a cloak of plausibility for such justifications by suggesting that though one knows in advance he is perpetrating (or preparing for) an atrocity beyond measure, he can evade moral responsibility by not "intending" it.

Bishop Carroll Dozier is right. The day of the just war, if there ever was such a day, is past.[4] The conditional clause is crucial to the pacifist, for he would hold there never was. From its beginnings the theory was an obvious—though possibly unconscious— device by which the behavior of Christians could be accommodated to the declared needs of the secular ruler by freeing the individual from the obligation to stand apart from and above the killing and destruction of war. Before long Christian practice would make a mockery of Origen's patient explanation that Christians did not engage in violence because they had been taught not to defend themselves against their enemies, because they were bound by higher laws that commanded gentleness and love of their fellow men.[5] Over the centuries accommodation too often became cooperation and even at times collaboration until Paul's vision of the Christian community as a universal mystical body of the Christ it professed to follow all but vanished in the spectacle of Christians killing Christians in almost every war that came along. All the scholarly tomes devoted to the development and exposition of the principles of the just war and its conditions were not enough to prevent Germany's bishops in Hitler's Third Reich from urging their flocks to fight for Folk and Fatherland as a Christian duty.

Not all theologians ignored the issue completely, of course. One assured his readers who might be troubled in conscience that a decision about the justice or injustice of Hitler's wars could be made only after the war was over and all the facts were at hand! This, I think, reveals the fatal flaw in the just-war tradition: it is useless during a war when the Christian has to decide what he is to do. For all the claims to realism and expertise made by its practitioners in dealing with what Father Bryan Hehir refers to as "the arcane details of the strategic debate," the just-war theory when taken in the context of an ongoing war becomes the theologian's equivalent of the Rubik cube, a dazzling display of intellectual dexterity with nothing to show for it when it is done. To cite Dozier again, it is time to file the just-war theory away in the same drawer that hides the flat-earth theory and the theories about the sun racing around the earth.

It is time to dismiss once and for all the just-war formulations as irrelevant to the realities of modern war. It might be well, too, to realize that it never was fully relevant to Christianity. As a source of moral guidance it found its source not in scripture but in the writings of pagan philosophers. The wisdom of Aristotle, not the teachings of Christ, provides the foundation for the carefully calibrated conditions developed by the scholastics. Helpful though it might have been, an ethical system which defined the morality of the "good pagan" does not, and never could, encompass the behavior to which the Christian is called. So, too, with such values as freedom and justice. Precious as they are and worthy of defending, they are not the ultimate values and must never be given precedence over Christ's call to sacrificial love even for (*especially* for?) the enemy and forgiveness for the unjust oppressor. We know that those who hunger and thirst after justice are promised their fill, but it is those who suffer persecutions and injustice for his sake who are assured of the kingdom of heaven.

Nowhere in the New Testament or in the writings of the early church fathers do we find anything that justifies the presumption of a *superseding* obligation to take up arms in defense of the secular power. The bishops' pastoral performs a great service in its recapitulation of the lessons of the pre-Constantinian centuries, its recognition of evangelical pacifism as a legitimate option for the Catholic, and its somewhat hesitant acknowledgment of the non-violent alternative and its potential. Unfortunately, to the extent that it seems to restore the preeminence of the just-war theory, it stumbles and falls short of the prophetic leadership the church and the world need at this critical "new moment" in time.

In his 1970 World Day of Peace Message, Pope Paul VI began with the lament, "Lord, it is true. We are not on the right path." Though the pope assuredly did not have this particular interpretation in mind, the pacifist would agree and suggest that the turning away from that right path came with the introduction and acceptance of the notion that war and violence could ever be justified for the Christian. The bishops' pastoral may not be enough to put us back on the right path, but at least it does represent a slight turn in the right direction.

NOTES

1. Michael Novak, "Draft Board Theology," in T. Quigley, ed, *American Catholics and Vietnam* (Grand Rapids: Eerdmans, 1968).

2. Father,
    I abandon myself into your hands;
        do with me what you will.
    Whatever you may do, I thank you:
        I am ready for all. I accept all.
    Let only your will be done in me,
        and in all your creatures—
    I wish no more than this, O Lord.

    Into your hands I commend my soul;
    I offer it to you with all the love
        of my heart,
        for I love you Lord,
        and so need to give myself,
        to surrender myself into your hands,
        without reserve,
        and with boundless confidence,

    For you are my Father.

3. Thomas Merton, *The Non-Violent Alternative* (New York: Farrar, Straus and Giroux, 1980), p. 75.

4. Most Rev. Carroll Dozier, Bishop of Memphis, "Gospel Non-Violence," speech given at the Pax Christi USA Assembly, Rochester, Minn., 8 October, 1982.

5. Origen, *Contra Celsum* 3,8.

JAMES FINN

Pacifism and Just War: Either or Neither

The whole Catholic doctrine of war is hardly more than a *Grenzmoral*, an effort to establish on a minimal basis of reason a form of action, the making of war, that remains always fundamentally irrational. (John Courtney Murray)

The Catholic bishops of the United States have done something new. A number of years after Vatican II, they have responded collectively and deliberately to the injunction of that council "to undertake a completely fresh appraisal of war" (#s 23, 66, 122). That fresh appraisal was undertaken, however, within the framework of a venerable tradition on war and peace. The declared intention of the bishops is to draw upon that tradition, to develop it, and to apply it to specific present issues. I propose to examine what their fresh appraisal means for the traditional doctrine and for U.S. policies.

There is no need to underline the gravity of the issues with which the bishops contend. They constitute questions of our survival, the matter of our politics, the tissue of our nightmares. Nor does the public response to the various drafts of the pastoral allow any doubt that what the bishops think and say will have consequences. Any Catholic who responds to the pastoral, who accepts what the bishops have called "both an invitation and a challenge" (# 4), should do so with the same sobriety that the bishops brought to their task, with the same willingness to make hard, clear judgments open to public examination and criticism.

The bishops say that they draw heavily on the Pastoral Constitution on the Church in the Modern World of Vatican II and on the popes of the nuclear age, from Pius XII to John Paul II. During the period from Pius XII to the present, Catholic teaching on war has changed significantly. It was Pius XII who reduced the legitimate causes of war to the single one of defense, but it was also Pius XII who disallowed pacifism as an acceptable choice for Catholic citizens. Given the history of the church on the pacifist option, the speed with which it has been not only legitimated but honored within the church is remarkable. It is a strength of the bishops' letter that it clarifies the terms of what was becoming a murky and tendentious debate. Pacifism, they assert, is an option for individuals but not for governments, which have an obligation to defend their people. That obligation is best informed by and understood within the moral option provided by just-war teaching. Although this distinction is welcome, it does not address the question of whether and how the pacifist position bears on public policy. This important point is never resolved in the pastoral. In fact, it is never clearly addressed, yet it permeates and colors much of the argument. It will be necessary to return to this point after an examination of how the bishops understand, develop, and apply the just-war tradition.

The just-war tradition posits the conditions under which war is justifiable and places constraints on what is justifiable in war. Understood as a work of reason consonant with the Gospel, it is intended to inform the Christian conscience and to establish the right terms for public debate. One of the criticisms frequently directed against this tradition is not that it is wrong but that it is irrelevant, that it has failed to establish any vital relation with public policies. This criticism is sufficiently accurate that upholders of that tradition must honor the bishops' attempt to show how just-war principles can get a grasp on and provide guidelines for specific policy decisions. But to honor the attempt is not yet to take the measure of the bishops' actual accomplishment. To do this we must look at any changes the bishops have made in just-war teaching and judge whether they are advances, retrogressions, or, possibly, temporary diversions. We must examine the application of the principles to specific issues the bishops address and attempt to assess their prudential judgments. Finally we must ask whether their recommendations, if they become policy, would move us "toward a more stable system of national and international security" (# 196), as the bishops intend, or toward some less desirable and more dangerous situation.

Framework for Analysis:
John Courtney Murray

To facilitate this analysis, to illuminate the argument, and to lend some historical perspective I am going to invoke some positions enunciated with intellectual rigor by John Courtney Murray, S.J. Not quite twenty-five years ago, in the course of presenting the thought of Pius XII, who gave sustained attention to the nature of contemporary war, Father Murray outlined the elements of statecraft present in just-war doctrine, showed how they dissolved false dilemmas and how they set proper terms for the moral/political debate.[1]

Murray stated that one could start an investigation of the problem of contemporary war by discussing (1) modern weapons technology, (2) Communism as a dominant fact in the present historical situation, and (3) the present mode of international organization. Considered in isolation from the others, each will lead to a distorted view. The likely distortions are (1) relative Christian pacifism. (2) support for a "holy" or preemptive war, or (3) the argument that war now having lost its legality is also invalid. Not only must all three lines of investigation be considered but they lead to three basic questions that must be considered in proper order. The first is the exact nature of the international conflict; this sets the perspective in which we must consider the other questions. This analysis

> will be [able] to furnish an answer to a complex of questions that must be answered before it is possible to consider the more narrow problem of war. What precisely are the values, in what hierarchical scale, that today are at stake in the international conflict? What is the degree of danger in which they stand? What is the mode of the menace itself—in particular, to what extent is it military, and to what extent is it posed by forms of force that are more subtle? If these questions are not carefully answered, one will have no standard against which to match the evils of war.

Only after we have answered these questions should we pass on to the array of means available to ensure the values at stake in the conflict. And only then to the third question, which concerns arms as the last resort.

The pastoral letter does not follow this order of analysis, and it is the weaker for it. For we must assess the values we are defending and the threats to which they are exposed before we can make prudential judgments about how to counter the threat—and whether and to what degree we can justifiably resort to the arms at our disposal. We must know the nature of our real or putative enemy before we can even negotiate on a realistic basis. Yet the bishops lay down many strictures on the use of tactical and strategic nuclear weapons, oppose specific proposals concerning our present deterrence system, and recommend various other measures before they even venture to describe the Soviet threat. Not until they turn to peace-keeping measures do they refer to the "fact of a Soviet threat, as well as the existence of a Soviet imperial drive for hegemony" (# 249). The realistic assessment of the Soviet system they offer here is an advance over that of earlier drafts, but it does not seem to have played a part in recommendations they had previously made. For what—given the nature of the Soviet tyranny as it has revealed itself to us over the decades—can it mean to recommend:

> Removal by all parties of short-range nuclear weapons which multiply dangers disproportionate to their deterrent value. (# 191)

To whom is this addressed? Does it refer to the cruise missiles and the Pershing 2's that the U.S. is scheduled to deploy in Europe in December 1983? Or the tactical nuclear weapons of NATO already in place? Or does it possibly refer to the SS 20's that the Soviet is continuing to produce at a fearsome rate, many of which they have installed in Central Europe? And if the latter, who is to persuade the Soviets that these weapons "multiply dangers disproportionate to their deterrent value"? The Soviet system and the Soviet policies so well described in the later pages of the pastoral are not likely to yield to the sweet voice of reason. What we can expect from the Soviets will depend upon our perception of their purposes and policies. And that perception should be enunciated *before* we make any recommendations that involve their behavior. For many of us, the history of negotiations with the Soviets shows that they will agree on reductions such as those recommended here only if they perceive them to be in their interest. The question then becomes one of how they are to be brought to that perception. And this cannot be answered satisfactorily until we have responded carefully to the set of questions that I have earlier quoted from Father Murray. The bishops have performed that task only indifferently well. On the basis of this pastoral, the reader is ill-prepared to accept or reject a number of the proposals that the bishops themselves oppose or recommend.

But it is when we come to the question of modern weapons systems that the great divide between Murray's position and that of the pastoral letter becomes most apparent. It is a divide that also and still exists between positions strongly advocated by the bishops and positions taken by many Americans, a number of whom are Catholics. They concern not the principles of just-war teaching but their application.

After positing the two moral options open to Catholics—in the course of which they lay down in familiar and abstract terms the tenets of justifiable war—the bishops turn to the problems and principles of war in the modern world. Although the many wars in which countries have been embroiled in the last four decades form a depressing lesson in what "modern war" encompasses, the bishops reveal the real focus of their concern by immediately turning to nuclear war. Their position, starkly put, is that "we must reject nuclear war" (# 132) but that "it is much less clear how we translate a 'no' to nuclear war into the *personal and public* choices which can move us in a new direction" (# 134; emphasis added). After thus acknowledging the difficulty, they proceed to lay out the path that they think will lead in that new direction. A summary of their overall position must necessarily neglect the reasoning that supports it and the nuances that qualify it. But the essentials include the following:

The bishops are led to "a strictly conditioned moral acceptance of nuclear deterrence" (# 186) as an interim measure. The acceptance is based on the assumption that the deterrence exists only to prevent the use of nuclear weapons by others. This flows from and leads to more closely defined positions. On the basis of non-combatant immunity, the bishops reject any policy that would make innocent civilians direct objects of attack. This might leave open the option of directing attacks only at military or militarily significant targets. While one might think the bishops would favor this as an alternative policy, they rule it out on two grounds. First, a nuclear strike against industrial and militarily significant economic targets within populated areas could cause morally disporportionate damage. Even with care, large numbers of civilians would be killed. Second, a strategy directed solely against the enemy's forces might seem to threaten their retaliatory power, making deterrence in a crisis unstable and a war more likely.

Limited Nuclear War
But what if, in order to strengthen the deterrence, reduce the likelihood

of war, and contain the injury to innocents within morally acceptable terms, one devised a limited-war strategy? Such a strategy would strengthen the deterrent by proving to an adversary that we were serious in our intentions; it would reduce the likelihood of war because the element of bluff would be diminished and our political will therefore less likely to be tested. If the deterrent failed, this strategy would limit the number of non-combatants killed because it would be based on specific and limited targets, using smaller and less destructive weapons with increasing accuracy.

This strategy, too, the bishops reject. A war-fighting capability as part of deterrence might support notions that nuclear war could be fought and won without transgressing acceptable human and moral limits. And even the limits originally intended are likely to be disregarded under conditions created by the initial nuclear strike.

And how does this apply to the smaller, tactical nuclear weapons which are included in the arsenal on which NATO now relies to deter both nuclear and conventional Soviet forces? To this question the bishops say two things. First, they "do not perceive any situation in which the deliberate initiation of nuclear war, on however restricted a scale, can be morally justified" (# 150). In standard terms they advocate a "no first use policy" (# 153). (It is to their credit that they recognize that this shift in NATO strategy would require NATO to develop an alternative mode of defense, that this alternative would require greater expenditure—nuclear weapons are cheaper in relative terms—and that it could not be implemented immediately.)

But if an opponent struck first with nuclear weapons, what then? Would any nuclear response be appropriate and morally justifiable? Acutely aware of the contingent judgments that are required to evaluate the possibilities of a limited nuclear exchange, the bishops pose a series of skeptical questions, their own responses to which incline them to a negative judgment. To cross from conventional to nuclear weapons is such a risk that they see "no moral justification for submitting the human community to this risk" (# 161). But what if smaller, more efficient and thus less destructive tactical weapons could be devised? Again, their judgment is no, because their development would, they fear, blur the distinction between conventional and nuclear weapons. Furthermore, they support what has loosely been termed the "freeze movement." They recommend "support for immediate, bilateral, verifiable agreements to halt the testing, production, and deployment of new nuclear weapons systems" (# 191), a program which, if accepted, would preclude the testing and development of more effective and less destructive nuclear weapons.

Having placed these restrictions on nuclear weapons, the bishops are concerned lest anyone think they are making the world safe for conventional war. This gap they also try to close. Reluctantly acknowledging that their restrictions might demand greater conventional defenses, but avoiding consideration of any burden this would necessarily place on budgets and policies, they "hope that a significant reduction in numbers of conventional arms and weaponry would go hand in hand with diminishing reliance on nuclear deterrence" (# 217). This remains, as many will say, a pious hope.

But if all these measures were carried out should we not develop civil defense measures that would include, for example, ballistic missiles defense, shelters, and relocation plans? This possibility, they say, should be studied while efforts to develop non-violent means of conflict resolution should be pursued.

Thus the bishops' attempt to say no to nuclear war. They are left with a nuclear weapons system that is intended to deter even though the declared policy forbids any use of nuclear weapons. It forbids nuclear strikes against cities and militarily significant targets near cities because these would violate non-combatant immunity, and it puts leashes on first use and retaliation because the risks of escalation are so great. It is a policy that separates the twinned elements of deterrence, the weapons and the political will to use them, and jettisons the political will. Furthermore it would play havoc with the weapons systems we have. Our aging missiles could not be improved or replaced by more reliable weapons because testing and deployment would have been halted.

The Pastoral and Murray's Framework
How does this square with or mark a departure from the traditional position as presented by Father Murray? I am no more able to present all the supporting arguments Father Murray employs than I was to present those of the bishops. Nevertheless, simply to present essential premises and conclusions of his argument will highlight the great divide I earlier mentioned.

Almost twenty-five years ago, Murray set forth the traditional teaching in the following way. Acknowledging that war remains a possibility "not to be exorcized even by prayer and fasting," the doctrine of the church continues to condemn war as an evil, to place limits on that evil, and as far as possible to humanize its conduct. Given our historical moment, the right terms for public debate are set by a dialectical process alternating between principle and fact. As a power-imperialism, the Soviet Union "must be confronted by power, steadily and at every point." The Soviet Union has already solved a major problem U.S. policy has yet to solve: without making survival one of the issues at stake, how do we prepare to use whatever force is necessary or desirable? The traditional doctrine asserts in principle that force remains the *ultima ratio* in human affairs and that we may be morally obligated to rely on it. The facts include the existence of nuclear weapons whose use is possible and may be necessary "lest a free field be granted to brutal violence and lack of conscience." The doctrine insists on certain limitations: ". . . thus the terms of public debate are set in two words, 'limited war.' All other terms of debate are fanciful or fallacious."

> There are those who say that the limitation of nuclear war, or any war, is today impossible, for a variety of reasons—technical, political, etc. In the face of this position, the traditional doctrine simply asserts again, "The problem today is limited war." But notice that the assertion is on a higher plane than that of sheer fact. It is a moral proposition, or better, a moral imperative. In other words, since limited nuclear war may be a necessity, it must be made a possibility. Its possibility must be created. And the creation of its possibility requires a work of intelligence, and the development of manifold action, on a whole series of policy levels—political (foreign and domestic), diplomatic, military, technological, scientific, fiscal, etc., with the important inclusion of the levels of public opinion and public education. To say that the possibility of limited war cannot be created by intelligence and energy, under the direction of a moral imperative, is to succumb to some sort of determinism in human affairs.

Dismissed also was "the special delusion proper to the nuclear age, that any use of nuclear weapons, however low in the kiloton range, must inevitably lead to world catastrophe. Hence the false dilemma: either to begin with catastrophe or to renounce all use of nuclear force."

In invoking this presentation of Father Murray twenty-five years after it was written, I do not presume that the bishops were ignorant of it or that Murray would steadfastly have maintained the same position today. I am sure that Murray's argument was known to the framers of the pastoral. As to what position he might have taken today, that is beyond anyone's divination. What is beyond any question is that Murray's insistence on "limited war" as the proper term for public debate diverges sharply from the bishops' insistence on "no nuclear war." The issue could not be put more starkly.

Current Military Realities

Since some readers of the pastoral might account for the movement the bishops have made in terms of the shifting events of the last twenty-five years, some word must be said about the historical moment in which the document situates itself. Any reader of the document who was ignorant of the developments of the last four decades might well conclude that a nuclear race has continued almost unabated; that there has been a "continuing upward spiral even in conventional arms"; that the deterrence system was accepted as stable and safe until today; that "the new evaluation of the arms race" flows from a new recognition of how destructive they can be and how narrow the political and moral choices presented; and that at the crest of this new moment the bishops speak a new word.

The reader would not learn from the letter that, measured in megatons, the American stockpile in 1980 was only one fourth of what it was twenty-five years earlier; that we have fewer nuclear weapons now than in the mid-sixties; that U.S. strategic budgets had spiraled consistently down in the early seventies; that in somewhat less than two decades the U.S. and its allies reduced their defense budgets by fifty percent; that the "arms race" does not follow the action-reaction pattern frequently ascribed to the U.S. and Soviet military forces; that the stability of the deterrent system was frequently questioned from the fifties on; that both specialists and average citizens criticized U.S. nuclear policies publicly and vigorously. Furthermore, they acknowledged the threat of nuclear weapons and the strict choices they imposed. Certainly Father Muray did.

The bishops are correct in saying that the present awareness of our plight is unprecedented in its breadth and depth. And it may prove to be more sustained than previous movements. But it has not produced essentially new positions. In its broad and continuing outline, the argument is that with which Murray concerned himself. The position of nuclear pacifism which the bishops espouse is not new; what is new is that the bishops espouse it. That it is not new does not, of course, mean that it is not valid, that it fails to observe and properly employ the doctrinal principles of traditional Catholic teaching. But those who attend to the teachings of the American bishops have a right, even an obligation, to ask whether the pastoral is the best available application of the teaching and whether it best provides for the security of our nation and the well-being of the international community.

Examining the Evidence

Since the arguments and conclusions of the bishops turn on matters more of judgment than of fact, one can approach the issue of that judgment in several ways. First, one can examine the supporting evidence they offer to see whether it actually does support their conclusions. For example, they quote from a study John Paul II commissioned from the Pontifical Academy of Sciences; "Recent talk about winning or even surviving a nuclear war must reflect a failure to appreciate a medical reality: Any nuclear war would inevitably cause death, disease and suffering of pandemonic proportions . . ." (# 130). Presumably, as medical scientists, the authors of the document intend to speak with scientific accuracy. We have a right, then, to ask what they mean by "*any* nuclear war." Would a nuclear strike at a surveillance or communications satellite hundreds of miles in space answer the description? Or a strike at naval forces at sea? Or a highly restricted strike at, say, some key element of one of America's allies, even if we did not respond? These are kinds of possibilities that would be considered in a limited war. There is no evidence that such limited strikes would cause damage of "pandemonic proportions." But perhaps the members of the commission assumed, as some people do, that escalation of the nuclear war would be inevitable and lead to the results they specify. If so, it must be pointed out that such a conclusion exceeds the realm of their medical competence. So far from inspiring trust in their competence, this speculation undermines the authority of their statement— and the authority of those who would depend upon it.

One could examine in this fashion the various kinds of evidence on which the bishops rely. Obviously an arduous and demanding task that would require one to duplicate much of the work that went into the letter initially.

Criteria for Judgment

One can approach the document in still another way. Recognizing that the policy debate is inconclusive and that our judgment of whether a nuclear war could remain limited turns on how one projects likely reactions in a nuclear exchange, the bishops posit a series of questions concerning information, stress, communications, human or computer error and the definition of "limited." Having listed what are real and very serious concerns, the bishops then conclude that "the burden of proof remains on those who assert that meaningful limitation is possible" (# 159).

This is a fair and useful procedure. It is a way of assessing risks and the moral responsibilities they entail. And one can, within the framework provided by just-war principles, develop a similar set of questions. One set, which could be further refined, would run like this.

Do the United States and its allies face an opponent that threatens their safety and the values which sustain them?

Does the nuclear element in our arsenals play a part in deterring actual or potential aggression?

Would the deterrent quality be diminished by:

    a. ruling out strikes and threats of strikes against military targets?

    b. declaring that we would not strike first?

    c. declaring that we would not retaliate with nuclear weapons?

    d. resisting modernization that would increase command control, reduce the risk of accident, and limit potential damage?

Would the risk of war be decreased by diminishing the deterrent, by disqualifying any use of strategic weapons, and by ruling out limited nuclear war?

The burden of proof that these procedures would reduce the risk of conventional and/or nuclear war rests on those who assert that such limitations are morally and militarily desirable.

Blending Pacifist and Just-War Options?

There is a third way to approach the pastoral letter. It is to examine the process by which the pastoral was shaped. This examination has led me slowly and reluctantly to the conclusion that the process itself is almost irremediably flawed. I say this as someone who was privileged to play a small part in that process. I was a witness before the five-member commission of the bishops; I received and commented upon successive drafts; I was impressed with the openness of the consultative process; I applauded the third draft and final document as marking a distinct improvement over earlier drafts. Nevertheless, I found that under the pressure of closer examination, certain fault lines appeared repeatedly and formed a pattern. I was forced to ask why. The answer I found is so central to the document that I will try to express it in several ways, but essentially it is that in the document the two traditions open to Catholics—pacifism and just war—are joined in such a way that they corrupt each other. The comprehensive view to which the document aspires leads to a compromise, not of positions the adherents of either tradition could make, but of the principles of each tradition.

Adherents of the two options do share an overall moral vision of peace, but on how best to incarnate that vision in this world they differ. They no longer travel together on one broad path but go in decidedly different directions. In an incisive essay that he prepared before the bishops' project was undertaken, Father J. Bryan Hehir analyzed this condition of pluralism within the church and formulated the crucial questions that it posed. The two traditions derive from and foster, he pointed out, different patterns of moral reasoning and lead to different practical resolutions. Conscientious objection and selective conscientious objection, for example, cannot logically be held by the same person. Furthermore, he pointed out that "the implications for public policy of a pacifist and a just-war position are significantly different. The distance which pacifist churches keep from the policy questions is testimony to this fact." A problem this presents to the church is how, out of this pluralist setting, it projects a policy position.

The pastoral would seem to have responded to this at least partially when, in referring to a choice between the two available options, it said, "We are referring to options open to individuals. . . . Governments threatened by armed, unjust aggression must defend their people" (# 75). Since pacifism is not an option for a government, its policy decisions in this area should, according to this approach, be developed within a just-war framework. Yet in preparing the pastoral letter bishops who are pacifists, bishops who have repudiated just-war doctrine, discussed and voted on crucial policy options for our defense structures. And their counterparts in the larger Catholic community were invited to submit their arguments and judgments on policy matters. The issue here should not be confused. Pacifists have a perfect right to address matters of war and peace and military preparedness. What is illegitimate and damaging to the integrity of both traditions is to have pacifists seeming to act within the just-war tradition while they define its tenets so narrowly as to strangle it. Gordon Zahn, for example, has termed Father Murray's statement on limited nuclear war "scandalous." And, given Zahn's pacifist position, this response is neither unexpected nor improper, but it does make him an unlikely candidate to apply the principles set forth by Murray.

To attempt to join the two traditions in this way is to follow the procedure adopted by two men who find themselves facing a wide ravine while some danger behind them fast approaches. They are faced with the choice of attempting to leap the ravine or to turn and face the danger. A good case can be made for either, but they differ on which to choose. Each failing to convince the other, they resolve their differences by deciding to jump half way.

To yoke the two traditions together as the pastoral does not only confounds the policy options, but confuses the distinct modes of moral reasoning to which Father Hehir referred. Two examples: (1) After exploring in rich detail various meanings and connotations of peace, the pastoral states that just-war teaching allows but also demands "extraordinarily strong reasons for overriding the presumption *in favor of peace* and *against* war" (# 83; emphasis in original). Precisely not! As Father Murray said, "the single inner attitude which is nourished by the traditional doctrine is a will to peace, which, in the extremity, bears within itself a will to enforce the precept of peace by arms." The traditional doctrine does not, therefore, override a presumption in favor of peace unless peace is understood merely as the absence of war, which has never been Catholic teaching. The just-war doctrine recognizes that a defensive use of arms is sometimes required for the restoration of peace.

(2) The bishops state: "As a people, we must refuse to legitimate the idea of nuclear war. Such a refusal will require not only new ideas and new vision, but what the Gospel calls conversion of heart" (# 131). Whatever one can say about expecting a people to undergo a conversion of heart, it does not flow from the application of just-war principles or from the patterns of moral reasoning which they encourage. Those principles encourage a critical procedure subject to reason, and open to discussion and debate in the political arena in which policy decisions are hammered out.

We will see some of the practical consequences of the approach adopted by the pastoral as individual bishops reassert their unchanged positions. "Yes, I signed the document and it does criticize even limited nuclear retaliation. But that is a particular application open to different judgments and under some circumstances I would favor such retaliation." Or, "Yes, I accepted the deterrence but I still think possession of those weapons is immoral, and if anyone thinks I'm going to campaign for increasing conventional weapons just because we've outlawed nuclear weapons, they can think again." Such reactions will reveal that the two traditions still live separately and that the forced homogenization of the pastoral was temporary.

Pacifists must continue to develop their positions within their *own* framework, using their own modes of moral reasoning. And so must those of us who adhere to just-war principles. Respecting the bishops, their authority and their purpose, I am, nevertheless, critical of their performance. I am unpersuaded that they have presented the only or best application of just-war doctrines. And I believe their recommendations, if pressed into operation, would weaken the security of the United States and its allies. I am left with the position enunciated by Father Murray and developed since then by a distinguished group of Christian moralists. The correct term for public debate at this time remains "limited war." This necessitates support for (1) a deterrent system strengthened by morally acceptable limited-war strategies upon which one could rely if the deterrent were to fail; (2) defensive measures to protect citizens and reduce military damage; (3) arms control approaches that will be built on the sturdy base of mutual interest; (4) unilateral initiatives that do not weaken the foregoing measures and that promise further safe reductions; (5) modernization measures that increase safety, limit damage, and improve command and control procedures; (6) strengthened regional and international agencies that might act as buffers and help resolve conflicts.

It is from this position that I and many who share it hope to continue the dialogue which the bishops have opened and in which the pastoral letter must be regarded as an initial stage.

NOTES

1. John Courtney Murray, S. J., *We Hold These Truths: Catholic Reflections on the American Proposition* (New York: Sheed and Ward, 1960). The quotations and the supporting arguments are in two chapters: "Doctrine and Policy in Communist Imperialism," pp. 221–47, and "The Use of Doctrine on the Use of Force," pp. 249–73.

V

Nuclear War and Deterrence

The Challenge of Peace

Part II.A-D, #s 122–199

Clearly Part II is the apex of the pastoral. Here, the letter accepts the challenge presented by the third of "the signs of the times": new problems posed by nuclear weapons "must be addressed by fresh applications of traditional moral principles."

The bishops cast the nuclear dilemma in terms of "a cosmic drama." On the one hand, humankind "possesses a power which should never be used" because of its enormous destructive capacity. Therefore, can it be used? On the other hand, its presence is alleged to be a deterrent to a war that threatens the planet. And can it even be possessed?

The letter approaches the resolution of the dilemma by making the tactical decision "to build a barrier against the concept of nuclear war as a viable strategy of defense." To implement this decision the pastoral proposes that stringent limits be set on governments' nuclear policies. From a compact, tightly reasoned application of just-war criteria, the letter offers a series of moral judgments about the use of nuclear weapons that are intended to define the limits and to shape the public debate.

The pastoral addresses the second horn of the nuclear dilemma, its deterrence value, in the form of a question: "May a nation possess what it may not use?" The letter's response, relying heavily upon Pope John Paul II's conditioned acceptance of balanced nuclear deterrence, offers a series of recommendations regarding U.S. nuclear policy.

BRUCE M. RUSSETT

The Doctrine of Deterrence

Deterrence Defined

Discussion of nuclear deterrence in this context must consider both the technical academic debate and the kind of normative or strategic analysis employed in the pastoral letter. We begin with the implications of a fairly standard definition of deterrence used by the letter: "Dissuasion of a potential adversary from initiating an attack or conflict, often by the threat of unacceptable retaliatory damage."[1] Several aspects of this definition deserve comment.

First, it refers to dissuading an adversary from *initiating* an attack or conflict. In other words, deterrence is an effort to prevent another party from doing something he or she has not yet done, rather than to persuade the party to do something new. Deterrence refers to the use of military means to achieve a necessarily uncertain psychological effect.

It is very hard to judge whether deterrence succeeds, or is even necessary. NATO deterrence of a Soviet military invasion of Western Europe well illustrates the difficulty. Very possibly the Soviet Union would long since have occupied Western Europe, but for NATO military strength. But very possibly it would *not* have done so even in the absence of significant Western military power. Perhaps the Soviets never had any serious interest in occupying such a large, populous territory where they are so unpopular; the daunting prospects of trying to govern such an overextended empire might alone have been enough to "deter" an invasion. Or perhaps not. As it is, we can confidently say only that NATO military deterrence has *not yet failed*: the Soviets have not invaded. Whether military deterrence has succeeded or been irrelevant, or whether it could have succeeded with a much lower level of military deterrent threat, we cannot know. Without access to the full archives, and minds, of the Kremlin, we can only have opinions.

It becomes an article of faith, not subject to empirical confirmation. In this sense the phrase "the doctrine of deterrence" is very apt. The result is not merely an academic point in logic-chopping. It cuts to the heart of military and political issues of deterrence.

Second, note the reference to the threat of "unacceptable" damage. How much is enough, or excessive? For successful deterrence must we have "the clear and present ability to destroy the attacker as a viable 20th century nation?"[2] Or would some much lower level of nuclear capability suffice? Former national security advisor McGeorge Bundy asserted that the explosion "of even one hydrogen bomb on one city of one's own country would be recognized in advance as a catastrophic blunder."[3] Or if some military deterrence is necessary, might not conventional (non-nuclear) means alone be enough? Continuing policy debates—what constitutes "overkill"; can we defend Western Europe without the threat of "first use" of nuclear weapons—stem from the impossibility of confident, concrete answers to the question, How much is enough? In doubt, there is a temptation to err, if at all, on the side of excessive deterrence. It may seen safer to have too much than too little. A consequence of having too much, however, is the possibility of enormous, thoroughly disproportionate, damage if for any reason deterrence fails. (Should we really blow up the world if the Russians invade Austria?)

An often neglected point is that what is enough to constitute "unacceptable" damage varies substantially. Presumably it would take a stronger threat to prevent an enemy from occupying an economically and strategically important area than from seizing a piece of useless desert. More subtly, deterrence of the *same act* may require stronger threats under *different circumstances*. In "normal" peacetime almost all countries have a great deal to gain from continuing peace, and from the prosperity that peacetime growth and international trade can provide. A Soviet attack "out of the blue" seems to offer costs to the Soviet Union entirely disproportionate to the economic and physical damage that country would suffer from even a blunted Western retaliation. In times of severe military and political crisis, however, the equation changes greatly.

Suppose, for example, the situation is not "normal" peacetime but a military confrontation, somewhat like the Cuban missile crisis of 1962, where each side fears the other may attack. Each might prefer continued peace. But if my nuclear retaliatory forces are vulnerable to an attack and I think that attack is imminent, I may feel it necessary to launch them in a "preemptive" strike: the "use it or lose it" situation. The temptation to launch a preemptive strike is even greater if my opponent's forces are also vulnerable to a first strike. That is, each side is more tempted to strike first if by doing so it can significantly diminish the other side's capacity to retaliate. If both sides' forces are vulnerable the temptation to shoot first in a crisis may become almost irresistible. This is precisely the reason so many analysts fear the destabilizing effects of vulnerable land-based missiles with high accuracy.[4]

Suppose, further, that the political situation is one of widespread revolts in Eastern Europe, aided by "volunteer" forces from Western Europe. Even very substantial NATO nuclear forces might not be enough to deter a Soviet attack on Western Europe if the Soviet alternative seemed to be the loss of its Eastern European empire. Both military and political conditions, which can change drastically within short time periods, affect a determination of what is "unacceptable retaliatory damage."

Third, the reference to broader economic and political conditions of peacetime should alert us to limitations of the purely military terms of the definition. The threat of direct military retaliation is surely *one* way to deter attack. Others may include the threat of an escalated arms race (American rearmament was one clear consequence of the North Korean attack on South Korea in 1950), and the prospective loss of markets and goods in peacetime international trade. Henry Kissinger tried to enmesh the Soviet Union in a web of interdependence with the West as a means of giving the Soviets something substantial to lose if they strayed too far from detente. Many of the most effective instruments of deterrence in international politics involve the subtle, and even un-conscious, manipulation of a broad range of non-military punish-ments—and rewards—for continuing good behavior.

Extended Deterrence

The definition is vague on the matter of *what* (other than "an attack or conflict") is to be deterred. In fact, the question of how much is enough depends critically on just what action we are trying to deter. On one level, nuclear powers surely develop and build nuclear weapons to deter other states from attacking them with nuclear weapons. Some-times we treat this as the principal obstacle to disarmament—"the Russians would bomb us if we couldn't bomb them back." But the history of nuclear deterrence shows that this is *not* the most common purpose for having nuclear weapons. The United States, for example, built atomic bombs and intercontinental bombers during the years 1945 to 1949, before the Soviets had even a single atom bomb. Israel is thought to be capable of deploying nuclear weapons in very short order (a matter of days), even though none of Israel's neighbors is remotely close to having operational nuclear weapons. In both cases, the purpose of nuclear weapons is to prevent large-scale *conventional* war or invasion rather than nuclear attack. And in the case of the United States in the 1940s (and even now) the perceived threat was not plausibly of a Soviet invasion of American home territory. Rather, nuclear weapons were intended to deter a Soviet invasion of our allies, most importantly those in Western Europe.

Nuclear weapons therefore may fulfill a variety of deterrent purposes: deterring a nuclear or conventional attack on oneself, or deterring a nuclear or conventional attack on allies, client states, or friendly neutrals. Deterrence of attack on states other than oneself has become known as "extended deterrence." It is a central and explicit part of both superpowers' logic.

Nuclear weapons are, relative to large-scale conventional forces, rather cheap. In the words of Secretary of Defense Charles Wilson in the 1950s, they give "more bang for the buck." They have seemed to promise, to a technologically superior West, an economically tolerable means of holding off numerically superior forces of the "Eastern hordes." The policy became official with Secretary of State John Foster Dulles's exposition of "massive retaliation" ("in a manner and at a place of our choosing") in 1954. It was refined with the United States deployment of tactical nuclear weapons in Europe during the 1950s under the doctrine of, if necessary, fighting a tactical nuclear war to repulse a conventional Soviet attack. The policy seemed somewhat more attractive during the short period before the Soviet Union deployed its own tactical nuclear weapons in Eastern Europe. Even so, NATO maintains an official policy of "flexible response": to reply, at whatever level of violence seems necessary, to any Soviet incursion. This means, explicitly, the threat to use nuclear weapons whether or not the Soviet Union's attacking forces have yet used them. The United States has also used the explicit or implicit threat of nuclear first use to deter war in various other parts of the world, such as Korea and, most recently, the perceived threat of Soviet invasion of Iran during the last year of the Carter administration.[5] Much of the debate about nuclear deterrence turns on the question of whether the threat of nuclear weapons is being employed too widely and cavalierly, or whether alternative (conventional) means of deterrence are really beyond the ability or willingness of the Western alliance. Doctrines of nuclear deterrence often are ambiguous about just what kind of attack is supposed to be prevented.

Counterforce and Counterpopulation Targeting

Even when the instruments of deterrence are nuclear weapons, there often is equal ambiguity about just what are the means of deterrence: the threat of strikes against what kinds of targets, by what kinds of nuclear weapons.

In the early days of the nuclear era only atomic bombs existed, and not many of them. They were to be delivered by long-range bombers to targets in the Soviet homeland, in an extension of the strategic bombing characteristic of World War II. They had to be targeted in a way that would have maximum effect on Soviet war-making capabilities. In the first conception—an extension of American success against Nazi Germany—that was thought to be against the Soviet petroleum industry, creating a severe bottleneck in industry, transportation, and military operations. Soon, however, Air Force planners gave more attention to the larger industrial and population damage ("bonus" effects) that would result from using atom bombs against targets in urban areas. Consideration of different kinds of damage melded the two, and in some plans, as in the first Strategic Air Command (SAC) operational plan, the aim points were "selected with the primary objective of the annihilation of population, with industrial targets incidental."[6] The target list of a war plan charmingly known as BROILER called for thirty-four bombs on twenty-four cities. The list was rapidly expanded as more bombs became available, with a combination of industrial and population damage being intended.

As the nuclear and later thermonuclear (hydrogen bomb) stockpiles of both superpowers grew, so did the number and kind of targets. Some strategists continued to emphasize the primary importance of crippling immediate Soviet war-making capability: military targets per se, transportation, petroleum and electrical generation facilities, and war-related industry. Others, like General Curtis LeMay, urged that "we should concentrate on industry itself which is located in urban areas," so that even if a bomb missed its target "a bonus will be derived from the use of the bomb."[7] "Bonus" in this instance clearly included the death of Soviet civilians.

In discussing nuclear deterrence policy we must distinguish between *declaratory* policy and *operational* policy, between what a government says it will do with weapons, and what it in fact plans or intends to do with those weapons in actual military operations.

American declaratory policy has, until very recently, been deliberately ambiguous about just what would be struck. In his famous 1962 statement at Ann Arbor, Michigan, Defense Secretary Robert McNamara said the principal military objective should be "the destruction of the enemy's forces, not of his population." He later retreated from this public declaration, and in the same statement cited earlier about destroying the attacker "as a viable 20th century nation" defined that as the ability to destroy one-fifth to one-fourth of the enemy's population and one-half of its industrial capacity.[8] This public characterization certainly was not unique to McNamara; similar words were expressed by many other officials before and after him.

Whether the effect of civilian casualties was deliberately sought as a deterrent, accepted as an unintended but welcome bonus, or reluctantly accepted as a relatively unavoidable consequence has varied with different strategists and different times. James Schlesinger, as Richard Nixon's secretary of defense, talked openly about the possibility of striking military targets while minimizing civilian casualties, and Harold Brown, defense secretary under Jimmy Carter, wrote that "we do not target civilian population centers *per se*."[9] The latter statement has been repeated frequently and publicly by the current administration, in words quoted in the pastoral letter. It would seem that declaratory deterrent policy clearly is no longer one of deliberate counterpopulation strikes.

We cannot be so sure what operational policy might become during the course of a nuclear war. But the expansion of the set of targets associated even with a purely counterforce deterrent strategy has been enormous, a thousandfold from operation BROILER. By the end of the 1950s SAC had identified over 20,000 targets in the Soviet Union, and 40,000 by 1980.[10] They included "militarily significant" industry, transportation and communication facilities, command centers, tactical military forces and support complexes, and of course Soviet submarine pens, airfields, and missile silos. The list of targets has regularly out-

paced—and driven upward—the number of strategic bombs and warheads available to hit them. (For example, the current inventory is
about 9,000 warheads and bombs on long-range delivery systems.)
Attempts to be selective have been overwhelmed by the number of
targets. For instance, the 1979 SIOP (Single Integrated Operational
Plan) identified 60 "military" targets within the city of Moscow alone.[11]

In the evolution of nuclear strategy, American planners had to confront a growing unpleasant fact. Whereas in the first years targeting
could be directed at Soviet war-making capability in general, it soon
became necessary for American strategists to think about nuclear "damage limitation"; that is, to limit the ability of the Soviet Union to hit
the United States with nuclear weapons. By 1950 first priority in targeting was assigned to Soviet capability to deliver atomic bombs.[12] But
this kind of targeting capability inevitably threatens to degrade Soviet
retaliatory capacity. As we noted earlier, stable deterrence, especially
in times of crisis, depends on the confidence each side has in its ability
to survive a first strike from its opponent with enough of its own
retaliatory forces intact to insure "unacceptable" damage to the attacker. If the ability of retaliatory forces to survive a first strike is not
assured, the temptation to initiate war oneself, in a preemptive strike,
is strong.

In the bomber age this was not a serious problem, especially once
both sides had good air defense and radar systems in place. An attacking bomber force could be spotted long before it reached targets
in either the Soviet Union or the United States. Intercontinental missiles, however, shortened the time between launching an attack and
the impact of incoming warheads to only about thirty minutes. With
the advent of highly accurate missiles (accurate within about .12 miles)
and MIRVs (Multiple Independently targeted Reentry Vehicles), whereby
one MIRV missile can hope, with ten warheads, to destroy five or even
ten enemy missiles on the ground, land-based missiles have become
highly vulnerable to attack. Previous attempts to "harden" missile silos
with steel and concrete to resist blast have essentially been overwhelmed. Missile silos cannot effectively be concealed from informa-
tion-gathering satellites, and most proposals to make land-based missiles
mobile, to evade precise targeting, have all seemed technically unpromising. Counterforce targeting, in the broad sense of a wide variety
of military and military-industrial targets, need not endanger retaliatory
capability. But these new technological developments, coupled with

deliberate targeting of an opponent's land-based missile silos, could do so and become profoundly destabilizing. Increasingly, therefore, assurance of retaliatory capability has come to rest on bombers (which might be launched, and if necessary recalled, in the face of impending attack), smaller more mobile cruise missiles, and especially sea-based missiles launched from submarines which can be kept moving and whose location can probably be kept secret.

"Acceptable" Deterrence

With these elements of the strategic debate on deterrence in mind, we are ready to consider some normative evaluations inherent in the pastoral letter. The letter makes central use of Pope John Paul II's June 1982 statement to the United Nations:

> In current conditions, "deterrence" based on balance, certainly not as an end in itself but as a step on the way toward a progressive disarmament, may still be judged morally acceptable. (173)

The letter appropriately calls this a "strictly conditioned" acceptance of deterrence (186). We must realize how little it explicitly accepts. It cannot be used to indicate a blanket acceptance of all, or even many, forms of deterrence.

Most obviously, and noted by virtually all commentators, is the condition that deterrence must be "a step on the way toward a progressive disarmament." Deterrence cannot be considered "an end in itself," nor can we resign ourselves to an indefinite future whereby we are condemned, in the pope's next words, to be "always susceptible to the real danger of explosion."

Another element of his statement is the phrase "based on balance." It implies a need, as recognized by most strategists and policy makers, to maintain some sort of "parity" or "essential equivalence" to the capability of one's opponent. But a further implication of the "based on balance" phrase is a willingness to concede such a capability to the opponent. In other words, one can reasonably read the Holy Father's words as rejecting notions of seeking "superiority" or means to "win" or "prevail" in nuclear wars. In the contemporary situation many observers contend that such notions can lead at best to a continuing upward spiral of the arms race as one power tries to establish such a capability and the other seeks to avoid being under such a threat, or to establish its own "winning" capability. At worst, attempts to achieve a "winning" capability would produce first-strike forces and "use it or lose it" situations of extreme danger in crisis.

There are other limitations implicit in the pope's words. He refers very generally to "deterrence," not to particular implements or strategies of nuclear deterrence. In the French original of his United Nations address the operative words are *une dissuasion—a* deterrent, some deterrent, not any and all deterrents. He does not even explicitly endorse *nuclear* deterrence. What we have here, in explicit words, is no more than a recognition that in competitive international relations states require, at least "in current conditions," *some* means to deter other states from aggressive action. The specific form of that deterrent is not specified. Moreover, deterrence *"may still be judged"* morally acceptable. Again, this is hardly a blanket endorsement of everything that is said, done, or planned in the name of deterrence.

The vague, general, and ambiguous content of the Holy Father's words must be fully appreciated. It may seem niggling to point out how little is truly endorsed. Possibly Pope John Paul II would explicitly accept various specific aspects of American or Soviet deterrent policy. The fact remains that he has not done so, and it would be dishonest to pretend that he has. The very restricted nature of his overt "acceptance" impels the kind of further normative analysis articulated by the bishops in their letter.

A Just-War Analysis of Deterrence
The bishops' analysis of deterrence is clearly based on the analytical categories of the just-war tradition. Three such categories are especially relevant.

First is the requirement of *discrimination*, or observing the principle of non-combatant immunity. This requirement is stated categorically as a general principle, not as a mere application subject to disagreement. The bishops could hardly do otherwise. It is a basic principle of Christian ethics that one may not directly and intentionally kill innocent human beings. Its relevance to nuclear deterrence follows from the same premise as does the Catholic condemnation of abortion. The fetus is innocent, and may not be deliberately killed, even to avert some great evil or achieve some good end. The same is true if children or adult civilians are deliberately killed in a bombing raid. In the words of Cardinal Bernardin's opening address to the Chicago, May 1983 meeting, it is "murder."

The condemnation of direct attacks on "civilian population centers as such" removes a great deal of deliberate ambiguity from past American deterrent policy. "Collateral" damage must be limited, not intended, and "bonus effects" may not be sought. While we have identified substantial past ambiguity both in declaratory and operational policy, only in the last year—in obvious response to the evolving position of the bishops' pastoral letter—has the American government so clearly and repeatedly disavowed any such intention. Morally, that disavowal has to be considered a major achievement, one with many implications for the direction of future policy.[13]

The second just-war category, of equal importance, is the principle of *proportionality*. By some (inevitably subjective and uncertain) calculation the harm done by an act, even unintentionally, may not be disproportionate to the good intended to be achieved or to the evil to be avoided. The principle of discrimination forbids counterpopulation warfare; the principle of proportionality puts sharp limits on counterforce warfare. The latter principle recognizes that in almost any war some civilians will unavoidably be killed if military targets are hit. This is clearly a case of "double effect," and admits that some civilian deaths can be accepted as a by-product of striking a military target. But just because civilians are not killed intentionally does not mean they can be killed without limit. Specifically, the pastoral letter expresses very grave reservations about the massive civilian casualties that would surely occur in any nuclear exchange, even one directed deliberately only to military targets. The section on deterrence is filled with references to the way military facilities and civilian living and working areas are interspersed, to the fact that the number of civilians who would necessarily be killed is "horrendous," and cites admissions by the administration that "once any substantial numbers of weapons were used, the civilian casualty levels would quickly become truly catastrophic." The principle of proportionality thus says that discrimination alone—merely limiting a nuclear strike to counterforce targets—is not enough to make that policy "morally acceptable."

Many strategists and government officials—especially, but not only, members of the current administration—have maintained that improvements in strategic weaponry are movements in the direction of greater moral acceptability. Specifically, improvements in accuracy, coupled with elimination of the very large warheads placed on older missiles like the Titan, will have the effect of limiting collateral damage. The number of (supposedly greatly reduced) civilian casualties sustained when military targets are hit could therefore be judged appropriate to some aims of war or deterrence. Nuclear deterrence could then be said to be both discriminating and proportionate.[14] Modernization of the strategic arsenal, with more accurate weapons like the MX, is therefore morally permissible and even required! Similar claims are made for "small" battlefield tactical nuclear weapons and, on occasion, for the neutron bomb.

On the first encounter, it is hard to disagree with this assessment. A reduction in unintended civilian deaths would be consistent with traditional moral principles. But on examination the problems are immense. One problem is the fact, as already mentioned, that any large-scale nuclear exchange, even of "discriminating" weapons, would inevitably produce millions or tens of millions of civilian casualties. Numerous studies, drawing on private and government material, reach this conclusion. Some of them are cited in the letter.[15] The combination of immediate casualties from blast and radiation, with longer-term casualties from fall-out, disruption of the medical, sanitation, transportation, and communication systems, ecological devastation, and so forth, would be very, very great—even from attacks that were "limited" to such "strictly military" targets as the 1050 American and 1400 Soviet land-based ICBMs. Actually, the Defense Department's list of military and militarily related industrial targets (remember, 40,000 of them) includes industry and utilities essential to the economic recuperation of the Soviet Union.[16] If the Soviet (American) economy is destroyed, tens of millions of Soviet (American) citizens will die of hunger and disease. To "prevail" in such a war would have little meaning. There are not many causes to which such megadeaths would be "proportionate."

One problem is therefore the illusion that any large-scale nuclear exchange could in any real sense be "limited" in its consequences. The other problem is with the expectation that nuclear war could be fought in some precise fashion of strike and counterstrike, that in any substantial nuclear exchange the war could be restricted to a limited number of strictly military targets. There are people in the government who imagine it could be done, with acceptable consequences.[17] The majority of analysts, however, consider the likelihood of such limitation, under wartime conditions of anger, confusion, ignorance, and loss of control, to be extremely small. One cannot definitively rule out the possibility, but neither should one bet the future of civilization on it. Probably the two most knowledgeable experts on this matter are Desmond Ball and John Steinbruner, who offer nearly identical skeptical views. In Steinbruner's words,

> Once the use of as many as 10 or more nuclear weapons directly against the USSR is seriously contemplated, U.S. strategic commanders will likely insist on attacking the full array of Soviet military targets. . . . If national commanders seriously attempted to implement this strategy (controlled response) in a war with existing and currently projected U.S. forces, the result would not be a finely controlled strategic campaign. The more likely result would be the collapse of U.S. forces into isolated units undertaking retaliation on their own initiative against a wide variety of targets at unpredictable moments.[18]

In a nutshell, limitation of nuclear war fails a third principle of the just-war tradition: *reasonable chance of success*.

So much for what could—or could not—morally be done in war. Is *deterrence*—as contrasted with what one actually *does* in war—different? After all, the purpose of deterrence, as we are so often reminded, is to prevent war.

The bishops have two answers to this. One is the fact that, whatever our good intentions, deterrence may fail. If we make plans—build weapons, construct strategic programs, proclaim doctrines, instruct commanders—on the basis of principles we would not be willing to act upon, we just may be called to act upon them anyway. Many things happen almost automatically in any war or defense establishment. In the 1914 crisis, the powers had competitive mobilization plans that worked automatically, making World War I unavoidable. Or we may contemplate recent talk about plans for launching nuclear weapons on warning. Plans adopted in the name of deterrence may come to fruition in action, whatever our desires at the time. If war should come as the result of some uncontrollable crisis, or a physical or human accident, plans calling in the name of deterrence for morally unacceptable acts would very likely be *realized* as morally unacceptable acts. The second answer is the traditional principle of Catholic moral theology that says one may not intend what one may not do. An intention to commit an immoral act in a particular event (even if one is confident that the triggering event will not transpire) is itself immoral. The argument from "mere deterrence" will not fly.

Another aspect of recent strategy that the bishops probably would reject is brinkmanship, or what Thomas Schelling called, "manipulating the shared risk of war."[19] Schelling recognizes that a would-be deterrer might well threaten to do something that, in the event deterrence failed, he would not in fact want to carry out. The United States might *threaten* to go to all-out nuclear war if the Soviet Union occupies West Germany. In the event the Soveit Union *did* occupy West Germany, the United States government might not want, for moral and/or practical reasons, to execute its threat. In fact, a government fully in control of its military forces probably would *not* want to initiate all-out nuclear war. One way to deal with this situation would be to build some variant of a "doomsday machine": commit oneself irrevocably and automatically to an act of mutual destruction that one would not want to carry out if one retained a choice at the time. Almost everyone rejects the doomsday machine solution as grossly imprudent and disproportionate.

But a less drastic solution would be to build into a situation an element of unpredictability and uncontrollability. In practice, a Soviet invasion of West Germany might very well trigger an all-out nuclear war whether or not the American government wished it to do so. American nuclear weapons would be widely dispersed, to low-level commanders who would very likely have operational control over the weapons. (The PAL [Permissive Action Link] codes that prevent unauthorized use in peacetime very likely would be released to low-level commanders in a time of high crisis in Europe.) One of those commanders, in the "fog of war" with his troops under siege, might very well use the weapons.[20] Or the Soviet Union, fearing they would be used, might stage a preemptive attack on them. Use of a few tactical or theatre nuclear weapons would be very likely to escalate into a strategic exchange between the American and Soviet homelands, as several military analysts cited in the pastoral letter have testified. The threat of unintended use of nuclear weapons in the event of a conventional war or even a high-level crisis in Europe provides a powerful deterrent to the deliberate initiation of war, of any kind, in the center of that continent. No rational Soviet leader would deliberately run such a risk.

If we believe that political crises (unlike military events) are always fully controllable, then perhaps such a deterrent seems prudent. But if we believe that political crises are not always controllable or avoidable (1914 again, or a revolt in East Germany that attracts support from West Germany, or a political breakdown in Yugoslavia that draws in regular or volunteer fighters from East and West), it does *not* seem prudent. The bishops termed "the deliberate initiation of nuclear war" to be morally unjustified. I believe they similarly would declare a deliberate posture of probable loss of control to be an unjustifiable moral risk. "Non-nuclear attacks by another state must be resisted by other than nuclear means."

Use, Threat, and Possession

Yet another question is whether one may threaten to perform acts which one could not licitly do or intend. The broad question of "bluffing" as a theological issue is not, I understand, settled. The bishops avoid it in their letter. On more narrowly pragmatic grounds we can ask whether making deterrent threats, of indiscriminate or disproportionate use of nuclear weapons, would be a prudent national policy. The answer, I believe, is clearly no. For one thing, if the threatener were known to adhere to other aspects of the Christian just-war tradition, it would be an obviously empty bluff—the threatener simply would not be believed. If the threatener were not a known adherent to the just-war tradition, the threat would gain greater credibility. But to be credible the threat would have to be supplemented by public orders and plans for the contingent use of nuclear weapons if deterrence failed. Declaratory policy would have to be contrary to operational policy, with only a very small circle of policy makers aware of the difference. It is very unlikely that such a policy could succeed. On the one hand, the fact that the threat was only a bluff probably would become known, through leaks or espionage. Or, if the secret were held tightly enough, the automaticity inherent in strategic nuclear planning very possibly would take over in the event of war, especially if war included (as it very likely would) a "decapitating" attack that removed the commander-in-chief. The use of nuclear weapons would then probably follow the lines of the declaratory policy rather than the secret operational policy—nuclear weapons would be used in a morally unacceptable manner. The circle cannot be squared.

To encourage belief in the probability of "morally acceptable limited nuclear war" would play into the hands of the war fighters, the "prevailers," who think "victory is possible." It would encourage those who want to continue to rely on a threat of first use of nuclear weapons to deter a wide range of acts in Europe, the Middle East, and elsewhere. It would encourage brinkmanship and crisis risk-taking at the expense of building up alternative, non-nuclear means of defending ourselves and our allies. The bishops very prudently avoid that trap.

The trap on the other end of the spectrum lies in the position that while a nation may continue to possess nuclear weapons it may not use them under any conceivable circumstances. This becomes the "you can have it but you can't use it" position. It is easily parodied. It falls under much the same objections as apply to expressing a threat one could not licitly execute. If it is known that the weapons would not be deliberately used under any circumstances, then the weapons lose most of their deterrent power. If—as is in fact virtually unavoidable in a complex military establishment—one leaves open the possibility that the weapons will be used despite the commander-in-chief's intention not to use them, the result is hardly better from a moral standpoint. Leaving something to chance inescapably involves moral responsibility for those who leave it to chance and intend to benefit from the chance. Again, the circle cannot be squared.

Some critics, including several conservative columnists, the *New York Times* in a 6 May 1983 editorial, and Albert Wohlstetter in his article cited earlier, have accused the bishops of adopting just such a "you can have it but you can't use it" position. It is true that the second draft (October 1982) of the pastoral letter was ambiguous—deliberately so—on this matter. While it contained no passage explicitly saying *no* use would be permissible, it was imbued (properly) with a strong rhetoric of saying no to nuclear war and contained a few passages whose full meaning was obscure.[21] The ambiguity was intended to mollify critics who chose to interpret some passages in the first draft—notably, "If nuclear weapons may be used at all, they may be used only after they had been used against our own country or our allies, and, even then, only in an extremely limited, discriminating manner against military targets"—as the bishops giving some Good Housekeeping Seal of Approval to limited nuclear war. In context it certainly was nothing of the kind. Predictably, the ambiguity of the second draft opened the bishops up, from conservative critics, to ridicule or mischievous charges that the bishops, despite their disclaimers, were "really" adopting a stance of unilateral nuclear disarmament. Fortunately this ambiguity was removed in the third draft and the form adopted in the final Chicago meeting. In fact, a proposed amendment by Archbishop Quinn, of "opposition on moral grounds to any use of nuclear weapons," was not adopted.[22]

A Dilemma Without Easy Resolution

These two traps—the extremes of counterforce as nuclear war winning and of possession without use—frame a fundamental dilemma that cannot easily be resolved. There *is no* good practical solution to the problem of nuclear deterrence. Moral considerations further complicate the problem. The bishops' position in the final letter is not so ambiguous as it is frankly conflicted.

One proposed deterrent has been through advocacy or adoption of an extreme version of MAD (Mutually Assured Destruction) that is expressly and solely a counterpopulation deterrent. But practically, it would mean abandonment of almost all forms of extended deterrence, since no state would initiate its own sure destruction in order to "defend" another. And morally, Christians must reject strategies of counterpopulation warfare.

Another possible way to ease, though not escape, the moral dilemma would be through adopting a posture of "tolerating" nuclear weaponry as a means to a good end (deterrence, or ultimate disarmament). There were hints of this kind of reasoning in the first and second drafts of the letter. But critics labeled that reasoning "consequentialist" and feared it would lead to wider application of "bad means justifying a good end" variants of moral theology. Consequentialist reasoning is widely condemned by traditionalist Catholic theologians. While it is not entirely clear that the early drafts depended on such reasoning, and there are respectable Catholic theologians who do not reject consequentialism, it was not a supportable basis for the bishops' letter. To avoid totally rejecting nuclear deterrence the bishops had to find some strategy that at least had a chance, in some hypothetical circumstances, of being morally neutral (discriminating, proportionate) rather than intrinsically evil.

A key and often neglected element of some acceptable resolution is the bishops' strong advocacy of a no first-use posture. They reject the notion of extended deterrence and require that non-nuclear attacks be resisted by other than nuclear means. If so, a purely counterforce deterrent has no need for prompt hard-kill capabilities, or any other seemingly first-strike forces which could endanger crisis stability. The risks of escalation are high under the best of circumstances. If the opponent should begin nuclear war, *some* of those risks would already have been taken. To deter that act, and to bring the war to a negotiated halt just as soon as possible, we may plan certain very restricted forms of retaliation. But the risks of first use of nuclear weapons are too high to justify us in ever setting the process in motion.

While understanding that "development of an alternative defense position will still take time," the bishops insist that NATO "move rapidly" toward such a position. They are willing—clearly if unenthusiastically—to consider that "some strengthening of conventional defense would be a proportionate price to pay, if this will reduce the possibility of nuclear war." This is an essential piece of realism. While many military experts differ as to whether non-nuclear defense of Western Europe really is possible, there are many cogent and informed arguments for its feasibility. The hurdles really are political rather than economic or military, and the lack of current political will, in America and in Europe, need not be taken as a given for all eternity.[23] Furthermore, there are also other ways to help defend Western Europe than by nuclear *or* non-nuclear forces. A general lowering of international political tensions would help, as would a structure of rewards implicit in the extension of East-West economic interdependence. Development of non-violent means of defense (see III.A.5 of the letter) may be a possibility. And if the United States were to abandon nuclear deterrence of non-nuclear threats, that act would contribute greatly to a worldwide delegitimization of nuclear weapons. It would help persuade potential nuclear powers that nuclear weapons "buy" more insecurity that security.

For myself, I repeat that I see no *good* solution overall. Every possibility contains practical and moral dangers. No one can be optimistic about the chances of surviving decades or generations of continuing reliance on nuclear deterrence in any form. People are prone to error, and machinery to accidents. An indefinite future of nuclear weapons seems intolerable. The bishops' insistence on a new way of thinking for the long run is absolutely necessary. Unilateral disarmament, accepting all its risks, does occasionally seem attractive, and a variant of that—some form of *nuclear* pacifism—more so. Yet on balance I cannot judge unilateral extremes to be desirable, and full mutual nuclear disarmament really does seem improbable. Pope John Paul II's statement that "deterrence may still be judged morally acceptable" still somehow rings true. That statement is in no way authoritatively binding. It is full of ambiguities, and even contradictions. But at the moment I can see no path other than one of continued wrestling with those ambiguities and contradictions.

NOTES

1. *The Challenge of Peace: God's Promise and Our Response*, #163, citing W. H. Kincade and J. D. Porro, *Negotiating Security: An Arms Control Reader* (Washington, 1979).
2. *Statement of Defense Secretary Robert S. McNamara on the Fiscal Year 1969–73 Defense Program and the 1969 Defense Budget* (Washington, 1968), p. 47. Secretary McNamara's words on this occasion were not peculiar to him, but rather typical of much of American deterrent rhetoric. In practice McNamara almost certainly thought this level of damage to be greater than necessary, or prudent.
3. McGeorge Bundy, "To Cap the Volcano," *Foreign Affairs* 48, no. 1 (Spring 1969): 10.
4. Note the fears in the pastoral letter (# 190) about "prompt hard-target kill" weapons and the footnote reference to MX and Pershing II missiles (n. 84).
5. Desmond Ball, "U.S. Strategic Forces: How Would They Be Used?" *International Security* 7, no. 3 (Winter 1982/83): 31–60.
6. Quoted in David Alan Rosenberg, "The Origins of Overkill: Nuclear Weapons and American Strategy, 1945–1960," *International Security* 7, no. 4 (Spring 1983): 15.
7. Quoted in ibid.
8. *Statement of Defense Secretary Robert S. McNamara*, p. 48.
9. *Department of Defense Authorization for Appropriations for Fiscal Year 1982: Hearings Before the Committee on Armed Services of the United States Senate*, 97th Congress, 1st Session (Washington, 1981), p. 80.
10. Rosenberg, "Origins of Overkill," p. 50, and Ball, "U.S. Strategic Forces," p. 36.
11. Sir Solly Zuckerman, *Nuclear Illusion and Reality* (New York, 1982).
12. An irony here is that we now know that the Soviet military forces only acquired operational atomic bombs in 1952. This is an example of frequent exaggeration of threat, and choosing to err on the side of too much deterrence rather than too little.
13. "No civilian targets" means no civilian targets *ever*, even in retaliation for attacks on American civilians. This last aspect will not be popular with many strategists, who understandably would like to retain the threat of purely retaliatory strikes against civilians as a means to insure Soviet good behavior during a "limited" nuclear war.
14. This argument is expressed by Albert Wohlstetter, "Bishops, Statesmen, and Other Strategists on the Bombing of Innocents," *Commentary*, June 1983, pp. 15–35.
15. See also Bruce Russett, *The Prisoners of Insecurity* (San Francisco, 1983), chap. 3 and materials cited there; Ruth Adams and Susan Cullen, *The Final Epidemic: Physicians and Scientists on Nuclear War* (Chicago, 1981); and Eric Chivian et al., *Last Aid: The Medical Dimensions of Nuclear War* (San Francisco, 1982).
16. Counterforce strategies have, in the past, repeatedly had the effect of enlarging the list of targets (Rosenberg, "Origins of Overkill," p. 50). That is therefore the trap inherent in contemporary counterforce policies.

17. For examples of this thinking see the interviews reported in Robert Scheer, *With Enough Shovels: Reagan, Bush, and Nuclear War* (New York, 1982).

18. "Nuclear Decapitation," *Foreign Policy* 45 (Winter 1981–82): 22–23; also see Desmond Ball, *Can Nuclear War Be Controlled?*, Adelphi Paper 161 (1981).

19. Thomas Schelling, *Arms and Influence* (New Haven, 1966), p. 99.

20. Paul Bracken, *The Command and Control of Nuclear Forces* (New Haven, 1983).

21. Most troublesome in this respect was the quotation from Cardinal Krol which said that "not only the *use* of strategic nuclear weapons, but also the *declared intent* to use them involved in our deterrence policy, are both wrong" (italics in original). This statement could be taken to refer to any use of nuclear weapons, or only the use of or declared intent to use weapons indiscriminately, i.e., against cities. Since counterpopulation warfare was still an element of American declaratory policy (and very possibly of operational policy) at the time of Cardinal Krol's statement, he is not necessarily condemning *any* use or threat. Similar ambiguity arose regarding advice, in the pastoral section at the end of the second draft, to men and women in defense industries: "You also have specific questions to face because your industry produces many of the weapons of massive and indiscriminate destruction which have concerned us in this letter. We have judged immoral even the threat to use such weapons. At the same time, we have held that the possession of nuclear weapons may be tolerated as deterrents while meaningful efforts are underway to achieve multilateral disarmament." I believe that, in context, the operative qualifier is "massive and indiscriminate destruction," but it is understandable how some readers could have taken this passage as a blanket condemnation.

22. It is nevertheless true that some critics, notably Wohlstetter and the *Times* editorial, ostensibly were responding to the third draft or final version. A charitable interpretation of their criticism is that they simply had not read the late versions carefully. McGeorge Bundy, "The Bishops and the Bomb," *New York Review of Books*, 16 June 1983, pp. 3–8, exhibits a much better understanding of the letter.

23. The pastoral letter (n. 67) cites some participants in this debate. Others include John Mearsheimer, "Why the Soviets Can't Win Quickly in Central Europe," *International Security* 7, no. 1 (Summer 1982): 3–39; Bernard W. Rogers, "The Atlantic Alliance: Prescriptions for a Difficult Decade," *Foreign Affairs* 60, no. 5 (Summer 1982), and the Report of the European Security Study, *Strengthening Conventional Deterrence: Proposals for the 1980s* (New York, 1983). General Rogers has reservations about whether a full no first-use policy is feasible, but has been campaigning vigorously for at least a no early first-use posture.

RICHARD A. McCORMICK

Nuclear Deterrence and the Problem of Intention: A Review of the Positions

The final form of the bishops' pastoral letter is the precipitate of a complex and very arduous process involving the input and reactions of many publics. Amidst much tugging and pulling for tone and emphasis, amidst the jostling and pressuring of special interest groups, the bishops and their drafting committee had to cling to a single constant: the Gospel's perspectives as they have been appropriated by the Christian community over the centuries in a variety of cultural and national-political circumstances. This appropriation has never been without tensions, especially between resisting the violent to protect the innocent and constraining one's own violence in the process. As various generations attempted to reconcile these apparently—and perhaps really—irreconcilable thrusts, rules of constraint were developed and are often referred to as the just-war theory. Playing a prominent role in these rules was the notion of intention, for example, in the rule about non-combatant immunity. The role of intention seems central in any discussion, not only of war but of deterrence of war. For deterrence *seems* to contain an implied threat, or a conditioned intention to use: if you use, we will. The problem stems from the rather traditional notion that it is wrong to threaten seriously or intend to do what it is morally wrong to do. Thus the person who says he will commit adultery if the weather is not good enough for tennis is an adulterer in moral terms. Unlike earlier drafts, the final version of the pastoral did not enter this question as it accepted or tolerated a nuclear deterrent. Indeed, it is safe to say that other ethical statements and conclusions of the pastoral left some "untidy loose ends." Whatever the case, the problem of intention will continue to be with us as the pastoral letter provides the basis for continuing public discussion of these matters. Because this is the case and because not a little of the literature prior to the final version of the pastoral touched on this question, it may be helpful to detail some of that literature as an aid to continuing discussion.

I should like to concentrate on some longer studies that have been composed as aids in the teaching-learning process of the church. But before doing so, I should advert to the excellent overview of the issue provided by Michael Mahon, S.J.[1] It is an absolutely first-rate summary of the moral issues: (1) the pure form of deterrence (mutually assured destruction and the problem of intentionality); (2) proposals for limited nuclear war; (3) discussion of first-strike scenarios. On this last point, for example, Mahon clearly and accurately reviews the exchange between Theodore Draper and the authors (McGeorge Bundy, George Kennan, Robert McNamara, Gerard Smith) of a highly publicized *Foreign Affairs* article urging a no-first-use policy.[2] Throughout Mahon expertly reviews the analyses of well-known authors in these discussions (e.g., Michael Walzer, Francis Winters, Francis Meehan, Michael Novak, Paul Ramsey, John Cardinal Krol, Bishop Roger Mahony, William O'Brien, and others).

Mahon's purpose is to lay out the issues, not to adjudicate them; so he exercises admirable restraint. But his personal reflection at the conclusion of the review is well worth the many months he must have labored to construct this overview. Mahon suggests that the nuclear discussion has centered on three principles: proportionality in the use of violence, the immunity from attack that non-combatants should enjoy, and that war should be a last resort. He further suggests that "the principle of right authority is due for a comeback." He means, of course, that the unimpeachable authority for nuclear policy should reside with the prospective victims. It is too serious a matter to be left to governments. The mass movements in Europe and the United States clearly indicate that the victims want to delegitimate the use of nuclear weapons by nation-states. Mahon's concern is shared by others, as will become clear below. If one has time for but a single article, Mahon's is the one to read.

A second writing by theologian Germain Grisez evaluates the present nuclear deterrent in an argument that unfolds like a syllogism.[3] It is always morally wrong to intend, even reluctantly and conditionally,

to kill the innocent. But present deterrent policy involves this murderous intent. Therefore, the present deterrent policy is morally wrong.
The minor is established by reference to the *United States Military Statement*, which refers to a focus of nuclear weapons on "Soviet values."
But even if the targeting was not aimed at cities, Grisez believes the
deaths of millions of innocents is essential to the deterrent and therefore
direct (intended). To the objection that it is possible to deter with mere
possession—and with no intent to use—he responds that this "might
have been helpful had it been offered before the present deterrent
policy was adopted."

It had been argued by John Cardinal Krol (September 1979) before
the U.S. Senate Committee on Foreign Relations that the deterrent
could be tolerated provided the deterrent is used to make progress on
arms limitation, reduction, and eventual abolition. Grisez rejects this
because it perverts the traditional notion of toleration into a justification
for one's own immoral activity. Nor can one argue that choosing to
kill innocents is the lesser evil; for "this position requires that one be
able to weigh (supposedly 'nonmoral') evils" against one another. This
we are unable to do rationally. Rather, this "proportionalist" position
calls for a choice before judgment. What we choose to do becomes
right.

In his continuing battle with "proportionalists," Grisez does not
seem to realize that his arguments bite back. For instance, if the proportionalist must choose before judgment, how is this any different
from the non-proportionalist who argues legitimate national self-defense against an aggressor? Does such a person not have to weigh
political freedom against the loss of human life in defending it and
decide that it is reasonable to suffer this evil for that good? If values
cannot be measured against one another, for the proportionalist, how
can they be compared by the person applying the fourth condition of
the double effect (proportionate reason)? In this study Grisez answers
as follows: "They may not do to any enemy's population (even as a
side effect) what they would not have the other nation's leaders do to
them and their people. In such cases, proportionality reduces to the
Golden Rule."

But that is not an adequate answer. The question—which requires
a rational answer if Grisez's critiques against proportionalists as arbitrary deciders are to carry any weight—is: *Why* would they not want
it done to themselves? Why would a war become "unduly burden-

some"?[4] Is it not because the overall evils do not stand in a proportionate relationship to the values to be protected or achieved? Does that not demand the very weighing and balancing Grisez says is rationally impossible? Was it proportionate or disproportionate for the Russians to lose twenty million lives defending the fatherland? Every episcopal and theological document that I have consulted in this summary involves the type of weighing and balancing Grisez excludes in principle. Determining what is proportionate is a matter of political prudence and sometimes imprecise but this does not mean that it is irrational or arbitrary.[5]

John Langan, S.J., reviews what he calls the "absolutist" position. Its basic claim, Langan asserts, is "that every use of nuclear weapons is morally wrong."[6] Langan admits that this position has power and clarity; but does it work? Its ruling out any use is precisely the weakness of the absolutist position. One can conceive of cases where nuclear weapons meet the controlling criteria of the just-war theory. While these may seem antiseptic and abstract (a kind of "two-battleships-at-sea scenario"), Langan regards them as "crucial for understanding the limits of the absolutist argument." If *some* use of nuclear weapons is in principle justifiable, "the possession and production of nuclear weapons must be allowable in principle," and the absolutist case collapses. Unattractive as this may seem, Langan sees it as freeing us to understand "the balancing of values which is required in shaping strategic policy."

Langan prefers a contextualist approach to deterrence, one in which the serious danger of a catastrophic exchange plays a central role, but not one that justifies an exceptionless moral rule. Dangers can be greater or less, and where policy is concerned one must get involved in the weighing and balancing of risks: for instance, the likelihood of enslavement of free political communities without a deterrent against the likelihood of nuclear catastrophe with one. We are faced with the danger of doing terrible things and the danger of suffering terrible things. Langan lists three things that no policy may do or threaten to do, and whose risk must be minimized: the destruction of humanity, the destruction of an entire society, direct attacks on non-combatants. If a policy involves doing or committing us to do these things, it is immoral. But it need not so involve us, because there is the possibility in principle of a moral use of nuclear weapons. Langan concludes by insisting that the American bishops should not ban the bomb "but should adopt a stance which affirms the limitations of violence that are central to the just-war tradition and which at the same time points to the dangers of using nuclear weapons and of allowing the arms race to continue."

Langan's study is carefully crafted and sensitive to the distinction between moral and political judgments. Grisez would doubtless regard him as a proportionalist, since Langan sees the need to weigh values and disvalues of very different kinds, as I believe anyone applying just-war criteria must.

I would raise a single point with Langan's essay. He is clarifying his position against something like a straw man. That is, there is probably no one who holds the absolutist position that *theoretically* any use of a nuclear weapon is clearly morally wrong. That would be a difficult, indeed impossible, position to defend once one had accepted the moral legitimacy of national self-defense. What many would hold is a universal moral prohibition (Langan's "exceptionless rule") against use of nuclear weapons because of the almost unavoidable danger of escalation. The single question to be put to Langan, then, is this: Does the *abstract* possibility of a morally justified use of a nuclear weapon really justify the *concrete* retention of an arsenal that has no relationship to the abstract scenario? In other words, what is morally allowable in fact must be related to what is likely to occur in fact. As the bishops' pastoral states, "The issue at stake is the *real* as opposed to the *theoretical* possibility of a 'limited nuclear exchange' " (# 157).

What Langan's argument does, then, is destroy a so-called pure absolutist position that asserts that any conceivable use of a nuclear weapon is morally wrong. It does not have the same effect on a universal prohibition based on real escalatory dangers. And if a universal moral prohibition of use can still be powerfully argued from escalatory risk, then what is to be said of production and possession of nuclear weapons?

Some of the points just mentioned are made in a challenging study by David Hollenbach, S.J.[7] Hollenbach concludes that any use of strategic counterforce weapons cannot be morally justified. Such strategy violates the *in bello* criteria of discrimination and proportionality and the *ad bellum* criterion of reasonable hope of success (because of probability of escalation to mass slaughter). He then turns to tactical nuclear weapons and draws the very same conclusion.

Next he turns to hypothetical cases such as those raised by Langan and states that "such hypotheses have little or nothing to do with the real international situation." Hollenbach's conclusion, that "the use of nuclear weapons can never be morally justified, " I agree with, even though I could imagine with Langan antiseptic cases where the use would be controlled.

But what about possession and the threat to use nuclear weapons as a deterrent? Hollenbach refers to the pastoral letter of the American bishops (1976) in which they condemned attacks on civilian populations and threats to do so. John Cardinal Krol repeated this in 1979 but distinguished between threatening and mere possession, justifying toleration of the latter as the lesser of two evils, providing that meaningful negotiations were taking place toward reduction and elimination of nuclear weapons. The Krol testimony, Hollenbach notes, sees in the *threat* to use such weapons the *intention* to do so; but it also assumes that possession is compatible with an intention not to use them.

Hollenbach wrestles with this testimony on two grounds. First, we must distinguish the intention to use nuclear weapons and the intention to deter their use. To pursue policies that make war less likely, even though they involve threat, "is to *intend* the avoidance of war." Making war less likely is what is to be judged where specific policies are concerned, not deterrence in the abstract. Second, with regard to toleration, Hollenbach feels that Krol's notion is essentially correct but that it could be formulated more helpfully. He means that the conditions of toleration should be: (1) any policy must make war less likely; (2) any policy must increase the possibility of arms reduction, not decrease it. These twin conditions acknowledge that the moral judgment about deterrence is one about *the direction in which we are moving*.

Hollenbach's study has the great virtue of locating the discussion within the strong overall presumption against violence central to the Christian tradition. The key to his conclusion (carefully conditioned toleration of possession) is the distinction between intent to use nuclear weapons (never permitted) and intent to avoid war. Will it stand up? Specifically, a wary critic might point out that there is a means-end relationship between the two, that the intent to avoid war is indeed the *ultimate* intent but that it is served and achieved by the intent to use necessarily involved in any serious threat. In other words, the instrumental intention is not swallowed up in or obliterated by the good of the consummatory intention. Is it not there and still problematic?

Hollenbach's study thrusts intention back to center stage. At this point of the discussion enters John R. Connery, S.J.[9] Connery asks whether the threat of use as a deterrent is morally legitimate. The deterrent comes from mere possession and "would not call for any express intention on the part of the country possessing it." Connery narrows the question by excluding any indiscriminate strikes (nuclear or other) and any first strike of an aggressive kind. The sole remaining question is that of a controlled, defensive response. He argues that nuclear response with tactical nuclear weapons can be controlled and discriminate. To make it so is our moral challenge.

For the assessment of the morality of practical policy, Connery has eliminated the problem of intention. How? In two ways. First, since no express intention is required by mere possession, that possession does not create an insuperable problem. Indeed, Connery states that it is hard to see how strategic weapons "could legitimately serve any other but deterrent purposes"—which presumably he would countenance. Second, where tactical weapons are concerned, there is no intention problem because their use is justifiable when discriminate. All we need do, in our possession of nuclear weapons, is have the intention to use them discriminately.

Connery's article did not go without response. In a letter to the editor, Dan DiLuzio referred to it as a "remarkable rationalization." The use of any weapon could be judged sufficiently controllable, but only in "some idealized construct of the world."[10] Similarly, Walter Sullivan protested that the article did "not seem to be touched by the nuclear reality" that arsenals are located near population centers, that limited exchange carries enormous risk of escalation.[11] Furthermore, he rejects the distinction between merely having the bomb and intending to use it. The bomb exists for one reason: to be used if necessary.

From what has been said above, it is clear that I would agree with Hollenbach against Connery that no use of nuclear weapons can be justified in the present circumstances because of the unjustifiable risk of escalation. Second, can mere possession be divorced from some intent to use, as Connery asserts along with Winters (below)? That is a key question in the moral analysis. Langan, Sullivan, and others believe that such divorce is not possible. Langan states that "a firm and settled intention not to use nuclear weapons in all foreseeable circumstances makes the possession of such weapons literally useless as well as irrational and needlessly provocative."[12] In other words, he argues that *some* intention is there. The problem of intention just will not go away.

Now enter Michael Novak and Joseph O'Hare, S.J.[13] Novak insists that the question is not Vatican II's "an entirely new attitude" toward war, but whether Catholic teaching is "moral, realistic, and prudent." After that little rhetorical salvo—involving false alternatives—he states the two purposes of deterrence: to deter military use of nuclear weapons, and secondarily to deter nuclear blackmail. To achieve these objectives, mere possession of nuclear weapons is not enough. "It must be intentional." Novak notes that intentionality when applied to political systems is only analogous to intention in individual subjects. It is like ("but not exactly like") the intentionality embedded in acts themselves: for example, in sexual intercourse as "objectively ordered to procreation" regardless of subjective intentions of individual agents.

Thus the objective intentionality of a nuclear deterrent is "readiness for use." It is this readiness that threatens and deters. The system is *designed* to convey a sense of readiness for use. But, he asks, is it moral to maintain a system whose very existence threatens use if it is immoral ever to use it? His answer: that depends on the purpose of the system. If it is to deter use of nuclear weapons, the threat aims at a high moral purpose (a good) and "does so in a morally sound way." Thus he justifies the nuclear deterrent but disagrees with Cardinal Krol on the condition. Krol had stipulated that possession is tolerable only if efforts are being made toward nuclear disarmament. Thus Krol's criterion would seem to apply only if other nuclear powers were willing to engage seriously in disarmament negotiations.

What move has Novak made? He has, if I understand him, attempted to finesse the classic problem of intention by shifting the "intention" from the agent to the system itself. But there are problems in doing that. Let me put it as follows. If one constructs a system that has inbuilt intentionality ("readiness to use"), does not the intention of the maintainer have to conform to this inbuilt intentionality? What sense does it make to construct a whole system whose very sense is "readiness to use" if the constructor is absolutely unready to use it? And if the constructor is ready to use it, is that not exactly what Novak would condemn?

Another way into my problem with Novak's analysis is his discussion of "the purpose of the system." May we, he asks, maintain such a system? "That," he says, "depends on the purpose of the system." If it is deterrence, then we may; if it is other than deterrence, no. But who decides this purpose other than the agent? And if it is clearly the agents (political authorities) who intend to deter, what else must they intend to achieve this? Must the agent not intend conditionally to use the system if the deterrence is to be credible? Here we are back to the question I put to Hollenbach. The intention to deter is obviously noble, but can it obliterate the instrumental intention to use? If not, we are back to the problem of the agent's intention, which Novak rather cavalierly dismissed at the outset as "rather traditional stuff."

Francis X. Meehan is very close to Novak's understanding of intention.[14] He believes that distinguishing mere possession from intention to use confuses individual with social morality. In individuals possession may be distinguished from threat or intention to use. Not so in social morality. At this level there are mechanisms beyond individual control (e.g., chains of command, planned operating procedures, computers), all of which carry an "inbuilt objective intention." To view the matter otherwise is Platonic. Meehan further suggests that the church may well be at an exciting "kairotic" moment. That is, we are literally pulled by historical circumstances to rediscover the early Christian witness and transform ourselves from within.

What does this dynamic mean with regard to arms possession? Meehan distinguishes the church's address to its own members from its address to the wider community (policymakers, the world at large). He understands the appeals of the "peace bishops" for unilateral disarmament to be addressed within the church (ad intra) and to be altogether appropriate. When, however, the church addresses a larger public (ad extra), she cannot realistically call for unilateral disarmament. But by addressing a clear moral message to her own adherents, the church can create a kind of "third force" that will bring pressure on governments of both superpowers. The only and obvious problem with Meehan's scenario is that there is virtually no effective public opinion in the Soviet Union.

Joseph O'Hare, editor of *America* magazine, has Novak in his sights in his companion article. He protests Novak's dismissal of Vatican II's call for "an entirely new attitude" by noting that war waged with nuclear weapons "would almost certainly be total." O'Hare believes that the preoccupation of Catholic debate with the purity of moral intention distracts us "from the actual moral choices available to us."

He rejects unilateral disarmament as morally irresponsible, defends the present deterrent as "the least dangerous of the choices available to us," but insists on unilateral initiatives toward arms reduction by the United States.

The key to O'Hare's analysis is the phrase "least dangerous." On the one hand, there are the dangers associated with unilateral disarmament—dangers that something would happen to us and the Western world. On the other hand, the danger involved in keeping a deterrent is that we would do something to others with it. The first seems to be a risk of enormous nonmoral evil; the second is the risk of doing moral evil. I can fairly hear Grisez shouting "consequentialist" at O'Hare's essay.

Francis Winters, S.J., also engages Novak's dispute with the bishops.[15] He believes that Novak is especially rankled by the "power of the bishops to articulate binding moral imperatives." Winters is startled at the first version of the proposed pastoral because it allows some retaliatory use of nuclear weapons even though it can be reasonably expected that it will escape human control, as "the professional consensus believes." This more permissive attitude, which one finds also in Connery's study, fails to deal with the condition that war be waged by competent authority. In a nuclear war competent authority will be *hors de combat* very quickly and the control will slip to the uncoordinated command of multiple subordinates—in a word, the control will be gone.

Winters argues that between an immoral military strategy and subjugation to godless communism, there still remains a third option: retention of the nuclear arsenal without any intent to use it. The arsenal *in itself* is "the necessary and sufficient condition of strategic deterrence." Novak had dismissed this by postulating that weapons do not deter apart from the public consensus to use them, because they have an inbuilt intentionality ("ready for use"). Winters believes this is a postulate without proof. Equivalently, then, Winters is reiterating the Krol distinction between threat/intention/use and mere possession. The latter need not involve the former.

* * *

This is the way the recent discussion has gone. It is a rich and lively literature. It represents a believing community trying agonizingly to discover God's will in a very complex and dangerous world. A few remarks might not be out of place here.

First, as noted, it would be unrealistic to see the American episcopal document as the final word on the subject. The bishops, like anyone else, discover the Christian truth on these questions through an arduous groping process. If anything is clear from the literature I have reviewed, it is that there is little theological unanimity to aid and inform this process. For this reason, I would qualify the assertion of Winters that the teaching "will be binding in conscience on American Catholics." No, bishops ought not shrink into harmless statements about "moral ambiguity" when matters are clear and certain. But not all matters are.

Second, given the different views within the Catholic community and the strong feelings that accompany those views, the bishops are in something of a no-win situation. Some, perhaps many, Catholics are surely disappointed. We will almost certainly hear further accusations either of "accommodationist" or of "political naiveté." But given the state of the discussion, that should not surprise us or lead to genuine divisions, even schism within the community, as some have suggested. Rather, it should make us aware of the fact that bishops, as a group, deliberate and speak from a certain "social location" within both the broader community and the church and are probably unavoidably sensitive to jostling and pressures from all sides, not excluding Rome, other national hierarchies, the government, etc.—sides where they would wish to retain credibility and effectiveness. That is one reason for viewing their final document as a transitional contribution to a still developing public opinion in the church.[16] It is also a reason for individual bishops—and all of us—to continue to explore and speak out on this most serious of all contemporary moral problems. The American bishops should not be viewed as closing the debate, as the always insightful George Higgins notes.[17]

Third, there is a growing conviction (popular, strategic, moral-theological) that any use of nuclear weapons is morally irresponsible. The issue most hotly debated is that of possession for deterrence and the conditioned intention apparently involved in it.[18] The possession question, as a moral question, raises and rests on three issues. (1) Does mere possession with no intention to use factually deter, as Winters and Connery would argue against Novak, Langan, and others? (2) Is it possible to possess weapons which do deter without intending (conditionally) to use them, as Winters, Krol, and others would maintain against Langan, Meehan, William O'Brien, Matthiesen,[19] and others? (3) Is it possible to threaten (something that seems essential to deterrence) the use of nuclear weapons without the intention to use them? In other words, is the notion of threat different from conditioned intention? It will be recalled that Dubarle proposed years ago that a threat does not necessarily involve such an intent.[20]

Fourth, it has become increasingly clear that the one instrumentality capable of influencing the bureaucratic paralysis that leads to superpower deadlock on nuclear weapons is public opinion.[21] There were 400,000 demonstrators in Amsterdam, 200,000 in Bonn, 200,000 in Rome, 150,000 in London, 200,000 in Brussels, 200,000 in Paris, 200,000 in Athens, 300,000 in Bucharest, and many more in the United States. These protests do have an effect. I believe that we need our prophets, politically naive and theologically imprecise as they may at times seem. They provoke public opinion out of its sense of powerlessness, a sense undoubtedly nourished by the "principalities and powers" because it ends in apathy. They provoke us to visualize in faith a different future and to challenge the endless wrangling of strategic experts mired in the mathematics of destruction.[22] George F. Kennan, former ambassador to the Soviet Union, proposed in 1981 that the president suggest to the Soviet government an immediate across-the-board fifty percent reduction of the superpowers' nuclear arsenals. We need that type of bold and sweeping gesture, just as we need the prodding of the Hunthausens, the Gumbletons, the Matthiesens, the Sullivans of the episcopate.[23]

Whatever the case, this roundup has summarized and critiqued the work of others, especially as they went about informing the bishops. It is only fair to expose to the favor of criticism my own suggestions to the bishops. My response had suggested the following episcopal wording on two matters touching nuclear weapons.[24]

> 1. Retaliatory defensive use. Some of our military and political consultants believe that the use of tactical nuclear weapons can be isolated and limited, and therefore that such use cannot be morally excluded. Much as this might be true in an abstract scenario, the lessons of history, both past and more recent, lead us to believe that any use of nuclear weapons is inseparable from the *danger* of escalation and totalized warfare. We can identify no human or political purpose that will purge this risk of irresponsibility.
>
> 2. Possession for deterrence. For us the very possession of nuclear weapons has been the most difficult of all problems. We are aware that many people of good will believe that possession of nuclear weapons has served as a deterrent for many years. Furthermore, they believe that unilateral disarmament would be destabilizing and would heighten the possibility of the use of weapons of mass de-

struction by an irresponsible and adverturesome political adversary. Others believe that since there can be no morally legitimate use of nuclear weapons, and no morally justifiable threat to use them—a belief we share—then even possession of nuclear weapons is morally unjustified. We believe that both sides of this discussion make valid points. That is the very meaning of a "sinful situation." It is a situation we should not be in in the first place. There is no choice without some regrettable and destructive aspect. We cannot justify any use of or any serious threat to use nuclear weapons. On the other hand, we cannot entertain the greater possibility of such use that would seem to be associated with the imbalance created by unilateral disarmament. This is a paradoxical situation. The very evil that must be avoided at all costs can only be avoided *for the present* by maintaining its own possibility. There are risks in retention of nuclear weapons. There are risks in their unilateral abandonment under present conditions. And the risk is the same—that nuclear weapons might ever be used. Perception and judgment of this risk differ amongst people of good will, people with hearts and minds firmly set on the maintenance of peace. In such a situation of difference of factual perception, moral clarity is agonizingly difficult to achieve.

We have been able to arrive at only the following clarities. (1) The possession of nuclear weapons is at the very best morally ambiguous, and therefore at best only tolerable. It may not even be that. (2) Such possession is tolerable only for the present and under certain conditions. (3) These conditions are: a firm resolve never to use nuclear weapons and a firm resolve to work immediately to assure their abolition, in law and in fact. (4) While unilateral disarmament may not be a clear moral mandate, unilateral steps toward multilateral disarmament certainly are.

We realize that some, perhaps many people will view this matter somewhat differently. We are aware that even some American bishops have taken a different individual stand. We encourage such forthrightness and courage. In a matter so morally problematic and ambiguous, this is understandable. There is room, even need, for a variety of approaches lest apathy freeze the status quo. Warfare of any kind represents the collapse of rational political discourse and in this sense it is always irrational. It is at the very fringe of the justifiable. Nuclear war is beyond that fringe. That being the case, it is understandable that there can be many people who believe that even possession of nuclear weapons is morally intolerable. We share that conviction, but as a goal to be achieved without increasing the threat that such weapons will be used as we move toward the goal. If our government does not take unilateral steps toward multilateral nuclear disarmament, the only morally acceptable option may soon become unilateral disarmament.[25]

It is to be noted that these suggestions state about possession of nuclear weapons that it is "at best only tolerable. It may not even be that."

Serious scholars disagree on the three questions raised concerning possession, threat, and intention. The proposed wording is a *rebus sic stantibus* matter meant to reflect this unclarity and leave the question open.

NOTES

Substantial portions of this chapter appeared in *Theological Studies* 44 (March 1983):100–113.

1. Michael Mahon, S.J., "Nuclear Morality: A Primer for the Perplexed," *National Jesuit News*, November 1982, special supplement.

2. "Nuclear Weapons and the Atlantic Alliance," *Foreign Affairs* 60 (1982):753–68.

3. G. Grisez, "Moral Implications of a Nuclear Deterrent," *Center Journal* 2: (1982-3):9–24.

4. That little phrase hides a weighing and balancing that we all make but that Grisez cannot admit *in principle* because, he claims, it involves incommensurables. "Unduly burdensome"? With regard to what? Concretely, if a war can become *"unduly* burdensome," it can become so only because the cost (in life, economic sacrifice, etc.) is not judged proportionate to the good being protected (e.g., political self-determination). But how does one measure such incommensurables? Grisez says that we cannot. Yet he does so. Otherwise there is no distinction between what is *unduly* burdensome and what is *appropriately* burdensome. Burdens are acceptable or not depending on what is gained or lost if the burden is not borne. David Hollenbach states this well when he notes: "According to this view [traditional double effect] one is still bound . . . to weigh the evil consequences which indirectly accompany the attack against the good effects which flow from it" ("Nuclear Weapons and Nuclear War: The Shape of the Catholic Debate," *Theological Studies* 43 [1982]: 577–605; 594). Hollenbach correctly states that these are prudential judgments "not subject to logically certain demonstration." That is not to say that they are not rational.

5. In his new book, *The Nuclear Delusion* (New York: Pantheon, 1982), George Kennan states: "There is no issue at stake in our political relations with the Soviet Union—no hope, no fear, nothing to which we aspire, nothing we would like to avoid—which could conceivably be worth a nuclear war" (see *New York Times Book Review*, 7 November 1982, p. 38). Surely there is a weighing going on here.

6. John Langan, S.J., "The American Hierarchy and Nuclear Weapons," *Theological Studies* 43 (1982):447–67.

7. See n. 4 above.

8. Robert L. Spaeth distinguishes between "the intention to launch nuclear missiles" and "a policy decision to launch them if attacked by nuclear weapons." This latter, he says, "shows a supremely moral aspect of deterrence." That is, it has a "moral goal." I fail to see Spaeth's distinction. For "a policy decision to launch if . . ." contains a conditioned intention. Can a "moral goal" eliminate this? ("Disarmament and the Catholic Bishops," *This World* 2 [Summer 1982]:5–17)

9. John R. Connery, S.J., "The Morality of *Nuclear Warpower*," *America* 147 (1982):25–28.

10. *America* 147 (1982):101.

11. Ibid., p. 61.

12. Langan, "American Hierarchy and Nuclear Weapons," p. 452.

13. Michael Novak, "Nuclear Morality," *America* 147 (1982):5–8. Joseph A. O'Hare, S.J., "One Man's Primer on Nuclear Morality," *America* 147 (1982):9–12.

14. Francis X. Meehan, "The Moral Dimensions of Disarmament," *New Catholic World* 226 (1982):68–70.

15. Francis X. Winters, S.J., "Catholic Debate and Division on Deterrence," *America* 147 (1982):127–31.

16. It is interesting to note here the pastoral letter of Francis T. Hurley (Anchorage), Robert L. Whelan, S.J. (Fairbanks), and Michael H. Kenny (Juneau). It concerns Proposition 6 and the withdrawal of public funding for abortion in Alaska. The bishops invite their diocesans to reflect and pray about this matter and "come to a decision." They are careful not to dictate the decision ("On Christian Life and Christian Responsibility," *Inside Passage* 13 [8 October 1982]:4–5). John Reedy, C.S.C., has properly called attention to the distinction between the religious and moral values involved in contemporary issues and specific political choices (e.g., a nuclear freeze, the Hatch Amendment). On these latter the bishops have no particular competence. When this distinction is not observed, there is a "degradation of teaching authority" ("Bishops and Public Issues," *Catholic Telegraph*, 25 June 1982, p. 4). For an interesting article in support of a nuclear freeze, see James L. Hart, S.J., "The Case for a Freeze on Nuclear Arms," *America* 147 (1982):226–28.

17. George Higgins, "Nuclear Debate: A Caution," *Catholic Standard*, 4 November 1982, p. 9.

18. It is interesting to note that the English bishops cite lack of clarity about a government's intention as a reason for their perplexity ("Désarmement et paix," *Documentation catholique* 64 [1982]:818).

19. Leroy Matthiesen states: "The possession of nuclear weapons is the same thing as a threat to use them" (*Time*, 8 November 1982, p. 18).

20. D. Dubarle, "La stratégie de la menace nucléaire devant la morale internationale," *Revue de l'action populaire*, 1964, pp. 645–60.

21. Two episcopal documents call attention to the importance of public opinion in this matter. See "Le désarmement," *Documentation catholique* 64 (1982):682, and "Le désarmement: Point de vue d'église de France," *ibid.*, pp. 787–88. When Robert S. McNamara was asked by Robert Scheer how the tremendous nuclear buildup occurred, he answered: "Because the potential victims have not been brought into the debate yet, and it's about time we brought them in" (see Kermit D. Johnson, "The Nuclear Reality: Beyond Niebuhr and the Just War," *Christian Century* 99 [1982]:1014–17). Johnson concludes his fine article by noting that if our politicians cannot exercise moral leadership on this matter, "then it is time for the leaders to be led." Similarly, Roger Ruston, O.P., in his study *Nuclear Deterrence: Right or Wrong* (published under the auspices of the Commission for International Justice and Peace of the Bishops' Conference of England and Wales) puts great emphasis on public opinion (see *Tablet* 236 [1982]:862 and 631).

22. For an excellent study of faith and visualization, see Walter Wink, "Faith and Nuclear Paralysis," *Christian Century* 99 (1982):234–37.

23. For other valuable suggestions, see Alan Geyer, "Disarmament Time at the U.N.: It's Never Enough to Say No," *Christianity and Crisis* 42 (1982):127–30. Geyer is one of our best informed and most influential Christian ethicists in the area of disarmament.

24. Personal communication to Bryan Hehir, 12 July 1982.

25. A Church of England report stated that Britain should renounce its independent nuclear deterrent. "The evils caused by this method of making war are greater than any conceivable evil which the war is intended to prevent." It also noted: "You may either decide for a nuclear component in deterrence and risk nuclear war, or decide against it and risk the political and human consequences and defeat by someone with fewer moral inhibitions." For a Christian the second risk is preferable, for "the issue is not whether we will die for our beliefs but whether we will kill for them." The committee included a Catholic moral theologian (Brendan Soane). Its report was expected to be hotly debated in the February 1983 general synod (*Catholic Review*, 22 October 1982, A2). Robert F. Rizzo argues that the momentum of just-war reasoning is carrying the American Catholic bishops toward pacifism, "which will reject the technological weapons of modern warfare, whether conventional or nuclear" ("Nuclear War: The Moral Dilemma," *Cross Currents* 32 [1982]:71–84).

VI

World Order

The Challenge of Peace

Part III, #s 200–273

The building of peace as a way to prevent war is the subject of Part III. This constructive project, in the bishops' view, places a high premium on commitment and expertise in three areas.

The first area is dismantlement. It is urgent that the existing array of nuclear weapons be dismantled. As an initial step, the two superpowers are urged to halt the testing, production, and deployment of new nuclear weapons. The quality of these negotiations, in terms of sincerity and effectiveness, can significantly prevent the spread of nuclear weapons to other nations. Agreement must occur about prohibiting the production of chemical-biological weapons, controlling the sale of arms, and reaching a balanced reduction of conventional weapons. The ultimate objective of dismantlement is disarmament.

The second area requires innovative skills. While nations have the right of self-defense, armed force is not the only available option. Innovative methods must be developed for peoples to defend against attack without using violence. In addition to advancing the traditional art of diplomacy, other methods must be explored: techniques of non-violent resistance, peaceful non-compliance to hinder an invading army, and strategies of "making the adversary a friend."

The third area involves reinforcement. Since the existing international structures are too fragile to protect the planet's common good, and individual nations cannot cope with global problems, the pastoral offers the blueprint of Pope John XXIII: the establishment of an effective public authority capable of operating on a world-wide basis. The United Nations is cited as one "edifice which . . . must not fail; it must be perfected and made equal to the needs. . . ." Its structures and those of other multilateral agencies need reinforcing, and the role of the United States in this regard is cited as crucial. Such structures are needed to broaden the global vision beyond the rivalry between East and West, which consumes enormous resources for self-defense, and to encompass the gap between North and South where millions are in "absolute poverty."

GEORGE F. KENNAN

America's Unstable Soviet Policy

The second Russian Revolution of 1917 (actually not a "revolution" but the Bolshevik-Communist seizure of power in the two greatest Russian cities) took place in the highly confused international atmosphere of the final year of World War I. It was followed by a three-year period of even greater confusion in Russian internal affairs, marked by such things as the Russian civil war, the Allied intervention, the Russo-Polish war of 1920, and a famine. It was not until 1921 that things sorted themselves out sufficiently to make it clear that the Communists were at least firmly installed throughout most of the former empire and to confront the American government with the necessity of clarifying its attitude toward the newly established Communist regime.

For the next twelve years—Republican years, all of them—the policy adopted in Washington was a simple one: no diplomatic recognition; no official relations at all. The principal reasons for this attitude were two. The first was the refusal of the Soviet regime to accept any obligation to meet the debts of previous Russian regimes or the claims arising from the Soviet nationalization of foreign properties in Russia. The second was the resentment engendered by the world revolutionary pretensions of the Soviet regime. After 1923, the promotion of world revolution gradually ceased, to be sure, to be the prime motivation of Soviet foreign policy. But the inflammatory rhetoric remained. So did the intensive efforts at instigation, support, and manipulation of Communist activities in other countries. The shameless hypocrisy with which the Communist Party leaders attempted to deny responsibility for these activities, pretending that the Communist International was something over which they, in their governmental positions, had no control, was

Reprinted, with permission, from *The Atlantic Monthly*, November 1982, pp. 71–80.

offensive to much American opinion, as was also the scarcely concealed contempt and hostility for all "capitalist" countries which rang through so much official Soviet rhetoric. In all of this were to be found the reasons for the decade-long denial of American diplomatic recognition to the Soviet regime.

Franklin Roosevelt, coming into office in 1933, soon changed the American policy. The change was explained by two facets of his thinking. He cared very little, in the first place, about the reasons that had animated his Republican predecessors in matters of policy toward the Soviet Union. The trouble over "debts and claims" disturbed him only insofar as he felt himself obliged to respond to congressional pressures along that line. Nor did the activities of the Communist International bother him much. Politician and pragmatist that he was, he was well aware of the political insignificance of Soviet-inspired radical activities in the United States ("Stamp out Trotskyism in Kansas" was a flaming headline in the *Daily Worker* one day in the early thirties). What seemed to him more important was the shadows of German national socialism and Japanese militarism rising on the horizon—both so offensive to influential segments of American opinion. It seemed to FDR that Americans had a bond in this respect with the Soviet leaders, who had their own reasons for fearing these emerging political forces. This bond, he thought, could be usefully developed by the establishment of diplomatic relations with the Soviet regime. So, at the end of 1933, after skillfully placating American opinion with the smoke screen of the largely meaningless exchanges of diplomatic notes known as the "Litvinov agreements," he proceeded to "recognize Russia": that is, to send an ambassador to Moscow, and to receive a Soviet one in Washington, thus establishing the formal diplomatic relationship that has endured to the present day.

During the initial years of this new relationship—the remaining years of the 1930s—the experiment of mutual diplomatic representation was not a particularly successful one. At the moment when relations were established, the Soviet leaders had been assailed by fears that the Japanese might be preparing to attack Russia's eastern provinces. This had accounted for some of their conciliatory disposition at that time. It soon became apparent, however, that the danger was less urgent than they had thought, and their enthusiasm for the new relationship declined. Little came of the rosy assurances embodied in the Litvinov agreements. Initially welcomed with an unusual show of cordiality, the new American Embassy in Moscow soon fell victim to the routine treatment of isolation, clandestine observation, and avoidance of all but the most perfunctory official contact to which foreign diplomatic representatives have traditionally been subjected in Moscow. The mission came to serve, in those years of 1930s, primarily as a place where a group of young American Foreign Service officers learned a few things about Russia and went through that unique schooling by means of which the Soviet government has contrived, over a period of half a century, to educate and to graduate from their period of service in Moscow one class after another of embittered diplomats, sending them out into the world to preach vigilance against the wiles and pretenses of Soviet policy.

The years immediately following American recognition were marked in the Soviet Union by the fearful and indescribable orgy of official terror and brutality known as "the purges." Their effect on the Soviet–American relationship was mixed. On those Americans who lived in Moscow at the time, the effect was one of utter and enduring horror coupled with a profound conviction that any regime capable of perpetrating such monstrous cruelties against its own people, and indeed against itself, was to be dealt with only at arm's length and with the utmost circumspection. That Franklin Roosevelt ever fully understood the nature and significance of these nightmarish events is doubtful. He appears never wholly to have departed, even in those terrible years, from his conviction that Stalin was probably really not such a bad fellow at heart, that what was needed to set him on the right track was a bit more relaxed treatment—a bit less suspicion and more cordiality than a snobbish upper-class American plutocracy (as FDR saw it) had been inclined to concede. Roosevelt seems never fully to have understood the limitations that rest upon the possibilities for intimacy or friendship with people who have a great deal of blood on their hands. This failure of understanding was to some extent shared by much of the remainder of the American liberal community. A greater shock was received by that community, actually, with the news of the conclusion of the German–Soviet Non-Aggression Pact, in 1939. Mistreatment of the Soviet population was one thing (much could be excused in the name of the Revolution), but that the Soviet Union, which for years had held itself out as the greatest opponent of German nazism and had encouraged others to go even further in that stance, should now have turned around and suddenly, after highly conspiratorial preparations, made a cynical deal with Hitler at the expense of the Poles and the Baltic peoples was a great blow not only to pro-Soviet liberal circles in the United States but to many Communists, there and elsewhere, as well.

Yet all this abruptly changed again when, in 1941, both the Soviet Union and the United States found themselves (involuntarily) at war with Nazi Germany. The "Russians" became, almost overnight, our great and good allies. The image of Stalin changed instantly from that of the "crafty giant" Churchill once correctly described to that of a benevolent hero of the resistance to Hitlerism. War psychology, to which the American public is no less prone than any other, at once led to the discovery of previously unknown virtues in a regime that was also now at war with America's principal military enemy. Considering that the Soviet Union was absorbing some 80 percent of the Nazi war effort while we and our Western allies were, up to 1944, unable even to mount a second front, the American official community (and particularly the military leadership) generally felt that the most important thing was to "get on" (that was the term then commonly used) with Moscow, politically and propagandistically as well as in point of military aid. In these circumstances, nothing was too good, in 1942 and 1943, for our valiant Soviet allies. Anyone who in those years attempted to remind others that Soviet ideas about the postwar future might be seriously in conflict with out own was sternly admonished that in wartime we Americans did not "take our eyes off the ball"—the ball being, in this instance, the earliest possible total defeat of Germany. Gone, now, were the resentments over Soviet aspirations for world revolution. Soviet demands, advanced by Stalin during the war, for the westward extension of the boundaries of the Soviet Union were accepted by Britain, and silently (though not happily) acquiesced to by the United States.

In the ensuing years of 1944 and 1945, other far-reaching concessions were made. The bitter implications of Soviet behavior at the time of the Warsaw uprising were largely ignored. There must be no attempt, while hostilities were in progress, to discuss realistically with our Soviet allies the sordid questions of the political arrangements that should prevail in Central and Eastern Europe when the war was over. Such discussions, it was insisted, might be destructive of the wartime intimacy; matters of this nature were to be taken care of, after the termination of hostilities, by general political collaboration among the

United States, Britain, the Soviet Union, and—at FDR's insistence—Chiang Kai-shek's China.

* * *

It is small wonder that in the face of such wishful and unrealistic attitudes there was, in the immediate post-hostilities period, a rude awakening and disillusionment. There is no need to recount the details. Soviet leaders, partially confused by the official pro-Soviet American rhetoric of the wartime years and misled by the ease with which they had obtained Western agreement to the extension of their borders and the ruthless consolidation of their political domination in the occupied areas, were somewhat dizzy with success. They were not sure how far they would be permitted to go. Their dreams ran to the acquisition of a dominant political position in Germany and the remainder of Western Europe. They had no thought of trying to achieve this by force of arms. Their thoughts were rather of political devices such as acquiring a share of the control over the Ruhr, taking advantage of the strong positions of the French and Italian Communist parties, exploiting Soviet military-control powers in Berlin and Vienna, and penetrating Western labor-union, intellectual, and student movements. They had, after all, been encouraged to expect an extensive withdrawal of American forces and of American involvement in European affairs when the war was over. This, they thought, would create a serious political vacuum; the rest might be accomplished, or so it was hoped, by the clever, ruthless exploitation of the political cards they now held in their hands.

Actually, those cards were not so strong as the Soviet leaders supposed. This was at once revealed by the Marshall Plan initiative, in 1947–1948, which wholly frustrated any dreams of the political takeover of Western Europe. The remaining Soviet efforts of the 1940s, outstandingly the crackdown on Czechoslovakia and the mounting of the Berlin blockade, were defensive in inspiration—attempts to play Moscow's last major political cards in anticipation of what they saw looming before them: a new division of power across the European continent.

These attempts reflected no Soviet desire for a full-fledged military showdown, or even for a division of the continent into opposing military alliances. It is entirely possible that had the Western European countries, while resisting the Berlin blockade, continued to concentrate steadily on Europe's economic and political recovery, Stalin, whose country had the most pressing need for at least several years of peaceful reconstruction, would have been prepared to make extensive compromises—compromises that would at least have obviated the necessity for such a military division of the continent. But the Western Europeans, conditioned by the experience of centuries to see any serious international tension as the forerunner of a war, immediately interpreted the existing evidence of Soviet political recalcitrance as a menace of invasion. And we Americans, always high-mindedly disinclined to make compromises with evil (except, of course, in our own domestic politics), were disinclined to go in for any political deals with what was rapidly coming to be seen as "the enemy." Thus the North Atlantic Treaty Organization came into existence, to be responded to, in its turn, by the Warsaw Pact. And thus the decision to take Western Germany into NATO, and to re-arm it, produced the inevitable countermeasures with respect to East Germany. These developments, together with the revelation, in 1949, of a Soviet nuclear capability, followed by the Korean War (the origins and purposes of which were seriously misinterpreted in the West), laid a firm and unshakable foundation for the militarization of the American attitude toward the Soviet problem that has been the dominant feature of American diplomacy ever since.

* * *

This might be a good place to pause and note the full import of the changes that by the end of the 1940s had come over the American-Soviet relationship. The factors that had been the determining ones in the early years of the relationship had been either removed or greatly weakened. The problem of what was once called "debts and claims" had been eclipsed by the traumatic experiences of World War II, and was rapidly falling victim to the tendency of international life that so often causes "insoluble" problems, if allowed to remain long enough unsolved, gradually to lose their significance. And as for "world revolution": the Comintern, once the symbol of all that Americans objected to in Soviet policy, had by this time been formally abolished. It had been Stalin's custom, in any case, to use the subservient foreign Communist parties as instruments for the support of Soviet foreign policy rather than as vehicles for the serious promotion of revolution. With the abolition of the Comintern, Moscow's relations with those foreign parties, previously channeled through the Comintern, had been turned over partly to the Soviet secret police, which used them for espionage and for other forms of its chartered skulduggery, and partly to a section of the apparatus of the Soviet Central Committee, to which was given the unpleasant task of holding the hands of the foreign Communist leaders and assuring their continued subservience while preventing them from either unduly influencing or embarrassing Soviet policy-makers. In these circumstances, no informed person, either in the Soviet Union or elsewhere, any longer took seriously Moscow's theoretical and rhetorical commitment to world revolution.

With these issues out of the way, the relationship was now destined to be shaped primarily by two factors: one old, one new.

The old factor was what might be called the substructure of tensions, misunderstandings, irritations, and minor conflicts flowing from the great disparity between the two political systems, not only in ideology but, even more important, in traditions, habits, customs, and methodology. This factor had never been absent at any time since the founding of the Soviet regime (indeed, to some extent it had been present in the czarist period as well). It continued to weigh upon the Soviet-American relationship in the postwar years, even in the post-Stalin period, almost as heavily as it had before the war. It must be regarded as a permanent burden on the relationship, probably never to be wholly overcome, certainly not to be importantly mitigated in any short space of time.

The new factor was the military and geopolitical situation arising from the circumstances of the war and its aftermath: a situation destined, as it turned out, to overshadow all other aspects of the relationship in intensity, in endurance, and in gravity—gravity for the two countries and for the world at large.

Prior to World War II, the respective military situations and interests of the two powers had not constituted a significant factor in their relations. The Soviet Union was then not a competitor or a threat to the United States in naval power; the same thing applied, the other way around, when it came to land power. By the end of the 1920s, the Soviet Union had acquired, to be sure, a formidable land army (in the Russian tradition)—an army that was already the greatest, numerically, in the world. But the two countries were so widely separated—in the

West by the Atlantic Ocean and the intervening powers of Europe, in the East by the Pacific Ocean plus China and Japan—that there was no consciousness on either side of a serious military rivalry.

With the conclusion of World War II, all that changed. The final stages of military operations had enabled the Soviet Union to overcome the communications-poor barrier of the territory between the Baltic and Black seas which had historically separated Central and Western Europe from the Russian armies. The traditional military power of Russia, now represented by the Soviet Union, had been projected into the heart of Europe, where there was nothing to oppose it at the time but a number of Western European peoples either shattered by the recent Hitlerian occupation or militarily exhausted or both. This Western Europe was unable to restore either its political self-confidence or its capacity for self-defense without American support. And the absence of any realistic agreement among the victors on a political future for the defeated Germany, or indeed for Central and Eastern Europe generally, left Soviet and American military forces confronting each other across a line through the middle of North-Central Europe—a line never originally meant to become the central demarcation of a divided Europe but destined, as we now know, to remain just that for at least several decades into the future.

This major geopolitical displacement marked a fundamental change in the Soviet-American relationship. It did not, as many seem to have supposed, render either necessary or inevitable a war between the two powers—then or at any other time. But it injected into the relationship a new factor: an immediate military proximity, made all the more delicate and dangerous insofar as it was superimposed upon the permanent substructure of friction referred to above. If, before the war, Washington had dealt with the Soviet Union primarily as a revolutionary political force, it was now obliged to deal with it as a traditional military great power, suddenly and unexpectedly poised on the very edge of America's own newly acquired sphere of political-military interest.

And this new geopolitical relationship was burdened by several further complications—all new, all serious.

The end of the war, in the first place, had left the United States with little in the way of military manpower (in view of its precipitous demobilization) but with a bloated military superstructure, and particularly with an expanded apparatus for military planning, for which use now had to be found. With Germany and Japan out of the way, there was need of a new prospective opponent with relation to whose military personality a new American military posture could be designed. The Soviet Union was the obvious, indeed the only plausible, candidate.

It is said that Woodrow Wilson was shocked to learn, in 1915, that the Army War College was studying plans for wars against other countries. The story, sometimes cited as an example of Mr. Wilson's naiveté, seems to be the somewhat distorted version of a real episode. But it is suggestive of a historically significant reality. When a military planner selects another country as the leading hypothetical opponent of his own country—the opponent against whom military preparations and operations are theoretically to be directed—the discipline of his profession obliges him to endow that opponent with extreme hostility and the most formidable of capabilities. In tens of thousands of documents, this image of the opponent is re-created, and depicted in all its implacable formidability, until it becomes hopelessly identified with the real country in question. In this way, the planner's hypothesis becomes, imperceptibly, the politician's and the journalist's reality. Even when there is *some* degree of substance behind the hypothesis, what emerges is invariably an overdrawn and distorted image.

And so it has been in the case of the Soviet Union, with the result that what began as a limited political conflict of interests and aspirations has evolved into a perceived total military hostility; and what was in actuality a Soviet armed-forces establishment with many imperfections and many limitations on its capabilities has come gradually to be perceived as an overpowering paragon of military efficiency, standing at the beck and call of a political regime consumed with no other purpose than to do us maximum harm. This sort of distortion has magnified inordinately, in the public eye, the dimensions of what was initially a serious political problem, and has created, and fed, the impression that the problem is one not to be solved otherwise than by some sort of a military showdown.

A second complication—and a tremendous one—has been the addition of nuclear weaponry to the arsenals of the two powers, and their competition in the development of it. This form of weaponry, with its suicidal and apocalyptic implications, has thrown such uncertainty and confusion into the whole field of military planning, and has aroused such extreme anxieties and such erratic reactions on the part of the public, that it has come close to obscuring the real political, and even military, conflicts of interest between the United States and the Soviet Union behind a fog of nuclear fears, suspicions, and fancied scenarios.

Finally, there was one other effect, this time political, of the outcome of World War II that must also be noted. In the two decades before the war, the western borders of the USSR were essentially those of the old Grand Duchy of Muscovy. They corresponded, in a rough way, to the real ethnic line between those who might be called "Russians" (Little and Great) and those to whom that term could not properly be applied. The wartime extension of the Soviet borders far to the west, together with the acquisition and consolidation of a Soviet hegemony over all of Eastern, and parts of Central, Europe, brought into the Soviet orbit a number of non-Russian nationalities—some formerly included in the czarist empire, some not—very much against the will of a great many of their members, especially those who fled and found refuge in the United States. The result was to add materially to those existing American political factions (some highly vocal and not without political influence) that were animated by a burning hatred of the Soviet Union and were anxious to enlist the political and military resources of the United States for the destruction of the Soviet empire.

* * *

In order that this new proximity of Soviet and American forces, together with its various complications, might be removed, and a more normal and less dangerous situation created in Central and Eastern Europe, three sorts of agreements would have been necessary between the United States and its allies, on the one hand, and the Soviet Union and (for formality's sake) its allies, on the other.

One would have been an agreement to assure the extensive retirement of both Soviet and American forces from the center of Europe. The Soviet side would never have agreed to this except on the condition that the Germany thus freed from the forces of the two powers should be a neutralized and disarmed one, not in alliance with the United States. But this was a condition that the Western powers, for their part, were never prepared even to consider; and with the rearming of Western Germany and the consolidation of its position as a member of NATO, all practical possibility for meeting this requirement passed, in any case. This precluded, as early as the first years of the 1950s, and has precluded ever since, any effective agreement over the German problem.

The second essential agreement would have been one assuring the extensive dismantling of the Soviet hegemony in Eastern Europe—i.e., the concession to the Eastern European governments of a full freedom of action, including at least the right to change their social systems at will. To this, too, Moscow would never have agreed in the absence of a settlement of the German problem.

The third agreement would have been one outlawing nuclear weapons and assuring their removal from the arsenals of all countries, first and foremost those of the United States and the Soviet Union. However, such has been the commitment of the United States government to nuclear weaponry as an indispensable component of its defense force that there has never been a time since 1950 when that government would have been prepared to consider its complete outlawing. The problem was subsequently further complicated by the proliferation of nuclear weapons into the hands of several other governments; so that today, the level of the largest of these peripheral arsenals of the two leading nuclear powers could in any case not be expected to sink.

In these circumstances, there has never been any conceivable basis for a one-time, general settlement of the military-political stalemate that World War II produced. It would obviously require some major alteration in the entire balance of power—some drastic internal breakdown or some new and overpowering external involvement of one side or the other—to make possible, even theoretically, any immediate untying of this knot. The peaceful resolution of this problem is conceivable today only under the benevolent influence of the passage of time, supported by such efforts as mere men can make to promote a greater measure of background confidence and understanding between the governments involved.

Given this situation, the best that men of good will were able to do over the two decades following the death of Stalin was to tinker around the edges of this unresolved and (for the moment) unresolvable military-political deadlock, trying, wherever opportunity seemed to present itself, to narrow the area to which the disagreements applied or to reduce their dangerousness (for dangerous they were and are) in other ways. This a number of these men did; and their successes, while always limited and modest, were more numerous and in some instances more extensive than many today recall.

In Khrushchev's time, there was, outstandingly, the negotiation of the Austrian peace treaty—a product of Khrushchev's own relative good will plus the patient efforts of several excellent Western negotiators, among them our own ambassador, Llewellyn Thompson, to whose exceptional skills and insights Europe probably owes more than to those of any other American of his time. This happily removed one strategically placed European country from the arena of Soviet-American conflict. In addition, there was the signing of the first nuclear-test-ban treaty, in 1963; and there were several early arrangements in the field of cultural exchange.

The ensuing Brezhnev era saw, of course, the spectacular summitry of Messrs. Nixon and Kissinger, marking the successful conclusion of a whole series of agreements in a number of fields—cultural, scientific, technological, and military—culminating in the first SALT agreement of 1972 and the initiation of negotiations for the second one. A number of these agreements proved valuable in one degree or another, and some might have yielded even greater positive results had they been given a longer period of trial and a bit more commitment from the American side. They were supplemented, of course, by the West German–Soviet agreements concluded around the same time, largely under the leadership of Willy Brandt—agreements that, among other things, gave to the western sectors of Berlin, for the first time, reasonably dependable communications with the remainder of West Germany, and thus alleviated one of the greatest, and least necessary, of the dangers of the postwar period.

* * *

These were, I reiterate, modest and limited gains. Their real significance was obscured, rather than enhanced, by the overdramatization to which they were often subjected, under the misleading heading of "détente." The Soviet-American relationship continued, of course, to be burdened at all times by the permanent substructure of friction. But the results of all these efforts to mitigate the prevailing tensions and to improve the atmosphere of Soviet-American relations were on balance positive, so much so that the record of achievement up to 1974 provided in itself no reason why they should not have been continued—rather the contrary.

This, however, was not to be. As we all know, the latter part of 1974 witnessed, together with the Watergate scandal, the beginning of a deterioration of Soviet-American relations that has lasted to the present day—a deterioration in which many of the achievements of the preceding years have been destroyed.

The deterioration was inaugurated by the Jackson-Vanik amendment to the 1974 Trade Reform Act—an amendment that had the effect of knocking out the Soviet-American trade agreement already negotiated in 1972 and of denying to the Soviet Union the concession of the normal customs treatment the agreement provided. Since then, there has been nothing but one long and dreary process of retrogression: rapidly declining trade; neglect or abandonment of cultural-exchange arrangement; throttling down of personal contacts; failure of ratification of the second SALT agreement; reckless acceleration of the weapons race; demonstrative tilting toward Communist China; angry polemic and propagandistic exchange, all culminating in the shrill denunciations and various anti-Soviet "sanctions" of the Carter and Reagan administrations. Of the list of constructive principles agreed upon eight years ago by Nixon and Brezhnev for the future peaceful and productive shaping of the relationship, not one is left that Mr. Nixon's successors have not denounced or abandoned, or both.

How is this sudden turnabout to be explained? The search for the answers to that question is a revealing exercise.

Was there, perhaps, some change in the nature of the Soviet regime with which we were dealing—some change that, alone, would have warranted a drastic departure from previous American policy? Not at all. On the contrary: the Brezhnev regime was marked expressly by an extraordinary steadiness and consistency of behavior. The entire personality of the Soviet structure of power, as distinct from the Soviet society, has shown very little alteration, in fact, since the first years of the post-Stalin epoch.

Was it perhaps that the men who conducted American policy in the years prior to 1974 were naive, or affected by pro-Soviet sympathies, or for some other reason blind to the negative sides of the Soviet personality and behavior? Again, the answer is no. These men were perfectly well aware of the negative aspects of the political regime with which they were dealing. They simply considered that in the light of the prevailing military-political stalemate, there were limits to the usefulness of heroic gestures of petulance and indignation over these various disagreements, whereas it might be useful to take advantage of whatever opportunities seemed to present themselves for the mitigation of existing tensions in ways not adverse to American interests. Their efforts were often, admittedly, experimental. Not all were fully expected to work out; but most of them did. And the gains were considered to be worth whatever minor sacrifices or concessions were involved.

Was it, then, that American public opinion had revolted against the policies pursued in earlier years? Here, too, the answer is no. There was at all times, of course, a hardline faction, or cluster of factions, not very large but violent in its opinions, that opposed any and every form of negotiation or compromise with Moscow, and looked to military intimidation, if not to the actual use of force, as the only means through which anything useful could be accomplished in relations with the Soviet Union. This faction had always existed; and it had recently been strengthened by new flurries of interest in some quarters in the Soviet "dissidents" and in the human-rights question. But the bulk of the American people had seemed to accept with understanding, if not with enthusiasm, these various efforts to diminish tension and to narrow the dangers of the military-political standoff. Even many of those who were not convinced initially of the usefulness of such efforts were willing to see them given a try by people—namely, the various American statesman and diplomats in question—who, they thought, knew more, or ought to know more, about the problem of Soviet-American relations than they themselves did, and who deserved a certain initial margin of confidence. This, plainly, was an instance in which people were inclined, by and large, to respond to political leadership; and there is no apparent reason to suppose that if that leadership had wished to continue to conduct, and to explain, the sort of policy that had prevailed prior to 1974, it would have failed to continue to enjoy an adequate measure of public acquiescence.

If one asks those who have presided over this process of deterioration why they viewed it as necessary or desirable, one receives a variety of answers. There was the human-rights problem; there were the restrictions on Jewish emigration; there were the expansionist tendencies of the Soviet regime with relation t the Third World; there was Afghanistan; there was the Jaruzelski take-over in Poland; there was, above all, the continued Soviet military buildup.

There is some degree of substance in most, if not all, of these charges, but not very much, particularly if taken in relation to Soviet policies prior to that benchmark of 1974. Certainly, there was no change in Soviet behavior in any of these respects drastic enough to justify a change in American policy as abrupt and drastic as the one that took place.

Human rights? The policies applied in the mid-1970s and since in this respect have been no more severe than in the preceding decades, and have actually been far more lenient than anything Russia knew in the Stalin era, when this was scarcely an issue in Soviet-American relations at all.

The treatment of Jews, and the problem of Jewish emigration? In proposing their trade amendment, Jackson and Vanik chose a moment when Jewish emigration was running at the highest rate since at least the 1950s. There was no reason to conclude that, barring this effort, it would not have continued at this rate, or possibly even have increased. Nor would the amendment appear to have been in any way useful to the people on whose behalf it was ostensibly advanced. On the contrary, it would seem to have set Jewish emigration back by some five years.

Soviet "adventurism" in the Third World? I know of no evidence that Soviet efforts to gain influence with Third World regimes were any more extensive in the 1970s, or since, than they were in earlier periods of Soviet history. Least of all is it evident that they were any more successful. The methods had indeed been changing—but changing in a direction (namely, the generous export of arms and advisers) that made them depressingly similar to some of our own.

Afghanistan? Yes, of course: a crude, bungled operation; an obvious mistake of Soviet policy, with origins not entirely dissimilar to those of our own involvement in Vietnam. But not one that impinged directly on American interests, particularly if it be considered that the alternative might have been the growing influence of a Khomeini type of violently anti-American Moslem fanaticism in that part of the world. And one no more serious in its consequences than the absorption of Outer Mongolia into the Soviet sphere of interest in the 1920s, or of Tibet into Communist China at a later date, both changes to which the United States found it possible to accommodate itself without violent repercussions on the bilateral relations with the respective countries.

Poland? Yes, indeed, a tragic situation, the product of a long series of mistakes—many, though not all, on the Soviet side. But this was not a situation that was suddenly created at the end of the 1970s; nor was it worse then than in earlier years. The fact is that Moscow, after being publicly warned by our government on dozens of occasions in 1980 not to intervene militarily in Poland, actually refrained from intervening, and was punished anyway. The theory offered as justification for this—that Jaruzelski undertook his crackdown on Moscow's orders and would not have done so in the absence of those orders—rests, so far as I am aware, solely on conjecture. And the resulting situation, while indeed onerous and even dangerous, is less so than it was a year ago, and no more so than the situation that prevailed in earlier decades.

Finally, the Soviet arms buildup? Yes, a reality, no doubt—some of it exaggerated by calculated leaks from Western military establishments, but another portion of it real enough, and parts of it, such as the mounting of the SS-20s in the western districts of the USSR, unnecessary and foolish. But this, too, did not begin in 1974, nor has the United States government done all that it could to prevent or discourage the buildup. It was, after all, we, and not the Soviet government, who declined to ratify the second SALT treaty. There was no reason why that agreement should not have been ratified (we are, after all, finding it possible to observe its provisions); and no reason why negotiations for further such agreements could not have been put in hand long ago and with a much greater evidence of enthusiasm than the Reagan administration has evinced. In the welter of mistakes, misconceptions, and fixations that has led to the present arms race, both sides have their hearty share of the blame; but there was never any reason why negotiations for the tempering and overcoming of this dangerous competition should not have gone forward, as they did in earlier years, without detriment to the remaining fabric of Soviet-American relations.

* * *

These points concerning the recent deterioration of relations are mentioned here because they illustrate a situation of great importance, the significance of which seems hardly to have been noted on this side of the water. This is that the fluctuations of official American attitudes and policies with relation to the Soviet Union would appear to have been responsive only in minor degree, if at all, to changes in the nature of the problem that country has presented for American statesmanship.

The Soviet Union with which we declined to have relations in the 1920s was not greatly different from that which we found it possible to recognize in 1933. The Stalin regime that aroused our indignation during the Non-Aggression Pact period was precisely the same as that in which we came to discern so many virtues during the war. This latter, in its turn, was no different from the one that we discovered, at the end of the 1940s, to be a great danger to us and to the free world in general.

There was, indeed, a certain real change in the nature of the regime by virtue of the transition from Stalin to Khrushchev in the years 1953 to 1957; and this, as we have seen, was taken advantage of by American statesmen in the ensuing years. But again, the Brezhnev that Messrs. Nixon and Kissinger did such extensive business with was very much the same as the one with whom subsequent American statesmen found it impossible to collaborate at all. There were, of course, over this entire period, important gradual changes in Soviet society and even in the relations between people and regime; but these changes were not pronounced in the structure of power itself, and even less so—except in the transition from the Stalin era to the succeeding ones—in the problem that this structure of power presented for the outside world. Yet American attitudes and policies were subject to abrupt, and sometimes drastic, alterations.

All this would seem to indicate that the motivations for American policy toward the Soviet Union from the start have been primarily subjective, not objective, in origin. They have represented for the most part not reactions to the nature of a certain external phenomenon (the Soviet regime) but rather the reflections of emotional and political impulses making themselves felt on the internal American scene. And these impulses would appear to have been not of American public opinion at large (for that opinion, good-humoredly tolerant but reserved and noncommittal, has exhibited no such violent fluctuations) but of the professional political establishment. This is explicable, perhaps, to the extent that policy toward the Soviet Union has been a partisan political issue; but this has been true only to a limited extent. More important would seem to have been the momentary violence of feeling on the part of politically influential lobbies and minorities to whose pressures the politicians of the moment were inclined to pander or defer.

However that may be, the record of American policy toward the Soviet Union over the six and a half decades of the existence of that body politic gives the impression that it was not really the nature of any external problem that concerned us but rather something we were anxious to prove to ourselves, about ourselves.

It is, surely, not unreasonable to point out that this state of affairs is not adequate as a response to the problem that the Soviet Union actually presents. Indeed, it holds great dangers for this country and for others as well. The problem presented by the need for a continued peaceful co-existence on the same planet of the Soviet Union and the United States is one that would challenge even the highest resources of this country for analysis, for it must be dealt with in ways conducive not just to American national interest in the narrow sense but to peace among the various great powers—a condition without which no American interest of any sort can be served. Vital prerequisites for the successful policy of a great power are stability and consistency. Even our allies cannot be helped by a policy that lacks these qualities. If there was ever a time in the history of this country when there was no place for the sort of self-conscious posturing, and the sort of abrupt changes of concept, that have marked our reaction to Soviet power in recent decades, that time is now.

To renounce this sort of self-indulgence, deeply ingrained as it is in American political behavior, is admittedly a big order. It will probably never be wholly satisfied. But there have been moments in American history when a bipartisan consciousness of national danger or necessity has enabled us, as in the case of the Marshall Plan, to face a problem objectively and to find the answer to it most responsive to the general interest—an answer, that is, broadly, imaginatively, and generously conceived, and consistently pursued. With a nuclear-weapons race increasingly out of control now staring us in the face—confronted as we are with accumulations of modern weapons, nuclear and otherwise, of such monstrous destructiveness that their detonation (and weapons have a way of being detonated in the end) could well put an end to civilization—we can no longer afford to address to the problem of Soviet-American relations anything less than the best, in the way of sobriety, objective analysis, steadiness, thoughtfulness, and practicality of purpose, that our society can produce. There is not much more time for the recognition of this fact to penetrate the national consciousness. The clock is ticking; the remaining ticks are numbered; the end of their number is already in sight. Only a thorough, open-minded, bipartisan re-examination of this whole problem, and a determined, imaginative promulgation of the results of such a re-examination, could bring a safe end to this ticking.

LESTER C. THUROW

The Arms Race and the Economic Order

If the arms race were to end, one can confidently maintain that the world could easily shift to civilian production with a minimum of disruption. What can be done is seen in what has been done.

In the aftermath of World War II there was a brief period before the Cold War began of almost complete demobilization. From 1945 to 1947 the armed forces of the United States fell from $11^1/_2$ million to $1^1/_2$ million men. Military purchases fell from over forty percent of the GNP to just four percent of the GNP. Yet there was only a slight increase in unemployment, from two to four percent of the labor force.

Practical experience is backed by analysis. If one looks at the skills that are used in the production of military goods and services, it is clear that those skills could be used, and are in fact needed, in the civilian economy. Engineers, skilled machinists, electronics technicians—they all are in demand, usually in short supply, in the civilian economy. For military production uses the people who are easiest to employ in our economy. It takes not a random sample of the American labor force but an above average group when it comes to skills and employability. That is true both in industries serving the military and in the military itself. Military recruiters, for example, will not take those with mental or physical handicaps and insist on minimum standards of literacy and personal behavior.

High Unemployment
Upon first reflection this assertion seems contradicted by an unemployment rate in excess of ten percent in the spring of 1983. How could we redeploy military and industrial manpower from military production when we cannot employ those who are now in the civilian economy? It is important to understand, however, that high unemployment

is not an accident or evidence of an inability to create civilian jobs. Those currently unemployed are not unemployed through our inability to expand the demand for goods and hence their services, but are unemployed through a deliberate decision to force them into unemployment in an effort to solve the inflation problem.

As a society we have adopted a strategy of stopping inflation that requires a certain fraction of the labor force to be unemployed. To stop inflation under this strategy the economy must be stopped with restrictive monetary and fiscal policies. This produces unemployed human and physical resources, and these idle resources serve as a stick to beat down the price and wage increases of those left in employment.

While one can question the morality of this technique for stopping inflation (it is only one of several possible strategies, and the social burden of stopping inflation is placed on a very limited group of individuals who tend to come disproportionally from the poorest segments of society), those currently unemployed, if one were to use a military metaphor, have essentially been drafted to be "Inflation Fighters for the U.S. of A."

While, given the current strategy, an army in excess of 11 million people seems necessary to fight the anti-inflationary wars, the size of the necessary army does not need to rise with a shift from military to civilian production. Policy makers could without worrying about more inflation allow civilian demands to expand to absorb the human and physical resources being released from the military sector, even if they were unwilling to allow civilian demand to expand to absorb those currently unemployed.

Costs of a Conventional Alternative
While we certainly would redeploy people from military to civilian production, this is unlikely to be the result of any American decision to rely less on nuclear arms or upon any Soviet-American agreement to limit the nuclear arms race. Put crudely, nuclear arms provide a "large bang for the buck." Their cheapness has in fact been one of the arguments for relying upon them in the doctrine of deterrence. Fewer troops have to be maintained in the Central European front with nuclear weapons than without them. To get the same deterrence bang from conventional arms would undoubtedly require a defense budget that was larger, not smaller, than the current defense budget. Thus the real problem is apt to be one of shifting resources from civilian to military uses rather than the reverse.

This is clearly the case in any unilateral decision by the United States to rely less on nuclear arms and is apt to be the case even if a joint Soviet-American agreement were reached to rely less on nuclear arms. The history of such agreements is that they tend to limit expenditures on the cheapest, most likely to be deployed, new weapons systems but leave the arms race itself intact. As a result, the race shifts from relatively cheap weapons systems that are within the arc of current scientific and engineering knowledge to relatively expensive weapons systems that are just beyond the arc of current scientific and engineering knowledge.

Ending the Arms Race
And an agreement to limit the arms race itself is almost a contradiction in terms. For that can come about not through agreement but only through a firm belief on both sides that one side is no threat to the other. The United States and Canada do not need a formal agreement stating that neither side needs to spend money on armaments to defend itself from the other. If they needed an agreement, they could not trust each other and no agreement would be possible or have any meaning, even if it were to exist on paper.

Trust that neither side threatens the other is not something that can be negotiated. It must be built upon a long history of events that gradually builds up confidence. And one must candidly admit that the events of the past decade have pushed the United States and the Soviet Union in precisely the opposite direction. There is clearly less mutual trust today than there was a decade ago.

While one can agree with the bishops' repetition of the judgment of Vatican II that "the arms race is one of the greatest curses on the human race" (# 13), the arms race, having gone on for the entire history of mankind (Egypt versus Assyria, Rome versus Carthage, France versus England), is not likely to stop. For the simple fact is that no one knows how to stop it without remaking human behavior. At least up to this point, religion has failed in that (its?) task.

If the main problems of the arms race were economic, the world's task would be simple. But, in fact, the economic problems are not even second-order problems. If the world wanted to stop the arms race, economic difficulties would not stop that shift for more than a brief instance. The problem is *will*, not economic obstacles to that *will*.

Justifying an End to the Arms Race

The section of the bishops' pastoral letter that is most directly relevant to economics and the arms race is entitled "Interdependence: From Fact to Policy"(III.B.3). Unfortunately, the section does not start with "fact" and therefore does not lead to "policy." The essence of the section is to be found in the second half of the quotation from Vatican II: "The arms race is one of the greatest curses on the human race and the harm that it inflicts upon the poor is more than can be endured." The section essentially implies that poor countries are poor (at least partially) because they have been exploited by rich, militarily powerful countries.

The evidence for this assertion is lacking in the bishops' letter and denied by historical research. All of our historical evidence indicates that it costs a country more to maintain an empire than it gains from having an empire. Investments in the empire always exceeded the economic gains from the empire. That was true in the days of nineteenth century colonialism (remember who built the railways across India) and is just as true today.

Colonies may be a source of home country power but they are not a source of home country wealth. If per capita consumption were the goal, no one would have ever set out to build an empire that had to be maintained by force.

Empires also gain by having wealthy colonies or allies rather than poor colonies and allies. To drive this point home let me pose a series of what the Germans call *Gedanken* experiments.

America's allies (NATO, Japan) are much wealthier than the allies (Eastern Europe, Cuba, North Vietnam) of the Soviet Union. Does that fact make America stronger or weaker, wealthier or poorer? Clearly it contributes to both our wealth and our strength.

Suppose that we could impose a magic curtain so that there would be absolutely no contact (no sales of goods and services, no visits, no exchange of knowledge or knowledge about each other) between the developed and the underdeveloped world. Would the underdeveloped world be better off? Would the standard of living and prospects for future development fall faster in the developed or underdeveloped countries? To ask the question is to answer it.

Minor adjustments would be necessary in the style and standards of living in the developed world. But almost everything that is imported from the underdeveloped countries could be relatively easily replaced.

Tropical fruit would be grown under glass and to a much greater extent in the tropical regions (such as Florida) of developed countries. Synthetic oil would be developed to replace oil imported from underdeveloped countries. The technologies are well known and were used by Germany in both World War I and II. They are simply expensive and lead to more costly gasoline—an inconvenience, but not a major disaster.

In contrast, major changes would be necessary in the underdeveloped world. Without the ability to buy spare parts, their existing industrial enterprises would grind to a halt. Without the ability to import technologies and send their students to the developed world, they would have to reinvent the knowledge that they can now quickly acquire. Many underdeveloped countries could not feed themselves if they could not trade tropical agricultural products such as cocoa for the grain of the developed world. Basic food grains such as wheat will not grow where luxury products such as cocoa will. Without the markets of the first world the oil of the second world would neither exist nor have value.

Consider the countries that once were among the world's richest and are now numbered among the world's poor—Egypt, Iraq (Babylon), China, Iran (Persia), and in more modern times Argentina. Did any of them become poor because they were exploited from outside or because two other countries were engaged in an arms race? Clearly not. It is more nearly accurate to say that they themselves became poor because they spent themselves into poverty in the arms race.

As a final *Gedanken* experiment ask yourself another question. What country do you know of that is so poor that it cannot and does not engage in its own little arms race with its own neighbors? I know of no country that isn't arming itself to its teeth against its neighbors. Have you ever heard of a country too poor to fight a war?

There is no doubt that the arms race hurts the poor, but the arms race that impacts the poor is not that between the Soviet Union and the United States but that among poor countries.

There is also a real question as to whether humanitarian aid can work in an environment dominated by "little" arms races. All foreign aid is by its very nature "fundable." If Americans pay to build a local school or hospital, the local government can use the resources that it otherwise would have had to use to build that school to buy armaments. Even if the local country wouldn't have built the hospital without aid, the aid comes in the form of dollars that can be used to buy armaments while most of the hospital is paid for in terms of local currencies that are often completely unusable in world markets. The net result is more funds available to buy arms.

While it does not present the human race with the prospect of self-annihilation, from the point of view of economics third-world arms races are clearly more destructive than first-world arms races. While we would all be smarter if we avoided arms races, in a very real sense we can afford our arms race while they cannot afford theirs.

The basic argument for helping poor individuals and poor countries has to be a moral one. We help them not because we are guilty of "causing" their poverty but because it is a "moral" duty to help those in need and because a world without poverty is a better world than one with it.

And when aid is given, conditions should be imposed even if we are not ourselves living up to those conditions. I can think of no humanitarian reason why we should give aid to any country with a rising military budget. For whatever we think we are doing, we are effectively subsidizing increases in their military budgets. At the moment, if we were to limit our aid to countries with falling military budgets, we would be giving aid to very few.

From an economic point of view one can argue as to whether we are wealthy enough to afford the arms race in which we are engaged, but when it comes to the third world there is no argument. They are not wealthy enough to afford the arms race in which they are engaged. And we certainly have both a right and a duty to use our foreign aid to stop their arms race even if we are not smart enough to stop our owns arms race.

Public Opinion
The bishops maintain that "as pastors who often appeal to our congregations for funds destined for international programs, we find good will and great generosity the prevailing characteristics. The spirit of generosity which shaped the Marshall Plan is still alive in the American public" (# 262). But "we must discover how to translate this personal sense of generosity and compassion into support for policies which would respond to papal teaching in international economic issues" (# 263).

The bishops seem to see the problem as one of how personal generosity can be translated into institutional generosity, but I suspect that the bishops are being too generous with their fellow human beings. The spirit of generosity simply is not there.

Looking at the bottom line, I know of no dimension upon which aid to the poor, whether in the form of private charity, social welfare programs, or foreign aid itself, is not falling as a percentage of personal income. Foreign aid is the least popular program with which Congress deals. Congress regularly finds itself unable to agree on even the old dollar levels of expenditures much less any increase to compensate even for the effects of inflation. And much of what we call foreign aid does not go to the poor but goes to countries such as Israel or Egypt that are supported for military and not humanitarian reasons.

As a society we seem willing to cut the food and nutritional programs for our own poor. And private charity has not exactly rushed to fill the gap left by shrinking public generosity. Let me respectfully suggest that a society that does not seem bothered by hunger among its own poor is unlikely to be interested in helping the poor of the rest of the world.

Economic Warfare
Interestingly, the bishops do not address themselves at all to one of the strong undercurrents of the arms race—most clearly expressed by President Reagan in his address to the British Parliament. In that address the president saw a Soviet economy about ready to collapse economically. If we just applied some economic pressure in the form of higher defense spending, the Soviets would be forced to respond with higher spending of their own and in the process bring their economy to a halt.

Thus the B-1 bomber may be technologically obsolete in the sense that the Soviets already know how to build a defense system that can defeat it, but if it costs the United States $50 billion to build the B-1 and it costs the Soviets $150 billion to build the necessary defenses, the weapon is a good weapon because it will add to the economic pressure on the Soviet economy. Put crudely, if we have a per capita GNP twice that of the Soviet Union and we spend fifty percent of our GNP on defense, they will have to spend one hundred percent and in the process go broke.

The responses to this argument are moral, historical, and economic. Using the sharp distinction that the bishops' pastoral letter makes between combatants and noncombatants, I would assume that the bishops would object to deliberate efforts to reduce the economy of one's adversary to ruin. For if Russians go hungry because of American actions it will not be the leaders of the Kremlin or the generals of the army but ordinary Russian citizens. Whatever the level of general animosity between America and the Soviet Union, these average individuals are clearly not our enemies.

As a result, deliberate actions to hobble another country's economy, such as our grain embargo, would seem to be subject to the same moral objection as nuclear war itself. Neither action makes a sharp distinction between combatant and noncombatant.

Yet I am not sure that the bishops' distinction between combatant and noncombatant is as "morally" useful as it first appears. When does one cease to be a combatant in a modern war? Are those involuntarily drafted into the armed forces combatants? Are workers in a defense plant combatants? Are the workers in plants who supply components to both defense and civilian plants combatants? If so, all farmers become combatants since some of their food will be used to feed the military. What if I voted for the leaders who are undertaking war? If I support the war am I a combatant?

Historically, the effort to beat the Soviets into submission economically would seem to make no sense. Repeatedly, Soviet citizens have demonstrated an ability and willingness (the response to Napoleon and Hitler are major examples) to make whatever sacrifices, economic or otherwise, that are necessary to avoid being dictated to from the outside. There is no reason to believe that American dictation will elicit any different response.

Economically, societies are much more resilient than they at first appear. They are not the fragile institutions sometimes depicted. The strategic bombing surveys of Germany after World War II indicated that the allied bombing did not succeed in reducing German production of military materials. It was far easier to kill people than it was to disrupt the economy. If such data needed to be confirmed it was confirmed in Vietnam. More tonnage of bombs was dropped than in all of World War II, yet North Vietnam still continued to function and provide what was necessary both for survival on the home front and military actions.

By being willing to make the necessary sacrifices in other areas any industrial economy can provide the items that are essential to its survival. The country may not be able to provide a high standard of personal consumption, but it can provide the resources necessary to conduct a war. What actual bombing cannot accomplish is unlikely to be accomplished by grain embargoes or attempts to spend one's adversary into bankruptcy.

The Real Economic Price of the Arms Race

Economically, the objection to the arms race is not what it does to others (I would be willing to bet that foreign aid would not go up a penny if the arms race were to end tomorrow), but what it does to ourselves. The problem is not so much that we divert resources to the arms race (being a rich society we can easily afford to waste five to ten percent of the GNP), but that we divert our very best talent.

Suppose that you are a new engineer just graduating from MIT. You have two job offers—one from a civilian firm, one from a military firm. Which are you going to take? One offers you a chance to build a better car and the other offers you a chance to build a laser weapon to knock Russian missiles out of space. In all likelihood you will take the defense job. It is simply more exciting—closer to the frontiers of scientific knowledge, less constrained by economics. One could design a great billion dollar car, but no one would buy it. If one designs a billion dollar laser, it gets bought.

High quality talent is in limited supply in any society. If the best engineers are building space weapons in the United States but automobiles in Japan, no one should be surprised when Japan conquers the auto industry. We dominate in space weapons, but there is a limited market for such weapons and they do not help raise the standard of living of the average American.

If such a situation continues for a long period of time, the process essentially undermines the economic foundations upon which it rests. The talent needed to produce a vibrant economy is gradually sucked out of the economy and, as the productive economy stagnates (either absolutely or relative to other countries), the economy base upon which the military superstructure sits rots—eventually pulling the military superstructure down with it.

If one examines the history of large, once dominant countries, it is difficult to find any who were conquered from without without first rotting from within. While it is certainly possible to conduct an arms race without rotting from within (Rome did it for many hundreds of years), the diversion of talent from productive to non-productive areas places a constant strain on the system.

One may find an arms race necessary. But whatever one thinks about the necessity of it, it is not productive. For more weapons, nuclear or non-nuclear, add nothing to our future ability to produce a higher standard of living for our citizens or the citizens of the rest of the world. Economically they are a waste.

VII

Church:
Conscience, Prayer, and Penance

The Challenge of Peace

Part IV and Conclusion, #s 274–339

The pastoral's concluding sections cite the challenges posed to U.S. Catholics because the nation is so heavily armed with modern weapons, and recommend some responses for consideration.

While the letter offers a series of traditional suggestions, such as calling for increased educational efforts, more prayer, and a return to Friday fast and abstinence, it includes two highly controversial public issues: one is political with moral overtones—abortion; the other is penitential with public consequences—the U.S. bombing of Hiroshima and Nagasaki.

Regarding the first issue, the letter asks "how long a nation willing to extend a constitutional guarantee to the 'right' to kill defenseless human beings by abortion is likely to refrain from adopting strategic warfare policies deliberately designed to kill millions of defenseless human beings. . . ." The letter calls for the millions who say "no" to nuclear war to say "no" also to abortion. The intensity of the bishops' interest in the subject can be measured by the fact that coverage of abortion received two sentences in the initial draft, whereas in the final text it was expanded to almost four hundred words.

The penitential issue with grave public consequences involves the U.S. atomic bombings in 1945. The pastoral reminds its readers that Pope Paul VI's described these events as "butchery of untold magnitude." The bishops boldly set out for themselves the incredible task to "shape the climate of opinion which will make it possible for our country to express profound sorrow" for these events. Without this confession of guilt and the consequent firm purpose of amendment, the bishops fear "there is no possibility of finding a way to repudiate future use of nuclear weapons. . . ."

A concluding note in the pastoral reflects the bishops' insistence that U.S. Catholics exercise their citizenship and the virtue of patriotism by asking the nation to "live up to its full potential as an agent of peace with justice for all people." In these ways, Catholics witness to the belief that "a better world is here for human hands and hearts and minds to make."

JOHN C. HAUGHEY

Disarmament of the Heart

"All of the values we are promoting in this letter rest ultimately in the disarmament of the human heart and the conversion of the human spirit to God who alone can give authentic peace. Indeed, to have peace in our world, we must first have peace within ourselves."[1] The two sets of means which the bishops' pastoral emphasizes for bringing about this disarmament are religious and philosophical. In the first part of this article I will elaborate on those which are of a religious nature. In the second part, on those which are of a philosophical nature.

Religious Resources
The religious means that the faithful are encouraged to use to bring about this disarmament of the human heart, especially their own, are treated in the fourth part of the pastoral. The notion of discipleship introduces the cluster of religious means which members of the body of Christ are to employ. Each member of the community of disciples is to hear Christ saying to him or to her: "Follow me." This following must take us "beyond where we are now."[2] We must separate "ourselves from all attachments and affiliations that could prevent us from hearing and following our authentic vocation."[3] And a costly discipleship it is. Each follower of Christ who hears the call to peacemaking must expect "a share in the cross."[4] "We must regard as normal even the path of persecution and the possibility of martyrdom."[5] In order to be sustained in the following of Christ "we must develop a sense of solidarity, cemented by relationships with mature and exemplary Christians who represent Christ and his way of life."[6] In other words, community is needed for Christians to be able to profess "full faith in an increasingly secularized society."[7]

The bishops emphasize that peacemaking "is a requirement of our faith"; it is not an optional commitment.[8] "We are called to be peacemakers, not by some movement of the moment, but by our Lord Jesus."[9]

The most important religious resource for this vocation to peace-making is the prayer life of Christians. "It is in prayer that we encounter Jesus, who is our peace, and learn from him the way to peace."[10] This prayer which is both personal and communal, is of several kinds. The most obvious, perhaps, is petitionary prayer. Prayer for peace is a frequent practice among believers. Less well known and practiced is what the bishops call contemplative prayer. "Contemplative prayer is especially valuable for advancing peace and harmony in the world."[11] It is by comtemplative prayer that Christians experience an unfolding of love which is the moving force of peace.[12] They also note the importance of devotional prayer, mentioning in that context the rosary as a form and Mary, Our Lady of Peace, as a particularly venerable object of our devotional prayer.

As a means toward peace, the eucharist is to be given considerable attention, according to the pastoral. Not only is the act of reconciliation with the risen Christ the whole import of the sacrament, but every celebration of the eucharist is to be an occasion for a further commitment to the cause of peace in our world. We must dedicate ourselves as a community to peace and reconciliation.[13] To this end the bishops encourage an increased awareness of "the sign of peace at Mass [as] an authentic sign of our reconciliation with God and with one another."[14]

The Christian vocation to peacemaking, however, is not an interior matter, merely spiritual, an affair of the heart. It involves action. It moves from heart to world. Christian peacemaking requires "doer[s] of the word."[15] What we must do must be done in relationship to the many expressions of violence, especially our own or those directed toward us. The sacrament of reconciliation, therefore, as well as communal penance services are prescribed. Forgiveness, God's of us, must flow from us to one another.

Fasting and abstinence are two other means prescribed by which we show ourselves doers of the word. "Every Friday should be a day significantly devoted to prayer, penance, and almsgiving for peace."[16] In addition to eating less and abstaining from meat this day, the peculiar form of fasting the bishops exhort us to is spelled out by the rich passage of Isaiah: "Is not the sort of fast that pleases me, to break unjust fetters and undo the thongs of the yoke, to let the oppressed go free and break every yoke, to share your bread with the hungry, and shelter the homeless poor, to clothe the person you see to be naked . . . ?" (Is. 58:6-7). Christian peacemaking must start at home, must roll back, so to speak, the hostilities that mount up between ourselves and peoples close at hand.

But if we are to respond with prayer, reconcilation, and fasting, and become doers of God's word of peace, we must hear this word. Hearing the Gospel of peace is an essential element in the disarmament of the heart. The bishops assure us that "we still recognize in the scriptures a unique source of revelation, a word of God which is addressed to us as surely as it has been through all preceding generations."[17] Although they believe that scripture is foundational for confronting the dilemma of war and peace, and a revelatory foundation at that, they suggest rather than develop some scriptural themes which can disclose more about this dilemma. Presumably, the pastoral is calling for the development of a theology of peace rather than presenting itself as such a synthesis.

Scriptural Themes

The pastoral merely hints at the great wealth that is contained in a number of different scriptural themes. For example, the theme of *covenant*. They note that peace is a special characteristic of covenant as it is treated in the Old Testament. Peace in the land is given by the one who brings us into his covenant of peace. Right relationship between God and his people obtains if Israel is willing to put its trust in God alone and to look only to him for its security.[18] Insofar as Israel trusted in God she lived in peace.

It was by her trust that Israel showed herself faithful to the covenant. She was called to live in the midst of hostile nations and still retain this posture of spirit toward God. As the pastoral notes both Jeremiah and Isaiah condemn Israel's leaders for depending on their own strength and on alliances with other nations rather than trusting in God.

For some Christians, trusting in God means that arms should not be used to obtain security. Although the letter legitimates the vocation of non-violence as a valid understanding of the Gospel of peace, their own implicit theology of providence does not have them opt for the pacifist position. "Respecting our freedom, [God] does not solve our problems, but sustains us as we take responsibility for his work of creation and try to shape it in the ways of the kingdom."[19] By its location in the pastoral, the bishops seem to be suggesting that our calculus about the use of nuclear arms must be rooted in our trust in God. Care must be taken that we not be accused of having it both ways, simply juxtaposing trust in God and trusting in our arms at the same time.

Love as lived and preached by Jesus is another of the pastoral's scriptural themes. It is an "active, life-giving, inclusive force." It is able to go beyond the pale of family and kind and begin to reach even to those who are enemies. It does not seek revenge or retaliation. Jesus is the incarnation of God's love and the exemplar of its power. Jesus' own resurrection shows that this love is stronger than death itself. It would appear to be the only force capable of moving people beyond the need to seek redress of their grievances through arms. It refuses to act out of fear of those who can kill the body because its fear and awe and eye are fixed on the one who raises up and tears down all human powers. The love of God incarnate in Jesus "refused to defend [itself] with force or with violence. He endured violence and cruelty so that God's love might be fully manifest."[20] It would be difficult to see how a Christian vocation to peacemaking could have any efficacy if it were not animated by this force and his example.

A third theme, at the core of the Christian vocation to peacemaking, is the *reconciling action of God in Christ*. "In his death-resurrection he gives God's peace to our world."[21] This act of reconciliation has already taken place but it is only slowly appropriated by Christians through faith. Growth in strength for the task of peacemaking presumes that we increasingly make our own this act of reconciliation which has been done to us and for our world in Christ. It is essential that we perceive the character of this ongoing action of God in us. A valuable metaphor for doing this can be found in the second chapter of the letter to the Ephesians: Christ is not only our peace once and for all, but he continues to be our peace precisely by knocking down the walls of hostility that develop in us. The barriers referred to in the text are between Jews and Gentiles, but the metaphor applies wherever there are walls of hostility. These can be within a person due to self-hatred or non-acceptance of oneself. These can be interpersonal or intergroup. So the primary action of reconciliation between ourselves and God which has been definitively won in Christ involves an ongoing wall-breaking power of God's spirit. That wall-breaking power of God's spirit extends the *shalom* of God, the peace of God, the human wholeness which Christ announced and made possible. But this peace must be expected, requisitioned, and allowed to operate in Christians' hearts and in their relationships. Not a once and for all action, but this reconciling action of God must be ongoing since the walls of hostility within ourselves, toward ourselves, and toward others can be erected at a moment's notice. We are capable of coming to grievance, fear, resentment, all the day long. Hence we are in need of this *shalom* power all the day long. Peace in our hearts is continually being threatened and must be won in dealing with the things which threaten it and by having recourse to the power of God's reconciling act in Christ whereby the threat can be overcome.

It would be a cheapening, even a trivialization, of this act of reconciliation, if Christians were to translate their desire for peace into a kind of a miraculous power that did not have to go through them out into concrete actions with other persons and peoples. The Christian vocation to peacemaking is not a simple projection of our hopes for peace onto God and a well wishing of those who feel called to action on behalf of this aspiration and a hope that the world doesn't blow up in the meantime. Rather, Christian peacemaking must have its headwaters in the continual appropriation of this power of reconciliation in concrete ways. Our peace is a false peace if we do not do peace, if we are not peacemakers concretely with one another. The *shalom* of God, this inner dynamism which impacts us through the reconciliation that Christ is continually extending to us is something that will be known by others and ourselves only to the extent that it is being done by us. Dealing with the spiraling arms race is only one aspect of the task of Christian peacemaking. Dealing with anger in our hearts and distrust of others is a much more universal experience. Christians have to deal with their fears, resentments, angers, and distrusts from within the act which makes them Christian and makes Christ their peace.

Peace Is a Gift
So far I have elaborated on three scriptural themes that are essential to giving a vision to the task of Christian peacemaking. What unifies them is that all three are ways of indicating that peace is a gift. It is a gift that God has wanted to give to humankind from the beginning. It has been bestowed irretrievably on us by the reconciling action of Christ. Since it is a gift it must be received. It is received by the active power of believing. It is received if we believe in the one who has won the gift for us and extends it to us. It is received if we let the reconciling power of God in Christ operate on our lives now. We let that reconciling power act on our lives if we make ourselves vulnerable to him by giving him access to the walls of hostility that grow up between us and others.

The precondition for receiving the gift is the realization that we cannot bestow this gift upon ourselves. Our need, taken to Christ, is met tangibly as Christ becomes our peace and as his power rolls against the walls of hostility which we find in ourselves. Acknowledging the walls, wanting them down, allowing him to pierce them, are all essential to Christian peacemaking. We cannot take this gift for granted. We take it for granted if we see the act of reconciliation won for us by Christ as a once and for all action. Although it is a definitive action, it is not single nor static. The gift of Christ's peace, furthermore, brings with it the giver of the gift. The gift cannot be disengaged from the giver. "He is our peace," his peace is not a gift apart from who he is.

Intrinsic to belief in Christ as our peace and to the receiving of the gift of peace is the action taken with what we have received. Gift becomes task. Task is the other side of gift. Peacemaking flows from peace receiving. The disarmament of the human heart breaks out into action.

The Gospel of John intuits the fact that there are constitutive parts to the gift. His Easter night Pentecost scene links peace, Spirit, and forgiveness.

"Peace be with you," the risen Christ says to his disciples on the evening of the first day of the week. "As the Father has sent me, so I send you." Then he breathed on them and said: "Receive the Holy Spirit, if you forgive men's sins, they are forgiven them; if you hold them bound, they are held bound" (John. 20:21–23). He promised he would not leave them orphans. He returns in the gift of peace and the gift of the Holy Spirit. He sends them forth to extend the reconciling act which he made possible between themselves and God, to the relationships between themselves and one another, and between themselves and the people to whom he sent them.

Once a separation takes place between gift and task, then almost certainly peace will become our task alone, and futility will be its consequence. But the converse is also true: if peace is not our task, then peace as gift will become more and more trivial and extrinsic. It then is reduced to an empty piety. We can fail in being Christian peacemakers either because we allow the work to be disengaged from the gift or because we try to receive the gift without taking on the tasks that flow from it. We must carry out the task of peace wherever there are walls of hostility. We simply cannot accept walls of hostility between ourselves and other individuals or peoples. I believe this is the religious core of the bishops' discomfort with resigning ourselves to nuclear deterrence as an ongoing policy. That would mean that we have decided to live with walls of hostility and, by doing so, manifest our disbelief in the reconciling action of God in Christ.

We do not deal with these hostilities and enemies by our own means but by the means to which our faith gives us access. Insofar as our enemy is the Soviet Union, we are to deal with this reality by the means which our faith provides us. Why walls obtain between the United States and the Soviet Union is easy enough to see. The bishops cite military expansionism as the main reason. In response to this we feel the need to "build and maintain overwhelming or at least counter-vailing military power."[22] The pastoral is not naive about the height or breadth of these walls. They do not gloss over the radical differences between us in political philosophy and understandings of morality.[23] They warn, however, of a "'hardness of heart' which can close us off to others or to the changes needed to make the future different from the past."[24] They remind us not to "underestimate both our human potential for creative diplomacy and God's action in our midst which can open the way to changes we could barely imagine."[25] Our desire for peace is not to be spiritualized but must be enfleshed in concrete action through which God's gift is expressed. The bishops cite especially Pope John Paul II's call for "lucid dialogue" which seeks "to unblock the situation and to work for the possible establishment of peace on particular points."[26]

A Caution
While each draft of the bishops' letter has been more satisfying than the previous one in the way they have treated scripture, even this final document leaves much to be desired. On the one hand they pray: "We call upon the spirit of God who speaks in the word and in our hearts to aid us in our listening."[27] Yet on the other hand, in what has to be the most inept observation in the entire pastoral, they observe, "[the scriptures] do not provide us with detailed answers to the specifics of the question which we face today. They do not speak specifically of nuclear war or nuclear weapons, for these were beyond the imagination of the communities in which the scriptures were formed."[28] It is not always clear what the bishops expect from scripture by the way they treat it in the pastoral. It seems there were two different mentalities at work in its composition. One expected much from scripture. With the fuller and fuller treatment in each successive draft, the words of scripture were accorded greater and greater importance. Nevertheless, the overall treatment of scripture in the pastoral also gives one the impression that it was part of a data-gathering process that was needed before they got down to the more important contribution of the analytic part

of the pastoral. Since the bishops see the pastoral as a first step of many we can only hope that in their subsequent direction of the church they will be more specific in what they expect from scripture and more specific in their guidance of the faithful in its use. It would be hard to find a more efficacious instrument for the disarming of the human heart than the word of God. Part of the disarming process is a need to be open to a change in questions which we bring to the word of God. The word must be given a chance to act as a sword cutting through even what we think are the important "questions which we face today."

Strategy and Spirituality

The letter is rich in its moral methodology, providing much light about the moral principles which form consciences and their application to the subject of violence. The pastoral is deficient in what might be called a "discernment" methodology. By this I mean several things. First of all, Catholics need guidance about how to pray the scriptures. There is widespread uncertainty in the Catholic church about the use of scripture by individuals and groups. This uncertainty leads to caution and non-use. Knowledge of the historical-critical method which enables one to see how the scriptures are conditioned by the situations in which they were written is not enough. It would seem, however, that if there is going to be any break in the impasse that we have come to with respect to our use of force, it will have to come from those who are growing in "zeal to propagate the Gospel of peace" (Eph. 6:15). But this Gospel requires "the sword of the Spirit, the word of God" (Eph. 6:17).

Discernment methodology, furthermore, requires that we take seriously the words of the bishops with respect to peace as a matter of vocation, a call from Christ to each of us. If this is the case, then the "norm ethics" which the pastoral is so helpful in providing must be complemented by a "call ethics." If individuals and communities of Christians are to go beyond where they are now and if the universal norms which are given a full treatment in the pastoral letter do not exhaust the gospel vision, then how do Catholic Christians proceed from there to hearing what they are being called to? Among other things, a call ethics would be concerned to spell out the spiritual disciplines which have developed in the history of the church for understanding and fulfilling vocation in Christ.

Philosophical Resources

The bishops' letter comes from a Catholic social tradition which as the bishops describe it "is a mix of biblical, theological, and philosophical elements which are brought to bear upon the concrete problems of the day."[29] The bulk of their letter is an elaboration of the philosophical elements. These philosophical elements are clustered around the principles of the just-war theory. The benefits which these principles and this theory furnish are several. First, they equip those who find themselves in a moral dilemma with principles from a tradition of reasoning about violence and what to do in the face of it. Second, they help to form consciences. Third,.they furnish us with a body of principles by which the bishops and the church can address the wider civil community. As moral principles they can be understood by those who are of the faith as well as those who are not. Fourth, since they are accessible to both believers and those who are not, they supply potential material for public moral discourse. Fifth, since they are rooted in reason these moral principles and this just-war theory give peacemaking a degree of objectivity.

Valuable as they are, it is important not to overlook the limitations of the just-war theory and its principles. First of all, their cogency begins to lessen as they go from the abstract to the concrete, there to be met by different facts, different interpretation of facts, and a wide range of disagreement about the application of the principles and theory to the facts. Second, the theory's ability to address reason can also leave those using the theory in the dark about what is going on in their own hearts. No one can deny that the just-war theory has been used by many to arrive at a justification for actions while leaving those using the theory unaware of the violence in themselves which at least partly accounts for the violence breaking out in the political order. Valuable as it is in itself, the just-war theory has been historically misused because it can address situations more easily than hearts. Furthermore, one would have to question whether these principles can furnish us with the power necessary for the "moral-about-face" which the bishops and the Holy Father see as necessary in the spiraling arms race.

The situation that the world faces is one of an almost universal feeling of helplessness. Most people of good will believe that the situation we are in is an immoral one and an intolerable one. Their question is not whether it is moral but where we will find the power to do something about it. The kind of power the bishops can evoke is the power of faith. We have to ask ourselves, both as citizens and Christians, whether we are up against poor moral reasoning which then calls for better moral reasoning or whether we are up against something more sinister which reasoning will not unearth or confront.

Catholic Christianity has always been concerned that faith and reason not be played off one against the other. Although it is not a product of reason, Catholicism has always sought to employ reason in order to give faith the intelligibility it needed to be understood and deepened by its own membership and made communicable to others who do not count themselves members. For Catholic Christians the relationship between faith and reason might be best seen in terms of employing reason to deepen faith. A case in point are the "philosophical elements" in the pastoral. The pastoral makes the point that the just-war theory has its origins in the church. Although it furnishes the material for public discourse and does not require faith to be understood or assented to, Catholic Christians who make use of the just-war theory will need to employ it from the perspective of faith. This theory is only one resource to be used to hear the call to peacemaking.

The pastoral is not merely an updated attempt to spell out the implications of the just-war theory for the present arms race, even though that is part of what is being attempted. But, more profoundly, it is an attempt to spell out more specifically what is entailed in following Christ, the peacemaker. It is an attempt to spell out the call coming to us "from Jesus Christ himself." The spiraling violence, seen especially in the arms race, is the occasion for the letter and the dismantling of these weapons of destruction is undoubtedly one consummation devoutly to be pursued. But if that is all that is entailed, few will respond since, even with the pastoral's help, most will feel an inability to comprehend the complex issues or will be overwhelmed by their sense of impotence before they even begin. For those few who will feel an ability to respond but who reduce vocation to this particular task, they will almost certainly focus largely on tactics and strategies keyed to the elimination of weapons if they concur with the bishops' evaluation of them. In the pastoral, the religious means recommended by the bishops require a fuller treatment than they have received here. There needs to be a clearer link between the philosophical elements and those which are religious. Without this link and understanding of the vocational nature of Christian peacemaking, the pastoral and its subject may become an occasion for much hostility and division.

Call to Peace

What will save us from such a development is a new appreciation of the saving act which has reconciled the world to God in Christ. It is the character of this act which is foundational to all our peacemaking. Wherever Christ's reconciling power is being received, the call to peace-making is being issued. That call begins in the daily, hourly experience of hostility or resentment or any of the negative emotions. It takes active faith for Christ to become and continue as our peace. Since we are always capable of losing this, his continual winning of his place in our hearts is where the vocation to peacemaking is renewed. He must be received as our peace in order for us to be ministers of reconciliation in our culture. The power of his reconciling action must be done to be known. The Soviet Union is only one of many walls we have allowed to be erected. There are many closer to home, starting with those in our own homes and communities. The means for this disarmament of the human heart and human relationships are many. Since it is unlikely that any of us will be called to Geneva to negotiate an arms accord, it would be better to begin now with the walls that are closer, those in us and between us. We can do this with confidence since the power we are relying on to penetrate them is immeasurable in its scope (Eph. 1:19).

NOTES

1. *The Challenge of Peace: God's Promise and Our Response*, # 284.
2. Ibid., # 276.
3. Ibid.
4. Ibid.
5. Ibid.
6. Ibid., # 277.
7. Ibid.
8. Ibid., Conclusion, # 333.
9. Ibid.
10. Ibid., # 290.
11. Ibid., # 294.
12. Ibid.
13. Ibid., # 295.
14. Ibid.
15. Ibid., # 276.
16. Ibid., # 298.
17. Ibid., # 29.
18. Ibid., # 34.
19. Ibid., Conclusion, # 339.

20. Ibid., # 49.
21. Ibid., # 54.
22. Ibid., # 248.
23. Ibid., #s 251-53.
24. Ibid., # 258.
25. Ibid.
26. Ibid., # 254.
27. Ibid., # 29.
28. Ibid., # 55.
29. Ibid., # 14.

HARRY A. FAGAN

Pastoral Possibilities:

Conscience Formation, Education, and Conflict Resolution

The U.S. bishops in their pastoral letter *The Challenge of Peace* are saying that the decisions about nuclear weapons are among the most pressing moral questions of our age. And while these decisions have obvious military and political aspects, they involve fundamental moral choices. In simple terms, the bishops' position is that good ends (defending one's country, protecting freedom, etc.) cannot justify immoral means (the use of weapons which kill indiscriminately and threaten whole societies). The bishops fear that our world and nation are headed in the wrong direction. They warn that more weapons with greater destructive potential are produced every day and that more and more nations are seeking to become nuclear powers. Consequently, in our quest for more and more security, they fear that we are actually becoming less and less secure and less and less able to act in a morally acceptable way.

Reasonable
Frankly, when people finally get a chance to sit down and read the bishops' pastoral in the calm of their own living rooms, their first reaction will probably be surprise at its overall reasonableness. After all the sensationalized "one liners" highlighted by the national media, people will probably have expected a much more radical document.

Granted, the mere fact that Catholic bishops are addressing the complex topics of nuclear weaponry and our national defense is provocative and seems a bit unusual, but as one reads the pastoral two points of reality begin to creep into one's consciousness. First, if people have even casually kept up with what has been written and said by popes, councils, bishops, and theologians since Vatican II, they will quickly realize that there is actually very little in this document that breaks new ground or sails naively into uncharted waters, as so many have claimed.

The second point of reality that becomes clear in pondering the words of the pastoral is that these opinions and feelings have been voiced before, but in much more traditional and everyday places. Beyond the boundaries of stereotypical conservative and liberal positions, most people have heard the pastoral's worries and cautions about war and the nuclear age expressed openly by very solid people who gather and talk at meetings in church basements, at the corner tavern, over lunch with fellow workers, or around the coffee pot in various neighborhood settings.

We begin to get the sense that 238 U.S. Catholic bishops (a group not known for its radicalism) voted for this pastoral, in part, to help articulate a national mood and a set of legitimate feelings held by many men and women in this country. The bishops have indeed furthered the national debate by clarifying the issues and offering very concrete suggestions that they believe will hold up under scrutiny. Their specific contribution, of course, is that they provide a *moral* framework for thinking about and discussing these issues.

Personal Choices
However, the reasonableness of the pastoral begins to be eclipsed as one grasps and starts to grapple with its stated and underlying intention. For the bishops have somewhat broken precedent and declared quite clearly that this pastoral is not entirely church doctrine demanding obedience. It is, rather, their invitation to all people to consider historical church teachings and basic moral principles as they form their own individual consciences about the application of these principles to the serious choices before them concerning war in the nuclear age. In their legitimate and traditional teaching role, the bishops have offered us a pastoral letter which is appropriately named and probably best described as *The Challenge of Peace*. They have interpreted the Gospel as a challenge for us to live our lives in a new way, a new way for us to think about peace and a new way for us to act for peace.

They have, in other words, presented a challenge to all people to form their own consciences regarding peace. This is different from simply making up our minds, for the argument of the pastoral is that a specifically moral aspect must be considered and is necessary regarding these matters. And a moral aspect means as much a way of acting as a way of thinking. Furthermore, we have come to realize that with many moral questions people are as likely to act their way into a new way of thinking as they are to think their way into a new way of acting. The bishops, in fact, seem to recognize this when they call for new ways of acting in the Christian community. We avoid, then, abstract notions of promoting peace by accentuating the available pastoral processes by which people can be helped to focus on the practical ways that they actually develop their opinions and act as peacemakers.

From Rhetoric to Action

> To be a Christian, according to the New Testament, is not simply to believe with one's mind, but also to become a doer of the word, a wayfarer with and a witness to Jesus. (*The Challenge of Peace,* # 276)

The pastoral has explicitly posed very tough questions to each of us. The bishops have moved the conversation about peace from a traditional but "fuzzy" longing we have been reading on banners for years to a much more substantive dialogue with specific choices and decisions for each of us.

This is not the first challenge for us to rethink what it means to be a contemporary Catholic. Our understanding of and commitment to Jesus Christ have been challenged a number of times since Vatican II, through such documents as Pope John XXIII's *Pacem in Terris* and *Mater et Magistra* or Pope Paul VI's encyclical "On the Development of Peoples" (*Populorum Progressio*), all dealing with the economic, social, and military policies of nations. Pope John Paul II's encyclical "On Human Work" has raised some serious challenges to the world of business and employment. And the U.S. bishops have spoken out frequently concerning such matters as: racism, capital punishment, gun control, the right to decent housing, welfare reform, health care, and the rights of the poor. We have had statements time after time that challenge us regarding our obligation to protect and promote the dignity of every person. Admittedly, few of these statements have been given the publicity and attention that has been accorded this pastoral on war and peace.

Yet, in spite of all these statements and express actions by the bishops to bring their views to bear on public policy, I think we must make two admissions. First, we have not been able to unify and distinguish ourselves as a church known specifically in this country for our courageous caring for people. And second, where we have been closely identified with issues, such as opposition to abortion or support for school aid, we have not been able to advance our cause very successfully.

I think these two phenomena are related. With regard to the impact of Catholics' perceived priorities on public policy, we must admit that, although Catholics constitute about 25 percent of the nation's population and Catholic leadership has publicly committed great resources to oppose abortion and acquire public aid for parochial schools, this leadership has not been able to speak with confidence that "all" Catholics will be united around these positions. Clearly, the issues involved are of great significance. Consider, for example, the fact that a city like Washington, D.C., records more abortions than live births and it is hard to avoid the conclusion that the matter is out of hand. Or reflect for a moment on the fact that our Catholic schools have become means for black and brown children in large urban centers to acquire the education necessary for them to become productive members of society, and one realizes that parochial schools are not exactly a parochial concern. But the main point is that we could not and did not "deliver" on a couple of issues that we had announced in various ways as priorities. The matter of a distinctive Catholic profile on issues of justice and the linkage between this and our capacity to influence public policy come together in what I regard as three important factors or problems that need to be solved before taking another plunge into rhetoric about making this pastoral on peace operative with present Catholics. The three factors are:

1. We did not deal with the tensions within the Catholic community.
2. We did not consider the development of our people a high enough priority.
3. We have not thought that building a unified constituency with the power to affect public policy was one of the clearest ways to promote the Gospel plea to protect the God-given dignity of every person.

Each of these factors, tensions within the Catholic community, development of people, and the formation of an active constituency should be carefully scrutinized. The past offers us a context for such consideration and provides some insight into how we can make the pastoral an occasion for greater growth in our church and more effective impact on public policy.

Dealing with Tensions

The church's overall vision of unity, of our being a covenant people who are one in the Lord, is certainly central to our theology and our sense of church. It is currently popular to celebrate our diversity, a diversity we have well nurtured (with some hesitation, we pride ourselves on being a church that offers daily communion to the Gallo brothers and to Cesar Chavez). Yet, there is no controversy about our basic unity in the family of God. In fact, much of the past history of the church in this country, often referred to as the "immigrant" church, has fostered a great sense of solidarity.

However, we cannot hide the tensions within the Catholic community and we must anticipate that many will disagree with the conclusions and even the intent of the pastoral. Our ideals of unity must be seen in the context of potential divisiveness. And, in fact, there have already arisen among us some serious divisions regarding matters of justice. The 1971 Synod of Bishops had declared that "Action on behalf of justice . . . is a constitutive part of the preaching of the Gospel." If such action is constitutive, then it is literally impossible to have an authentic Catholic parish without such action. We could not have a parish with a liturgy committee but no social concerns committee, or a spiritual renewal program which did not give serious attention to the needs of the poor, the elderly, the handicapped, or other people suffering from want or injustice.

What has happened frequently, however, was the emergence of two "churches"—what we can call an A church and a B church. The A church was perceived to be ideologically on the right and focused its spiritual renewal efforts on a personalized relationship with Jesus, giving little attention to the social mission of the church, to the protection and promotion of the dignity of the poor in our midst. The B church, probably still smarting from the tumultuous sixties, was perceived to be ideologically on the left, with much attention to peace and justice activity, often claiming a kind of prophetic style, but with very little attention to the sacramentality of the church. The A and B churches were allowed to grow and coexist in dioceses while being isolated from each other and, in most cases, were uprooted from parishes.

The theology of unity has, in many ways, given way to basic division along standard ideological, political, and economic lines. As Catholics lost the feeling of being embattled minorities with clear enemies, unity gave way to these basic and timeworn divisions. Further, there is almost no chance to rekindle the past blind loyalty to the institutional church in this post–*Humanae Vitae*, voluntary church, where everything from Mass attendance to birth control seems to be openly regarded as optional in the attitudes and behaviors of Catholics. Consequently, we must both face the tensions within the Catholic community, recognizing that these tensions could be aggravated by the pastoral, and look within ourselves for the means of unity, cohesion, and motivation, rather than look elsewhere for such direction.

We have to look within the life and words of Jesus and begin to speak openly about conversion. Yet, the conversion we seek is not a conversion to private testimony but one that leads to public action. The action we take, which can both express and deepen our commitments of conscience, must find their roots in both the warmth of Jesus in Galilee and the fire of Jesus in Jerusalem: in his healing, preaching, teaching, caring in Galilee, and his strength and outspoken challenge in Jerusalem. We will, in fact, miss the point of the pastoral if we allow it to be discussed in traditional liberal/conservative terms, which is already happening. Rather, we must struggle to help people deal with the pastoral in gospel/strategy terms, for example, in terms of the importance of faith and its relevance to our discussion of strategy, as well as its promotion of a particular Catholic identity in our country.

Part of the challenge of the pastoral is its specificity. There is a certain logic to the argument that, for the sake of unity, the bishops should treat problems in a general way and not focus on specific issues or on particular solutions or actions regarding these issues. There would be little controversy if bishops were to speak out on the importance of employment to family life, viable neighborhoods, or peace. It is when they translate their concerns into positions on plant closings, bank and insurance company red-lining of neighborhoods, or specific elements of our defense policy that controversy arises.

A church seeking tranquility will settle for general pronouncements. A church committed to truth and challenge will be specific. This specificity is essential to building a church that will thrive in the future. Not only will the youth of our day move away faster from a "safe" church that avoids the challenge of being specific, but Catholics in their thirties and forties also yearn to belong to a church that calls them to be prayerful, to be different, to be strong, and identifiably unique.

They do not want to settle into the typical morass of today's lifestyles.

There is no denying the challenge of the specific, the demands of the pastoral. I suggest that we face the challenge and confront the tensions within the church in a number of ways.

First, we must locate the pastoral in a spirituality. Our approach to the pastoral should be related to the tensions between sin and grace in our lives. People need to be able to see that sin presents an opportunity for grace. A theology that avoids the darkness in the world will reduce the church to nice people singing sentimental songs, sending up balloons with trite messages, and, in general, reducing our solid traditions to wishy-washy slogans. We need to be reminded that we cannot get to the glory of the Resurrection without going through the darkness and pain of the Crucifixion. We need to see the cross as a reminder to grow deeper in our understanding of what it means to be tested and found worthy.

Perhaps we need to recover an awareness that life is not simply a matter of nice opinions and easy alternatives. Sin exists, negatives abound; central to our faith is an attitude, a deep sense of hope, a conviction that it is possible to turn negatives into positives, sinfulness into grace, the Crucifixion into the Resurrection, with the power of God that we share.

There is, in short, no strategy regarding the pastoral that can be effective without a clear spirituality. Fundamental to any effort to face the tensions within the church and the controversy around the pastoral will be our starting where the pastoral starts with careful, personal reflection on the wisdom of God that appears to be foolishness to most of the world.

Second, our facing the tensions within the church and the potential divisiveness of the pastoral requires that we be able to face and handle the predictable conflicts. To the extent that we can regard tension and conflict as opportunities for growth, the pastoral can be regarded as a "teachable moment," an occasion for growth in the church. Typically, seminaries, novitiates, and training programs for lay leadership are devoid of any effort to prepare people for managing and resolving conflict. The ideal of harmony is so much a part of our images and feelings regarding the church that we are reluctant to prepare ministers to be comfortable with and to handle conflict. In fact, the degree to which we understand conflict and our own particular leadership role regarding it will clearly correspond with our effectiveness as a church that chooses to dialogue, to relate faith to the concrete realities of life, to urge people to form their consciences. A spirituality that is specific depends on a pastoral style that does not run away from conflict or tension. A few basic rules or guides regarding conflict should be recalled.

Both conflict resolution and conscience formation involve honest dialogue and real listening. We cannot seriously help people to form their consciences without observing basic rules of communication; we must enter into conversation with people. This is essential to the resolution of any conflict. Pastoral leaders, priests, discussion leaders, adult education directors, will be successful in helping people to grasp what the bishops are saying to the extent that they take the time and make the effort to hear what people are saying. If people are having difficulty with a principle or its application, is their dispute intellectual, is it emotional, is it a matter of faulty information, or is it an expression of some other deeper concern? It has been said that the best preacher is the one who is the best listener. Whether in preaching, teaching, individual counseling, or group discussion, pastoral leaders will be able to help people confront the challenge of the pastoral and to cope with the conflicts that will arise to the extent that they are prepared to listen to every person carefully. Conflict resolution places the burden on the listener to immediately convey a sense of empathy with or understanding of what the other person is saying in order for communication to begin.

Further, in the disputes and conflicts that can arise among participants in any discussion, it will be important to be able to distinguish among the three types of conflict identified by social psychologist Anatol Rappaport: games, debates, and fights. A game occurs when people are simply interested in the challenging competition of ideas. They are arguing for argument's sake. The key points of a game are the way success is measured and the cooperation of a good opponent. A debate occurs when people are truly trying to persuade each other. Truth and accuracy regarding information and judgments are at stake. A fight is in progress when people are trying to "destroy" each other physically or emotionally. No longer is their interest in the issue or the challenge of ideas. Clearly, it is the debate that we want to encourage—the engagement with the issues and ideas, information and judgments. Pastoral leaders will need to be able to move beyond games and away from fights. A game is unproductive conflict, a fight destructive conflict, a debate can be useful conflict if it is sincerely perceived as an effort to get at the truth.

A final factor regarding internal tensions, and obviously related to the other two, is the matter of leadership. For, skills and competence aside, it is our understanding and style of leadership that will eventually produce a meaningful dialogue on these very difficult social issues.

In relation to the peace pastoral the stance of the recognized leadership in our church (priests, religious, and lay) will be most critical. If dialogue within and through tensions is our goal, then the single most harmful posture will be one of defensiveness. While this is a very individual decision, I suggest that every pastoral leader should be able to form his or her own individual conscience regarding the issues raised in the pastoral without being particularly threatened or annoyed by any differing opinion. This calm openness will demonstrate a Christian style and call others to a similar posture.

Development of People
The peace pastoral is not only an opportunity to deal with our internal tensions, but quite significantly it presents us with the means to achieve the development of our people. And I suggest that we must use the very real problems or tensions—and specifically (but not only) the issues raised in the peace pastoral—which daily confront each of us as the arena in which we develop and empower all the people in our church, or drastically adjust our mission. In my opinion, the pastoral offers us the choice of development of our people or serious division in our church.

The development of people that I am pleading for is an evolving, unfolding, maturing, training, growing, reminding formation process that rekindles in us the very best of our Catholic and American traditions. It is a process that helps us understand better the "meaning" of our lives and nurtures in us a belief that we are responsible for our time and have the capacity to do something about it. It is a process that focuses our lives on and connects them to God and to each other, and to each other's rights and problems. This development of our people must therefore include a practical spirituality, a realistic social analysis, and a set of skills that will promote a deep-seated conviction that our church's integrity is concretized when we collectively act for peace and the protection of everyone's God-given dignity.

Adult education, approached properly, must become a reality in every diocese with programs in every parish, if implementation of the pastoral and the developement of people is to be a priority of our church. Understandably, the notion of adult education as a fresh solution creates little enthusiasm. Especially is this so if we consider the study of parish life done by the University of Note Dame in 1982: it found that while two-thirds of all Catholic parishes had some kind of religious adult education programming, the median number of parishioners attending was only 16. From any slant, those numbers indicate that about 6,000 parishes are doing absolutely nothing about adult education, another 6,000 are so ineffective in their programming they attract something less than 16 parishioners, and worse yet, it is easy to conclude that only about 1 percent of our total U.S. Catholic church is attending any real religious education conducted in parishes. It has often been said that Jesus taught adults and played with children. Somehow, for a number of generations, the church seems to be doing exactly the opposite.

Specifically, in order for the pastoral to have an impact on the lives of the majority of Catholics in our country, every diocese and every parish will need to decide whether it wishes to *maneuver carefully to avoid*, or *participate in cautiously*, or *promote enthusiastically* an adult education process which will generate a true dialogue on peace. The specific stance of every diocese and parish will be obvious and will determine whether the full range of diocesan or parish resources will be integrated and utilized to allow the pastoral to become an opportunity for people development.

Consequently, our church's adult education programming must be reexamined and reconstructed. This new thrust in adult education will have to be well planned in order to create an opportunity for people to acquire the spiritual grounding they seek and the skills they need to deal with the real issues they face in everyday living. Who participates in adult education? How do they participate? What are the issues and what is the content? Who presents it and how is it presented? What is the purpose? How is this education integrated into the total life of the parish? How will it develop and unify people rather than manipulate or further divide them? These are all important questions that should be thoroughly discussed and carefully decided.

Adult education program participants should be a mixed audience of old and young, men and women, white and people of color, and, most importantly, of priest, lay, and religious. There is no special message for any one segment of the church, and if we want to develop a unified people, then we all need to grow together—especially in our understanding of each other's needs and dreams. While there will always, and should always be educational occasions just for priests, or for religious, or for lawyers, or for whomever, to insure psychological support of peers and spiritual or ministry development around the specialized functions of each, the essential information and strategies about the social mission of the church, and particularly this peace pastoral, most probably will be lived out and acted on in the parish. Effective parish activity depends on the well coordinated action of priests, religious, and lay people all working together.

The content of adult education programming should "hold up" as objective and primarily explanatory. While the trap of inflammatory rhetoric and accusatory "finger pointing" seems so prevalant today, it would be helpful if the parish audience was analyzed carefully and educational information was produced that people could hear and use. Let us, for example, assume that 5 percent of the parish or diocese is extremely liberal and 5 percent is extremely conservative, with the remaining 90 percent somewhere in the middle and relatively confused about all the heat created by those two opposite extremes. Nothing an educational program could say will be urgent enough or relevant enough to appease these liberals; nothing it could say will maintain the status quo enough or be balanced enough to appeal to these conservatives. Therefore, I suggest we forget the more strident liberals and conservatives and gear the main thrust of education efforts toward the concerned, blasé, or slightly confused 90 percent in the middle who are anxiously awaiting an unbiased, easily understood explanation of how and why the church ever got itself embroiled in all these peace and social action controversies in the first place.

Today's Catholics have demonstrated a healthy desire to connect a spiritual dimension to the realities of their everyday lives. Adult education programming should help people who have grown up with a sense only of the "institutional church" to be introduced to the spirit of the Gospels. This will require a gentle but firm introduction to and immersion in scriptual reflection and prayerful style as integral components of any educational or developmental process. There is plenty of spiritual room in which to operate between the two poles of fundamentalism and secularism. By connecting our faith and traditions to the concrete social issues of our day and the specifics of the peace pastoral, we will begin to develop a workable, usable, and practical spirituality that will nourish people through all the current tension and confusion. Undoubtedly, for many Catholics the most comfortable connection of social issues to this new spirituality could occur during weekend liturgies. Special attention should be given to well-coordinated liturgies with well-prepared challenging homilies which could encourage attendance at adult education programs and an openness to the topics. Special vigils and prayer services focused on peace could also help to connect our spiritual customs with current social issues. But nothing will appear more hollow than an educational approach in a parish that is contradicted in Sunday's sermon or negated by a pronouncement of the parish council. We must strive for consistency in our liturgies, apostolates, fund raising, recreational activities, and other education programs within the parish and throughout the diocese.

The content of adult education must be planned to be developmental rather than theoretical. Highlighting the principles or the ideals of the peace pastoral without being specific about the attitudinal and behavioral changes necessary to accomplish peace, and how each person begins that individual process, will only add to the immobilization of people and further promote the "paralysis by analysis" syndrome. Development through education means that concrete skills to work effectively on specific "real life" issues should be discussed, made an object of training, practiced extensively, and evaluated. Also the development of the pastoral leader's "enabling-of-others" or training skills must become a much clearer priority if these adult education programs are to be successful. Pastoral leaders must learn and practice how to pass on the leadership skills of recruitment, running good meetings, researching issues, public speaking, designing effective strategies, gathering resources, creating quality parish programs on other issues, and forming working coalitions around these topics or issues. These skills must be taught to all those who are responsible for adult education. Quite simply, if pastoral leaders have to organize the second peace adult education program, or the second community service project in the parish, or again design next year's peace liturgy or prayer vigil, then they must have done something wrong the first time. The people they worked with the first time should have learned how it was done and be ready and anxious to practice those new skills, with the pastoral leader only having to serve as a friendly consultant. Adult education should not create dependency, but rather be focused on the empowering of others to think and act for themselves.

A style or process of listening as well as informing will have to be an integral part of every adult education program. Lectures, readings, scripture, films, and various visual-type presentations should be used as stimulants to instigate and guide the participant's discussion. Not only does the church need to hear from people about what they think of the peace pastoral's message, and which other social issues interest them the most, but we should also recall that adults usually learn and internalize new information much better when they have an opportunity to discuss, test, and determine for themselves how the issues relate to their own personal experiences.

The process of adult education must be designed to lead to action. For if the process is really developmental, people will need to test the new information, practice their new skills, and, in general, become comfortable with putting their faith into action. One of the most important facets of an education-leading-to-action process is the clearness of the invitation for participants to become involved in a specific parish or community activity as an integral part of the educational program. A well-structured, diocese or parish supported, follow-up action strategy might include these options:

1. An invitation to continue to grow in both their understanding of the peace pastoral's issues and their own spirituality by forming a new, or joining an existing, Parish Social Concerns group. These groups could encourage others in the parish to become involved in the peace discussions and collectively explore appropriate community activities.
2. An invitation to volunteer and participate in a worthwhile social service program which is ministering to needy people in the parish or community.
3. An invitation to become involved in a specific advocacy effort attempting to change an institutional policy or practice which would promote peace and alleviate pressure on poor people.
4. An invitation to join in the legislative processes of our country by forming voter registration projects or creating well-organized legislative information networks in the parish and throughout the diocese.
5. An invitation to explore new ways for people and families to live as peacemakers, along the lines of Jim and Kathy McGinnis's Institute for Peace and Justice in St. Louis, which connects prayer, action, and reflection with everyday family life.

All five action options should be offered as a part of every diocesan or parish adult education program. Two additional action options, more national in scope, could also be considered. Actually, both these activities or programs have existed for more than a decade, but their relevance right now to the peace pastoral is striking. The Campaign for Human Development (CHD) is the Catholic church's main way to address the problems and solutions of poverty in the United States. Every diocese and parish conducting adult education programs on the peace pastoral would do well to coordinate their efforts and highlight CHD's educational approach and give special attention to its annual fall collection. There also exists in Washington a staff of women religious who have organized a national educational and lobbying effort called NETWORK. This organization researches the issues, is politically savvy, and has demonstrated a capacity to deal effectively with public policy matters. In addition to offering NETWORK financial support, every diocese and parish should consider ways to participate appropriately in such national legislative efforts.

To summarize, if we are to develop people, develop our church rather than divide it over this peace pastoral, then we must rethink our adult education programming. We must eliminate the segregation of priests, religious, and lay people in our educational gatherings. We must offer education about the very real issues that are currently pushing families and people to the wall. We must develop people with the specific skills training that they need to deal effectively with these issues, and we must be prepared as a church to support them in their direct actions on these issues. A new mix, with new and meaningful issues, with a new sense of empowerment training, deliverability, and action.

Constituency Development

The dimensions of our faith which require us to promote peace and protect everyone's God-given dignity demand the building of a unified constituency with the power to affect public policy. For peace and dignity are matters of public policy.

The unprecedented consultative process of the U.S. bishops as they drafted the pastoral has successfully demonstrated that the church has both the capacity and the ability to determine priorities, secure professional expertise, integrate various religious and political philosophies, listen and respond to people's concerns, and make a unique contribution to the debates and decisions on public policy.

Now, the church must have a plan in this regard with a long-range view. If we were to focus on racism one year, evangelization the next, family ministry the next, peace the next, and the capitalist economy the next, then we will have no focus at all. We should have clear and well-thought-out goals and objectives, with definite and measurable timelines and realistic expectations of making a difference. Certainly, the living of our faith and the promotion of our values deserve more focused attention than our backing into an issue and being somewhat surprised when we happen to be effective.

While membership and participation in the Catholic church within the United States will remain voluntary, people will respond positively to a specific request to meet a difficult challenge which requires them to put their values into action. There is, in fact, a longing for this challenge.

Through extensive consultation and genuine listening, program or issue priorities could be achieved that would offer the church a strategical focus. This overall focusing on both a goal and its timing would encourge, indeed necessitate, the coordination and integration of all national, diocesan, and parish resources.

For the purpose of speculation (maybe as an organizer's fantasy) imagine the impact of a coordinated front that utilized the Catholic press and all the journals and periodicals, Catholic universities, all the departments of the U.S. Catholic Conference, seminaries, religious orders, national Catholic organizations and specific ministry associations, novitiates, priests' and sisters' senates, diocesan pastoral and parish councils, all the special apostolates, liturgy offices, clergy continuing education programs, social concerns groups, vocation offices, high school religious education directors, parish committees, state Catholic conferences, grade schools, senior citizen programs, and on and on and on.

The peace and justice mission of the church—meaning the way we connect God and our faith to the everyday happenings of people trying to be peacemakers while simultaneously: holding a marriage together; keeping a job or building a career; raising a healthy and happy gang of kids; making the house payment or paying the rent without having to use their little savings to cover ever-rising utility, transportation, and food costs; taking care of elderly parents; maintaining a sense of charity and justice to others in the face of a world full of violence and robbery; dealing with unscrupulous corporations; coping with politicians constantly appealing to our worst instincts; and trying to understand military minds that seem to be much too open to the unthinkable possibility of a nuclear war—is indeed a very difficult mission today.

The church must be seen as, and actually perform as, an ally of all of us who face very real everyday human conditions. Our character is not the main issue, it's the condition in which we're all trying to hold onto ourselves and what we believe in that requires the most focused attention.

Many people in diocesan agencies and parishes throughout the country have been working diligently for years to develop people and assist in their spiritual formation and productive organization so that these issues and needs can be addressed. Now is the time for those who have been working, those who have been wondering what to do, and those who have been hanging back waiting for just the "right" time to all join forces and produce a unified people that are "doers of the word, wayfarers with and witnesses to Jesus."

The peace pastoral is certainly an exciting opportunity.

The Challenge of Peace: God's Promise and Our Response

A Pastoral Letter on War and Peace

May 3, 1983
National Conference of Catholic Bishops

CONTENTS

Summary

The Second Vatican Council opened its evaluation of modern warfare with the statement: "The whole human race faces a moment of supreme crisis in its advance toward maturity." We agree with the council's assessment; the crisis of the moment is embodied in the threat which nuclear weapons pose for the world and much that we hold dear in the world. We have seen and felt the effects of the crisis of the nuclear age in the lives of people we serve. Nuclear weaponry has drastically changed the nature of warfare, and the arms race poses a threat to human life and human civilization which is without precedent.

We write this letter from the perspective of Catholic faith. Faith does not insulate us from the daily challenges of life but intensifies our desire to address them precisely in light of the gospel which has come to us in the person of the risen Christ. Through the resources of faith and reason we desire in this letter to provide hope for people in our day and direction toward a world freed of the nuclear threat.

As Catholic bishops we write this letter as an exercise of our teaching ministry. The Catholic tradition on war and peace is a long and complex one; it stretches from the Sermon on the Mount to the statements of Pope John Paul II. We wish to explore and explain the resources of the moral-religious teaching and to apply it to specific questions of our day. In doing this we realize, and we want readers of this letter to recognize, that not all statements in this letter have the same moral authority. At times we state universally binding moral principles found in the teaching of the Church; at other times the pastoral letter makes specific applications, observations and recommendations which allow for diversity of opinion on the part of those who assess the factual data of a situations differently. However, we expect, Catholics to give our moral judgments serious consideration when they are forming their own views on specific problems.

The experience of preparing this letter has manifested to us the range of strongly held opinion in the Catholic community on questions of fact and judgment concerning issues of war and peace. We urge mutual respect among individuals and groups in the Church as this letter is analyzed and discussed. Obviously, as bishops, we believe that such differences should be expressed within the framework of Catholic moral teaching. We need in the Church not only conviction and commitment but also civility and charity.

While this letter is addressed principally to the Catholic community, we want it to make a contribution to the wider public debate in our country on the dangers and dilemmas of the nuclear age. Our contribution will not be primarily technical or political, but we are convinced that there is no satisfactory answer to the human problems of the nuclear age which fails to consider the moral and religious dimensions of the questions we face.

Although we speak in our own name, as Catholic bishops of the Church in the United States, we have been conscious in the preparation of this letter of the consequences our teaching will have not only for the United States but for other nations as well. One important expression of this awareness has been the consultation we have had, by correspondence and in an important meeting held at the Vatican (January 18–19, 1983), with representatives of European bishops' conferences. This consultation with bishops of other countries, and, of course, with the Holy See, has been very helpful to us.

Catholic teaching has always understood peace in positive terms. In the words of Pope John Paul II: "Peace is not just the absence of war. . . . Like a cathedral, peace must be constructed patiently and with unshakable faith." (Coventry, England, 1982) Peace is the fruit of order. Order in human society must be shaped on the basis of respect for the transcendence of God and the unique dignity of each person, understood in terms of freedom, justice, truth and love. To avoid war in our day we must be intent on building peace in an increasingly interdependent world. In Part III of this letter we set forth a positive vision of peace and the demands such a vision makes on diplomacy, national policy, and personal choices.

While pursuing peace incessantly, it is also necessary to limit the use of force in a world comprised of nation states, faced with common problems but devoid of an adequate international political authority. Keeping the peace in the nuclear age is a moral and political imperative. In Parts I and II of this letter we set forth both the principles of Catholic teaching on war and a series of judgments, based on these principles, about concrete policies. In making these judgments we speak as moral teachers, not as technical experts.

I. SOME PRINCIPLES, NORMS AND PREMISES OF CATHOLIC TEACHING

A. On War

1. Catholic teaching begins in every case with a presumption against war and for peaceful settlement of disputes. In exceptional cases, determined by the moral principles of the just-war tradition, some uses of force are permitted.

2. Every nation has a right and duty to defend itself against unjust aggression.

3. Offensive war of any kind is not morally justifiable.

4. It is never permitted to direct nuclear or conventional weapons to "the indiscriminate destruction of whole cities or vast areas with their populations. . . ." (*Pastoral Constitution*, #80.) The intentional killing of innocent civilians or non-combatants is always wrong.

5. Even defensive response to unjust attack can cause destruction which violates the principle of proportionality, going far beyond the limits of legitimate defense. This judgment is particularly important when assessing planned use of nuclear weapons. No defensive strategy, nuclear or conventional, which exceeds the limits of proportionality is morally permissible.

B. On Deterrence

1. "In current conditions 'deterrence' based on balance, certainly not as an end in itself but as a step on the way toward a progressive disarmament, may still be judged morally acceptable. Nonetheless, in order to ensure peace, it is indispensable not to be satisfied with this minimum which is always susceptible to the real danger of explosion." (Pope John Paul II, "Message to U.N. Special Session on Disarmament," #8, June 1982.)

2. No *use* of nuclear weapons which would violate the principles of discrimination or proportionality may be *intended* in a strategy of deterrence. The moral demands of Catholic teaching require resolute willingness not to intend or to do moral evil even to save our own lives or the lives of those we love.

3. Deterrence is not an adequate strategy as a long-term basis for peace; it is a transitional strategy justifiable only in conjunction with resolute determination to pursue arms control and disarmament. We are convinced that "the fundamental principle on which our present peace depends must be replaced by another, which declares that the true and solid peace of nations consists not in equality of arms but in mutual trust alone." (Pope John XXIII, *Peace on Earth*, #113.)

C. The Arms Race and Disarmament

1. The arms race is one of the greatest curses on the human race; it is to be condemned as a danger, an act of aggression against the poor, and a folly which does not provide the security it promises. (Cf: *Pastoral Constitution*, #81, *Statement of the Holy See to the United Nations*, 1976.)

2. Negotiations must be pursued in every reasonable form possible; they should be governed by the "demand that the arms race should cease; that the stockpiles which exist in various countries should be reduced equally and simultaneously by the parties concerned; that nuclear weapons should be banned; and that a general agreement should eventually be reached about progressive disarmament and an effective method of control." (Pope John XXIII, *Peace On Earth*, #112.)

D. On Personal Conscience

1. *Military Service:* "All those who enter the military service in loyalty to their country should look upon themselves as the custodians of the security and freedom of their fellow countrymen; and when they carry out their duty properly, they are contributing to the maintenance of peace." (*Pastoral Constitution, #79.*)

2. *Conscientious Objection:* "Moreover, it seems just that laws should make humane provision for the case of conscientious objectors who refuse to carry arms, provided they accept some other form of community service." (*Pastoral Constitution, #79.*)

3. *Non-violence:* "In this same spirit we cannot but express our admiration for all who forego the use of violence to vindicate their rights and resort to other means of defense which are available to weaker parties, provided it can be done without harm to the rights and duties of others and of the community." (*Pastoral Constitution, #78.*)

4. *Citizens and Conscience:* "Once again we deem it opportune to remind our children of their duty to take an active part in public life, and to contribute towards the attainment of the common good of the entire human family as well as to that of their own political community. . . . In other words, it is necessary that human beings, in the intimacy of their own consciences, should so live and act in their temporal lives as to create a synthesis between scientific, technical and professional elements on the one hand, and spiritual values on the other." (Pope John XXIII, *Peace On Earth, #146, 150.*)

II.   MORAL PRINCIPLES AND POLICY CHOICES

As bishops in the United States, assessing the concrete circumstances of our society, we have made a number of observations and recommendations in the process of applying moral principles to specific policy choices.

A. On the Use of Nuclear Weapons

1. *Counter Population Use:* Under no circumstances may nuclear weapons or other instruments of mass slaughter be used for the purpose of destroying population centers or other predominantly civilian targets. Retaliatory action which would indiscriminately and disproportionately take many wholly innocent lives, lives of people who are in no way responsible for reckless actions of their government, must also be condemned.

2. *The Initiation of Nuclear War:* We do not perceive any situation in which the deliberate initiation of nuclear war, on however restricted a scale, can be morally justified. Non-nuclear attacks by another state must be resisted by other than nuclear means. Therefore, a serious moral obligation exists to develop non-nuclear defensive strategies as rapidly as possible. In this letter we urge

NATO to move rapidly toward the adoption of a "no first use" policy, but we recognize this will take time to implement and will require the development of an adequate alternative defense posture.

3. *Limited Nuclear War:* Our examination of the various arguments on this question makes us highly skeptical about the real meaning of "limited." One of the criteria of the just-war teaching is that there must be a reasonable hope of success in bringing about justice and peace. We must ask whether such a reasonable hope can exist once nuclear weapons have been exchanged. The burden of proof remains on those who assert that meaningful limitation is possible. In our view the first imperative is to prevent any use of nuclear weapons and we hope that leaders will resist the notion that nuclear conflict can be limited, contained or won in any traditional sense.

B. On Deterrence

In concert with the evaluation provided by Pope John Paul II, we have arrived at a strictly conditional moral acceptance of deterrence. In this letter we have outlined criteria and recommendations which indicate the meaning of conditional acceptance of deterrence policy. We cannot consider such a policy adequate as a long-term basis for peace.

C. On Promoting Peace

1. We support immediate, bilateral verifiable agreements to halt the testing, production and deployment of new nuclear weapons systems. This recommendation is not to be identified with any specific political initiative.

2. We support efforts to achieve deep cuts in the arsenals of both superpowers; efforts should concentrate first on systems which threaten the retaliatory forces of either major power.

3. We support early and successful conclusion of negotiations of a comprehensive test ban treaty.

4. We urge new efforts to prevent the spread of nuclear weapons in the world, and to control the conventional arms race, particularly the conventional arms trade.

5. We support, in an increasingly interdependent world, political and economic policies designed to protect human dignity and to promote the human rights of every person, especially the least among us. In this regard, we call for the establishment of some form of global authority adequate to the needs of the international common good.

This letter includes many judgments from the perspective of ethics, politics and strategy needed to speak concretely and correctly to the "moment of supreme crisis" identified by Vatican II. We stress again that readers should be aware, as we have been, of the distinction between our statement of moral principles and of official Church teaching and our application of these to concrete issues. We urge that special care be taken not to use passages out of context; neither should brief portions of this document be cited to support positions it does not intend to convey or which are not truly in accord with the spirit of its teaching.

In concluding this summary we respond to two key questions often asked about this pastoral letter:

Why do we address these matters fraught with such complexity, controversy and passion? We speak as pastors, not politicians. We are teachers, not technicians. We cannot avoid our responsibility to lift up the moral dimensions of the choices before our world and nation. The nuclear age is an era of moral as well as physical danger. We are the first generation since Genesis with the power to threaten the created order. We cannot remain silent in the face of such danger. Why do we address these issues? We are simply trying to live up to the call of Jesus to be peacemakers in our own time and situation.

What are we saying? Fundamentally, we are saying that the decisions about nuclear weapons are among the most pressing moral questions of our age. While these decisions have obvious military and political aspects, they involve fundamental moral choices. In simple terms, we are saying that good ends (defending one's country, protecting freedom, etc.) cannot justify immoral means (the use of weapons which kill indiscriminately and threaten whole societies). We fear that our world and nation are headed in the wrong direction. More weapons with greater destructive potential are produced every day. More and more nations are seeking to become nuclear powers. In our quest for more and more security we fear we are actually becoming less and less secure.

In the words of our Holy Father, we need a "moral about-face." The whole world must summon the moral courage and technical means to say no to nuclear conflict; no to weapons of mass destruction; no to an arms race which robs the poor and the vulnerable; and no to the moral danger of a nuclear age which places before humankind indefensible choices of constant terror or surrender. Peacemaking is not an optional commitment. It is a requirement of our faith. We are called to be peacemakers, not by some movement of the moment, but by our Lord Jesus. The content and context of our peacemaking is set not by some political agenda or ideological program, but by the teaching of his Church.

Ultimately, this letter is intended as an expression of Christian faith, affirming the confidence we have that the risen Lord remains with us precisely in moments of crisis. It is our belief in his presence and power among us which sustain us in confronting the awesome challenge of the nuclear age. We speak from faith to provide hope for all who recognize the challenge and are working to confront it with the resources of faith and reason.

To approach the nuclear issue in faith is to recognize our absolute need for prayer: we urge and invite all to unceasing prayer for peace with justice for all people. In a spirit of prayerful hope we present this message of peace.

INTRODUCTION

1.   "The whole human race faces a moment of supreme crisis in its advance toward maturity." Thus the Second Vatican Council opened its treatment of modern warfare.[1] Since the council, the dynamic of the nuclear arms race has intensified. Apprehension about nuclear war is almost tangible and visible today. As Pope John Paul II said in his message to the United Nations concerning disarmament: "Currently, the fear and preoccupation of so many groups in various parts of the world reveals that people are more frightened about what would happen if irresponsible parties unleash some nuclear war."[2]

2.   As bishops and pastors ministering in one of the major nuclear nations, we have encountered this terror in the minds and hearts of our people—indeed, we share it. We write this letter because we agree that the world is at a moment of crisis, the effects of which are evident in people's lives. It is not our intent to play on fears, however, but to speak words of hope and encouragement in time of fear. Faith does not insulate us from the challenges of life; rather, it intensifies our desire to help solve them precisely in light of the good news which has come to us in the person of Jesus, the Lord of history. From the resources of our faith we wish to provide hope and strength to all who seek a world free of the nuclear threat. Hope sustains one's capacity to live with danger without being overwhelmed by it; hope is the will to struggle against obstacles even

1. Vatican II, the *Pastoral Constitution on the Church in the Modern World* (hereafter cited: *Pastoral Constitution*), #77. Papal and conciliar texts will be referred to by title with paragraph number. Several collections of these texts exist although no single collection is comprehensive; see the following: *Peace and Disarmament: Documents of the World Council of Churches and the Roman Catholic Church* (Geneva and Rome: 1982) (hereafter cited: *Documents*, with page number); J. Gremillion, *The Gospel of Peace and Justice: Catholic Social Teaching Since Pope John* (Maryknoll, N.Y.: 1976); D. J. O'Brien and T. A. Shannon, eds., *Renewing the Earth: Catholic Documents on Peace, Justice and Liberation* (New York: 1977); A. Flannery, O.P., ed., *Vatican Council II: The Conciliar and Post Conciliar Documents* (Collegeville, Minn.: 1975); W. Abbot, ed., *The Documents of Vatican II* (New York: 1966). Both the Flannery and Abbot translations of the *Pastoral Constitution* are used in this letter.

2. John Paul II, "Message to the Second Special Session of the United Nations General Assembly Devoted to Disarmament" (June 1982) (hereafter cited: "Message U.N. Special Session 1982"), #7.

when they appear insuperable. Ultimately our hope rests in the God who gave us life, sustains the world by his power, and has called us to revere the lives of every person and all peoples.

3.   The crisis of which we speak arises from this fact: nuclear war threatens the existence of our planet; this is a more menacing threat than any the world has known. It is neither tolerable nor necessary that human beings live under this threat. But removing it will require a major effort of intelligence, courage, and faith. As Pope John Paul II said at Hiroshima: "From now on it is only through a conscious choice and through a deliberate policy that humanity can survive."[3]

4.   As Americans, citizens of the nation which was first to produce atomic weapons, which has been the only one to use them and which today is one of the handful of nations capable of decisively influencing the course of the nuclear age, we have grave human, moral and political responsibilities to see that a "conscious choice" is made to save humanity. This letter is therefore both an invitation and a challenge to Catholics in the United States to join with others in shaping the conscious choices and deliberate policies required in this "moment of supreme crisis."

3. John Paul II, "Address to Scientists and Scholars," #4, *Origins* 10 (1981):621.

I. Peace in the Modern World: Religious Perspectives and Principles

5.   The global threat of nuclear war is a central concern of the universal Church, as the words and deeds of recent popes and the Second Vatican Council vividly demonstrate. In this pastoral letter we speak as bishops of the universal Church, heirs of the religious and moral teaching on modern warfare of the last four decades. We also speak as bishops of the Church in the United States, who have both the obligation and the opportunity to share and interpret the moral and religious wisdom of the Catholic tradition by applying it to the problems of war and peace today.

6.   The nuclear threat transcends religious, cultural, and national boundaries. To confront its danger requires all the resources reason and faith can muster. This letter is a contribution to a wider common effort, meant to call Catholics and all members of our political community to dialogue and specific decisions about this awesome question.

7.   The Catholic tradition on war and peace is a long and complex one, reaching from the Sermon on the Mount to the statements of Pope John Paul II. Its development cannot be sketched in a straight line and it seldom gives a simple answer to complex questions. It speaks through many voices and has produced multiple forms of religious witness. As we locate ourselves in this tradition, seeking to draw from it and to develop it, the document which provides profound inspiration and guidance for us is the *Pastoral Constitution on the Church in the Modern World* of Vatican II, for it is based on doctrinal principles and addresses the relationship of the Church to the world with respect to the most urgent issues of our day.[4]

8.   A rule of interpretation crucial for the *Pastoral Constitution* is equally important for this pastoral letter although the authority inherent in these two documents is quite distinct. Both documents use principles of Catholic moral

---

4. The *Pastoral Constitution* is made up of two parts; yet it constitutes an organic unity. By way of explanation: the constitution is called "pastoral" because, while resting on doctrinal principles, it seeks to express the relation of the Church to the world and modern mankind. The result is that, on the one hand, a pastoral slant is present in the first part and, on the other hand, a doctrinal slant is present in the second part. *Pastoral Constitution*, note 1 above.

257

teaching and apply them to specific contemporary issues. The bishops at Vatican II opened the *Pastoral Constitution* with the following guideline on how to relate principles to concrete issues:

> In the first part, the Church develops her teaching on man, on the world which is the enveloping context of man's existence, and on man's relations to his fellow men. In Part II, the Church gives closer consideration to various aspects of modern life and human society; special consideration is given to those questions and problems which, in this general area, seem to have a greater urgency in our day. As a result, in Part II the subject matter which is viewed in the light of doctrinal principles is made up of diverse elements. Some elements have a permanent value; others, only a transitory one. Consequently, the constitution must be interpreted according to the general norms of theological interpretion. Interpreters must bear in mind—especially in Part II—the changeable circumstances which the subject matter, by its very nature, involves.[5]

9.   In this pastoral letter, too, we address many concrete questions concerning the arms race, contemporary warfare, weapons systems, and negotiating strategies. We do not intend that our treatment of each of these issues carry the same moral authority as our statement of universal moral principles and formal Church teaching. Indeed, we stress here at the beginning that not every statement in this letter has the same moral authority. At times we reassert universally binding moral principles (e.g., non-combatant immunity and proportionality). At still other times we reaffirm statements of recent popes and the teaching of Vatican II. Again, at other times we apply moral principles to specific cases.

10.   When making applications of these principles we realize—and we wish readers to recognize—that prudential judgments are involved based on specific circumstances which can change or which can be interpreted differently by people of good will (e.g., the treatment of "no first use"). However, the moral judgments that we make in specific cases, while not binding in conscience, are to be given serious attention and consideration by Catholics as they determine whether their moral judgments are consistent with the Gospel.

11.   We shall do our best to indicate, stylistically and substantively, whenever we make such applications. We believe such specific judgments are an important part of this letter, but they should be interpreted in light of another passage from the *Pastoral Constitution*:

> Often enough the Christian view of things will itself suggest some specific solution in certain circumstances. Yet it happens rather frequently, and legitimately so, that with equal sincerity some of the faithful will disagree with others on a given matter. Even against the intention of their proponents, however, solutions proposed on one side or another may be easily confused by many people with the Gospel message. Hence it is necessary for people to remember that no one is allowed in the aforementioned situations to appropriate the Church's authority for his opinion. They should always try to enlighten one another through honest discussion, preserving mutual charity and caring above all for the common good.[6]

5. Ibid.

6. Ibid., #43.

12.   This passage acknowledges that, on some complex social questions, the Church expects a certain diversity of views even though all hold the same universal moral principles. The experience of preparing this pastoral letter has shown us the range of strongly held opinion in the Catholic community on questions of war and peace. Obviously, as bishops we believe that such differences should be expressed within the framework of Catholic moral teaching. We urge mutual respect among different groups in the Church as they analyze this letter and the issues it addresses. Not only conviction and commitment are needed in the Church, but also civility and charity.

13.   The *Pastoral Constitution* calls us to bring the light of the gospel to bear upon "the signs of the times." Three signs of the times have particularly influenced the writing of this letter. The first, to quote Pope John Paul II at the United Nations, is that "the world wants peace, the world needs peace."[7] The second is the judgment of Vatican II about the arms race: "The arms race is one of the greatest curses on the human race and the harm it inflicts upon the poor is more than can be endured."[8] The third is the way in which the unique dangers and dynamics of the nuclear arms race present qualitatively new problems which must be addressed by fresh applications of traditional moral principles. In light of these three characteristics, we wish to examine Catholic teaching on peace and war.

14.   The Catholic social tradition, as exemplified in the *Pastoral Constitution* and recent papal teachings, is a mix of biblical, theological, and philosophical elements which are brought to bear upon the concrete problems of the day. The biblical vision of the world, created and sustained by God, scarred by sin, redeemed in Christ and destined for the kingdom, is at the heart of our religious heritage. This vision requires elaboration, explanation, and application in each age; the important task of theology is to penetrate ever more adequately the nature of the biblical vision of peace and relate it to a world not yet at peace. Consequently, the teaching about peace examines both how to construct a more peaceful world and how to assess the phenomenon of war.

15.   At the center of the Church's teaching on peace and at the center of all Catholic social teaching are the transcendence of God and the dignity of the human person. The human person is the clearest reflection of God's presence in the world; all of the Church's work in pursuit of both justice and peace is designed to protect and promote the dignity of every person. For each person not only reflects God, but is the expression of God's creative work and the meaning of Christ's redemptive ministry. Christians approach the problem of war and peace with fear and reverence. God is the Lord of life, and so each human life is sacred; modern warfare threatens the obliteration of human life on a previously unimaginable scale. The sense of awe and "fear of the Lord" which former generations felt in approaching these issues weighs upon us with new urgency. In the words of the *Pastoral Constitution*:

7. John Paul II, "Message U.N. Special Session 1982," #2.
8. *Pastoral Constitution*, #81.

> Men of this generation should realize that they will have to render an account
> of their warlike behavior; the destiny of generations to come depends largely
> on the decisions they make today.[9]

16.   Catholic teaching on peace and war has had two purposes: to help
Catholics form their consciences and to contribute to the public policy debate
about the morality of war. These two purposes have led Catholic teaching to
address two distinct but overlapping audiences. The first is the Catholic faithful,
formed by the premises of the gospel and the principles of Catholic moral
teaching. The second is the wider civil community, a more pluralistic audience,
in which our brothers and sisters with whom we share the name Christian,
Jews, Moslems, other religious communities, and all people of good will also
make up our polity. Since Catholic teaching has traditionally sought to address
both audiences, we intend to speak to both in this letter, recognizing that
Catholics are also members of the wider political community.
17.   The conviction, rooted in Catholic ecclesiology, that both the community
of the faithful and the civil community should be addressed on peace and war
has produced two complementary but distinct styles of teaching. The religious
community shares a specific perspective of faith and can be called to live out
its implications. The wider civil community, although it does not share the same
vision of faith, is equally bound by certain key moral principles. For all men
and women find in the depth of their consciences a law written on the human
heart by God.[10] From this law reason draws moral norms. These norms do not
exhaust the gospel vision, but they speak to critical questions affecting the
welfare of the human community, the role of states in international relations,
and the limits of acceptable action by individuals and nations on issues of war
and peace.
18.   Examples of these two styles can be found in recent Catholic teaching.
At times the emphasis is upon the problems and requirements for a just public
policy (e.g., Pope John Paul II at the U.N. Special Session 1982); at other times
the emphasis is on the specific role Christians should play (e.g., Pope John Paul
II at Coventry, England, 1982). The same difference of emphasis and orientation
can be found in Pope John XXIII's *Peace on Earth* and Vatican II's *Pastoral Constitution*.
19.   As bishops we believe that the nature of Catholic moral teaching, the
principles of Catholic ecclesiology, and the demands of our pastoral ministry
require that this letter speak both to Catholics in a specific way and to the wider
political community regarding public policy. Neither audience and neither mode
of address can be neglected when the issue has the cosmic dimensions of the
nuclear arms race.
20.   We propose, therefore, to discuss both the religious vision of peace among
peoples and nations and the problems associated with realizing this vision in

9. Ibid., #80.
10. Ibid., #16.

a world of sovereign states, devoid of any central authority and divided by ideology, geography, and competing claims. We believe the religious vision has an objective basis and is capable of progressive realization. Christ is our peace, for he has "made us both one, and has broken down the dividing wall of hostility . . . that he might create in himself one new man in place of the two, so making peace, and might reconcile us both to God" (Eph. 2:14-16). We also know that this peace will be achieved fully only in the kingdom of God. The realization of the kingdom, therefore, is a continuing work, progressively accomplished, precariously maintained, and needing constant effort to preserve the peace achieved and expand its scope in personal and political life.

21. Building peace within and among nations is the work of many individuals and institutions; it is the fruit of ideas and decisions taken in the political, cultural, economic, social, military, and legal sectors of life. We believe that the Church, as a community of faith and social institution, has a proper, necessary, and distinctive part to play in the pursuit of peace.

22. The distinctive contribution of the Church flows from her religious nature and ministry. The Church is called to be, in a unique way, the instrument of the kingdom of God in history. Since peace is one of the signs of that kingdom present in the world, the Church fulfills part of her essential mission by making the peace of the kingdom more visible in our time.

23. Because peace, like the kingdom of God itself, is both a divine gift and a human work, the Church should continually pray for the gift and share in the work. We are called to be a Church at the service of peace, precisely because peace is one manifestation of God's word and work in our midst. Recognition of the Church's responsibility to join with others in the work of peace is a major force behind the call today to develop a theology of peace. Much of the history of Catholic theology on war and peace has focused on limiting the resort to force in human affairs; this task is still necessary, and is reflected later in this pastoral letter, but it is not a sufficient response to Vatican II's challenge "to undertake a completely fresh reappraisal of war."[11]

24. A fresh reappraisal which includes a developed theology of peace will require contributions from several sectors of the Church's life: biblical studies, systematic and moral theology, ecclesiology, and the experience and insights of members of the Church who have struggled in various ways to make and keep the peace in this often violent age. This pastoral letter is more an invitation to continue the new appraisal of war and peace than a final synthesis of the results of such an appraisal. We have some sense of the characteristics of a theology of peace, but not a systematic statement of their relationships.

25. A theology of peace should ground the task of peacemaking solidly in the biblical vision of the kingdom of God, then place it centrally in the ministry of the Church. It should specify the obstacles in the way of peace, as these are understood theologically and in the social and political sciences. It should both identify the specific contributions a community of faith can make to the work

11. Ibid., #80.

of peace and relate these to the wider work of peace pursued by other groups and institutions in society. Finally, a theology of peace must include a message of hope. The vision of hope must be available to all, but one source of its content should be found in a Church at the service of peace.

26.   We offer now a first step toward a message of peace and hope. It consists of a sketch of the biblical conception of peace; a theological understanding of how peace can be pursued in a world marked by sin; a moral assessment of key issues facing us in the pursuit of peace today; and an assessment of the political and personal tasks required of all people of good will in this most crucial period of history.

A.   PEACE AND THE KINGDOM

27.   For us as believers, the sacred scriptures provide the foundation for confronting war and peace today. Any use of scripture in this area is conditioned by three factors. *First*, the term "peace" has been understood in different ways at various times and in various contexts. For example, peace can refer to an individual's sense of well-being or security, or it can mean the cessation of armed hostility, producing an atmosphere in which nations can relate to each other and settle conflicts without resorting to the use of arms. For men and women of faith, peace will imply a right relationship with God, which entails forgiveness, reconciliation, and union. Finally, the scriptures point to eschatological peace, a final, full realization of God's salvation when all creation will be made whole. Among these various meanings, the last two predominate in the scriptures and provide direction to the first two.

28.   *Second*, the scriptures as we have them today were written over a long period of time and reflect many varied historical situations, all different from our own. Our understanding of them is both complicated and enhanced by these differences, but not in any way obscured or diminished by them. *Third*, since the scriptures speak primarily of God's intervention in history, they contain no specific treatise on war and peace. Peace and war must always be seen in light of God's intervention in human affairs and our response to that intervention. Both are elements within the ongoing revelation of God's will for creation.

29.   Acknowledging this complexity, we still recognize in the scriptures a unique source of revelation, a word of God which is addressed to us as surely as it has been to all preceding generations. We call upon the spirit of God who speaks in that word and in our hearts to aid us in our listening. The sacred texts have much to say to us about the ways in which God calls us to live in union with and in fidelity to the divine will. They provide us with direction for our lives and hold out to us an object of hope, a final promise, which guides and directs our actions here and now.

1. Old Testament

30.   War and peace are significant and highly complex elements within the

multilayered accounts of the creation and development of God's people in the Old Testament.

a. War

31.   Violence and war are very much present in the history of the people of God, particularly from the Exodus period to the monarchy. God is often seen as the one who leads the Hebrews in battle, protects them from their enemies, makes them victorious over other armies (see, for example, Deut. 1:30; 20:4; Jos. 2:24; Jgs. 3:28). The metaphor of warrior carried multifaceted connotations for a people who knew themselves to be smaller and weaker than the nations which surrounded them. It also enabled them to express their conviction about God's involvement in their lives and his desire for their growth and development. This metaphor provided the people with a sense of security; they had a God who would protect them even in the face of overwhelming obstacles. It was also a call to faith and to trust; the mighty God was to be obeyed and followed. No one can deny the presence of such images in the Old Testament nor their powerful influence upon the articulation of this people's understanding of the involvement of God in their history. The warrior God was highly significant during long periods of Israel's understanding of its faith. But this image was not the only image, and it was gradually transformed, particularly after the experience of the exile, when God was no longer identified with military victory and might. Other images and other understandings of God's activity became predominant in expressing the faith of God's people.

b. Peace

32.   Several points must be taken into account in considering the image of peace in the Old Testament. First, all notions of peace must be understood in light of Israel's relation to God. Peace is always seen as a gift from God and as fruit of God's saving activity. Secondly, the individual's personal peace is not greatly stressed. The well-being and freedom from fear which result from God's love are viewed primarily as they pertain to the community and its unity and harmony. Furthermore, this unity and harmony extend to all of creation; true peace implied a restoration of the right order not just among peoples, but within all of creation. Third, while the images of war and the warrior God become less dominant as a more profound and complex understanding of God is presented in the texts, the images of peace and the demands upon the people for covenantal fidelity to true peace grow more urgent and more developed.

c. Peace and Fidelity to the Covenant

33.   If Israel obeyed God's laws, God would dwell among them. "I will walk among you and will be your God and you shall be my people" (Lv. 26:12). God would strengthen the people against those who opposed them and would give peace in the land. The description of life in these circumstances witnesses to unity among peoples and creation, to freedom from fear and to security (Lv. 26:3-16). The right relationship between the people and God was grounded in

and expressed by a covenantal union. The covenant bound the people to God in fidelity and obedience; God was also committed in the covenant, to be present with the people, to save them, to lead them to freedom. Peace is a special characteristic of this covenant; when the prophet Ezekiel looked to the establishment of the new, truer covenant, he declared that God would establish an everlasting covenant of peace with the people (Ez. 37:26).

34.   Living in covenantal fidelity with God had ramifications in the lives of the people. It was part of fidelity to care for the needy and helpless; a society living with fidelity was one marked by justice and integrity. Furthermore, covenantal fidelity demanded that Israel put its trust in God alone and look only to him for its security. When Israel tended to forget the obligations of the covenant, prophets arose to remind the people and call them to return to God. True peace is an image which they stressed.

35.   Ezekiel, who promised a covenant of peace, condemned in no uncertain terms the false prophets who said there was peace in the land while idolatry and injustice continued (Ez. 13:16). Jeremiah followed in this tradition and berated those who "healed the wounds of the people lightly" and proclaimed peace while injustice and infidelity prevailed (Jer. 6:14; 8:10-12). Jeremiah and Isaiah both condemned the leaders when, against true security, they depended upon their own strength or alliances with other nations rather than trusting in God (Is. 7:1-9; 30:1-4; Jer. 37:10). The lament of Isaiah 48:18 makes clear the connection between justice, fidelity to God's law, and peace; he cries out: "O that you had hearkened to my commandments! Then your peace would have been like a river, and your righteousness like the waves of the sea."

d. Hope for Eschatological Peace

36.   Experience made it clear to the people of God that the covenant of peace and the fullness of salvation had not been realized in their midst. War and enmity were still present, injustices thrived, sin still manifested itself. These same experiences also convinced the people of God's fidelity to a covenant which they often neglected. Because of this fidelity, God's promise of a final salvation involving all peoples and all creation and of an ultimate reign of peace became an integral part of the hope of the Old Testament. In the midst of their failures and sin, God's people strove for greater fidelity to him and closer relationship with him; they did so because, believing in the future they had been promised, they directed their lives and energies toward an eschatological vision for which they longed. Peace is an integral component of that vision.

37.   The final age, the Messianic time, is described as one in which the "Spirit is poured on us from on high." In this age, creation will be made whole, "justice will dwell in the wilderness," the effect of righteousness will be peace, and the people will "abide in a peaceful habitation and in secure dwellings and in quiet resting places" (Is. 32:15-20). There will be no need for instruments of war (Is. 2:4; Mi. 4:3),[12] God will speak directly to the people and "righteousness and

---

12. The exact opposite of this vision is presented in Joel 3:10 where the foreign nations are told that their weapons will do them no good in the face of God's coming wrath.

peace will embrace each other" (Ps. 85:10-11). A messiah will appear, a servant of God upon whom God has placed his spirit and who will faithfully bring forth justice to the nations: "He will not cry or lift up his voice, or make it heard in the street; a bruised reed he will not break and a dimly burning wick he will not quench; he will faithfully bring forth justice." (Is. 42:2-3).

38.   The Old Testament provides us with the history of a people who portrayed their God as one who intervened in their lives, who protected them and led them to freedom, often as a mighty leader in battle. They also appear as a people who longed constantly for peace. Such peace was always seen as a result of God's gift which came about in fidelity to the covenantal union. Furthermore, in the midst of their unfulfilled longing, God's people clung tenaciously to hope in the promise of an eschatological time when, in the fullness of salvation, peace and justice would embrace and all creation would be secure from harm. The people looked for a messiah, one whose coming would signal the beginning of that time. In their waiting, they heard the prophets call them to love according to the covenantal vision, to repent, and to be ready for God's reign.

2. New Testament

39.   As Christians we believe that Jesus is the messiah or Christ so long awaited. God's servant (Mt. 12:18-21), prophet and more than prophet (Jn. 4:19-26), the one in whom the fullness of God was pleased to dwell, through whom all things in heaven and on earth were reconciled to God, Jesus made peace by the blood of the cross (Col. 1:19-20). While the characteristics of the *shalom* of the Old Testament (gift from God, inclusive of all creation, grounded in salvation and covenantal fidelity, inextricably bound up with justice) are present in the New Testament traditions, all discussion of war and peace in the New Testament must be seen within the context of the unique revelation of God that is Jesus Christ and of the reign of God which Jesus proclaimed and inaugurated.

a. War
40.   There is no notion of a warrior God who will lead the people in an historical victory over its enemies in the New Testament. The only war spoken of is found in apocalyptic images of the final moments, especially as they are depicted in the Book of Revelation. Here war stands as image of the eschatological struggle between God and Satan. It is a war in which the Lamb is victorious (Rv. 17:14).

41.   Military images appear in terms of the preparedness which one must have for the coming trials (Lk. 14:31; 22:35-38). Swords appear in the New Testament as an image of division (Mt. 12:34; Heb. 4:12); they are present at the arrest of Jesus, and he rejects their use (Lk. 22:51 and parallel texts); weapons are transformed in Ephesians, when the Christians are urged to put on the whole armor of God which includes the breastplate of righteousness, the helmet of salvation, the sword of the Spirit, "having shod your feet in the equipment of the gospel of peace" (Eph. 6:10-17; cf. I Thes. 5:8-9). Soldiers, too, are present in the New Testament. They are at the crucifixion of Jesus, of course, but they

are also recipients of the baptism of John, and one centurion receives the healing of his servant (Mt. 8:5-13 and parallel texts; cf. Jn. 4:46-53).

42.   Jesus challenged everyone to recognize in him the presence of the reign of God and to give themselves over to that reign. Such a radical change of allegiance was difficult for many to accept and families found themselves divided, as if by a sword. Hence, the gospels tell us that Jesus said he came not to bring peace but rather the sword (Mt. 10:34). The peace which Jesus did not bring was the false peace which the prophets had warned against. The sword which he did bring was that of the division caused by the word of God which, like a two-edged sword, "pierces to the division of soul and spirit, of joints and marrow, and discerns the thoughts and intentions of the heart" (Heb. 4:12).

43.   All are invited into the reign of God. Faith in Jesus and trust in God's mercy are the criteria. Living in accord with the demands of the kingdom rather than those of one's specific profession is decisive.[13]

b. Jesus and Reign of God

44.   Jesus proclaimed the reign of God in his words and made it present in his actions. His words begin with a call to conversion and a proclamation of the arrival of the kingdom. "The time is fulfilled, and the kingdom of God is at hand; repent, and believe in the gospel" (Mk. 1:15, Mt. 4:17). The call to conversion was at the same time an invitation to enter God's reign. Jesus went beyond the prophets' cries for conversion when he declared that, in him, the reign of God had begun and was in fact among the people (Lk. 17:20-21; 12:32).

45.   His words, especially as they are preserved for us in the Sermon on the Mount, describe a new reality in which God's power is manifested and the longing of the people is fulfilled. In God's reign the poor are given the kingdom, the mourners are comforted, the meek inherit the earth, those hungry for righteousness are satisfied, the merciful know mercy, the pure see God, the persecuted know the kingdom, and peacemakers are called the children of God (Mt. 5:3-10).

46.   Jesus' words also depict for us the conduct of one who lives under God's reign. His words call for a new way of life which fulfills and goes beyond the law. One of the most striking characteristics of this new way is forgiveness. All who hear Jesus are repeatedly called to forgive one another, and to do so not just once, but many, many times (Mt. 6:14-15; Lk. 6:37; Mt. 18:21-22; Mk. 11:25; Lk. 11:4; 17:3-4). The forgiveness of God, which is the beginning of salvation, is manifested in communal forgiveness and mercy.

---

13. An omission in the New Testament is significant in this context. Scholars have made us aware of the presence of revolutionary groups in Israel during the time of Jesus. Barabbas, for example, was "among the rebels in prison who had committed murder in the insurrection" (Mk. 15:7). Although Jesus had come to proclaim and to bring about the true reign of God which often stood in opposition to the existing order, he makes no reference to nor does he join in any attempts such as those of the Zealots to overthrow authority by violent means. See M. Smith, "Zealots and Sicarii, Their Origins and Relations," *Harvard Theological Review* 64 (1971):1-19.

47.   Jesus also described God's reign as one in which love is an active, life-giving, inclusive force. He called for a love which went beyond family ties and bonds of friendship to reach even those who were enemies (Mt. 5:44-48; Lk. 6:27-28). Such a love does not seek revenge but rather is merciful in the face of threat and opposition (Mt. 5:39-42; Lk. 6:29-31). Disciples are to love one another as Jesus has loved them (Jn. 15:12).

48.   The words of Jesus would remain an impossible, abstract ideal were it not for two things: the actions of Jesus and his gift of the spirit. In his actions, Jesus showed the way of living in God's reign; he manifested the forgiveness which he called for when he accepted all who came to him, forgave their sins, healed them, released them from the demons who possessed them. In doing these things, he made the tender mercy of God present in a world which knew violence, oppression, and injustice. Jesus pointed out the injustices of his time and opposed those who laid burdens upon the people or defiled true worship. He acted aggressively and dramatically at times, as when he cleansed the temple of those who had made God's house into a "den of robbers" (Mt. 21:12-17 and parallel texts; Jn. 3:13-25).

49.   Most characteristic of Jesus' actions are those in which he showed his love. As he had commanded others, his love led him even to the giving of his own life to effect redemption. Jesus' message and his actions were dangerous ones in his time, and they led to his death—a cruel and viciously inflicted death, a criminal's death (Gal. 3:13). In all of his suffering, as in all of his life and ministry, Jesus refused to defend himself with force or with violence. He endured violence and cruelty so that God's love might be fully manifest and the world might be reconciled to the One from whom it had become estranged. Even at his death, Jesus cried out for forgiveness for those who were his executioners: "Father, forgive them . . ." (Lk. 23:34).

50.   The resurrection of Jesus is the sign to the world that God indeed does reign, does give life in death, and that the love of God is stronger even than death (Rom. 8:36-39).

51.   Only in light of this, the fullest demonstration of the power of God's reign, can Jesus' gift of peace—a peace which the world cannot give (Jn. 14:27)—be understood. Jesus gives that peace to his disciples, to those who had witnessed the helplessness of the crucifixion and the power of the resurrection (Jn. 20:19, 20, 26). The peace which he gives to them as he greets them as their risen Lord is the fullness of salvation. It is the reconciliation of the world and God (Rom. 5:1-2; Col. 1:20); the restoration of the unity and harmony of all creation which the Old Testament spoke of with such longing. Because the walls of hostility between God and humankind were broken down in the life and death of the true, perfect servant, union and well-being between God and the world were finally fully possible (Eph. 2:13-22; Gal. 3:28).

c. Jesus and the Community of Believers

52.   As his first gift to his followers, the risen Jesus gave his gift of peace. This gift permeated the meetings between the risen Jesus and his followers (Jn.

20:19-29). So intense was that gift and so abiding was its power that the remembrance of that gift and the daily living of it became the hallmark of the community of faith. Simultaneously, Jesus gave his spirit to those who followed him. These two personal and communal gifts are inseparable. In the spirit of Jesus the community of believers was enabled to recognize and to proclaim the savior of the world.

53.　　Gifted with Jesus' own spirit, they could recognize what God had done and know in their own lives the power of the One who creates from nothing. The early Christian communities knew that this power and the reconciliation and peace which marked it were not yet fully operative in their world. They struggled with external persecution and with interior sin, as do all people. But their experience of the spirit of God and their memory of the Christ who was with them nevertheless enabled them to look forward with unshakable confidence to the time when the fullness of God's reign would make itself known in the world. At the same time, they knew that they were called to be ministers of reconciliation (2 Cor. 5:19-20), people who would make the peace which God had established visible through the love and the unity within their own communities.

54.　　Jesus Christ, then, is our peace, and in his death-resurrection he gives God's peace to our world. In him God has indeed reconciled the world, made it one, and has manifested definitively that his will is this reconciliation, this unity between God and all peoples, and among the peoples themselves. The way to union has been opened, the covenant of peace established. The risen Lord's gift of peace is inextricably bound to the call to follow Jesus and to continue the proclamation of God's reign. Matthew's gospel (Mt. 28:16-20; cf. Lk. 24:44-53) tells us that Jesus' last words to his disciples were a sending forth and a promise: "I shall be with you all days." In the continuing presence of Jesus, disciples of all ages find the courage to follow him. To follow Jesus Christ implies continual conversion in one's own life as one seeks to act in ways which are consonant with the justice, forgiveness, and love of God's reign. Discipleship reaches out to the ends of the earth and calls for reconciliation among all peoples so that God's purpose, "a plan for the fullness of time, to unite all things in him" (Eph. 1:10), will be fulfilled.

3. Conclusion

55.　　Even a brief examination of war and peace in the scriptures makes it clear that they do not provide us with detailed answers to the specifics of the questions which we face today. They do not speak specifically of nuclear war or nuclear weapons, for these were beyond the imagination of the communities in which the scriptures were formed. The sacred texts do, however, provide us with urgent direction when we look at today's concrete realities. The fullness of eschatological peace remains before us in hope and yet the gift of peace is already ours in the reconciliation effected in Jesus Christ. These two profoundly religious meanings of peace inform and influence all other meanings for Christians. Because we have been gifted with God's peace in the risen Christ, we are called to our own peace and to the making of peace in our world. As disciples and as children of God, it is our task to seek for ways in which to make the forgiveness, justice and mercy and love of God visible in a world where violence and enmity are too often the norm. When we listen to God's word, we hear again and always the call to repentance and to belief: to repentance because although we are redeemed we continue to need redemption; to belief, because although the reign of God is near, it is still seeking its fullness.

B. KINGDOM AND HISTORY

56.   The Christian understanding of history is hopeful and confident but also sober and realistic. "Christian optimism based on the glorious cross of Christ and the outpouring of the Holy Spirit is no excuse for self-deception. For Christians, peace on earth is always a challenge because of the presence of sin in man's heart."[14] Peace must be built on the basis of justice in a world where the personal and social consequences of sin are evident.

57.   Christian hope about history is rooted in our belief in God as creator and sustainer of our existence and our conviction that the kingdom of God will come in spite of sin, human weakness, and failure. It is precisely because sin is part of history that the realization of the peace of the kingdom is never permanent or total. This is the continuing refrain from the patristic period to Pope John Paul II:

> For it was sin and hatred that were an obstacle to peace with God and with others: he destroyed them by the offering of life on the cross; he reconciled in one body those who were hostile (cf. Eph. 2:16; Rom. 12:5) . . . Although Christians put all their best energies into preventing war or stopping it, they do not deceive themselves about their ability to cause peace to triumph, nor about the effect of their efforts to this end. They therefore concern themselves with all human initiatives in favor of peace and very often take part in them. But they regard them with realism and humility. One could almost say that they relativize them in two senses: they relate them both to the self-deception of humanity and to God's saving plan.[15]

58.   Christians are called to live the tension between the vision of the reign of God and its concrete realization in history. The tension is often described in terms of "already but not yet": i.e., we already live in the grace of the kingdom, but it is not yet the completed kingdom. Hence, we are a pilgrim people in a world marked by conflict and injustice. Christ's grace is at work in the world; his command of love and his call to reconciliation are not purely future ideals but call us to obedience today.

14. John Paul II, "World Day of Peace Message 1982," #12, *Origins* 11 (1982): 477.

15. Ibid., #11-12, pp. 477-78.

59.   With Pope Paul VI and Pope John Paul II we are convinced that "peace is possible."[16] At the same time, experience convinces us that "in this world a totally and permanently peaceful human society is unfortunately a utopia, and that ideologies that hold up that prospect as easily attainable are based on hopes that cannot be realized, whatever the reason behind them."[17]

60.   This recognition—that peace is possible but never assured and that its possibility must be continually protected and preserved in the face of obstacles and attacks upon it—accounts in large measure for the complexity of Catholic teaching on warfare. In the kingdom of God, peace and justice will be fully realized. Justice is always the foundation of peace. In history, efforts to pursue both peace and justice are at times in tension, and the struggle for justice may threaten certain forms of peace.

61.   It is within this tension of kingdom and history that Catholic teaching has addressed the problem of war. Wars mark the fabric of human history, distort the life of nations today, and, in the form of nuclear weapons, threaten the destruction of the world as we know it and the civilization which has been patiently constructed over centuries. The causes of war are multiple and not easily identified. Christians will find in any violent situation the consequences of sin: not only sinful patterns of domination, oppression or aggression, but the conflict of values and interests which illustrate the limitations of a sinful world. The threat of nuclear war which affects the world today reflects such sinful patterns and conflicts.

62.   In the "already but not yet" of Christian existence, members of the Church choose different paths to move toward the realization of the kingdom in history. As we examine both the positions open to individuals for forming their consciences on war and peace and the Catholic teaching on the obligation of the state to defend society, we draw extensively on the *Pastoral Constitution* for two reasons.

63.   First, we find its treatment of the nature of peace and the avoidance of war compelling, for it represents the prayerful thinking of bishops of the entire world and calls vigorously for fresh new attitudes, while faithfully reflecting traditional Church teaching. Secondly, the council fathers were familiar with more than the horrors of World Wars I and II. They saw conflicts continuing "to produce their devastating effect day by day somewhere in the world," the increasing ferocity of warfare made possible by modern scientific weapons, guerrilla warfare "drawn out by new methods of deceit and subversion," and terrorism regarded as a new way to wage war.[18] The same phenomena mark our day.

64.   For similar reasons we draw heavily upon the popes of the nuclear age, from Pope Pius XII through Pope John Paul II. The teaching of popes and

16. John Paul II, "Message U.N. Special Session 1982," #13; Pope Paul VI, "World Day of Peace Message 1973."

17. John Paul II, "World Day of Peace Message 1982," #12, cited, p. 478.

18. *Pastoral Constitution*, #79.

councils must be incarnated by each local church in a manner understandable to its culture. This allows each local church to bring its unique insights and experience to bear on the issues shaping our world. From 1966 to the present, American bishops, individually and collectively, have issued numerous statements on the issues of peace and war, ranging from the Vietnam War to conscientious objection and the use of nuclear weapons. These statements reflect not only the concerns of the hierarchy but also the voices of our people who have increasingly expressed to us their alarm over the threat of war. In this letter we wish to continue and develop the teaching on peace and war which we have previously made, and which reflects both the teaching of the universal Church and the insights and experience of the Catholic community of the United States.

65. It is significant that explicit treatment of war and peace is reserved for the final chapter of the *Pastoral Constitution*. Only after exploring the nature and destiny of the human person does the council take up the nature of peace, which it sees not as an end in itself, but as an *indispensable condition* for the task "of constructing for all men everywhere a world more genuinely human."[19] An understanding of this task is crucial to understanding the Church's view of the moral choices open to us as Christians.

C. THE MORAL CHOICES FOR THE KINGDOM

66. In one of its most frequently quoted passages, the *Pastoral Constitution* declares that it is necessary "to undertake a completely fresh reappraisal of war."[20] The council's teaching situates this call for a "fresh reappraisal" within the context of a broad analysis of the dignity of the human person and the state of the world today. If we lose sight of this broader discussion we cannot grasp the council's wisdom. For the issue of war and peace confronts everyone with a basic question: what contributes to, and what impedes, the construction of a more genuinely human world? If we are to evaluate war with an entirely new attitude, we must be serious about approaching the human person with an entirely new attitude. The obligation for all of humanity to work toward universal respect for human rights and human dignity is a fundamental imperative of the social, economic, and political order.

67. It is clear, then, that to evaluate war with a new attitude, we must go far beyond an examination of weapons systems or military strategies. We must probe the meaning of the moral choices which are ours as Christians. In accord with the vision of Vatican II, we need to be sensitive to both the danger of war and the conditions of true freedom within which moral choices can be made.[21] Peace is the setting in which moral choice can be most effectively exercised.

19. Ibid., #77.
20. Ibid., #80.
21. Ibid., #17.

How can we move toward that peace which is indispensable for true human freedom? How do we define such peace?

1. The Nature of Peace

68. The Catholic tradition has always understood the meaning of peace in positive terms. Peace is both a gift of God and a human work. It must be constructed on the basis of central human values: truth, justice, freedom, and love. The *Pastoral Constitution* states the traditional conception of peace:

> Peace is not merely the absence of war. Nor can it be reduced solely to the maintenance of a balance of power between enemies. Nor is it brought about by dictatorship. Instead, it is rightly and appropriately called "an enterprise of justice" (Is. 32:7). Peace results from that harmony built into human society by its divine founder and actualized by men as they thirst after ever greater justice.[22]

69. Pope John Paul II has enhanced this positive conception of peace by relating it with new philosophical depth to the Church's teaching on human dignity and human rights. The relationship was articulated in his 1979 Address to the General Assembly of the United Nations and also in his "World Day of Peace Message 1982":

> Unconditional and effective respect for each one's unprescriptable and inalienable rights is the necessary condition in order that peace may reign in a society. Vis-a-vis these basic rights all others are in a way derivatory and secondary. In a society in which these rights are not protected, the very idea of universality is dead, as soon as a small group of individuals set up for their own exclusive advantage a principle of discrimination whereby the rights and even the lives of others are made dependent on the whim of the stronger.[23]

70. As we have already noted, however, the protection of human rights and the preservation of peace are tasks to be accomplished in a world marked by sin and conflict of various kinds. The Church's teaching on war and peace establishes a strong presumption against war which is binding on all; it then examines when this presumption may be overridden, precisely in the name of preserving the kind of peace which protects human dignity and human rights.

2. The Presumption against War and the Principle of Legitimate Self-Defense

71. Under the rubric, "curbing the savagery of war," the council contemplates the "melancholy state of humanity." It looks at this world as it is, not simply as we would want it to be. The view is stark: ferocious new means of warfare

22. Ibid., #78.

23. John Paul II, "World Day of Peace Message 1982," #9, cited. The *Pastoral Constitution* stresses that peace is not only the fruit of justice, but also love, which commits us to engage in "the studied practice of brotherhood" (#78).

threatening savagery surpassing that of the past, deceit, subversion, terrorism, genocide. This last crime, in particular, is vehemently condemned as horrendous, but all activities which deliberately conflict with the all-embracing principles of universal natural law, which is permanently binding, are criminal, as are all orders commanding such action. Supreme commendation is due the courage of those who openly and fearlessly resist those who issue such commands. All individuals, especially government officials and experts, are bound to honor and improve upon agreements which are "aimed at making military activity and its consequences less inhuman" and which "better and more workably lead to restraining the frightfulness of war."[24]

72.   This remains a realistic appraisal of the world today. Later in this section the council calls for us "to strain every muscle as we work for the time when all war can be completely outlawed by international consent." We are told, however, that this goal requires the establishment of some universally recognized public authority with effective power "to safeguard, on the behalf of all, security, regard for justice, and respect for rights."[25] *But what of the present?* The council is exceedingly clear, as are the popes:

> Certainly, war has not been rooted out of human affairs. As long as the danger of war remains and there is no competent and sufficiently powerful authority at the international level, governments cannot be denied the right to legitimate defense once every means of peaceful settlement has been exhausted. Therefore, government authorities and others who share public responsibility have the duty to protect the welfare of the people entrusted to their care and to conduct such grave matters soberly.
>
> But it is one thing to undertake military action for the just defense of the people, and something else again to seek the subjugation of other nations. Nor does the possession of war potential make every military or political use of it lawful. Neither does the mere fact that war has unhappily begun mean that all is fair between the warring parties.[26]

73.   The Christian has no choice but to defend peace, properly understood, against aggression. This is an inalienable obligation. It is the *how* of defending peace which offers moral options. We stress this principle again because we observe so much misunderstanding about both those who resist bearing arms and those who bear them. Great numbers from both traditions provide examples of exceptional courage, examples the world continues to need. Of the millions of men and women who have served with integrity in the armed forces, many have laid down their lives. Many others serve today throughout the world in the difficult and demanding task of helping to preserve that "peace of a sort" of which the council speaks. We see many deeply sincere individuals who, far from being indifferent or apathetic to world evils, believe strongly in conscience that they are best defending true peace by refusing to bear arms. In some cases they are motivated by their understanding of the gospel and the life and death

24. *Pastoral Constitution,* #79.

25. Ibid., #82.

26. Ibid., #79.

of Jesus as forbidding all violence. In others, their motivation is simply to give personal example of Christian forbearance as a positive, constructive approach toward loving reconciliation with enemies. In still other cases, they propose or engage in "active non-violence" as programmed resistance to thwart aggression, or to render ineffective any oppression attempted by force of arms. No government, and certainly no Christian, may simply assume that such individuals are mere pawns of conspiratorial forces or guilty of cowardice.

74.   Catholic teaching sees these two distinct moral responses as having a complementary relationship, in the sense that both seek to serve the common good. They differ in their perception of how the common good is to be defended most effectively, but both responses testify to the Christian conviction that peace must be pursued and rights defended within moral restraints and in the context of defining other basic human values.

75.   In all of this discussion of distinct choices, of course, we are referring to options open to individuals. The council and the popes have stated clearly that governments threatened by armed, unjust aggression must defend their people. This includes defense by armed force if necessary as a last resort. We shall discuss below the conditions and limits imposed on such defense. Even when speaking of individuals, however, the council is careful to preserve the fundamental *right* of defense. Some choose not to vindicate their rights by armed force and adopt other methods of defense, but they do not lose the right of defense nor may they renounce their obligations to others. They are praised by the council, as long as the rights and duties of others or of the community itself are not injured.

76.   Pope Pius XII is especially strong in his conviction about the responsibility of the Christian to resist unjust aggression:

> *A people threatened with an unjust aggression, or already its victim, may not remain passively indifferent, if it would think and act as befits a Christian.* All the more does the solidarity of the family of nations forbid others to behave as mere spectators, in any attitude of apathetic neutrality. Who will ever measure the harm already caused in the past by such indifference to war of aggression, which is quite alien to the Christian instinct? How much more keenly has it brought any advantage in recompense? On the contrary, it has only reassured and encouraged the authors and fomentors of aggression, while it obliges the several peoples, left to themselves, to increase their armaments indefinitely . . . Among (the) goods (of humanity) some are of such importance for society, that it is perfectly lawful to defend them against unjust aggression. *Their defense is even an obligation for the nations as a whole, who have a duty not to abandon a nation that is attacked.*[27]

27. Pius XII, "Christmas Message," 1948; The same theme is reiterated in Pius XII's "Message" of October 3, 1953: "The community of nations must reckon with unprincipled criminals who, in order to realize their ambitious plans, are not afraid to unleash total war. This is the reason why other countries if they wish to preserve their very existence and their most precious possessions, and unless they are prepared to accord free action to international criminals, have no alternative but to get ready for the day when they must defend themselves. *This right to be prepared for self-defense cannot be denied, even in these days, to any state.*"

77.   None of the above is to suggest, however, that armed force is the only defense against unjust aggression, regardless of circumstances. Well does the council require that grave matters concerning the protection of peoples be conducted *soberly*. The council fathers were well aware that in today's world, the "horror and perversity of war are immensely magnified by the multiplication of scientific weapons. For acts of war involving these weapons can inflict massive and indiscriminate destruction far exceeding the bounds of legitimate defense."[28] Hence, we are warned: "Men of our time must realize that they will have to give a somber reckoning for their deeds of war. For the course of the future will depend largely on the decisions they make today."[29] There must be serious and continuing study and efforts to develop programmed methods for both individuals and nations to defend against unjust aggression without using violence.

78.   We believe work to develop non-violent means of fending off aggression and resolving conflict best reflects the call of Jesus both to love and to justice. Indeed, each increase in the potential destructiveness of weapons and therefore of war serves to underline the rightness of the way that Jesus mandated to his followers. But, on the other hand, the fact of aggression, oppression and injustice in our world also serves to legitimate the resort to weapons and armed force in defense of justice. We must recognize the reality of the paradox we face as Christians living in the context of the world as it presently exists; we must continue to articulate our belief that love is possible and the only real hope for all human relations, and yet accept that force, even deadly force, is sometimes justified and that nations must provide for their defense. It is the mandate of Christians, in the face of this paradox, to strive to resolve it through an even greater commitment to Christ and his message. As Pope John Paul II said:

> Christians are aware that plans based on aggression, domination and the manipulation of others lurk in human hearts, and sometimes even secretly nourish human intentions, in spite of certain declarations or manifestations of a pacifist nature. For Christians know that in this world a totally and permanently peaceful human society is unfortunately a utopia, and that ideologies that hold up that prospect as easily attainable are based on hopes that cannot be realized, whatever the reason behind them. It is a question of a mistaken view of the human condition, a lack of application in considering the question as a whole; or it may be a case of evasion in order to calm fear, or in still other cases a matter of calculated self-interest. Christians are convinced, if only because they have learned from personal experience, that these deceptive hopes lead straight to the false peace of totalitarian regimes. But this realistic view in no way prevents Christians from working for peace; instead, it stirs up their ardor, for they also know that Christ's victory over deception, hate and death gives those in love with peace a more decisive motive for action than what the most generous theories about man have to offer; Christ's victory likewise gives a hope more surely based than any hope held out by the most audacious dreams.
>
> This is why Christians, even as they strive to resist and prevent every form of warfare, have no hesitation in recalling that, in the name of an elementary

28. *Pastoral Constitution*, #80.

29. Ibid.

requirement of justice, peoples have a right and even a duty to protect their existence and freedom by proportionate means against an unjust aggressor.[30]

79.   In light of the framework of Catholic teaching on the nature of peace, the avoidance of war, and the state's right of legitimate defense, we can now spell out certain moral principles within the Catholic tradition which provide guidance for public policy and individual choice.

3. The Just-War Criteria

80.   The moral theory of the "just-war" or "limited-war" doctrine begins with the presumption which binds all Christians: we should do no harm to our neighbors; how we treat our enemy is the key test of whether we love our neighbor; and the possibility of taking even one human life is a prospect we should consider in fear and trembling. How is it possible to move from these presumptions to the idea of a justifiable use of lethal force?

81.   Historically and theologically the clearest answer to the question is found in St. Augustine. Augustine was impressed by the fact and the consequences of sin in history—the "not yet" dimension of the kingdom. In his view war was both the result of sin and a tragic remedy for sin in the life of political societies. War arose from disordered ambitions, but it could also be used, in some cases at least, to restrain evil and protect the innocent. The classic case which illustrated his view was the use of lethal force to prevent aggression against innocent victims. Faced with the fact of attack on the innocent, the presumption that we do no harm, even to our enemy, yielded to the command of love understood as the need to restrain an enemy who would injure the innocent.

82.   The just-war argument has taken several forms in the history of Catholic theology, but this Augustinian insight is its central premise.[31] In the twentieth century, papal teaching has used the logic of Augustine and Aquinas[32] to articulate a right of self-defense for states in a decentralized international order and to state the criteria for exercising that right. The essential position was stated

30. John Paul II, "World Day of Peace Message 1982," #12, cited, p. 478.

31. Augustine called it a Manichaean heresy to assert that war is intrinsically evil and contrary to Christian charity, and stated: "War and conquest are a sad necessity in the eyes of men of principle, yet it would be still more unfortunate if wrongdoers should dominate just men." (The City of God, Book IV, C. 15)

Representative surveys of the history and theology of the just-war tradition include: F. H. Russell, The Just War in the Middle Ages (New York: 1975); P. Ramsey, War and the Christian Conscience (Durham, N.C.: 1961); P. Ramsey, The Just War: Force and Political Responsibility (New York: 1968), James T. Johnson, Ideology, Reason and the Limitation of War (Princeton: 1975), Just War Tradition and the Restraint of War: A Moral and Historical Inquiry (Princeton: 1981); L. B. Walters, Five Classic Just-War Theories (Ph.D. Dissertation, Yale University, 1971); W. O'Brien, War and/or Survival (New York: 1969), The Conduct of Just and Limited War (New York: 1981); J. C. Murray, "Remarks on the Moral Problem of War," Theological Studies 20 (1959):40-61.

32. Aquinas treats the question of war in the Summa Theologica, II-IIae, q. 40; also cf. II-IIae, q. 64.

by Vatican II: "As long as the danger of war persists and there is no international authority with the necessary competence and power, governments cannot be denied the right of lawful self-defense, once all peace efforts have failed."[33] We have already indicated the centrality of this principle for understanding Catholic teaching about the state and its duties.

83. Just-war teaching has evolved, however, as an effort to prevent war; only if war cannot be rationally avoided, does the teaching then seek to restrict and reduce its horrors. It does this by establishing a set of rigorous conditions which must be met if the decision to go to war is to be morally permissible. Such a decision, especially today, requires extraordinarily strong reasons for overriding the presumption *in favor of peace* and *against* war. This is one significant reason why valid just-war teaching makes provision for conscientious dissent. It is presumed that all sane people prefer peace, never *want* to initiate war, and accept even the most justifiable defensive war only as a sad necessity. Only the most powerful reasons may be permitted to override such objection. In the words of Pope Pius XII:

> The Christian will for peace . . . is very careful to avoid recourse to the force of arms in the defense of rights which, however legitimate, do not offset the risk of kindling a blaze with all its spiritual and material consequences.[34]

84. The determination of *when* conditions exist which allow the resort to force in spite of the strong presumption against it is made in light of *jus ad bellum* criteria. The determination of *how* even a justified resort to force must be conducted is made in light of the *jus in bello* criteria. We shall briefly explore the meaning of both.[35]

Jus ad Bellum

85. Why and when recourse to war is permissible.

86. **a) Just Cause:** War is permissible only to confront "a real and certain danger," i.e., to protect innocent life, to preserve conditions necessary for decent human existence, and to secure basic human rights. As both Pope Pius XII and Pope John XXIII made clear, if war of retribution was ever justifiable, the risks of modern war negate such a claim today.

87. **b) Competent Authority:** In the Catholic tradition the right to use force has always been joined to the common good; war must be declared by those with responsibility for public order, not by private groups or individuals.

88. The requirement that a decision to go to war must be made by competent authority is particularly important in a democratic society. It needs detailed treatment here since it involves a broad spectrum of related issues. Some of the

33. *Pastoral Constitution*, #79.

34. Pius XII, "Christmas Message," 1948.

35. For an analysis of the content and relationship of these principles cf.: R. Potter, "The Moral Logic of War," *McCormick Quarterly* 23 (1970):203-33; J. Childress, "Just War Criteria," in T. Shannon, ed., *War or Peace: The Search for New Answers* (N.Y.: 1980).

bitterest divisions of society in our own nation's history, for example, have been provoked over the question of whether or not a president of the United States has acted constitutionally and legally in involving our country in a *de facto* war, even if—indeed, especially if—war was never formally declared. Equally perplexing problems of conscience can be raised for individuals expected or legally required to go to war even though our duly elected representatives in Congress have, in fact, voted for war.

89.   The criterion of competent authority is of further importance in a day when revolutionary war has become commonplace. Historically, the just-war tradition has been open to a "just revolution" position, recognizing that an oppressive government may lose its claim to legitimacy. Insufficient analytical attention has been given to the moral issues of revolutionary warfare. The mere possession of sufficient weaponry, for example, does not legitimize the initiation of war by "insurgents" against an established government, any more than the government's systematic oppression of its people can be carried out under the doctrine of "national security."

90.   While the legitimacy of revolution in some circumstances cannot be denied, just-war teachings must be applied as rigorously to revolutionary-counterrevolutionary conflicts as to others. The issue of who constitutes competent authority and how such authority is exercised is essential.

91.   When we consider in this letter the issues of conscientious objection (C.O.) and selective conscientious objection (S.C.O.), the issue of competent authority will arise again.

92.   c) **Comparative Justice:** Questions concerning the *means* of waging war today, particularly in view of the destructive potential of weapons, have tended to override questions concerning the comparative justice of the positions of respective adversaries or enemies. In essence: which side is sufficiently "right" in a dispute, and are the values at stake critical enough to override the presumption against war? The question in its most basic form is this: do the rights and values involved justify killing? For whatever the means used, war, by definition, involves violence, destruction, suffering, and death.

93.   The category of comparative justice is designed to emphasize the presumption against war which stands at the beginning of just-war teaching. In a world of sovereign states recognizing neither a common moral authority nor a central political authority, comparative justice stresses that no state should act on the basis that it has "absolute justice" on its side. Every party to a conflict should acknowledge the limits of its "just cause" and the consequent requirement to use *only* limited means in pursuit of its objectives. Far from legitimizing a crusade mentality, comparative justice is designed to relativize absolute claims and to restrain the use of force even in a "justified" conflict.[36]

94.   Given techniques of propaganda and the ease with which nations and

36. James T. Johnson, *Ideology, Reason and the Limitation of War*, cited; W. O'Brien, *The Conduct of Just and Limited War*, cited, pp. 13-30; W. Vanderpol, *La doctrine scolastique du droit de guerre*, p. 387ff; J. C. Murray, "Theology and Modern Warfare," in W. J. Nagel, ed., *Morality and Modern Warfare*, p. 80ff.

individuals either assume or delude themselves into believing that God or right is clearly on their side, the test of comparative justice may be extremely difficult to apply. Clearly, however, this is not the case in every instance of war. Blatant aggression from without and subversion from within are often enough readily identifiable by all reasonably fair-minded people.

95.   d) **Right Intention:** Right intention is related to just cause—war can be legitimately intended only for the reasons set forth above as a just cause. During the conflict, right intention means pursuit of peace and reconciliation, including avoiding unnecessarily destructive acts or imposing unreasonable conditions (e.g., unconditional surrender).

96.   e) **Last Resort:** For resort to war to be justified, all peaceful alternatives must have been exhausted. There are formidable problems in this requirement. No international organization currently in existence has exercised sufficient internationally recognized authority to be able either to mediate effectively in most cases or to prevent conflict by the intervention of United Nations or other peacekeeping forces. Furthermore, there is a tendency for nations or peoples which perceive conflict between or among other nations as advantageous to themselves to attempt to prevent a peaceful settlement rather than advance it.

97.   We regret the apparent unwillingness of some to see in the United Nations organization the potential for world order which exists and to encourage its development. Pope Paul VI called the United Nations the last hope for peace. The loss of this hope cannot be allowed to happen. Pope John Paul II is again instructive on this point:

> I wish above all to repeat my confidence in you, the leaders and members of the International Organizations, and in you, the international officials! In the course of the last ten years, your organizations have too often been the object of attempts at manipulation on the part of nations wishing to exploit such bodies. However it remains true that the present multiplicity of violent clashes, divisions and blocks on which bilateral relations founder, offer the great International Organizations the opportunity to engage upon the qualitative change in their activities, even to reform on certain points their own structures in order to take into account new realities and to enjoy effective power.[37]

98.   f) **Probability of Success:** This is a difficult criterion to apply, but its purpose is to prevent irrational resort to force or hopeless resistance when the outcome of either will clearly be disproportionate or futile. The determination includes a recognition that at times defense of key values, even against great odds, may be a "proportionate" witness.

99.   g) **Proportionality:** In terms of the *jus ad bellum* criteria, proportionality means that the damage to be inflicted and the costs incurred by war must be proportionate to the good expected by taking up arms. Nor should judgments concerning proportionality be limited to the temporal order without regard to a spiritual dimension in terms of "damage," "cost," and "the good expected." In today's interdependent world even a local conflict can affect people every-

37. John Paul II, "World Day of Peace Message 1983," #11.

where; this is particularly the case when the nuclear powers are involved. Hence a nation cannot justly go to war today without considering the effect of its action on others and on the international community.

100.   This principle of proportionality applies throughout the conduct of the war as well as to the decision to begin warfare. During the Vietnam war our bishops' conference ultimately concluded that the conflict had reached such a level of devastation to the adversary and damage to our own society that continuing it could not be justified.[38]

Jus in Bello

101.   Even when the stringent conditions which justify resort to war are met, the conduct of war (i.e., strategy, tactics, and individual actions) remains subject to continuous scrutiny in light of two principles which have special significance today precisely because of the destructive capability of modern technological warfare. These principles are proportionality and discrimination. In discussing them here, we shall apply them to the question of *jus ad bellum* as well as *jus in bello*; for today it becomes increasingly difficult to make a decision to use any kind of armed force, however limited initially in intention and in the destructive power of the weapons employed, without facing at least the possibility of escalation to broader, or even total, war and to the use of weapons of horrendous destructive potential. This is especially the case when adversaries are "superpowers," as the council clearly envisioned:

> Indeed, if the kind of weapons now stocked in the arsenals of the great powers were to be employed to the fullest, the result would be the almost complete reciprocal slaughter of one side by the other, not to speak of the widespread devastation that would follow in the world and the deadly after-effects resulting from the use of such weapons.[39]

102.   It should not be thought, of course, that massive slaughter and destruction would result only from the extensive use of nuclear weapons. We recall with horror the carpet and incendiary bombings of World War II, the deaths of hundreds of thousands in various regions of the world through "conventional" arms, the unspeakable use of gas and other forms of chemical warfare, the destruction of homes and of crops, the utter suffering war has wrought during the centuries before and the decades since the use of the "atom bomb." Nevertheless, every honest person must recognize that, especially given the proliferation of modern scientific weapons, we now face possibilities which are appalling to contemplate. Today, as never before, we must ask not merely what *will* happen, but what *may* happen, especially if major powers embark on war. Pope John Paul II has repeatedly pleaded that world leaders confront this reality:

38. United States Catholic Conference, *Resolution on Southeast Asia* (Washington, D.C.: 1971).

39. *Pastoral Constitution*, #80.

[I]n view of the difference between classical warfare and nuclear or bacterio-logical war—a difference so to speak of nature—and in view of the scandal of the arms race seen against the background of the needs of the Third World, this right [of defense], which is very real in principle, only underlines the urgency of world society to equip itself with effective means of negotiation. In this way the nuclear terror that haunts our time can encourage us to enrich our common heritage with a very simple discovery that is within our reach, namely that war is the most barbarous and least effective way of resolving conflicts.[40]

103.   The Pontifical Academy of Sciences reaffirmed the Holy Father's theme, in its November 1981 "Statement on the Consequences of Nuclear War." Then, in a meeting convoked by the Pontifical Academy, representatives of national academies of science from throughout the world issued a "Declaration on the Prevention of Nuclear War" which specified the meaning of Pope John Paul II's statement that modern warfare differs by nature from previous forms of war. The scientists said:

> Throughout its history humanity has been confronted with war, but since 1945 the nature of warfare has changed so profoundly that the future of the human race, of generations yet unborn, is imperiled. . . . For the first time it is possible to cause damage on such a catastrophic scale as to wipe out a large part of civilization and to endanger its very survival. The large-scale use of such weapons could trigger major and irreversible ecological and genetic changes whose limits cannot be predicted.[41]

And earlier, with such thoughts plainly in mind, the council had made its own "the condemnation of total war already pronounced by recent popes."[42] This condemnation is demanded by the principles of proportionality and discrimi-nation. Response to aggression must not exceed the nature of the aggression. To destroy civilization as we know it by waging a "total war" as today it *could* be waged would be a monstrously disproportionate response to aggression on the part of any nation.

104.   Moreover, the lives of innocent persons may never be taken directly, regardless of the purpose alleged for doing so. To wage truly "total" war is by definition to take huge numbers of innocent lives. Just response to aggression must be discriminate; it must be directed against unjust aggressors, not against innocent people caught up in a war not of their making. The council therefore issued its memorable declaration:

> Any act of war aimed indiscriminately at the destruction of entire cities or of extensive areas along with their population is a crime against God and man himself. It merits unequivocal and unhesitating condemnation.[43]

40. John Paul II, "World Day of Peace Message 1982," #12, cited.

41. "Declaration on Prevention of Nuclear War" (Sept. 24, 1982).

42. *Pastoral Constitution*, #80.

43. Ibid.

105. When confronting choices among specific military options, the question asked by proportionality is: once we take into account not only the military advantages that will be achieved by using this means but also all the harms reasonably expected to follow from using it, can its use still be justified? We know, of course, that no end can justify means evil in themselves, such as the executing of hostages or the targeting of non-combatants. Nonetheless, even if the means adopted is not evil in itself, it is necessary to take into account the probable harms that will result from using it and the justice of accepting those harms. It is of utmost importance, in assessing harms and the justice of accepting them, to think about the poor and the helpless, for they are usually the ones who have the least to gain and the most to lose when war's violence touches their lives.

106. In terms of the arms race, if the *real* end in view is legitimate defense against unjust aggression, and the means to this end are not evil in themselves, we must still examine the question of proportionality concerning attendant evils. Do the exorbitant costs, the general climate of insecurity generated, the possibility of accidental detonation of highly destructive weapons, the danger of error and miscalculation that could provoke retaliation and war—do such evils or others attendant upon and indirectly deriving from the arms race make the arms race itself a disproportionate response to aggression? Pope John Paul II is very clear in his insistence that the exercise of the right and duty of a people to protect their existence and freedom is contingent on the use of proportionate means.[44]

107. Finally, another set of questions concerns the interpretation of the principle of discrimination. The principle prohibits directly intended attacks on non-combatants and non-military targets. It raises a series of questions about the term "intentional," the category of "non-combatant," and the meaning of "military."

108. These questions merit the debate occurring with increasing frequency today. We encourage such debate, for concise and definitive answers still appear to be wanting. Mobilization of forces in modern war includes not only the military, but to a significant degree the political, economic, and social sectors. It is not always easy to determine who is directly involved in a "war effort" or to what degree. Plainly, though, not even by the broadest definition can one rationally consider combatants entire classes of human beings such as schoolchildren, hospital patients, the elderly, the ill, the average industrial worker producing goods not directly related to military purposes, farmers, and many others. They may never be directly attacked.

109. Direct attacks on military targets involve similar complexities. Which targets are "military" ones and which are not? To what degree, for instance, does the use (by either revolutionaries or regular military forces) of a village or housing in a civilian populated area invite attack? What of a munitions factory in the heart of a city? Who is directly responsible for the deaths of noncombatants should the attack be carried out? To revert to the question raised earlier, how

44. John Paul II, "World Day of Peace Message 1982," #12, cited.

many deaths of non-combatants are "tolerable" as a result of indirect attacks—attacks directed against combat forces and military targets, which nevertheless kill non-combatants at the same time?

110.   These two principles, in all their complexity, must be applied to the range of weapons—conventional, nuclear, biological, and chemical—with which nations are armed today.

4. The Value of Non-violence

111.   Moved by the example of Jesus' life and by his teaching, some Christians have from the earliest days of the Church committed themselves to a non-violent lifestyle.[45] Some understood the gospel of Jesus to prohibit all killing. Some affirmed the use of prayer and other spiritual methods as means of responding to enmity and hostility.

112.   In the middle of the second century, St. Justin proclaimed to his pagan readers that Isaiah's prophecy about turning swords into ploughshares and spears into sickles had been fulfilled as a consequence of Christ's coming:

> And we who delighted in war, in the slaughter of one another, and in every other kind of iniquity have in every part of the world converted our weapons into implements of peace—our swords into ploughshares, our spears into farmers' tools—and we cultivate piety, justice, brotherly charity, faith and hope, which we derive from the Father through the crucified Savior . . .[46]

113.   Writing in the third century, St. Cyprian of Carthage struck a similar note when he indicated that the Christians of his day did not fight against their enemies. He himself regarded their conduct as proper:

> They do not even fight against those who are attacking since it is not granted to the innocent to kill even the aggressor, but promptly to deliver up their souls and blood that, since so much malice and cruelty are rampant in the world, they may more quickly withdraw from the malicious and the cruel.[47]

114.   Some of the early Christian opposition to military service was a response to the idolatrous practices which prevailed in the Roman army. Another powerful motive was the fact that army service involved preparation for fighting and

45. Representative authors in the tradition of Christian pacifism and non-violence include: R. Bainton, *Christian Attitudes Toward War and Peace* (Abington: 1960), chs. 4, 5, 10; J. Yoder, *The Politics of Jesus* (Grand Rapids: 1972), *Nevertheless: Varieties of Religious Pacifism* (Scottsdale: 1971); T. Merton, *Faith and Violence: Christian Teaching and Christian Practice* (Notre Dame: 1968); G. Zahn, *War, Conscience and Dissent* (New York: 1967); E. Egan, "The Beatitudes: Works of Mercy and Pacifism," in T. Shannon, ed., *War or Peace: The Search for New Answers* (New York: 1980), pp. 169-187; J. Fahey, "The Catholic Church and the Arms Race," *Worldview* 22 (1979):38-41; J. Douglass, *The Nonviolent Cross: A Theology of Revolution and Peace* (New York: 1966).

46. Justin, *Dialogue with Trypho*, ch. 110; cf. also *The First Apology*, chs. 14, 39.

47. Cyprian, *Collected Letters*; Letters to Cornelius.

killing. We see this in the case of St. Martin of Tours during the fourth century, who renounced his soldierly profession with the explanation: "Hitherto I have served you as a soldier. Allow me now to become a soldier of God . . . I am a soldier of Christ. It is not lawful for me to fight."[48]

115.   In the centuries between the fourth century and our own day, the theme of Christian non-violence and Christian pacifism has echoed and re-echoed, sometimes more strongly, sometimes more faintly. One of the great non-violent figures in those centuries was St. Francis of Assisi. Besides making personal efforts on behalf of reconciliation and peace, Francis stipulated that laypersons who became members of his Third Order were not "to take up lethal weapons, or bear them about, against anybody."

116.   The vision of Christian non-violence is not passive about injustice and the defense of the rights of others; it rather affirms and exemplifies what it means to resist injustice through non-violent methods.

117.   In the twentieth century, prescinding from the non-Christian witness of a Mahatma Ghandi and its worldwide impact, the nonviolent witness of such figures as Dorothy Day and Martin Luther King has had a profound impact upon the life of the Church in the United States. The witness of numerous Christians who had preceded them over the centuries was affirmed in a remarkable way at the Second Vatican Council.

118.   Two of the passages which were included in the final version of the *Pastoral Constitution* gave particular encouragement for Catholics in all walks of life to assess their attitudes toward war and military service in the light of Christian pacifism. In paragraph 79 the council fathers called upon governments to enact laws protecting the rights of those who adopted the position of conscientious objection to all war: "Moreover, it seems right that laws make humane provisions for the case of those who for reasons of conscience refuse to bear arms, provided, however, that they accept some other form of service to the human community."[49] This was the first time a call for legal protection of conscientious objection had appeared in a document of such prominence. In addition to its own profound meaning this statement took on even more significance in the light of the praise that the council fathers had given in the preceding section "to those who renounce the use of violence and the vindication of their rights."[50] In *Human Life in Our Day* (1968) we called for legislative provision to recognize selective conscientious objectors as well.[51]

119.   As Catholic bishops it is incumbent upon us to stress to our own community and to the wider society the significance of this support for a pacifist option for individuals in the teaching of Vatican II and the reaffirmation that the popes have given to nonviolent witness since the time of the council.

48. Sulpicius Severus, *The Life of Martin*, 4.3.

49. *Pastoral Constitution*, #79.

50. Ibid., #78.

51. United States Catholic Conference, *Human Life in Our Day* (Washington, D.C.: 1968), p. 44.

120.   In the development of a theology of peace and the growth of the Christian pacifist position among Catholics, these words of the *Pastoral Constitution* have special significance: "All these factors force us to undertake a completely fresh reappraisal of war."[52] The council fathers had reference to "the development of armaments by modern science (which) has immeasurably magified the horrors and wickedness of war."[53] While the just-war teaching has clearly been in possession for the past 1,500 years of Catholic thought, the "new moment" in which we find ourselves sees the just-war teaching and non-violence as distinct but interdependent methods of evaluating warfare. They diverge on some specific conclusions, but they share a common presumption against the use of force as a means of settling disputes.

121.   Both find their roots in the Christian theological tradition; each contributes to the full moral vision we need in pursuit of a human peace. We believe the two perspectives support and complement one another, each preserving the other from distortion. Finally, in an age of technological warfare, analysis from the viewpoint of non-violence and analysis from the viewpoint of the just-war teaching often converge and agree in their opposition to methods of warfare which are in fact indistinguishable from total warfare.

52. *Pastoral Constitution*, #80.
53. Ibid.

II. War and Peace in the Modern World: Problems and Principles

122.   Both the just-war teaching and non-violence are confronted with a unique challenge by nuclear warfare. This must be the starting point of any further moral reflection: nuclear weapons particularly and nuclear warfare as it is planned today, raise new moral questions. No previously conceived moral position escapes the fundamental confrontation posed by contemporary nuclear strategy. Many have noted the similarity of the statements made by eminent scientists and Vatican II's observation that we are forced today "to undertake a completely fresh reappraisal of war." The task before us is not simply to repeat what we have said before; it is first to consider anew whether and how our religious-moral tradition can assess, direct, contain, and, we hope, help to eliminate the threat posed to the human family by the nuclear arsenals of the world. Pope John Paul II captured the essence of the problem during his pilgrimage to Hiroshima:

> In the past it was possible to destroy a village, a town, a region, even a country. Now it is the whole planet that has come under threat.[54]

123.   The Holy Father's observation illustrates why the moral problem is also a religious question of the most profound significance. In the nuclear arsenals of the United States or the Soviet Union alone, there exists a capacity to do something no other age could imagine: we can threaten the entire planet.[55] For people of faith this means we read the Book of Genesis with a new awareness; the moral issue at stake in nuclear war involves the meaning of sin in its most graphic dimensions. Every sinful act is a confrontation of the creature and the creator. Today the destructive potential of the nuclear powers threatens the human person, the civilization we have slowly constructed, and even the created order itself.

124.   We live today, therefore, in the midst of a cosmic drama; we possess a power which should never be used, but which might be used if we do not reverse our direction. We live with nuclear weapons knowing we cannot afford to make one serious mistake. This fact dramatizes the precariousness of our position, politically, morally, and spiritually.

54. John Paul II, "Address to Scientists and Scholars," #4, cited, p. 621.
55. Cf. "Declaration on Prevention of Nuclear War."

125.   A prominent "sign of the times" today is a sharply increased awareness of the danger of the nuclear arms race. Such awareness has produced a public discussion about nuclear policy here and in other countries which is unprecedented in its scope and depth. What has been accepted for years with almost no question is now being subjected to the sharpest criticism. What previously had been defined as a safe and stable system of deterrence is today viewed with political and moral skepticism. Many forces are at work in this new evaluation, and we believe one of the crucial elements is the gospel vision of peace which guides our work in this pastoral letter. The nuclear age has been the theater of our existence for almost four decades; today it is being evaluated with a new perspective. For many the leaven of the gospel and the light of the Holy Spirit create the decisive dimension of this new perspective.

A.   THE NEW MOMENT

126.   At the center of the new evaluation of the nuclear arms race is a recognition of two elements: the destructive potential of nuclear weapons, and the stringent choices which the nuclear age poses for both politics and morals.

127.   The fateful passage into the nuclear age as a military reality began with the bombing of Nagasaki and Hiroshima, events described by Pope Paul VI as a "butchery of untold magnitude."[56] Since then, in spite of efforts at control and plans for disarmament (e.g., the Baruch Plan of 1946), the nuclear arsenals have escalated, particularly in the two superpowers. The qualitative superiority of these two states, however, should not overshadow the fact that four other countries possess nuclear capacity and a score of states are only steps away from becoming "nuclear nations."

128.   This nuclear escalation has been opposed sporadically and selectively but never effectively. The race has continued in spite of carefully expressed doubts by analysts and other citizens and in the face of forcefully expressed opposition by public rallies. Today the opposition to the arms race is no longer selective or sporadic, it is widespread and sustained. The danger and destructiveness of nuclear weapons are understood and resisted with new urgency and intensity. There is in the public debate today an endorsement of the position submitted by the Holy See at the United Nations in 1976: the arms race is to be condemned as a danger, an act of aggression against the poor, and a folly which does not provide the security it promises.[57]

129.   Papal teaching has consistently addressed the folly and danger of the arms race; but the new perception of it which is now held by the general public is due in large measure to the work of scientists and physicians who have

56. Paul VI, "World Day of Peace Message 1976," in *Documents*, p. 198.

57. "Statement of the Holy See to the United Nations" (1976), in *The Church and the Arms Race*; Pax Christi-USA (New York: 1976), pp. 23-24.

described for citizens the concrete human consequences of a nuclear war.[58]

130.   In a striking demonstration of his personal and pastoral concern for preventing nuclear war, Pope John Paul II commissioned a study by the Pontifical Academy of Sciences which reinforced the findings of other scientific bodies. The Holy Father had the study transmitted by personal representative to the leaders of the United States, the Soviet Union, the United Kingdom, and France, and to the president of the General Assembly of the United Nations. One of its conclusions is especially pertinent to the public debate in the United States:

> Recent talk about winning or even surviving a nuclear war must reflect a failure to appreciate a medical reality: Any nuclear war would inevitably cause death, disease and suffering of pandemonic proportions and without the possibility of effective medical intervention. That reality leads to the same conclusion physicians have reached for life-threatening epidemics throughout history. Prevention is essential for control.[59]

131.   This medical conclusion has a moral corollary. Traditionally, the Church's moral teaching sought first to prevent war and then to limit its consequences if it occurred. Today the possibilities for placing political and moral limits on nuclear war are so minimal that the moral task, like the medical, is prevention: as a people, we must refuse to legitimate the idea of nuclear war. Such a refusal will require not only new ideas and new vision, but what the gospel calls conversion of the heart.

132.   To say "no" to nuclear war is both a necessary and a complex task. We are moral teachers in a tradition which has always been prepared to relate moral principles to concrete problems. Particularly in this letter we could not be content with simply restating general moral principles or repeating well-known requirements about the ethics of war. We have had to examine, with the assistance of a broad spectrum of advisors of varying persuasions, the nature of existing and proposed weapons systems, the doctrines which govern their use, and the consequences of using them. We have consulted people who engage their lives in protest against the existing nuclear strategy of the United States, and we have consulted others who have held or do hold responsibility for this strategy. It has been a sobering and perplexing experience. In light of the evidence which witnesses presented and in light of our study, reflection, and consultation, we must reject nuclear war. But we feel obliged to relate our judgment to the specific elements which comprise the nuclear problem.

133.   Though certain that the dangerous and delicate nuclear relationship the superpowers now maintain should not exist, we understand how it came to exist. In a world of sovereign states, devoid of central authority and possessing the knowledge to produce nuclear weapons, many choices were made, some clearly objectionable, others well-intended with mixed results, which brought the world to its present dangerous situation.

58. R. Adams and S. Cullen, *The Final Epidemic: Physicians and Scientists on Nuclear War* (Chicago: 1981).

59. Pontifical Academy of Sciences, "Statement on the Consequences of the Use of Nuclear Weapons," in *Documents*, p. 241.

134.   We see with increasing clarity the political folly of a system which threatens mutual suicide, the psychological damage this does to ordinary people, especially the young, the economic distortion of priorities—billions readily spent for destructive instruments while pitched battles are waged daily in our legislatures over much smaller amounts for the homeless, the hungry, and the helpless here and abroad. But it is much less clear how we translate a "no" to nuclear war into the personal and public choices which can move us in a new direction, toward a national policy and an international system which more adequately reflect the values and vision of the kingdom of God.

135.   These tensions in our assessment of the politics and strategy of the nuclear age reflect the conflicting elements of the nuclear dilemma and the balance of terror which it has produced. We have said earlier in this letter that the fact of war reflects the existence of sin in the world. The nuclear threat and the danger it poses to human life and civilization exemplify in a qualitatively new way the perennial struggle of the political community to contain the use of force, particularly among states.

136.   Precisely because of the destructive nature of nuclear weapons, strategies have been developed which previous generations would have found unintelligible. Today military preparations are undertaken on a vast and sophisticated scale, but the declared purpose is not to use the weapons produced. Threats are made which would be suicidal to implement. The key to security is no longer only military secrets, for in some instances security may best be served by informing one's adversary publicly what weapons one has and what plans exist for their use. The presumption of the nation-state system, that sovereignty implies an ability to protect a nation's territory and population, is precisely the presumption denied by the nuclear capacities of both superpowers. In a sense each is at the mercy of the other's perception of what strategy is "rational," what kind of damage is "unacceptable," how "convincing" one side's threat is to the other.

137.   The political paradox of deterrence has also strained our moral conception. May a nation threaten what it may never do? May it possess what it may never use? Who is involved in the threat each superpower makes: government officials? or military personnel? or the citizenry in whose defense the threat is made?

138.   In brief, the danger of the situation is clear; but how to prevent the use of nuclear weapons, how to assess deterrence, and how to delineate moral responsibility in the nuclear age are less clearly seen or stated. Reflecting the complexity of the nuclear problem, our arguments in this pastoral must be detailed and nuanced; but our "no" to nuclear war must, in the end, be definitive and decisive.

B.   RELIGIOUS LEADERSHIP AND THE PUBLIC DEBATE

139.   Because prevention of nuclear war appears, from several perspectives, to be not only the surest but only way to limit its destructive potential, we see

our role as moral teachers precisely in terms of helping to form public opinion with a clear determination to resist resort to nuclear war as an instrument of national policy. If "prevention is the only cure," then there are diverse tasks to be performed in preventing what should never occur. As bishops we see a specific task defined for us in Pope John Paul II's "World Day of Peace Message 1982":

> Peace cannot be built by the power of rulers alone. Peace can be firmly constructed only if it corresponds to the resolute determination of all people of good will. Rulers must be supported and enlightened by a public opinion that encourages them or, where necessary, expresses disapproval.[60]

140.   The pope's appeal to form public opinion is not an abstract task. Especially in a democracy, public opinion can passively acquiesce in policies and strategies or it can, through a series of measures, indicate the limits beyond which a government should not proceed. The "new moment" which exists in the public debate about nuclear weapons provides a creative opportunity and a moral imperative to examine the relationship between public opinion and public policy. We believe it is necessary, for the sake of prevention, to build a barrier against the concept of nuclear war as a viable strategy for defense. There should be a clear public resistance to the rhetoric of "winnable" nuclear wars, or unrealistic expectations of "surviving" nuclear exchanges, and strategies of "protracted nuclear war." We oppose such rhetoric.

141.   We seek to encourage a public attitude which sets stringent limits on the kind of actions our own government and other governments will take on nuclear policy. We believe religious leaders have a task in concert with public officials, analysts, private organizations, and the media to set the limits beyond which our military policy should not move in word or action. Charting a moral course in a complex public policy debate involves several steps. We will address four questions, offering our reflections on them as an invitation to a public moral dialogue:

    1) the use of nuclear weapons;
    2) the policy of deterrence in principle and in practice;
    3) specific steps to reduce the danger of war;
    4) long-term measures of policy and diplomacy.

C.   THE USE OF NUCLEAR WEAPONS

142.   Establishing moral guildelines in the nuclear debate means addressing first the question of the use of nuclear weapons. That question has several dimensions.

143.   It is clear that those in the Church who interpret the gospel teaching as forbidding all use of violence would oppose any use of nuclear weapons under

60. John Paul II, "World Day of Peace Message 1982," #6, cited, p. 476.

any conditions. In a sense the existence of these weapons simply confirms and reinforces one of the initial insights of the non-violent position, namely, that Christians should not use lethal force since the hope of using it selectively and restrictively is so often an illusion. Nuclear weapons seem to prove this point in a way heretofore unknown.

144.   For the tradition which acknowledges some legitimate use of force, some important elements of contemporary nuclear strategies move beyond the limits of moral justification. A justifiable use of force must be both discriminatory and proportionate. Certain aspects of both U.S. and Soviet strategies fail both tests as we shall discuss below. The technical literature and the personal testimony of public officials who have been closely associated with U.S. nuclear strategy have both convinced us of the overwhelming probability that major nuclear exchange would have no limits.[61]

145.   On the more complicated issue of "limited" nuclear war, we are aware of the extensive literature and discussion which this topic has generated.[62] As a general statement, it seems to us that public officials would be unable to refute the following conclusion of the study made by the Pontifical Academy of Sciences:

> Even a nuclear attack directed only at military facilities would be devastating to the country as a whole. This is because military facilities are widespread rather than concentrated at only a few points. Thus, many nuclear weapons would be exploded.

61. The following quotations are from public officials who have served at the highest policy levels in recent administrations of our government: "It is time to recognize that no one has ever succeeded in advancing any persuasive reason to believe that any use of nuclear weapons, even on the smallest scale, could reliably be expected to remain limited." M. Bundy, G. F. Kennan, R. S. McNamara and G. Smith, "Nuclear Weapons and the Atlantic Alliance," *Foreign Affairs* 60 (1982):757.

"From my experience in combat there is no way that [nuclear escalation] . . . can be controlled because of the lack of information, the pressure of time and the deadly results that are taking place on both sides of the battle line." Gen. A. S. Collins, Jr. (former deputy commander in chief of U.S. Army in Europe), "Theatre Nuclear Warfare: The Battlefield," in J. F. Reichart and S. R. Sturn, eds., *American Defense Policy*, 5th ed., (Baltimore: 1982), pp. 359-60.

"None of this potential flexibility changes my view that a full-scale thermonuclear exchange would be an unprecedented disaster for the Soviet Union as well as for the United States. Nor is it at all clear that an initial use of nuclear weapons—however selectively they might be targeted—could be kept from escalating to a full-scale thermonuclear exchange, especially if command-and-control centers were brought under attack. The odds are high, whether weapons were used against tactical or strategic targets, that control would be lost on both sides and the exchange would become unconstrained." Harold Brown, *Department of Defense Annual Report FY 1979* (Washington, D.C.: 1978).

Cf. also: *The Effects of Nuclear War* (Washington, D.C.: 1979, U.S. Government Printing Office).

62. For example, cf.: H. A. Kissinger, *Nuclear Weapons and Foreign Policy* (New York: 1957), *The Necessity for Choice* (New York: 1960); R. Osgood and R. Tucker, *Force, Order and Justice* (Baltimore: 1967); R. Aron, *The Great Debate: Theories of Nuclear Strategy* (New York: 1965); D. Ball, *Can Nuclear War Be Controlled?* Adelphi Paper #161 (London: 1981); M. Howard, "On Fighting a Nuclear War," *International Security* 5 (1981):3-17.

Furthermore, the spread of radiation due to the natural winds and atmospheric mixing would kill vast numbers of people and contaminate large areas. The medical facilities of any nation would be inadequate to care for the survivors. An objective examination of the medical situation that would follow a nuclear war leads to but one conclusion: prevention is our only recourse.[63]

Moral Principles and Policy Choices

146. In light of these perspectives we address three questions more explicitly: (1) counter population warfare; (2) initiation of nuclear war; and (3) limited nuclear war.

1. Counter Population Warfare

147. Under no circumstances may nuclear weapons or other instruments of mass slaughter be used for the purpose of destroying population centers or other predominantly civilian targets. Popes have repeatedly condemned "total war" which implies such use. For example, as early as 1954 Pope Pius XII condemned nuclear warfare "when it entirely escapes the control of man," and results in "the pure and simple annihilation of all human life within the radius of action."[64] The condemnation was repeated by the Second Vatican Council:

> Any act of war aimed indiscriminately at the destruction of entire cities or of extensive areas along with their population is a crime against God and man himself. It merits unequivocal and unhesitating condemnation.[65]

148. Retaliatory action whether nuclear or conventional which would indiscriminately take many wholly innocent lives, lives of people who are in no way responsible for reckless actions of their government, must also be condemned. This condemnation, in our judgment, applies even to the retaliatory use of weapons striking enemy cities after our own have already been struck. No Christian can rightfully carry out orders or policies deliberately aimed at killing non-combatants.[66]

149. We make this judgment at the beginning of our treatment of nuclear strategy precisely because the defense of the principle of noncombatant immunity is so important for an ethic of war and because the nuclear age has posed such extreme problems for the principle. Later in this letter we shall discuss specific aspects of U.S. policy in light of this principle and in light of recent U.S. policy statements stressing the determination not to target directly or strike directly against civilian populations. Our concern about protecting the moral value of noncombatant immunity, however, requires that we make a clear reassertion of the principle our first word on this matter.

63. "Statement on the Consequences of the Use of Nuclear Weapons," cited, p. 243.

64. Pius XII, "Address to the VIII Congress of the World Medical Association," in *Documents*, p. 131.

65. *Pastoral Constitution*, #80.

66. Ibid.

2. The Initiation of Nuclear War

150.   We do not perceive any situation in which the deliberate initiation of nuclear warfare, on however restricted a scale, can be morally justified. Non-nuclear attacks by another state must be resisted by other than nuclear means. Therefore, a serious moral obligation exists to develop non-nuclear defensive strategies as rapidly as possible.

151.   A serious debate is under way on this issue.[67] It is cast in political terms, but it has a significant moral dimension. Some have argued that at the very beginning of a war nuclear weapons might be used, only against military targets, perhaps in limited numbers. Indeed it has long been American and NATO policy that nuclear weapons, especially so-called tactical nuclear weapons, would likely be used if NATO forces in Europe seemed in danger of losing a conflict that until then had been restricted to conventional weapons. Large numbers of tactical nuclear weapons are now deployed in Europe by the NATO forces and about as many by the Soviet Union. Some are substantially smaller than the bomb used on Hiroshima, some are larger. Such weapons, if employed in great numbers, would totally devastate the densely populated countries of Western and Central Europe.

152.   Whether under conditions of war in Europe, parts of Asia or the Middle East, or the exchange of strategic weapons directly between the United States and the Soviet Union, the difficulties of limiting the use of nuclear weapons are immense. A number of expert witnesses advise us that commanders operating under conditions of battle probably would not be able to exercise strict control; the number of weapons used would rapidly increase, the targets would be expanded beyond the military, and the level of civilian casualties would rise enormously.[68] No one can be certain that this escalation would not occur, even in the face of political efforts to keep such an exchange "limited." The chances of keeping use limited seem remote, and the consequences of escalation to mass destruction would be appalling. Former public officials have testified that it is improbable that any nuclear war could actually be kept limited. Their testimony and the consequences involved in this problem lead us to conclude that the danger of escalation is so great that it would be morally unjustifiable to initiate nuclear war in any form. The danger is rooted not only in the technology of our weapons systems but in the weakness and sinfulness of human communities. We find the moral responsibility of beginning nuclear war not justified by rational political objectives.

153.   This judgment affirms that the willingness to initiate nuclear war entails a distinct, weighty moral responsibility; it involves transgressing a fragile barrier—political, psychological, and moral—which has been constructed since 1945. We express repeatedly in this letter our extreme skepticism about the

67. M. Bundy, et al., "Nuclear Weapons," cited; K. Kaiser, G. Leber, A. Mertes, F. J. Schulze, "Nuclear Weapons and the Preservation of Peace," *Foreign Affairs* 60 (1982):1157-70; cf. other responses to Bundy article in the same issue of *Foreign Affairs*.

68. Testimony given to the National Conference of Catholic Bishops Committee during preparation of this pastoral letter. The testimony is reflected in the quotes found in note 61.

prospects for controlling a nuclear exchange, however limited the first use might be. Precisely because of this skepticism, we judge resort to nuclear weapons to counter a conventional attack to be morally unjustifiable.[69] Consequently we seek to reinforce the barrier against any use of nuclear weapons. Our support of a "no first use" policy must be seen in this light.

154.   At the same time we recognize the responsibility the United States has had and continues to have in assisting allied nations in their defense against either a conventional or a nuclear attack. Especially in the European theater, the deterrence of a *nuclear* attack may require nuclear weapons for a time, even though their possession and deployment must be subject to rigid restrictions.

155.   The need to defend against a conventional attack in Europe imposes the political and moral burden of developing adequate, alternative modes of defense to present reliance on nuclear weapons. Even with the best coordinated effort— hardly likely in view of contemporary political division on this question—development of an alternative defense position will still take time.

156.   In the interim, deterrence against a conventional attack relies upon two factors: the not inconsiderable conventional forces at the disposal of NATO and the recognition by a potential attacker that the outbreak of large scale conventional war could escalate to the nuclear level through accident or miscalculation by either side. We are aware that NATO's refusal to adopt a "no first use" pledge is to some extent linked to the deterrent effect of this inherent ambiguity. Nonetheless, in light of the probable effects of initiating nuclear war, we urge NATO to move rapidly toward the adoption of a "no first use" policy, but doing so in tandem with development of an adequate alternative defense posture.

3. Limited Nuclear War

157.   It would be possible to agree with our first two conclusions and still not be sure about retaliatory use of nuclear weapons in what is called a "limited exchange." The issue at stake is the *real* as opposed to the *theoretical* possibility of a "limited nuclear exchange."

158.   We recognize that the policy debate on this question is inconclusive and that all participants are left with hypothetical projections about probable reactions in a nuclear exchange. While not trying to adjudicate the technical debate, we are aware of it and wish to raise a series of questions which challenge the actual meaning of "limited" in this discussion.

—Would leaders have sufficient information to know what is happening in a nuclear exchange?

—Would they be able under the conditions of stress, time pressures, and fragmentary information to make the extraordinarily precise decision needed to keep the exchange limited if this were technically possible?

—Would military commanders be able, in the midst of the destruction

---

69. Our conclusions and judgments in this area although based on careful study and reflection of the application of moral principles do not have, of course, the same force as the principles themselves and therefore allow for different opinions, as the Summary makes clear.

and confusion of a nuclear exchange, to maintain a policy of "discriminate targeting"? Can this be done in modern warfare, waged across great distances by aircraft and missiles?

—Given the accidents we know about in peacetime conditions, what assurances are there that computer errors could be avoided in the midst of a nuclear exchange?

—Would not the casualties, even in a war defined as limited by strategists, still run in the millions?

—How "limited" would be the long-term effects of radiation, famine, social fragmentation, and economic dislocation?

159.   Unless these questions can be answered satisfactorily, we will continue to be highly skeptical about the real meaning of "limited." One of the criteria of the just-war tradition is a reasonable hope of success in bringing about justice and peace. We must ask whether such a reasonable hope can exist once nuclear weapons have been exchanged. The burden of proof remains on those who assert that meaningful limitation is possible.

160.   A nuclear response to either conventional or nuclear attack can cause destruction which goes far beyond "legitimate defense." Such use of nuclear weapons would not be justified.

161.   In the face of this frightening and highly speculative debate on a matter involving millions of human lives, we believe the most effective contribution or moral judgment is to introduce perspectives by which we can assess the empirical debate. Moral perspective should be sensitive not only to the quantitative dimensions of a question but to its psychological, human, and religious characteristics as well. The issue of limited war is not simply the size of weapons contemplated or the strategies projected. The debate should include the psychological and political significance of crossing the boundary from the conventional to the nuclear arena in any form. To cross this divide is to enter a world where we have no experience of control, much testimony against its possibility, and therefore no moral justification for submitting the human community to this risk.[70] We therefore express our view that the first imperative is to prevent any use of nuclear weapons and our hope that leaders will resist the notion that nuclear conflict can be limited, contained, or won in any traditional sense.

D.   DETERRENCE IN PRINCIPLE AND PRACTICE

162.   The moral challenge posed by nuclear weapons is not exhausted by an

70. Undoubtedly aware of the long and detailed technical debate on limited war, Pope John Paul II highlighted the unacceptable moral risk of crossing the threshold to nuclear war in his "Angelus Message" of December 13, 1981: "I have, in fact, the deep conviction that, in the light of a nuclear war's effects, which can be scientifically foreseen as certain, the only choice that is morally and humanly valid is represented by the reduction of nuclear armaments, while waiting for their future complete elimination, carried out simultaneously by all the parties, by means of explicit agreements and with the commitment of accepting effective controls." In *Documents*, p. 240.

analysis of their possible uses. Much of the political and moral debate of the nuclear age has concerned the strategy of deterrence. Deterrence is at the heart of the U.S.-Soviet relationship, currently the most dangerous dimension of the nuclear arms race.

1. The Concept and Development of Deterrence Policy

163.   The concept of deterrence existed in military strategy long before the nuclear age, but it has taken on a new meaning and significance since 1945. Essentially, deterrence means "dissuasion of a potential adversary from initiating an attack or conflict, often by the threat of unacceptable retaliatory damage."[71] In the nuclear age, deterrence has become the centerpiece of both U.S. and Soviet policy. Both superpowers have for many years now been able to promise a retaliatory response which can inflict "unacceptable damage." A situation of stable deterrence depends on the ability of each side to deploy its retaliatory forces in ways that are not vulnerable to an attack (i.e., protected against a "first strike"); preserving stability requires a willingness by both sides to refrain from deploying weapons which appear to have a first strike capability.

164.   This general definition of deterrence does not explain either the elements of a deterrence strategy or the evolution of deterrence policy since 1945. A detailed description of either of these subjects would require an extensive essay, using materials which can be found in abundance in the technical literature on the subject of deterrence.[72] Particularly significant is the relationship between "declaratory policy" (the public explanation of our strategic intentions and capabilities) and "action policy" (the actual planning and targeting policies to be followed in a nuclear attack).

165.   The evolution of deterrence strategy has passed through several stages of declaratory policy. Using the U.S. case as an example, there is a significant difference between "massive retaliation" and "flexible response," and between "mutual assured destruction" and "countervailing strategy." It is also possible to distinguish between "counterforce" and "countervalue" targeting policies; and to contrast a posture of "minimum deterrence" with "extended deterrence." These terms are well known in the technical debate on nuclear policy; they are less well known and sometimes loosely used in the wider public debate. It is important to recognize that there has been substantial continuity in U.S. action policy in spite of real changes in declaratory policy.[73]

166.   The recognition of these different elements in the deterrent and the

71. W. H. Kincade and J. D. Porro, *Negotiating Security: An Arms Control Reader* (Washington, D.C.: 1979).

72. Several surveys are available, for example cf.: J. H. Kahin, *Security in the Nuclear Age: Developing U.S. Strategic Policy* (Washington, D.C.: 1975); M. Mandelbaum, *The Nuclear Question: The United States and Nuclear Weapons 1946-1976* (Cambridge, England: 1979); B. Brodie, "Development of Nuclear Strategy," *International Security* 2 (1978):65-83.

73. The relationship of these two levels of policy is the burden of an article by D. Ball, "U.S. Strategic Forces: How Would They Be Used?" *International Security* 7 (1982/83):31-60.

evolution of policy means that moral assessment of deterrence requires a series of distinct judgments. They include: an analysis of the *factual character* of the deterrent (e.g., what is involved in targeting doctrine); analysis of the *historical development* of the policy (e.g., whether changes have occurred which are significant for moral analysis of the policy): the relationship of deterrence policy and other aspects of *U.S.-Soviet affairs*; and determination of the key *moral questions* involved in deterrence policy.

2. The Moral Assessment of Deterrence

167. The distinctively new dimensions of nuclear deterrence were recognized by policymakers and strategists only after much reflection. Similarly, the moral challenge posed by nuclear deterrence was grasped only after careful deliberation. The moral and political paradox posed by deterrence was concisely stated by Vatican II:

> Undoubtedly, armaments are not amassed merely for use in wartime. Since the defensive strength of any nation is thought to depend on its capacity for immediate retaliation, the stockpiling of arms which grows from year to year serves, in a way hitherto unthought of, as a deterrent to potential attackers. Many people look upon this as the most effective way known at the present time for maintaining some sort of peace among nations. Whatever one may think of this form of deterrent, people are convinced that the arms race, which quite a few countries have entered, is no infallible way of maintaining real peace and that the resulting so-called balance of power is no sure genuine path to achieving it. Rather than eliminate the causes of war, the arms race serves only to aggravate the position. As long as extravagent sums of money are poured into the development of new weapons, it is impossible to devote adequate aid in tackling the misery which prevails at the present day in the world. Instead of eradicating international conflict once and for all, the contagion is spreading to other parts of the world. New approaches, based on reformed attitudes, will have to be chosen in order to remove this stumbling block, to free the earth from its pressing anxieties, and give back to the world a genuine peace.[74]

168. Without making a specific moral judgment on deterrence, the council clearly designated the elements of the arms race: the tension between "peace of a sort" preserved by deterrence and "genuine peace" required for a stable international life; the contradiction between what is spent for destructive capacity and what is needed for constructive development.

169. In the post-conciliar assessment of war and peace, and specifically of deterrence, different parties to the political-moral debate within the Church and in civil society have focused on one aspect or another of the problem. For some, the fact that nuclear weapons have not been used since 1945 means that deterrence has worked, and this fact satisfies the demands of both the political and the moral order. Others contest this assessment by highlighting the risk of failure involved in continued reliance on deterrence and pointing out how politically

74. *Pastoral Constitution,* #81.

and morally catastrophic even a single failure would be. Still others note that the absence of nuclear war is not necessarily proof that the policy of deterrence has prevented it. Indeed, some would find in the policy of deterrence the driving force in the superpower arms race. Still other observers, many of them Catholic moralists, have stressed that deterrence may not morally include the intention of deliberately attacking civilian populations or non-combatants.

170.   The statements of the NCCB/USCC over the past several years have both reflected and contributed to the wider moral debate on deterrence. In the NCCB pastoral letter, *To Live In Christ Jesus* (1976), we focused on the moral limits of declaratory policy while calling for stronger measures of arms control.[75] In 1979 John Cardinal Krol, speaking for the USCC in support of SALT II ratification, brought into focus the other element of the deterrence problem: the actual use of nuclear weapons may have been prevented (a moral good), but the risk of failure and the physical harm and moral evil resulting from possible nuclear war remained. "This explains," Cardinal Krol stated, "the Catholic dissatisfaction with nuclear deterrence and the urgency of the Catholic demand that the nuclear arms race be reversed. It is of the utmost importance that negotiations proceed to meaningful and continuing reductions in nuclear stockpiles, and eventually to the phasing out altogether of nuclear deterrence and the threat of mutual-assured destruction."[76]

171.   These two texts, along with the conciliar statement, have influenced much of Catholic opinion expressed recently on the nuclear question.

172.   In June 1982, Pope John Paul II provided new impetus and insight to the moral analysis with his statement to the United Nations Second Special Session on Disarmament. The pope first situated the problem of deterrence within the context of world politics. No power, he observes, will admit to wishing to start a war, but each distrusts others and considers it necessary to mount a strong defense against attack. He then discusses the notion of deterrence:

> Many even think that such preparations constitute the way—even the only way—to safeguard peace in some fashion or at least to impede to the utmost in an efficacious way the outbreak of wars, especially major conflicts which might lead to the ultimate holocaust of humanity and the destruction of the civilization that man has constructed so laboriously over the centuries.
>
> In this approach one can see the "philosophy of peace" which was proclaimed in the ancient Roman principle: *Si vis pacem, para bellum.* Put in modern terms, this "philosophy" has the label of "deterrence" and one can find it in various guises of the search for a "balance of forces" which sometimes has been called, and not without reason, the "balance of terror."[77]

173.   Having offered this analysis of the general concept of deterrence, the Holy Father introduces his considerations on disarmament, especially, but not

75. United States Catholic Conference, *To Live in Christ Jesus* (Washington, D.C.: 1976), p. 34.

76. John Cardinal Krol, "Testimony on Salt II," *Origins* (1979):197.

77. John Paul II, "Message U.N. Special Session 1982," #3.

only, nuclear disarmament. Pope John Paul II makes this statement about the morality of deterrence:

> In current conditions "deterrence" based on balance, certainly not as an end in itself but as a step on the way toward a progressive disarmament, may still be judged morally acceptable. Nonetheless in order to ensure peace, it is indispensable not to be satisfied with this minimum which is always suscep-tible to the real danger of explosion.[78]

174.   In Pope John Paul II's assessment we perceive two dimensions of the contemporary dilemma of deterrence. One dimension is the danger of nuclear war, with its human and moral costs. The possession of nuclear weapons, the continuing quantitative growth of the arms race, and the danger of nuclear proliferation all point to the grave danger of basing "peace of a sort" on deter-rence. The other dimension is the independence and freedom of nations and entire peoples, including the need to protect smaller nations from threats to their independence and integrity. Deterrence reflects the radical distrust which marks international politics, a condition identified as a major problem by Pope John XIII in *Peace on Earth* and reaffirmed by Pope Paul VI and Pope John Paul II. Thus a balance of forces, preventing either side from achieving superiority, can be seen as a means of safeguarding both dimensions.

175.   The moral duty today is to prevent nuclear war from ever occurring *and* to protect and preserve those key values of justice, freedom and independence which are necessary for personal dignity and national integrity. In reference to these issues, Pope John Paul II judges that deterrence may still be judged morally acceptable, "certainly not as an end in itself but as a step on the way toward a progressive disarmament."

176.   On more than one occasion the Holy Father has demonstrated his aware-ness of the fragility and complexity of the deterrence relationship among nations. Speaking to UNESCO in June 1980, he said:

> Up to the present, we are told that nuclear arms are a force of dissuasion which have prevented the eruption of a major war. And that is probably true. Still, we must ask if it will always be this way.[79]

In a more recent and more specific assessment Pope John Paul II told an international meeting of scientists on August 23, 1982:

> You can more easily ascertain that the logic of nuclear deterrence cannot be considered a final goal or an appropriate and secure means for safeguarding international peace.[80]

177.   Relating Pope John Paul's general statements to the specific policies of the

78. Ibid., #8.

79. John Paul II, "Address to UNESCO, 1980," #21.

80. John Paul II, "Letter to International Seminar on the World Implications of a Nuclear Conflict," August 23, 1982, text in *NC News Documentary*, August 24, 1982.

U.S. deterrent requires both judgments of fact and an application of moral principles. In preparing this letter we have tried, through a number of sources, to determine as precisely as possible the factual character of U.S. deterrence strategy. Two questions have particularly concerned us: 1) the targeting doctrine and strategic plans for the use of the deterrent, particularly their impact on civilian casualties; and 2) the relationship of deterrence strategy and nuclear war-fighting capability to the likelihood that war will in fact be prevented.

Moral Principles and Policy Choices

178.   Targeting doctrine raises significant moral questions because it is a significant determinant of what would occur if nuclear weapons were ever to be used. Although we acknowledge the need for deterrent, not all forms of deterrence are morally acceptable. There are moral limits to deterrence policy as well as to policy regarding use. Specifically, it is not morally acceptable to intend to kill the innocent as part of a strategy of deterring nuclear war. The question of whether U.S. policy involves an intention to strike civilian centers (directly targeting civilian populations) has been one of our factual concerns.

179.   This complex question has always produced a variety of responses, official and unofficial in character. The NCCB Committee has received a series of statements of clarification of policy from U.S. government officials.[81] Essentially these statements declare that it is not U.S. strategic policy to target the Soviet civilian population as such or to use nuclear weapons deliberately for the purpose of destroying population centers. These statements respond, in principle at least, to one moral criterion for assessing deterrence policy: the immunity of non-combatants from direct attack either by conventional or nuclear weapons.

180.   These statements do not address or resolve another very troublesome moral problem, namely, that an attack on military targets or militarily significant industrial targets could involve "indirect" (i.e., unintended) but massive civilian casualties. We are advised, for example, that the United States strategic nuclear targeting plan (SIOP—Single Integrated Operational Plan) has identified 60 "military" targets within the city of Moscow alone, and that 40,000 "military" targets for nuclear

---

81. Particularly helpful was the letter of January 15, 1983, of Mr. William Clark, national security adviser, to Cardinal Bernardin. Mr. Clark stated: "For moral, political and military reasons, the United States does not target the Soviet civilian population as such. There is no deliberately opaque meaning conveyed in the last two words. We do not threaten the existence of Soviet civilization by threatening Soviet cities. Rather, we hold at risk the war-making capability of the Soviet Union—its armed forces, and the industrial capacity to sustain war. It would be irresponsible for us to issue policy statements which might suggest to the Soviets that it would be to their advantage to establish privileged sanctuaries within heavily populated areas, thus inducing them to locate much of their war-fighting capability within those urban sanctuaries." A reaffirmation of the administration's policy is also found in Secretary Weinberger's *Annual Report to the Congress* (Caspar Weinberger, *Annual Report to the Congress*, February 1, 1983, p. 55): "The Reagan Administration's policy is that under no circumstances may such weapons be used deliberately for the purpose of destroying populations." Also the letter of Mr. Weinberger to Bishop O'Connor of February 9, 1983, has a similar statement.

weapons have been identified in the whole of the Soviet Union.[82] It is important to recognize that Soviet policy is subject to the same moral judgment; attacks on several "industrial targets" or politically significant targets in the United States could produce massive civilian casualties. The number of civilians who would necessarily be killed by such strikes is horrendous.[83] This problem is unavoidable because of the way modern military facilities and production centers are so thoroughly interspersed with civilian living and working areas. It is aggravated if one side deliberately positions military targets in the midst of a civilian population. In our consultations, administration officials readily admitted that, while they hoped any nuclear exchange could be kept limited, they were prepared to retaliate in a massive way if necessary. They also agreed that once any substantial numbers of weapons were used, the civilian casualty levels would quickly become truly catastrophic, and that even with attacks limited to "military" targets, the number of deaths in a substantial exchange would be almost indistinguishable from what might occur if civilian centers had been deliberately and directly struck. These possibilities pose a different moral question and are to be judged by a different moral criterion: the principle of proportionality.

181.   While any judgment of proportionality is always open to differing evaluations, there are actions which can be decisively judged to be disproportionate. A narrow adherence exclusively to the principle of noncombatant immunity as a criterion for policy is an inadequate moral posture for it ignores some evil and unacceptable consequences. Hence, we cannot be satisfied that the assertion of an intention not to strike civilians directly, or even the most honest effort to implement that intention, by itself constitutes a "moral policy" for the use of nuclear weapons.

182.   The location of industrial or militarily significant economic targets within heavily populated areas or in those areas affected by radioactive fallout could well involve such massive civilian casualties that, in our judgment, such a strike would be deemed morally disproportionate, even though not intentionally indiscriminate.

183.   The problem is not simply one of producing highly accurate weapons that might minimize civilian casualties in any single explosion, but one of increasing the likelihood of escalation at a level where many, even "discriminating," weapons would cumulatively kill very large numbers of civilians. Those civilian deaths would occur both immediately and from the long-term effects of social and economic devastation.

184.   A second issue of concern to us is the relationship of deterrence doctrine to war-fighting strategies. We are aware of the argument that war-fighting capabilities enhance the credibility of the deterrent, particularly the strategy of extended deterrence. But the development of such capabilities raises other strategic and

82. S. Zuckerman, *Nuclear Illusion and Reality* (New York: 1982); D. Ball, cited, p. 36; T. Powers, "Choosing a Strategy for World War III," *The Atlantic Monthly*, November 1982, pp. 82-110.

83. Cf. the comments in Pontifical Academy of Sciences "Statement on the Consequences of the Use of Nuclear Weapons," cited.

moral questions. The relationship of war-fighting capabilities and targeting doctrine exemplifies the difficult choices in this area of policy. Targeting civilian populations would violate the principle of discrimination—one of the central moral principles of a Christian ethic of war. But "counterforce targeting," while preferable from the perspective of protecting civilians, is often joined with a declaratory policy which conveys the notion that nuclear war is subject to precise rational and moral limits. We have already expressed our severe doubts about such a concept. Furthermore, a purely counterforce strategy may seem to threaten the viability of other nations' retaliatory forces, making deterrence unstable in a crisis and war more likely.

185.   While we welcome any effort to protect civilian populations, we do not want to legitimize or encourage moves which extend deterrence beyond the specific objective of preventing the use of nuclear weapons or other actions which could lead directly to a nuclear exchange.

186.   These considerations of concrete elements of nuclear deterrence policy, made in light of John Paul II's evaluation, but applying it through our own prudential judgments, lead us to a strictly conditioned moral acceptance of nuclear deterrence. We cannot consider it adequate as a long-term basis for peace.

187.   This strictly conditioned judgment yields *criteria* for morally assessing the elements of deterrence strategy. Clearly, these criteria demonstrate that we cannot approve of every weapons system, strategic doctrine, or policy initiative advanced in the name of strengthening deterrence. On the contrary, these criteria require continual public scrutiny of what our government proposes to do with the deterrent.

188.   *On the basis of these criteria we wish now to make some specific evaluations*:

1) If nuclear deterrence exists only to prevent the *use* of nuclear weapons by others, then proposals to go beyond this to planning for prolonged periods of repeated nuclear strikes and counter-strikes, or "prevailing" in nuclear war, are not acceptable. They encourage notions that nuclear war can be engaged in with tolerable human and moral consequences. Rather, we must continually say "no" to the idea of nuclear war.

2) If nuclear deterrence is our goal, "sufficiency" to deter is an adequate strategy; the quest for nuclear superiority must be rejected.

3) Nuclear deterrence should be used as a step on the way toward progressive disarmanent. Each proposed addition to our strategic system or change in strategic doctrine must be assessed precisely in light of whether it will render steps toward "progressive disarmament" more or less likely.

189.   Moreover, these criteria provide us with the means to make some judgments and recommendations about the present direction of U.S. strategic policy. Progress toward a world freed of dependence on nuclear deterrence must be carefully carried out. But it must not be delayed. There is an urgent moral and political responsibility to use the "peace of a sort" we have as a framework to move toward authentic peace through nuclear arms control, reductions, and disarmament. Of primary importance in this process is the need to prevent the development and deployment of destabilizing weapons systems on either side; a second require-

ment is to insure that the more sophisticated command and control systems do not become mere hair triggers for automatic launch on warning; a third is the need to prevent the proliferation of nuclear weapons in the international system.

190.   In light of these general judgments *we oppose* some specific proposals in respect to our present deterrence posture:

1) The addition of weapons which are likely to be vulnerable to attack, yet also possess a "prompt hard-target kill" capability that threatens to make the other side's retaliatory forces vulnerable. Such weapons may seem to be useful primarily in a first strike;[84] we resist such weapons for this reason and we oppose Soviet deployment of such weapons which generate fear of a first strike against U.S. forces.

2) The willingness to foster strategic planning which seeks a nuclear war-fighting capability that goes beyond the limited function of deterrence outlined in this letter.

3) Proposals which have the effect of lowering the nuclear threshold and blurring the difference between nuclear and conventional weapons.

191.   In support of the concept of "sufficiency" as an adequate deterrent, and in light of the present size and composition of both the U.S. and Soviet strategic arsenals, *we recommend*:

1) Support for immediate, bilateral, verifiable agreements to halt the testing, production, and deployment of new nuclear weapons systems.[85]

2) Support for negotiated bilateral deep cuts in the arsenals of both superpowers, particularly those weapons systems which have destabilizing characteristics; U.S. proposals like those for START (Strategic Arms Reduction Talks) and INF (Intermediate-range Nuclear Forces) negotiations in Geneva are said to be designed to achieve deep cuts;[86] our hope is that they will be pursued in a manner which will realize these goals.

3) Support for early and successful conclusion of negotiations of a comprehensive test ban treaty.

4) Removal by all parties of short-range nuclear weapons which multiply dangers disproportionate to their deterrent value.

5) Removal by all parties of nuclear weapons from areas where they are likely to be overrun in the early stages of war, thus forcing rapid and uncontrollable decisions on their use.

6) Strengthening of command and control over nuclear weapons to prevent inadvertent and unauthorized use.

84. Several experts in strategic theory would place both the MX missile and Pershing II missiles in this category.

85. In each of the successive drafts of this letter we have tried to state a central moral imperative: that the arms race should be stopped and disarmament begun. The implementation of this imperative is open to a wide variety of approaches. Hence we have chosen our own language in this paragraph, not wanting either to be identified with one specific political initiative or to have our words used against specific political measures.

86. Cf. President Reagan's "Speech to the National Press Club" (November 18, 1981) and "Address at Eureka College" (May 9, 1982), Department of State, *Current Policy #346* and #387.

192.   These judgments are meant to exemplify how a lack of unequivocal condemnation of deterrence is meant only to be an attempt to acknowledge the role attributed to deterrence, but not to support its extension beyond the limited purpose discussed above. Some have urged us to condemn all aspects of nuclear deterrence. This urging has been based on a variety of reasons, but has emphasized particularly the high and terrible risks that either deliberate use or accidental detonation of nuclear weapons could quickly escalate to something utterly disproportionate to any acceptable moral purpose. That determination requires highly technical judgments about hypothetical events. Although reasons exist which move some to condemn reliance on nuclear weapons for deterrence, we have not reached this conclusion for the reasons outlined in this letter.

193.   Nevertheless, there must be no misunderstanding of our profound skepticism about the moral acceptability of any use of nuclear weapons. It is obvious that the use of any weapons which violate the principle of discrimination merits unequivocal condemnation. We are told that some weapons are designed for purely "counterforce" use against military forces and targets. The moral issue, however, is not resolved by the design of weapons or the planned intention for use; there are also consequences which must be assessed. It would be a perverted political policy or moral casuistry which tried to justify using a weapon which "indirectly" or "unintentionally" killed a million innocent people because they happened to live near a "militarily significant target."

194.   Even the "indirect effects" of initiating nuclear war are sufficient to make it an unjustifiable moral risk in any form. It is not sufficient, for example, to contend that "our" side has plans for "limited" or "discriminate" use. Modern warfare is not readily contained by good intentions or technological designs. The psychological climate of the world is such that mention of the term "nuclear" generates uneasiness. Many contend that the use of one tactical nuclear weapon could produce panic, with completely unpredictable consequences. It is precisely this mix of political, psychological, and technological uncertainty which has moved us in this letter to reinforce with moral prohibitions and prescriptions the prevailing political barrier against resort to nuclear weapons. Our support for enhanced command and control facilities, for major reductions in strategic and tactical nuclear forces, and for a "no first use" policy (as set forth in this letter) is meant to be seen as a complement to our desire to draw a moral line against nuclear war.

195.   Any claim by any government that it is pursuing a morally acceptable policy of deterrence must be scrutinized with the greatest care. We are prepared and eager to participate in our country in the ongoing public debate on moral grounds.

196.   The need to rethink the deterrence policy of our nation, to make the revisions necessary to reduce the possibility of nuclear war, and to move toward a more stable system of national and international security will demand a substantial intellectual, political, and moral effort. It also will require, we believe, the willingness to open ourselves to the providential care, power and word of God, which call us to recognize our common humanity and the bonds of mutual

responsibility which exist in the international community in spite of political differences and nuclear arsenals.

197.   Indeed, we do acknowledge that there are many strong voices within our own episcopal ranks and within the wider Catholic community in the United States which challenge the strategy of deterrence as an adequate response to the arms race today. They highlight the historical evidence that deterrence has not, in fact, set in motion substantial processes of disarmament.

198.   Moreover, these voices rightly raise the concern that even the conditional acceptance of nuclear deterrence as laid out in a letter such as this might be inappropriately used by some to reinforce the policy of arms buildup. In its stead, they call us to raise a prophetic challenge to the community of faith—a challenge which goes beyond nuclear deterrence, toward more resolute steps to actual bilateral disarmament and peacemaking. We recognize the intellectual ground on which the argument is built and the religious sensibility which gives it its strong force.

199.   The dangers of the nuclear age and the enormous difficulties we face in moving toward a more adequate system of global security, stability and justice require steps beyond our present conceptions of security and defense policy. In the following section we propose a series of steps aimed at a more adequate policy for preserving peace in a nuclear world.

III. The Promotion of Peace: Proposals and Policies

200.   In a world which is not yet the fulfillment of God's kingdom, a world where both personal actions and social forces manifest the continuing influence of sin and disorder among us, consistent attention must be paid to preventing and limiting the violence of war. But this task, addressed extensively in the previous section of this letter, does not exhaust Catholic teaching on war and peace. A complementary theme, reflected in the Scriptures and the theology of the Church and significantly developed by papal teaching in this century, is the building of peace as the way to prevent war. This traditional theme was vividly reasserted by Pope John Paul in his homily at Coventry Cathedral:

> Peace is not just the absence of war. It involves mutual respect and confidence between peoples and nations. It involves collaboration and binding agreements. Like a cathedral, peace must be constructed patiently and with unshakable faith.[87]

201.   This positive conception of peacemaking profoundly influences many people in our time. At the beginning of this letter we affirmed the need for a more fully developed theology of peace. The basis of such a theology is found in the papal teaching of this century. In this section of our pastoral we wish to illustrate how the positive vision of peace contained in Catholic teaching provides direction for policy and personal choices.

A.   SPECIFIC STEPS TO REDUCE THE DANGER OF WAR

202.   The dangers of modern war are specific and visible; our teaching must be equally specific about the needs of peace. Effective arms control leading to mutual disarmament, ratification of pending treaties,[88] development of nonvi-

---

87. John Paul II, "Homily at Bagington Airport," Coventry, #2, *Origins* 12 (1982):55.

88. The two treaties are the Threshold Test Ban Treaty signed July 3, 1974, and the Treaty on Nuclear Explosions for Peaceful Purposes (P.N.E.) signed May 28, 1976.

olent alternatives, are but some of the recommendations we would place before the Catholic community and all men and women of good will. These should be part of a foreign policy which recognizes and respects the claims of citizens of every nation to the same inalienable rights we treasure, and seeks to ensure an international security based on the awareness that the creator has provided this world and all its resources for the sustenance and benefit of the entire human family. The truth that the globe is inhabited by a single family in which all have the same basic needs and all have a right to the goods of the earth is a fundamental principle of Catholic teaching which we believe to be of increasing importance today. In an interdependent world all need to affirm their common nature and destiny; such a perspective should inform our policy vision and negotiating posture in pursuit of peace today.

1. Accelerated Work for Arms Control, Reduction, and Disarmament

203. Despite serious efforts, starting with the Baruch plans and continuing through SALT I and SALT II, the results have been far too limited and partial to be commensurate with the risks of nuclear war. Yet efforts for negotiated control and reduction of arms must continue. In his 1982 address to the United Nations, Pope John Paul II left no doubt about the importance of these efforts:

> Today once again before you all I reaffirm my confidence in the power of true negotiations to arrive at just and equitable solutions.[89]

204. In this same spirit, we urge negotiations to halt the testing, production, and deployment of new nuclear weapons systems. Not only should steps be taken to end development and deployment, but the numbers of existing weapons must be reduced in a manner which lessens the danger of war.

205. Arms control and disarmament must be a process of verifiable agreements especially between two superpowers. While we do not advocate a policy of unilateral disarmament, we believe the urgent need for control of the arms race requires a willingness for each side to take some first steps. The United States has already taken a number of important independent initiatives to reduce some of the gravest dangers and to encourage a constructive Soviet response; additional initiatives are encouraged. By independent initiatives we mean carefully chosen limited steps which the United States could take for a defined period of time, seeking to elicit a comparable step from the Soviet Union. If an appropriate response is not forthcoming, the United States would no longer be bound by steps taken. Our country has previously taken calculated risks in favor of freedom and of human values; these have included independent steps taken to reduce some of the gravest dangers of nuclear war.[90] Certain risks are required today to help free the world from bondage to nuclear deterrence and the risk

---

89. John Paul II, "Message to U.N. Special Session 1982," #8.

90. Mr. Weinberger's letter to Bishop O'Connor specifies actions taken on command and control facilities designed to reduce the chance of unauthorized firing of nuclear weapons.

of nuclear war. Both sides, for example, have an interest in avoiding deployment of destabilizing weapons systems.

206.   There is some history of successful independent initiatives which have beneficially influenced the arms race without a formal public agreement. In 1963 President Kennedy announced that the United States would unilaterally forgo further nuclear testing; the next month Soviet Premier Nikita Khrushchev proposed a limited test ban which eventually became the basis of the U.S.-Soviet partial test ban treaty. Subsequently, both superpowers removed about 10,000 troops from Central Europe and each announced a cut in production of nuclear material for weapons.

207.   a) Negotiation on arms control agreements in isolation, without persistent and parallel efforts to reduce the political tensions which motivate the buildup of armaments, will not suffice. The United States should therefore have a continuing policy of maximum political engagement with governments of potential adversaries, providing for repeated, systematic discussion and negotiation of areas of friction. This policy should be carried out by a system of periodic, carefully prepared meetings at several levels of government, including summit meetings at regular intervals. Such channels of discussion are too important to be regarded by either of the major powers as a concession or an event made dependent on daily shifts in international developments.

208.   b) The Nuclear Non-Proliferation Treaty of 1968 (NPT) acknowledged that the spread of nuclear weapons to hitherto non-nuclear states (horizontal proliferation) could hardly be prevented in the long run in the absence of serious efforts by the nuclear states to control and reduce their own nuclear arsenals (vertical proliferation). Article VI of the NPT pledged the superpowers to serious efforts to control and to reduce their own nuclear arsenals; unfortunately, this promise has not been kept. Moreoever, the multinational controls envisaged in the treaty seem to have been gradually relaxed by the states exporting fissionable materials for the production of energy. If these tendencies are not constrained, the treaty may eventually lose its symbolic and practical effectiveness. For this reason the United States should, in concert with other nuclear exporting states, seriously re-examine its policies and programs and make clear its determination to uphold the spirit as well as the letter of the treaty.

2. Continued Insistence on Efforts to Minimize the Risk of Any War

209.   While it is right and proper that priority be given to reducing and ultimately eliminating the likelihood of nuclear war, this does not of itself remove the threat of other forms of warfare. Indeed, negotiated reduction in nuclear weapons available to the superpowers could conceivably increase the danger of non-nuclear wars.

210.   a) Because of this we strongly support negotiations aimed at reducing and limiting conventional forces and at building confidence between possible adversaries, especially in regions of potential military confrontations. We urge that prohibitions outlawing the production and use of chemical and biological weapons be reaffirmed and observed. Arms control negotiations must take

account of the possibility that conventional conflict could trigger the nuclear confrontation the world must avoid.

211.   b) Unfortunately, as is the case with nuclear proliferation, we are witnessing a relaxation of restraints in the international commerce in conventional arms. Sales of increasingly sophisticated military aircraft, missiles, tanks, anti-tank weapons, anti-personnel bombs, and other systems by the major supplying countries (especially the Soviet Union, the United States, France, and Great Britain) have reached unprecedented levels.

212.   Pope John Paul II took specific note of the problem in his U.N. address:

> The production and sale of conventional weapons throughout the world is a truly alarming and evidently growing phenomenon . . . . Moreover the traffic in these weapons seems to be developing at an increasing rate and seems to be directed most of all toward developing countries.[91]

213.   It is a tragic fact that U.S. arms sales policies in the last decade have contributed significantly to the trend the Holy Father deplores. We call for a reversal of this course. The United States should renew earlier efforts to develop multilateral controls on arms exports, and should in this case also be willing to take carefully chosen independent initiatives to restrain the arms trade. Such steps would be particularly appropriate where the receiving government faces charges of gross and systematic human rights violations.[92]

214.   c) Nations must accept a limited view of those interests justifying military force. True self-defense may include the protection of weaker states, but does not include seizing the possessions of others, or the domination of other states or peoples. We should remember the caution of Pope John Paul II: "In alleging the threat of a potential enemy, is it really not rather the intention to keep for itself a means of threat, in order to get the upper hand with the aid of one's own arsenal of destruction?"[93] Central to a moral theory of force is the principle that it must be a last resort taken only when *all* other means of redress have been exhausted. Equally important in the age of modern warfare is the recognition that the justifiable reasons for using force have been restricted to instances of self-defense or defense of others under attack.

3. The Relationship of Nuclear and Conventional Defenses

215.   The strong position we have taken against the use of nuclear weapons, and particularly the stand against the initiation of nuclear war in any form, calls for further clarification of our view of the requirements for conventional defense.

216.   Nuclear threats have often come to take the place of efforts to deter or defend against non-nuclear attack with weapons that are themselves non-nuclear,

91. Ibid. Cf. United States Catholic Conference, *At Issue #2: Arms Export Policies—Ethical Choices* (Washington, D.C.: 1978) for suggestions about controlling the conventional arms trade.

92. The International Security Act of 1976 provides for such human rights review.

93. John Paul II, "Address to the United Nations General Assembly," *Origins* 9 (1979):268.

particularly in the NATO-Warsaw Pact confrontation. Many analysts conclude that, in the absence of nuclear deterrent threats, more troops and conventional (non-nuclear) weapons would be required to protect our allies. Rejection of some forms of nuclear deterrence could therefore conceivably require a willingness to pay higher costs to develop conventional forces. Leaders and peoples of other nations might also have to accept higher costs for their own defense, particularly in Western Europe, if the threat to use nuclear weapons first were withdrawn. We cannot judge the strength of these arguments in particular cases. It may well be that some strengthening of conventional defense would be a proportionate price to pay, if this will reduce the possibility of a nuclear war. We acknowledge this reluctantly, aware as we are of the vast amount of scarce resources expended annually on instruments of defense in a world filled with other urgent, unmet human needs.

217.   It is not for us to settle the technical debate about policy and budgets. From the perspective of a developing theology of peace, however, we feel obliged to contribute a moral dimension to the discussion. We hope that a significant reduction in numbers of conventional arms and weaponry would go hand in hand with diminishing reliance on nuclear deterrence. The history of recent wars (even so-called "minor" or "limited" wars) has shown that conventional war can also become indiscriminate in conduct and disproportionate to any valid purpose. We do not want in any way to give encouragement to a notion of "making the world safe for conventional war," which introduces its own horrors.

218.   Hence, we believe that any program directed at reducing reliance on nuclear weapons is not likely to succeed unless it includes measures to reduce tensions, and to work for the balanced reduction of conventional forces. We believe that important possibilities exist which, if energetically pursued, would ensure against building up conventional forces as a concomitant of reductions in nuclear weapons. Examples are to be found in the ongoing negotiations for mutual balanced force reductions, the prospects for which are certainly not dim and would be enhanced by agreements on strategic weapons, and in the confidence-building measures still envisaged under the Helsinki agreement and review conference.

219.   We must re-emphasize with all our being, nonetheless, that it is not only nuclear war that must be prevented, but war itself. Therefore, with Pope John Paul II we declare:

> Today, the scale and the horror of modern warfare—whether nuclear or not—makes it totally unacceptable as a means of settling differences between nations. War should belong to the tragic past, to history; it should find no place on humanity's agenda for the future.[94]

Reason and experience tell us that a continuing upward spiral, even in conventional arms, coupled with an unbridled increase in armed forces, instead of securing true peace will almost certainly be provocative of war.

94. John Paul II, "Homily at Bagington Airport," Coventry, 2; cited, p. 55.

4. Civil Defense

220.   Attention must be given to existing programs for civil defense against nuclear attack, including blast and fall-out shelters and relocation plans. It is unclear in the public mind whether these are intended to offer significant protection against at least some forms of nuclear attack or are being put into place to enhance the credibility of the strategic deterrent forces by demonstrating an ability to survive attack. This confusion has led to public skepticism and even ridicule of the program and casts doubt on the credibility of the government. An independent commission of scientists, engineers, and weapons experts is needed to examine if these or any other plans offer a realistic prospect of survival for the nation's population or its cherished values, which a nuclear war would presumably be fought to preserve.

5. Efforts to Develop Non-violent Means of Conflict Resolution

221.   We affirm a nation's right to defend itself, its citizens, and its values. Security is the right of all, but that right, like everything else, must be subject to divine law and the limits defined by that law. We must find means of defending peoples that do not depend upon the threat of annihilation. Immoral means can never be justified by the end sought; no objective, however worthy of good in itself, can justify sinful acts or policies. Though our primary concern through this statement is war and the nuclear threat, these principles apply as well to all forms of violence, including insurgency, counter-insurgency, "destabilization," and the like.

222.   a) The Second Vatican Council praised "those who renounce the use of violence in the vindication of their rights and who resort to methods of defense which are otherwise available to weaker parties, provided that this can be done without injury to the rights and duties of others or of the community itself."[95] To make such renunciation effective and still defend what must be defended, the arts of diplomacy, negotiation, and compromise must be developed and fully exercised. Non-violent means of resistance to evil deserve much more study and consideration than they have thus far received. There have been significant instances in which people have successfully resisted oppression without recourse to arms.[96] Non-violence is not the way of the weak, the cowardly, or the impatient. Such movements have seldom gained headlines, even though they have left their mark on history. The heroic Danes who would not turn Jews over to the Nazis and the Norwegians who would not teach Nazi propaganda in schools serve as inspiring examples in the history of non-violence.

223.   Non-violent resistance, like war, can take many forms depending upon the demands of a given situation. There is, for instance, organized popular defense instituted by government as part of its contingency planning. Citizens

95. *Pastoral Constitution*, #78.

96. G. Sharp, *The Politics of Nonviolent Action* (Boston: 1973); R. Fisher and W. Ury, *Getting to Yes: Negotiating Agreement Without Giving In* (Boston: 1981).

would be trained in the techniques of peaceable non-compliance and non-cooperation as a means of hindering an invading force or non-democratic government from imposing its will. Effective non-violent resistance requires the united will of a people and may demand as much patience and sacrifice from those who practice it as is now demanded by war and preparation for war. It may not always succeed. Nevertheless, before the possibility is dismissed as impractical or unrealistic, we urge that it be measured against the almost certain effects of a major war.

224.   b) Non-violent resistance offers a common ground of agreement for those individuals who choose the option of Christian pacifism even to the point of accepting the need to die rather than to kill, and those who choose the option of lethal force allowed by the theology of just war. Non-violent resistance makes clear that both are able to be committed to the same objective: defense of their country.

225.   c) Popular defense would go beyond conflict resolution and compromise to a basic synthesis of beliefs and values. In its practice, the objective is not only to avoid causing harm or injury to another creature, but, more positively, to seek the good of the other. Blunting the aggression of an adversary or oppressor would not be enough. The goal is winning the other over, making the adversary a friend.

226.   It is useful to point out that these principles are thoroughly compatible with—and to some extent derived from—Christian teachings and must be part of any Christian theology of peace. Spiritual writers have helped trace the theory of non-violence to its roots in scripture and tradition and have illustrated its practice and success in their studies of the church fathers and the age of martyrs. Christ's own teachings and example provide a model way of life incorporating the truth, and a refusal to return evil for evil.

227.   Non-violent popular defense does not insure that lives would not be lost. Nevertheless, once we recognize that the almost certain consequences of existing policies and strategies of war carry with them a very real threat to the future existence of humankind itself, practical reason as well as spiritual faith demand that it be given serious consideration as an alternative course of action.

228.   d) Once again we declare that the only true defense for the world's population is the rejection of nuclear war and the conventional wars which could escalate into nuclear war. With Pope John Paul II, we call upon educational and research institutes to take a lead in conducting peace studies: "Scientific studies on war, its nature, causes, means, objectives and risks have much to teach us on the conditions for peace . . ."[97] To achieve this end, we urge that funds equivalent to a designated percentage (even one-tenth of one percent) of current budgetary allotments for military purposes be set aside to support such peace research.

229.   In 1981, the Commission on Proposals for the National Academy of Peace and Conflict Resolution recommended the establishment of the U.S. Academy of Peace, a recommendation nearly as old as this country's constitution. The

97. John Paul II, "World Day of Peace Message 1982," #7, cited, p. 476.

commission found that "peace is a legitimate field of learning that encompasses rigorous, interdisciplinary research, education, and training directed toward peacemaking expertise."[98] We endorse the commission's recommendation and urge all citizens to support training in conflict resolution, non-violent resistance, and programs devoted to service to peace and education for peace. Such an academy would not only provide a center for peace studies and activities, but also be a tangible evidence of our nation's sincerity in its often professed commitment to international peace and the abolition of war. We urge universities, particularly Catholic universities, in our country to develop programs for rigorous, interdisciplinary research, education and training directed toward peacemaking expertise.

230.   We, too, must be prepared to do our part to achieve these ends. We encourage churches and educational institutions, from primary schools to colleges and institutes of higher learning, to undertake similar programs at their own initiative. Every effort must be made to understand and evaluate the arms race, to encourage truly transnational perspectives on disarmament, and to explore new forms of international cooperation and exchange. No greater challenge or higher priority can be imagined than the development and perfection of a theology of peace suited to a civilization poised on the brink of self-destruction. It is our prayerful hope that this document will prove to be a starting point and inspiration for that endeavor.

6. The Role of Conscience

231.   A dominant characteristic of the Second Vatican Council's evaluation of modern warfare was the stress it placed on the requirement for proper formation of conscience. Moral principles are effective restraints on power only when policies reflect them and individuals practice them. The relationship of the authority of the state and the conscience of the individual on matters of war and peace takes a new urgency in the face of the destructive nature of modern war.

232.   a) In this connection we reiterate the position we took in 1980. Catholic teaching does not question the right in principle of a government to require military service of its citizens provided the government shows it is necessary. A citizen may not casually disregard his country's conscientious decision to call its citizens to acts of "legitimate defense." Moreover, the role of Christian citizens in the armed forces is a service to the common good and an exercise of the virtue of patriotism, so long as they fulfill this role within defined moral norms.[99]

233.   b) At the same time, no state may demand blind obedience. Our 1980 statement urged the government to present convincing reasons for draft registration, and opposed reinstitution of conscription itself except in the case of

98. *To Establish the United States Academy of Peace: Report of the Commission on Proposals for the National Academy of Peace and Conflict Resolution* (Washington, D.C.: 1981), pp. 119-20.

99. United States Catholic Conference, *Statement on Registration and Conscription for Military Service* (Washington, D.C.: 1980). Cf. also *Human Life in Our Day*, cited, pp. 42-45.

a national defense emergency. Moreover, it reiterated our support for conscientious objection in general and for selective conscientious objection to participation in a particular war, either because of the ends being pursued or the means being used. We called selective conscientious objection a moral conclusion which can be validly derived from the classical teaching of just-war principles. We continue to insist upon respect for and legislative protection of the rights of both classes of conscientious objectors. We also approve requiring alternative service to the community—not related to military needs—by such persons.

B.   SHAPING A PEACEFUL WORLD

234.   Preventing nuclear war is a moral imperative; but the avoidance of war, nuclear or conventional, is not a sufficient conception of international relations today. Nor does it exhaust the content of Catholic teaching. Both the political needs and the moral challenge of our time require a positive conception of peace, based on a vision of a first world order. Pope Paul VI summarized classical Catholic teaching in his encyclical, *The Development of Peoples*: "Peace cannot be limited to a mere absence of war, the result of an ever precarious balance of forces. No, peace is something built up day after day, in the pursuit of an order intended by God, which implies a more perfect form of justice among men and women."[100]

1. World Order in Catholic Teaching

235.   This positive conception of peace sees it as the fruit of order; order, in turn, is shaped by the values of justice, truth, freedom and love. The basis of this teaching is found in sacred scripture, St. Augustine and St. Thomas. It has found contemporary expression and development in papal teaching of this century. The popes of the nuclear age, from Pius XII through John Paul II have affirmed pursuit of international order as the way to banish the scourge of war from human affairs.[101]

236.   The fundamental premise of world order in Catholic teaching is a theological truth: the unity of the human family—rooted in common creation, destined for the kingdom, and united by moral bonds of rights and duties. This basic truth about the unity of the human family pervades the entire teaching on war and peace: for the pacifist position it is one of the reasons why life cannot be taken, while for the just-war position, even in a justified conflict bonds of responsibility remain in spite of the conflict.

237.   Catholic teaching recognizes that in modern history, at least since the Peace of Westphalia (1648) the international community has been governed by

100. Paul VI, *The Development of Peoples* (1967), #76.

101. Cf. V. Yzermans, ed., *Major Addresses of Pius XII*, 2 vols. (St. Paul: 1961) and J. Gremillion, *The Gospel of Peace and Justice*, cited.

nation-states. Catholic moral theology, as expressed for example in chapters 2 and 3 of *Peace on Earth*, accords a real but relative moral value to sovereign states. The value is real because of the functions states fulfill as sources of order and authority in the political community; it is relative because boundaries of the sovereign state do not dissolve the deeper relationships of responsibility existing in the human community. Just as within nations the moral fabric of society is described in Catholic teaching in terms of reciprocal rights and duties—between individuals, and then between the individual and the state—so in the international community *Peace on Earth* defines the rights and duties which exist among states.[102]

238.   In the past twenty years Catholic teaching has become increasingly specific about the content of these international rights and duties. In 1963, *Peace on Earth* sketched the political and legal order among states. In 1966, *The Development of Peoples* elaborated on order of economic rights and duties. In 1979, Pope John Paul II articulated the human rights basis of international relations in his "Address to the United Nations General Assembly."

239.   These documents and others which build upon them, outlined a moral order of international relations, i.e., how the international community *should* be organized. At the same time this teaching has been sensitive to the actual pattern of relations prevailing among states. While not ignoring present geopolitical realities, one of the primary functions of Catholic teaching on world order has been to point the way toward a more integrated international system.

240.   In analyzing this path toward world order, the category increasingly used in Catholic moral teaching (and, more recently, in the social sciences also) is the interdependence of the world today. The theological principle of unity has always affirmed a human interdependence; but today this bond is complemented by the growing political and economic interdependence of the world, manifested in a whole range of international issues.[103]

241.   An important element missing from world order today is a properly constituted political authority with the capacity to shape our material interdependence in the direction of moral interdependence. Pope John XXIII stated the case in the following way:

> Today the universal common good poses problems of world-wide dimensions, which cannot be adequately tackled or solved except by the efforts of public authority endowed with a wideness of powers, structure and means of the same proportions: that is, of public authority which is in a position to operate in an effective manner on a world-wide basis. The moral order itself, therefore, demands that such a form of public authority be established.[104]

---

102. Cf. John XXIII, *Peace on Earth* (1963), esp. #80-145.

103. A sampling of the policy problems and possibilities posed by interdependence can be found in: R. O. Keohane and J. S. Nye, Jr., *Power and Interdependence* (Boston: 1977); S. Hoffmann, *Primacy or World Order* (New York: 1978); The Overseas Development Council, *The U.S. and World Development* 1979; 1980; 1982 (Washington, D.C.).

104. John XXIII, *Peace on Earth* (1963), #137.

242.   Just as the nation-state was a step in the evolution of government at a time when expanding trade and new weapons technologies made the feudal system inadequate to manage conflicts and provide security, so we are now entering an era of new, global interdependencies requiring global systems of governance to manage the resulting conflicts and ensure our common security. Major global problems such as worldwide inflation, trade and payments deficits, competition over scarce resources, hunger, widespread unemployment, global environmental dangers, the growing power of transnational corporations, and the threat of international financial collapse, as well as the danger of world war resulting from these growing tensions—cannot be remedied by a single nation-state approach. They shall require the concerted effort of the whole world community. As we shall indicate below, the United Nations should be particularly considered in this effort.
243.   In the nuclear age, it is in the regulation of interstate conflicts and ultimately the replacement of military by negotiated solutions that the supreme importance and necessity of a moral as well as a political concept of the international common good can be grasped. The absence of adequate structures for addressing these issues places even greater responsiblity on the policies of individual states. By a mix of political vision and moral wisdom, states are called to interpret the national interest in light of the larger global interest.
244.   We are living in a global age with problems and conflicts on a global scale. Either we shall learn to resolve these problems together, or we shall destroy one another. Mutual security and survival require a new vision of the world as one interdependent planet. We have rights and duties not only within our diverse national communities but within the larger world community.

2. The Superpowers in a Disordered World

245.   No relationship more dramatically demonstrates the fragile nature of order in international affairs today than that of the United States and the Soviet Union. These two sovereign states have avoided open war, nuclear or conventional, but they are divided by philosophy, ideology and competing ambitions. Their competition is global in scope and involves everything from comparing nuclear arsenals to printed propaganda. Both have been criticized in international meetings because of their policies in the nuclear arms race.[105]
246.   In our 1980 pastoral letter on Marxism, we sought to portray the significant differences between Christian teaching and Marxism; at the same time we addressed the need for states with different political systems to live together in an interdependent world:

> The Church recognizes the depth and dimensions of the ideological differences that divide the human race, but the urgent practical need for cooperative efforts in the human interest overrules these differences. Hence Catholic teaching seeks to avoid exacerbating the ideological opposition and to focus upon the

105. This has particularly been the case in the two U.N. Special Sessions on Disarmament, 1979, 1982.

problems requiring common efforts across the ideological divide: keeping the peace and empowering the poor.[106]

247.   We believe this passage reflects the teaching of *Peace on Earth*, the continuing call for dialogue of Pope Paul VI and the 1979 address of Pope John Paul II at the United Nations. We continue to stress this theme even while we recognize the difficulty of realizing its objectives.

248.   The difficulties are particularly severe on the issue of the arms race. For most Americans, the danger of war is commonly defined primarily in terms of the threat of Soviet military expansionism and the consequent need to deter or defend against a Soviet military threat. Many assume that the existence of this threat is permanent and that nothing can be done about it except to build and maintain overwhelming or at least countervailing military power.[107]

249.   The fact of a Soviet threat, as well as the existence of a Soviet imperial drive for hegemony, at least in regions of major strategic interest, cannot be denied. The history of the Cold War has produced varying interpretations of which side caused which conflict, but whatever the details of history illustrate, the plain fact is that the memories of Soviet policies in Eastern Europe and recent events in Afghanistan and Poland have left their mark in the American political debate. Many peoples are forcibly kept under communist domination despite their manifest wishes to be free. Soviet power is very great. Whether the Soviet Union's pursuit of military might is motivated primarily by defensive or aggressive aims might be debated, but the effect is nevertheless to leave profoundly insecure those who must live in the shadow of that might.

250.   Americans need have no illusions about the Soviet system of repression

106. United States Catholic Conference, *Marxist Communism* (Washington, D.C.: 1980), p. 19.

107. The debate on U.S.-Soviet relations is extensive; recent examples of it are found in: A. Ulam, "U.S.-Soviet Relations: Unhappy Coexistence," *America and the World, 1978*; *Foreign Affairs* 57 (1979):556-71; W. G. Hyland, "U.S.-Soviet Relations: The Long Road Back," *America and the World, 1981*; *Foreign Affairs* 60 (1982):525-50; R. Legvold, "Containment Without Confrontation," *Foreign Policy* 40 (1980):74-98; S. Hoffmann, "Muscle and Brains," *Foreign Policy* 37 (1979-80):3-27; P. Hassner, "Moscow and The Western Alliance," *Problems of Communism* 30 (1981):37-54; S. Bialer, "The Harsh Decade: Soviet Policies in the 1980s," *Foreign Affairs* 59 (1981):999-1020; G. Kennan, *The Nuclear Delusion: Soviet-American Relations in the Atomic Age* (New York: 1982); N. Podhoretz, *The Present Danger* (New York: 1980); P. Nitze, "Strategy in the 1980s," *Foreign Affairs* 59 (1980):82-101; R. Strode and C. Gray, "The Imperial Dimension of Soviet Military Power," *Problems of Communism* 30 (1981):1-15; International Institute for Strategic Studies, *Prospects of Soviet Power in the 1980s*, Parts I and II, Adelphi Papers #151 and 152 (London: 1979); S. S. Kaplan, ed., *Diplomacy of Power: Soviet Armed Forces as a Political Instrument* (Washington, D.C.: 1981); R. Barnet, *The Giants: Russia and America* (New York: 1977); M. McGwire, *Soviet Military Requirements*, The Brookings Institution (Washington, D.C.: 1982); R. Tucker, "The Purposes of American Power," *Foreign Affairs* 59 (1980/81):241-74; A. Geyer, *The Idea of Disarmament: Rethinking the Unthinkable* (Washington, D.C.: 1982). For a review of Soviet adherence to treaties cf.: "The SALT Syndrome Charges and Facts: Analysis of an 'Anti-SALT Documentary,'" report prepared by U.S. government agencies (State, Defense, CIA, ACDA and NSC), reprinted in *The Defense Monitor* 10, #8A, Center for Defense Information.

and the lack of respect in that system for human rights, or about Soviet covert operations and pro-revolutionary activities. To be sure, our own system is not without flaws. Our government has sometimes supported repressive governments in the name of preserving freedom, has carried out repugnant covert operations of its own, and remains imperfect in its domestic record of ensuring equal rights for all. At the same time, there is a difference. NATO is an alliance of democratic countries which have freely chosen their association; the Warsaw Pact is not.

251.   To pretend that as a nation we have lived up to all our own ideals would be patently dishonest. To pretend that all evils in the world have been or are now being perpetrated by dictatorial regimes would be both dishonest and absurd. But having said this, and admitting our own faults, it is imperative that we confront reality. The facts simply do not support the invidious comparisons made at times, even in our own society, between our way of life, in which most basic human rights are at least recognized even if they are not always adequately supported, and those totalitarian and tyrannical regimes in which such rights are either denied or systematically suppressed. Insofar as this is true, however, it makes the promotion of human rights in our foreign policy, as well as our domestic policy, all the more important. It is the acid test of our commitment to our democratic values. In this light, any attempts to justify, for reasons of state, support for regimes that continue to violate human rights is all the more morally reprehensible in its hypocrisy.

252.   A glory of the United States is the range of political freedoms its system permits us. We, as bishops, as Catholics, as citizens, exercise those freedoms in writing this letter, with its share of criticisms of our government. We have true freedom of religion, freedom of speech, and access to a free press. We could not exercise the same freedoms in contemporary Eastern Europe or in the Soviet Union. Free people must always pay a proportionate price and run some risks—responsibly—to preserve their freedom.

253.   It is one thing to recognize that the people of the world do not want war. It is quite another thing to attribute the same good motives to regimes or political systems that have consistently demonstrated precisely the opposite in their behavior. There are political philosophies with understandings of morality so radically different from ours, that even negotiations proceed from different premises, although identical terminology may be used by both sides. This is no reason for not negotiating. It is a very good reason for not negotiating blindly or naively.

254.   In this regard, Pope John Paul II offers some sober reminders concerning dialogue and peace:

> [O]ne must mention the tactical and deliberate lie, which misuses language, which has recourse to the most sophisticated techniques of propaganda, which deceives and distorts dialogue and incites to aggression . . . while certain parties are fostered by ideologies which, in spite of their declarations, are opposed to the dignity of the human person, ideologies which see in struggle the motive force of history, that see in force the source of rights, that see in the discernment of the enemy the ABC of politics, dialogue is fixed and sterile.

Or, if it still exists, it is a superficial and falsified reality. It becomes very difficult, not to say impossible, therefore. There follows almost a complete lack of communication between countries and blocs. Even the international institutions are paralyzed. And the setback to dialogue then runs the risk of serving the arms race. However, even in what can be considered as an impasse to the extent that individuals support such ideologies, the attempt to have a lucid dialogue seems still necessary in order to unblock the situation and to work for the possible establishment of peace on particular points. This is to be done by counting upon common sense, on the possibilities of danger for everyone and on the just aspirations to which the peoples themselves largely adhere.[108]

255.   The cold realism of this text, combined with the conviction that political dialogue and negotiations must be pursued, in spite of obstacles, provides solid guidance for U.S.-Soviet relations. Acknowledging all the differences between the two philosophies and political systems, the irreducible truth is that objective mutual interests do exist between the superpowers. Proof of this concrete if limited convergence of interest can be found in some vitally important agreements on nuclear weapons which have already been negotiated in the areas of nuclear testing and nuclear explosions in space as well as the SALT I agreements.

256.   The fact that the Soviet union now possesses a huge arsenal of strategic weapons as threatening to us as ours may appear to them does not exclude the possibility of success in such negotiations. The conviction of many European observers that a *modus vivendi* (often summarized as "detente") is a practical possibility in political, economic, and scientific areas should not be lightly dismissed in our country.

257.   Sensible and successful diplomacy, however, will demand that we avoid the trap of a form of anti-Sovietism which fails to grasp the central danger of a superpower rivalry in which both the U.S. and the U.S.S.R. are the players, and fails to recognize the common interest both states have in never using nuclear weapons. Some of those dangers and common interests would exist in any world where two great powers, even relatively benign ones, competed for power, influence, and security. The diplomatic requirement for addressing the U.S.-Soviet relationship is not romantic idealism about Soviet intentions and capabilities but solid realism which recognizes that everyone will lose in a nuclear exchange.

258.   As bishops we are concerned with issues which go beyond diplomatic requirements. It is of some value to keep raising in the realm of the political debate truths which ground our involvement in the affairs of nations and peoples. Diplomatic dialogue usually sees the other as a potential or real adversary. Soviet behavior in some cases merits the adjective reprehensible, but the Soviet people and their leaders are human beings created in the image and likeness of God. To believe we are condemned in the future only to what has been the past of U.S.-Soviet relations is to underestimate both our human potential for creative diplomacy and God's action in our midst which can open the way to changes we could barely imagine. We do not intend to foster illusory ideas that the road ahead in superpower

108. John Paul II, "World Day of Peace Message 1983," #7.

relations will be devoid of tension or that peace will be easily achieved. But we do warn against that "hardness of heart" which can close us or others to the changes needed to make the future different from the past.

3. Interdependence: From Fact to Policy

259. While the nuclear arms race focuses attention on the U.S.-Soviet relationship, it is neither politically wise nor morally justifiable to ignore the broader international context in which that relationship exists. Public attention, riveted on the big powers, often misses the plight of scores of countries and millions of people simply trying to survive. The interdependence of the world means a set of interrelated human questions. Important as keeping the peace in the nuclear age is, it does not solve or dissolve the other major problems of the day. Among these problems the pre-eminent issue is the continuing chasm in living standards between the industrialized world (East and West) and the developing world. To quote Pope John Paul II:

> So widespread is the phenomenon that it brings into question the financial, monetary, production and commercial mechanisms that, resting on various political pressures, support the world economy. These are proving incapable either of remedying the unjust social situations inherited from the past or of dealing with the urgent challenges and ethical demands of the present.[109]

260. The East-West competition, central as it is to world order and important as it is in the foreign policy debate, does not address this moral question which rivals the nuclear issue in its human significance. While the problem of the developing nations would itself require a pastoral letter, Catholic teaching has maintained an analysis of the problem which should be identified here. The analysis acknowledges internal causes of poverty, but also concentrates on the way the larger international economic structures affect the poor nations. These particularly involve trade, monetary, investment and aid policies.

261. Neither of the superpowers is conspicuous in these areas for initiatives designed to address "the absolute poverty" in which millions live today.[110]

262. From our perspective and experience as bishops, we believe there is a much greater potential for response to these questions in the minds and hearts of Americans than has been reflected in U.S. policy. As pastors who often appeal to our congregations for funds destined for international programs, we find good will and great generosity the prevailing characteristics. The spirit of generosity which shaped the Marshall Plan is still alive in the American public.

263. We must discover how to translate this personal sense of generosity and compassion into support for policies which would respond to papal teaching in international economic issues. It is precisely the need to expand our conception of international charity and relief to an understanding of the need for social

109. John Paul II, "The Redeemer of Man," #16, *Origins* 8 (1980):635.

110. The phrase and its description are found in R. S. McNamara, *Report to the Board of Governors of the World Bank 1978*; cf. also 1979; 1980 (Washington, D.C.).

justice in terms of trade, aid and monetary issues which was reflected in Pope John Paul II's call to American Catholics in Yankee Stadium:

> Within the framework of your national institutions and in cooperation with all your compatriots, you will also want to seek out the structural reasons which foster or cause the different forms of poverty in the world and in your own country, so that you can apply the proper remedies. You will not allow yourselves to be intimidated or discouraged by over-simplified explanations which are more ideological than scientific—explanations which try to account for a complex evil by some single cause. But neither will you recoil before the reforms—even profound ones—of attitudes and structures that may prove necessary in order to recreate over and over again the conditions needed by the disadvantaged if they are to have a fresh chance in the hard struggle of life. The poor of the United States and of the world are your brothers and sisters in Christ.[111]

264.   The Pope's words highlight an intellectual, moral, and political challenge for the United States. Intellectually, there is a need to rethink the meaning of national interest in an interdependent world. Morally, there is a need to build upon the spirit of generosity present in the U.S. public, directing it toward a more systematic response to the major issues affecting the poor of the world. Politically, there is a need for U.S. policies which promote the profound structural reforms called for by recent papal teaching.

265.   Precisely in the name of international order papal teaching has, by word and deed, sought to promote multilateral forms of cooperation toward the developing world. The U.S. capacity for leadership in multilateral institutions is very great. We urge much more vigorous and creative response to the needs of the developing countries by the United States in these institutions.

266.   The significant role the United States could play is evident in the daily agenda facing these institutions. Proposals addressing the relationship of the industrialized and developing countries on a broad spectrum of issues, all in need of "profound reforms," are regularly discussed in the United Nations and other international organizations. Without U.S. participation, significant reform and substantial change in the direction of addressing the needs of the poor will not occur. Meeting these needs is an essential element for a peaceful world.

267.   Papal teaching of the last four decades has not only supported international institutions in principle, it has supported the United Nations specifically. Pope Paul VI said to the U.N. General Assembly:

> The edifice which you have constructed must never fail; it must be perfected and made equal to the needs which world history will present. You mark a stage in the development of mankind for which retreat must never be admitted, but from which it is necessary that advance be made.[112]

268.   It is entirely necessary to examine the United Nations carefully, to recognize its limitations and propose changes where needed. Nevertheless, in light

111. John Paul II, "Homily at Yankee Stadium," #4, *Origins* 9 (1979):311.

112. Paul VI, "Address to the General Assembly of the United Nations" (1965), #2.

of the continuing endorsement found in papal teaching, we urge that the United States adopt a stronger supportive leadership role with respect to the United Nations. The growing interdependence of the nations and peoples of the world, coupled with the extra-governmental presence of multinational corporations, requires new structures of cooperation. As one of the founders of and major financial contributors to the United Nations, the United States can, and should, assume a more positive and creative role in its life today.

269.   It is in the context of the United Nations that the impact of the arms race on the prospects for economic development is highlighted. The numerous U.N. studies on the relationship of development and disarmament support the judgment of Vatican II cited earlier in this letter: "The arms race is one of the greatest curses on the human race and the harm it inflicts upon the poor is more than can be endured."[113]

270.   We are aware that the precise relationship between disarmament and development is neither easily demonstrated nor easily reoriented. But the fact of a massive distortion of resources in the face of crying human need creates a moral question. In an interdependent world, the security of one nation is related to the security of all. When we consider how and what we pay for defense today, we need a broader view than the equation of arms with security.[114] The threats to the security and stability of an interdependent world are not all contained in missiles and bombers.

271.   If the arms race in all its dimensions is not reversed, resources will not be available for the human needs so evident in many parts of the globe and in our own country as well. But we also know that making resources available is a first step; policies of wise use would also have to follow. Part of the process of thinking about the economics of disarmament includes the possibilities of conversion of defense industries to other purposes. Many say the possibilities are great if the political will is present. We say the political will to reorient resources to human needs and redirect industrial, scientific, and technological capacity to meet those needs is part of the challenge of the nuclear age. Those whose livelihood is dependent upon industries which can be reoriented should rightfully expect assistance in making the transition to new forms of employment. The economic dimension of the arms race is broader than we can assess here, but these issues we have raised are among the primary questions before the nation.[115]

272.   An interdependent world requires an understanding that key policy questions today involve mutuality of interest. If the monetary and trading sys-

---

113. *Pastoral Constitution*, #81.

114. Cf. Hoffman, cited; Independent Commission on Disarmament and Security Issues, *Common Security* (New York: 1982).

115. For an analysis of the policy problems of reallocating resources, cf: Bruce M. Russett, *The Prisoners of Insecurity* (San Francisco: 1983). Cf.: *Common Security*, cited; Russett, cited; *U.N. Report on Disarmament and Development* (New York: 1982); United Nations, *The Relationship Between Disarmament and Development: A Summary*, Fact Sheet #21 (New York: 1982).

tems are not governed by sensitivity to mutual needs, they can be destroyed. If the protection of human rights and the promotion of human needs are left as orphans in the diplomatic arena, the stability we seek in increased armaments will eventually be threatened by rights denied and needs unmet in vast sectors of the globe. If future planning about conservation of and access to resources is relegated to a pure struggle of power, we shall simply guarantee conflict in the future.

273.   The moral challenge of interdependence concerns shaping the relationships and rules of practice which will support our common need for security, welfare, and safety. The challenge tests our idea of human community, our policy analysis, and our political will. The need to prevent nuclear war is absolutely crucial, but even if this is achieved, there is much more to be done.

IV. The Pastoral Challenge and Response

A. THE CHURCH: A COMMUNITY OF CONSCIENCE, PRAYER AND PENANCE

274.   Pope John Paul II, in his first encyclical, recalled with gratitude the teaching of Pius XII on the Church. He then went on to say:

> Membership in that body has for its source a particular call, united with the saving action of grace. Therefore, if we wish to keep in mind this community of the People of God, which is so vast and so extremely differentiated, we must see first and foremost Christ saying in a way to each member of the community: "Follow Me." It is the community of the disciples, each of whom in a different way—at times very consciously and consistently, at other times not very consciously and very consistently—is following Christ. This shows also the deeply "personal" aspect and dimension of this society.[116]

275.   In the following pages we should like to spell out some of the implications of being a community of Jesus' disciples in a time when our nation is so heavily armed with nuclear weapons and is engaged in a continuing development of new weapons together with strategies for their use.

276.   It is clear today, perhaps more than in previous generations, that convinced Christians are a minority in nearly every country of the world—including nominally Christian and Catholic nations. In our own country we are coming to a fuller awareness that a response to the call of Jesus is both personal and demanding. As believers we can identify rather easily with the early Church as a company of witnesses engaged in a difficult mission. To be disciples of Jesus requires that we continually go beyond where we now are. To obey the call of Jesus means separating ourselves from all attachments and affiliation that could prevent us from hearing and following our authentic vocation. To set out on the road to discipleship is to dispose oneself for a share in the cross (cf. Jn. 16:20). To be a Christian, according to the New Testament, is not simply to believe with

116. John Paul II, "The Redeemer of Man," #21, cited, p. 641. Much of the following reflects the content of A. Dulles, *A Church to Believe in: Discipleship and the Dynamics of Freedom* (New York: 1982), ch. 1.

one's mind, but also to become a doer of the word, a wayfarer with and a witness to Jesus. This means, of course, that we never expect complete success within history and that we must regard as normal even the path of persecution and the possibility of martyrdom.

277.   We readily recognize that we live in a world that is becoming increasingly estranged from Christian values. In order to remain a Christian, one must take a resolute stand against many commonly accepted axioms of the world. To become true disciples, we must undergo a demanding course of induction into the adult Christian community. We must continually equip ourselves to profess the full faith of the Church in an increasingly secularized society. We must develop a sense of solidarity, cemented by relationships with mature and exemplary Christians who represent Christ and his way of life.

278.   All of these comments about the meaning of being a disciple or a follower of Jesus today are especially relevant to the quest for genuine peace in our time.

B.   ELEMENTS OF A PASTORAL RESPONSE

279.   We recommend and endorse for the faithful some practical programs to meet the challenge to their faith in this area of grave concern.

1. Educational Programs and Formation of Conscience

280.   Since war, especially the threat of nuclear war, is one of the central problems of our day, how we seek to solve it could determine the mode, and even the possibility, of life on earth. God made human beings stewards of the earth; we cannot escape this responsibility. Therefore we urge every diocese and parish to implement balanced and objective educational programs to help people at all age levels to understand better the issues of war and peace. Development and implementation of such programs must receive a high priority during the next several years. They must teach the full impact of our Christian faith. To accomplish this, this pastoral letter in its entirety, including its complexity, should be used as a guide and a framework for such programs, as they lead people to make moral decisions about the problems of war and peace, keeping in mind that the applications of principles in this pastoral letter do not carry the same moral authority as our statements of universal moral principles and formal Church teaching.

281.   In developing educational programs, we must keep in mind that questions of war and peace have a profoundly moral dimension which responsible Christians cannot ignore. They are questions of life and death. True, they also have a political dimension because they are embedded in public policy. But the fact that they are also political is no excuse for denying the Church's obligation to provide its members with the help they need in forming their consciences. We must learn together how to make correct and responsible moral judgments. We reject, therefore, criticism of the Church's concern with these issues on the

ground that it "should not become involved in politics." We are called to move from discussion to witness and action.

282.   At the same time, we recognize that the Church's teaching authority does not carry the same force when it deals with technical solutions involving particular means as it does when it speaks of principles or ends. People may agree in abhorring an injustice, for instance, yet sincerely disagree as to what practical approach will achieve justice. Religious groups are as entitled as others to their opinion in such cases, but they should not claim that their opinions are the only ones that people of good will may hold.

283.   The Church's educational programs must explain clearly those principles or teachings about which there is little question. Those teachings, which seek to make explicit the gospel call to peace and the tradition of the Church, should then be applied to concrete situations. They must indicate what the possible legitimate options are and what the consequences of those options may be. While this approach should be self-evident, it needs to be emphasized. Some people who have entered the public debate on nuclear warfare, at all points on the spectrum of opinion, appear not to understand or accept some of the clear teachings of the Church as contained in papal or conciliar documents. For example, some would place almost no limits on the use of nuclear weapons if they are needed for "self-defense." Some on the other side of the debate insist on conclusions which may be legitimate options but cannot be made obligatory on the basis of actual Church teaching.

2. True Peace Calls for "Reverence for Life"

284.   All of the values we are promoting in this letter rest ultimately in the disarmament of the human heart and the conversion of the human spirit to God who alone can give authentic peace. Indeed, to have peace in our world, we must first have peace within ourselves. As Pope John Paul II reminded us in his 1982 World Day of Peace message, world peace will always elude us until peace becomes a reality for each of us personally. "It springs from the dynamism of free wills guided by reason towards the common good that is to be attained in truth, justice and love."[117] Interior peace becomes possible only when we have a conversion of spirit. We cannot have peace with hate in our hearts.

285.   No society can live in peace with itself, or with the world, without a full awareness of the worth and dignity of every human person, and of the sacredness of all human life (Jas. 4:1-2). When we accept violence in any form as commonplace, our sensitivities become dulled. When we accept violence, war itself can be taken for granted. Violence has many faces: oppression of the poor, deprivation of basic human rights, economic exploitation, sexual exploitation and pornography, neglect or abuse of the aged and the helpless, and innumerable other acts of inhumanity. Abortion in particular blunts a sense of the sacredness of human life. In a society where the innocent unborn are killed wantonly, how can we expect people to feel righteous revulsion at the act or

117. John Paul II, "World Day of Peace Message 1982," #4, cited, p. 475.

threat of killing noncombatants in war?

286.   We are well aware of the differences involved in the taking of human life in warfare and the taking of human life through abortion. As we have discussed throughout this document, even justifiable defense against aggression may result in the indirect or unintended loss of innocent human lives. This is tragic, but may conceivably be proportionate to the values defended. Nothing, however, can justify direct attack on innocent human life, in or out of warfare. Abortion is precisely such an attack.

287.   We know that millions of men and women of good will, of all religious persuasions, join us in our commitment to try to reduce the horrors of war, and particularly to assure that nuclear weapons will never again be used, by any nation, anywhere, for any reason. Millions join us in our "no" to nuclear war, in the certainty that nuclear war would inevitably result in the killing of millions of innocent human beings, directly or indirectly. Yet many part ways with us in our efforts to reduce the horror of abortion and our "no" to war on innocent human life in the womb, killed not indirectly, but directly.

288.   We must ask how long a nation willing to extend a constitutional guarantee to the "right" to kill defenseless human beings by abortion is likely to refrain from adopting strategic warfare policies deliberately designed to kill millions of defenseless human beings, if adopting them should come to seem "expedient." Since 1973, approximately 15 million abortions have been performed in the United States, symptoms of a kind of disease of the human spirit. And we now find ourselves seriously discussing the pros and cons of such questions as infanticide, euthanasia, and the involvement of physicians in carrying out the death penalty. Those who would celebrate such a national disaster can only have blinded themselves to its reality.

289.   Pope Paul VI was resolutely clear: *If you wish peace, defend life.*[118] We plead with all who would work to end the scourge of war to begin by defending life at its most defenseless, the life of the unborn.

3. Prayer

290.   A conversion of our hearts and minds will make it possible for us to enter into a closer communion with our Lord. We nourish that communion by personal and communal prayer, for it is in prayer that we encounter Jesus, who is our peace, and learn from him the way to peace.

291.   In prayer we are renewed in faith and confirmed in our hope in God's promise.

292.   The Lord's promise is that he is in our midst when we gather in prayer. Strengthened by this conviction, we beseech the risen Christ to fill the world with his peace. We call upon Mary, the first disciple and the Queen of Peace, to intercede for us and for the people of our time that we may walk in the way of peace. In this context, we encouage devotion to Our Lady of Peace.

293.   As believers, we understand peace as a gift of God. This belief prompts us to pray constantly, personally and communally, particularly through the

118. Paul VI, "World Day of Peace Message 1977."

reading of scripture and devotion to the rosary, especially in the family. Through these means and others, we seek the wisdom to begin the search for peace and the courage to sustain us as instruments of Christ's peace in the world.

294.   The practice of contemplative prayer is especially valuable for advancing harmony and peace in the world. For this prayer rises, by divine grace, where there is total disarmament of the heart and unfolds in an experience of love which is the moving force of peace. Contemplation fosters a vision of the human family as united and interdependent in the mystery of God's love for all people. This silent, interior prayer bridges temporarily the "already" and "not yet," this world and God's kingdom of peace.

295.   The Mass in particular is a unique means of seeking God's help to create the conditions essential for true peace in ourselves and in the world. In the eucharist we encounter the risen Lord, who gave us his peace. He shares with us the grace of the redemption, which helps us to preserve and nourish this precious gift. Nowhere is the Church's urgent plea for peace more evident in the liturgy than in the Communion Rite. After beginning this rite of the Mass with the Lord's Prayer, praying for reconciliation now and in the kingdom to come, the community asks God to "grant us peace in our day," not just at some time in the distant future. Even before we are exhorted "to offer each other the sign of peace," the priest continues the Church's prayer for peace, recalling the Lord Jesus Christ's own legacy of peace:

> Lord Jesus Christ, you said to your apostles: I leave you peace, my peace I give you. Look not on our sins, but on the faith of your Church, and grant us the peace and unity of your kingdom.

Therefore we encourage every Catholic to make the sign of peace at Mass an authentic sign of our reconciliation with God and with one another. This sign of peace is also a visible expression of our commitment to work for peace as a Christian community. We approach the table of the Lord only after having dedicated ourselves as a Christian community to peace and reconciliation. As an added sign of commitment, we suggest that there always be a petition for peace in the general intercessions at every eucharistic celebration.

296.   We implore other Christians and everyone of good will to join us in this continuing prayer for peace, as we beseech God for peace within ourselves, in our families and community, in our nation, and in the world.

4. Penance

297.   Prayer by itself is incomplete without penance. Penance directs us toward our goal of putting on the attitudes of Jesus himself. Because we are all capable of violence, we are never totally conformed to Christ and are always in need of conversion. The twentieth century alone provides adequate evidence of our violence as individuals and as a nation. Thus, there is continual need for acts of penance and conversion. The worship of the Church, particularly through the sacrament of reconciliation and communal penance services, offers us multiple ways to make reparation for the violence in our own lives and in our world.

298.   As a tangible sign of our need and desire to do penance we, for the cause of peace, commit ourselves to fast and abstinence on each Friday of the year. We call upon our people voluntarily to do penance on Friday by eating less food and by abstaining from meat. This return to a traditional practice of penance, once well observed in the U.S. Church, should be accompanied by works of charity and service toward our neighbors. Every Friday should be a day significantly devoted to prayer, penance, and almsgiving for peace.

299.   It is to such forms of penance and conversion that the Scriptures summon us. In the words of the prophet Isaiah:

> Is not the sort of fast that pleases me, to break unjust fetters and undo the thongs of the yoke, to let the oppressed go free and break every yoke, to share your bread with the hungry, and shelter the homeless poor, to clothe the person you see to be naked and not turn from your own kin? Then will your light shine like the dawn and your wound be quickly healed over. If you do away with the yoke, the clenched fist, the wicked word, if you give your bread to the hungry and relief to the oppressed, your light will rise in the darkness, and your shadows become like noon (Is. 58:6-8; 10).

300.   The present nuclear arms race has distracted us from the words of the prophets, has turned us from peace-making, and has focused our attention on a nuclear buildup leading to annihilation. We are called to turn back from this evil of total destruction and turn instead in prayer and penance toward God, toward our neighbor, and toward the building of a peaceful world:

> I set before you life or death, a blessing or a curse. Choose life then, so that you and your descendants may live in the love of Yahweh your God, obeying His voice, clinging to Him; for in this your life consists, and on this depends your long stay in the land which Yahweh swore to your fathers Abraham, Isacc and Jacob, He would give them (Dt. 30:19–20).

C.   CHALLENGE AND HOPE

301.   The arms race presents questions of conscience we may not evade. As American Catholics, we are called to express our loyalty to the deepest values we cherish: peace, justice and security for the entire human family. National goals and policies must be measured against that standard.

302.   We speak here in a specific way to the Catholic community. After the passage of nearly four decades and a concomitant growth in our understanding of the ever growing horror of nuclear war, we must shape the climate of opinion which will make it possible for our country to express profound sorrow over the atomic bombing in 1945. Without that sorrow, there is no possibility of finding a way to repudiate future use of nuclear weapons or of conventional weapons in such military actions as would not fulfill just-war criteria.

303.   **To Priests, Deacons, Religious and Pastoral Ministers:** We recognize the unique role in the Church which belongs to priests and deacons by reason of

the sacrament of holy orders and their unique responsibility in the community of believers. We also recognize the valued and indispensable role of men and women religious. To all of them and to all other pastoral ministers we stress that the cultivation of the gospel vision of peace as a way of life for believers and as a leaven in society should be a major objective. As bishops, we are aware each day of our dependence upon your efforts. We are aware, too, that this letter and the new obligations it could present to the faithful may create difficulties for you in dealing with those you serve. We have confidence in your capacity and ability to convert these difficulties into an opportunity to give a fuller witness to our Lord and his message. This letter will be known by the faithful only as well as you know it, preach and teach it, and use it creatively.

304. **To Educators:** We have outlined in this letter Catholic teaching on war and peace, but this framework will become a living message only through your work in the Catholic community. To teach the ways of peace is not "to weaken the nation's will" but to be concerned for the nation's soul. We address theologians in a particular way, because we know that we have only begun the journey toward a theology of peace; without your specific contributions this desperately needed dimension of our faith will not be realized. Through your help we may provide new vision and wisdom for church and state.

305. We are confident that all the models of Catholic education which have served the Church and our country so well in so many ways will creatively rise to the challenge of peace.

306. **To Parents:** Your role, in our eyes, is unsurpassed by any other; the foundation of society is the family. We are conscious of the continuing sacrifices you make in the efforts to nurture the full human and spiritual growth of your children. Children hear the gospel message first from your lips. Parents who consciously discuss issues of justice in the home and who strive to help children solve conflicts through non-violent methods enable their children to grow up as peacemakers. We pledge our continuing pastoral support in the common objective we share of building a peaceful world for the future of children everywhere.

307. **To Youth:** Pope John Paul II singles you out in every country where he visits as the hope of the future; we agree with him. We call you to choose your future work and professions carefully. How you spend the rest of your lives will determine, in large part, whether there will any longer be a world as we know it. We ask you to study carefully the teachings of the Church and the demands of the gospel about war and peace. We encourage you to seek careful guidance as you reach conscientious decisions about your civic responsibilities in this age of nuclear military forces.

308. We speak to you, however, as people of faith. We share with you our deepest conviction that in the midst of the dangers and complexities of our time God is with us, working through us and sustaining us all in our efforts of building a world of peace with justice for each person.

309. **To Men and Women in Military Service:** Millions of you are Catholics serving in the armed forces. We recognize that you carry special responsibilities for the issues we have considered in this letter. Our perspective on your profes-

sion is that of Vatican II: "All those who enter the military service in loyalty to their country should look upon themselves as the custodians of the security and freedom of their fellow-countrymen; and where they carry out their duty properly, they are contributing to the maintenance of peace."[119]

310.   It is surely not our intention in writing this letter to create problems for Catholics in the armed forces. Every profession, however, has its specific moral questions and it is clear that the teaching on war and peace developed in this letter poses a special challenge and opportunity to those in the military profession. Our pastoral contact with Catholics in military service, either through our direct experience or through our priests, impresses us with the demanding moral standards we already see observed and the commitment to Catholic faith we find. We are convinced that the challenges of this letter will be faced conscientiously. The purpose of defense policy is to defend the peace; military professionals should understand their vocation this way. We believe they do, and we support this view.

311.   We remind all in authority and in the chain of command that their training and field manuals have long prohibited, and still do prohibit, certain actions in the conduct of war, especially those actions which inflict harm on innocent civilians. The question is not whether certain measures are unlawful or forbidden in warfare, but which measures: to refuse to take such actions is not an act of cowardice or treason but one of courage and patriotism.

312.   We address particularly those involved in the exercise of authority over others. We are aware of your responsibilities and impressed by the standard of personal and professional duty you uphold. We feel, therefore, that we can urge you to do everything you can to assure that every peaceful alternative is exhausted before war is even remotely considered. In developing battle plans and weapons systems, we urge you to try to ensure that these are designed to reduce violence, destruction, suffering, and death to a minimum, keeping in mind especially non-combatants and other innocent persons.

313.   Those who train individuals for military duties must remember that the citizen does not lose his or her basic human rights by entrance into military service. No one, for whatever reason, can justly treat a military person with less dignity and respect than that demanded for and deserved by every human person. One of the most difficult problems of war involves defending a free society without destroying the values that give it meaning and validity. Dehumanization of a nation's military personnel by dulling their sensibilities and generating hatred toward adversaries in an effort to increase their fighting effectiveness robs them of basic human rights and freedoms, degrading them as persons.

314.   Attention must be given to the effects on military personnel themselves of the use of even legitimate means of conducting war. While attacking legitimate targets and wounding or killing opposed combat forces may be morally justified, what happens to military persons required to carry out these actions? Are they treated merely as instruments of war, insensitive as the weapons they use? With

119. *Pastoral Constitution*, #79.

what moral or emotional experiences do they return from war and attempt to resume normal civilian lives? How does their experience affect society? How are they treated by society?

315.   It is not only basic human rights of adversaries that must be respected, but those of our own forces as well. We re-emphasize, therefore, the obligation of responsible authorities to ensure appropriate training and education of combat forces and to provide appropriate support for those who have experienced combat. It is unconscionable to deprive those veterans of combat whose lives have been severely disrupted or traumatized by their combat experiences of proper psychological and other appropriate treatment and support.

316.   Finally, we are grateful for the sacrifice so many in military service must make today and for the service offered in the past by veterans. We urge that those sacrifices be mitigated so far as possible by the provision of appropriate living and working conditions and adequate financial recompense. Military persons and their families must be provided continuing opportunity for full spiritual growth, the exercise of their religious faith, and a dignified mode of life.

317.   We especially commend and encourage our priests in military service. In addition to the message already addressed to all priests and religious, we stress the special obligations and opportunities you face in direct pastoral service to the men and women of the armed forces. To complement a teaching document of this scope, we shall need the sensitive and wise pastoral guidance only you can provide. We promise our support in facing this challenge.

318.   **To Men and Women in Defense Industries:** You also face specific questions, because the defense industry is directly involved in the development and production of the weapons of mass destruction which have concerned us in this letter. We do not presume or pretend that clear answers exist to many of the personal, professional and financial choices facing you in your varying responsibilities. In this letter we have ruled out certain uses of nuclear weapons, while also expressing conditional moral acceptance for deterrence. All Catholics, at every level of defense industries, can and should use the moral principles of this letter to form their consciences. We realize that different judgments of conscience will face different people, and we recognize the possibility of diverse concrete judgments being made in this complex area. We seek as moral teachers and pastors to be available to all who confront these questions of personal and vocational choice. Those who in conscience decide that they should no longer be associated with defense activities should find support in the Catholic community. Those who remain in these industries or earn a profit from the weapons industry should find in the Church guidance and support for the ongoing evaluation of their work.

319.   **To Men and Women of Science:** At Hiroshima Pope John Paul said: "Criticism of science and technology is sometimes so severe that it comes close to condemning science itself. On the contrary, science and technology are a wonderful product of a God-given human creativity, since they have provided us with wonderful possibilities and we all gratefully benefit from them. But we know that this potential is not a neutral one: it can be used either for man's

progress or for his degradation."[120] We appreciate the efforts of scientists, some of whom first unlocked the secret of atomic power and others of whom have developed it in diverse ways, to turn the enormous power of science to the cause of peace.

320. Modern history is not lacking scientists who have looked back with deep remorse on the development of weapons to which they contributed, sometimes with the highest motivation, even believing that they were creating weapons that would render all other weapons obsolete and convince the world of the unthinkableness of war. Such efforts have ever proved illusory. Surely, equivalent dedication of scientific minds to reverse current trends, and to pursue concepts as bold and adventuresome in favor of peace as those which in the past have magnified the risks of war, could result in dramatic benefits for all of humanity. We particularly note in this regard the extensive efforts of public education undertaken by physicians and scientists on the medical consequences of nuclear war.

321. We do not, however, wish to limit our remarks to the physical sciences alone. Nor do we limit our remarks to physical scientists. In his address at the United Nations University in Hiroshima, Pope John Paul II warned about misuse of "the social sciences and the human behavioral sciences when they are utilized to manipulate people, to crush their mind, souls, dignity and freedom . . ."[121] The positive role of social science in overcoming the dangers of the nuclear age is evident in this letter. We have been dependent upon the research and analysis of social scientists in our effort to apply the moral principles of the Catholic tradition to the concrete problems of our day. We encourage social scientists to continue this work of relating moral wisdom and political reality. We are in continuing need of your insights.

322. **To Men and Women of the Media:** We have directly felt our dependence upon you in writing this letter; all the problems we have confronted have been analyzed daily in the media. As we have grappled with these issues, we have experienced some of the responsibility you bear for interpreting them. On the quality of your efforts depends in great measure the opportunity the general public will have for understanding this letter.

323. **To Public Officials:** Vatican II spoke forcefully of "the difficult yet noble art of politics."[122] No public issue is more difficult than avoiding war; no public task more noble than building a secure peace. Public officials in a democracy must both lead and listen; they are ultimately dependent upon a popular consensus to sustain policy. We urge you to lead with courage and to listen to the public debate with sensitivity.

324. Leadership in a nuclear world means examining with great care and objectivity every potential initiative toward world peace, regardless of how unpromising it might at first appear. One specific initiative which might be

---

120. John Paul II, "Address to Scientists and Scholars," #3, cited, p. 621.

121. Ibid.

122. *Pastoral Constitution*, #75.

taken now would be the establishment of a task force including the public sector, industry, labor, economists and scientists with the mandate to consider the problems and challanges posed by nuclear disarmament to our economic well-being and industrial output. Listening includes being particularly attentive to the consciences of those who sincerely believe that they may not morally support warfare in general, a given war, or the exercise of a particular role within the armed forces. Public officials might well serve all of our fellow citizens by proposing and supporting legislation designed to give maximum protection to this precious freedom, true freedom of conscience.

325. In response to public officials who both lead and listen, we urge citizens to respect the vocation of public service. It is a role easily maligned but not easily fulfilled. Neither justice nor peace can be achieved with stability in the absence of courageous and creative public servants.

326. **To Catholics as Citizens:** All papal teaching on peace has stressed the crucial role of public opinion. Pope John Paul II specified the tasks before us: "There is no justification for not raising the question of the responsibility of each nation and each individual in the face of possible wars and of the nuclear threat."[123] In a democracy, the responsibility of the nation and that of its citizens coincide. Nuclear weapons pose especially acute questions of conscience for American Catholics. As citizens we wish to affirm our loyalty to our country and its ideals, yet we are also citizens of the world who must be faithful to the universal principles proclaimed by the Church. While some other countries also possess nuclear weapons, we may not forget that the United States was the first to build and to use them. Like the Soviet Union, this country now possesses so many weapons as to imperil the continuation of civilization. Americans share responsibility for the current situation, and cannot evade responsibility for trying to resolve it.

327. The virtue of patriotism means that as citizens we respect and honor our country, but our very love and loyalty make us examine carefully and regularly its role in world affairs, asking that it live up to its full potential as an agent of peace with justice for all people.

> Citizens must cultivate a generous and loyal spirit of patriotism, but without being narrow-minded. This means that they will always direct their attention to the good of the whole human family, united by the different ties which bind together races, people, and nations.[124]

328. In a pluralistic democracy like the United States, the Church has a unique opportunity, precisely because of the strong constitutional protection of both religious freedom and freedom of speech and the press, to help call attention to the moral dimensions of public issues. In a previous pastoral letter, *Human Life In Our Day*, we said: "In our democratic system, the fundamental right of political dissent cannot be denied, nor is rational debate on public policy deci-

123. John Paul II, "Address at Hiroshima," #2, *Origins* 10 (1981):620.

124. *Pastoral Constitution*, #75.

sions of government in the light of moral and political principles to be discouraged. It is the duty of the governed to analyze responsibly the concrete issues of public policy."[125] In fulfilling this role, the Church helps to create a community of conscience in the wider civil community. It does this in the first instance by teaching clearly within the Church the moral principles which bind and shape the Catholic conscience. The Church also fulfills a teaching role, however, in striving to share the moral wisdom of the Catholic tradition with the larger society.

329.   In the wider public discussion, we look forward in a special way to cooperating with all other Christians with whom we share common traditions. We also treasure cooperative efforts with Jewish and Islamic communities, which possess a long and abiding concern for peace as a religious and human value. Finally, we reaffirm our desire to participate in a common public effort with all men and women of good will who seek to reverse the arms race and secure the peace of the world.

---

125. *Human Life in Our Day*, cited, p. 41.

CONCLUSION

330. As we close this lengthy letter, we try to answer two key questions as directly as we can.

331. Why do we address these matters fraught with such complexity, controversy and passion? We speak as pastors, not politicians. We are teachers, not technicians. We cannot avoid our responsibility to lift up the moral dimensions of the choices before our world and nation. The nuclear age is an era of moral as well as physical danger. We are the first generation since Genesis with the power to virtually destroy God's creation. We cannot remain silent in the face of such danger. Why do we address these issues? We are simply trying to live up to the call of Jesus to be peacemakers in our own time and situation.

332. What are we saying? Fundamentally, we are saying that the decisions about nuclear weapons are among the most pressing moral questions of our age. While these decisions have obvious military and political aspects, they involve fundamental moral choices. In simple terms, we are saying that good ends (defending one's country, protecting freedom, etc.) cannot justify immoral means (the use of weapons which kill indiscriminately and threaten whole societies). We fear that our world and nation are headed in the wrong direction. More weapons with greater destructive potential are produced every day. More and more nations are seeking to become nuclear powers. In our quest for more and more security, we fear we are actually becoming less and less secure.

333. In the words of our Holy Father, we need a "moral about-face." The whole world must summon the moral courage and technical means to say "no" to nuclear conflict; "no" to weapons of mass destruction; "no" to an arms race which robs the poor and the vulnerable; and "no" to the moral danger of a nuclear age which places before humankind indefensible choices of constant terror or surrender. Peacemaking is not an optional commitment. It is a requirement of our faith. We are called to be peacemakers, not by some movement of the moment, but by our Lord Jesus. The content and context of our peacemaking is set, not by some political agenda or ideological program, but by the teaching of his Church.

334. Thus far in this pastoral letter we have made suggestions we hope will be helpful in the present world crisis. Looking ahead to the long and productive future of humanity for which we all hope, we feel that a more all-inclusive and final solution is needed. We speak here of the truly effective international author-

336

ity for which Pope John XXIII ardently longed in *Peace on Earth*,[126] and of which Pope Paul VI spoke to the United Nations on his visit there in 1965.[127] The hope for such a structure is not unrealistic, because the point has been reached where public opinion sees clearly that, with the massive weaponry of the present, war is no longer viable. There *is* a substitute for war. There is negotiation under the supervision of a global body realistically fashioned to do its job. It must be given the equipment to keep constant surveillance on the entire earth. Present technology makes this possible. It must have the authority, freely conferred upon it by all the nations, to investigate what seems to be preparations for war by any one of them. It must be empowered by all the nations to enforce its commands on every nation. It must be so constituted as to pose no threat to any nation's sovereignty. Obviously the creation of such a sophisticated instrumentality is a gigantic task, but is it hoping for too much to believe that the genius of humanity, aided by the grace and guidance of God, is able to accomplish it? To create it may take decades of unrelenting daily toil by the world's best minds and most devoted hearts, but it shall never come into existence unless we make a beginning now.

335. As we come to the end of our pastoral letter we boldly propose the beginning of this work. The evil of the proliferation of nuclear arms becomes more evident every day to all people. No one is exempt from their danger. If ridding the world of the weapons of war could be done easily, the whole human race would do it gladly tomorrow. Shall we shrink from the task because it is hard?

336. We turn to our own government and we beg it to propose to the United Nations that it begin this work immediately; that it create an international task force for peace; that this task force, with membership open to every nation, meet daily through the years ahead with one sole agenda: the creation of a world that will one day be safe from war. Freed from the bondage of war that holds it captive in its threat, the world will at last be able to address its problems and to make genuine human progress, so that every day there may be more freedom, more food, and more opportunity for every human being who walks the face of the earth.

337. Let us have the courage to believe in the bright future and in a God who wills it for us—not a perfect world, but a better one. The perfect world, we Christians believe, is beyond the horizon, in an endless eternity where God will be all in all. But a better world is here for human hands and hearts and minds to make.

338. For the community of faith the risen Christ is the beginning and end of all things. For all things were created through him and all things will return to the Father through him.

339. It is our belief in the risen Christ which sustains us in confronting the

---

126. John XXIII, *Peace on Earth* (1963), #137.

127. Paul VI, "Address to the General Assembly of the United Nations," (1965), #2.

awesome challenge of the nuclear arms race. Present in the beginning as the word of the Father, present in history as the word incarnate, and with us today in his word, sacraments, and spirit, he is the reason for our hope and faith. Respecting our freedom, he does not solve our problems but sustains us as we take responsibility for his work of creation and try to shape it in the ways of the kingdom. We believe his grace will never fail us. We offer this letter to the Church and to all who can draw strength and wisdom from it in the conviction that we must not fail him. We must subordinate the power of the nuclear age to human control and direct it to human benefit. As we do this we are conscious of God's continuing work among us, which will one day issue forth in the beautiful final kingdom prophesied by the seer of the Book of Revelation:

> Then I saw a new heaven and a new earth; for the first heaven and the first earth had passed away and the sea was no more. And I saw the holy city, new Jerusalem, coming down out of heaven from God, prepared as a bride adorned for her husband; and I heard a great voice from the throne saying, "Behold, the dwelling of God is with men. He will dwell with them, and they shall be his people, and God himself will be with them, he will wipe away every tear from their eyes, and death shall be no more, neither shall there be mourning nor crying nor pain any more, for the former things have passed away." And he who sat upon the throne said, "Behold, I make all things new" (Rv. 21:1-5).

APPENDIX 1

Declaration on Prevention of Nuclear War

Presented to His Holiness the Pope by an assembly of Presidents of Scientific Academies and other scientists from all over the world convened by the Pontifical Academy of Sciences (24 September 1982)

I. Preamble

Throughout its history, humanity has been confronted with war, but since 1945 the nature of warfare has changed so profoundly that the future of the human race, of generations yet unborn, is imperilled. At the same time, mutual contacts and means of understanding between peoples of the world have been increasing. This is why the yearning for peace is now stronger than ever. Humanity is confronted today with a threat unprecedented in history, arising from the massive and competitive accumulation of nuclear weapons. The existing arsenals, if employed in a major war, could result in the immediate deaths of many hundreds of millions of people, and of untold millions more later through a variety of after-effects. For the first time, it is possible to cause damage on such a catastrophic scale as to wipe out a large part of civilization and to endanger its very survival. The large-scale use of such weapons could trigger major and irreversible ecological and genetic changes, whose limits cannot be predicted.

Science can offer the world no real defense against the consequences of nuclear war. There is no prospect of making defenses sufficiently effective to protect cities since even a single penetrating nuclear weapon can cause massive destruction. There is no prospect that the mass of the population could be protected against a major nuclear attack or that devastation of the cultural, economic and industrial base of society could be prevented. The breakdown of social organization, and the magnitude of casualties, will be so large that no medical system can be expected to cope with more than a minute fraction of the victims.

There are now some 50,000 nuclear weapons, some of which have yields a thousand times greater than the bomb that destroyed Hiroshima. The total explosive content of these weapons is equivalent to a million Hiroshima bombs, which corresponds to a yield of some three tons of TNT for every person on earth. Yet these stockpiles continue to grow. Moreover, we face the increasing danger that many additional countries will acquire nuclear weapons or develop the capability of producing them.

There is today an almost continuous range of explosive power from the smallest battlefield nuclear weapons to the most destructive megaton warhead. Nuclear weapons are regarded not only as a deterrent, but also as a tactical weapon for use in a general war under so-called controlled conditions. The immense and increasing stockpiles of nuclear weapons, and their broad dispersal in the armed forces, increase the probability of their being used through accident or miscalculation in times of heightened political or military tension. The risk is very great that any use of nuclear weapons, however limited, would escalate to general nuclear war.

The world situation has deteriorated. Mistrust and suspicion between nations have grown. There is a breakdown of serious dialogue between the East and West and between North and South. Serious inequities among nations and within nations, shortsighted national or partisan ambitions, and lust for power are the seeds of conflict which may lead to general and nuclear warfare. The scandal of poverty, hunger, and degradation is in itself becoming an increasing threat to peace. There appears to be a growing fatalistic acceptance that war is inevitable and that wars will be fought with nuclear weapons. In any such war there will be no winners.

Not only the potentialities of nuclear weapons, but also those of chemical, biological and even conventional weapons are increasing by the steady accumulation of new knowledge. It is therefore to be expected that the means of non-nuclear war, as horrible as they already are, will also become more destructive if nothing is done to prevent it. Human wisdom, however, remains comparatively limited, in dramatic contrast with the apparently inexorable growth of the power of destruction. It is the duty of scientists to help prevent the perversion of their achievements and to stress that the future of mankind depends upon the acceptance by all nations of moral principles transcending all other considerations. Recognizing the natural rights of human beings to survive and to live in dignity, science must be used to assist humanity towards a life of fulfillment and peace.

Considering these overwhelming dangers that confront all of us, it is the duty of every person of good will to face this threat. All disputes that we are concerned with today, including political, economical, ideological and religious ones, are small compared to the hazards of nuclear war. It is imperative to reduce distrust and to increase hope and confidence through a succession of steps to curb the development, testing, production and deployment of nuclear weapons systems, and to reduce them to substantially lower levels, with the ultimate hope of their complete elimination.

To avoid wars and achieve a meaningful peace, not only the powers of intelligence are needed, but also the powers of ethics, morality and conviction.

The catastrophe of nuclear war can and must be prevented, and leaders and governments have a grave responsibility in this regard. But it is humanity as a whole which must act for its survival; it faces its greatest moral issue, and there is no time to be lost.

II. In view of these threats of global nuclear catastrophe, we declare:

–Nuclear weapons are fundamentally different from conventional weapons. They must not be regarded as acceptable instruments of warfare. Nuclear warfare would be a crime against humanity.

–It is of utmost importance that there be no armed conflict between nuclear powers because of the danger that nuclear weapons would be used.

–The use of force anywhere as a method of settling international conflicts entails the risk of military confrontation of nuclear powers.

–The proliferation of nuclear weapons to additional countries seriously increases the risk of nuclear war and could lead to nuclear terrorism.

–The current arms race increases the risk of nuclear war. The race must be stopped, the development of new more destructive weapons must be curbed, and nuclear forces must be reduced, with the ultimate goal of complete nuclear disarmament. The sole purpose of nuclear weapons, as long as they exist, must be to deter nuclear war.

III. Recognizing that excessive conventional forces that increase mistrust and could lead to confrontation with the risk of nuclear war, and that all differences and territorial disputes should be resolved by negotiation, arbitration or other peaceful means, we call upon all nations:

–Never to be the first to use nuclear weapons;

–To seek termination of hostilities immediately in the appalling event that nuclear weapons are ever used;

–To abide by the principle that force or the threat of force will not be used against the territorial integrity or political independence of another state;

–To renew and increase efforts to reach verifiable agreements curbing the arms race and reducing the numbers of nuclear weapons and delivery systems. These agreements should be monitored by the most effective technical means. Political differences or territorial disputes must not be allowed to interfere with this objective;

–To find more effective ways and means to prevent the further proliferation of nuclear weapons. The nuclear powers, and in particular the superpowers, have a special obligation to set an example in reducing armaments and to create a climate conducive to non-proliferation. Moreover, all nations have the duty to prevent the diversion of peaceful uses of nuclear energy to the proliferation of nuclear weapons;

–To take all practical measures that reduce the possibility of nuclear war by accident, miscalculation or irrational action;

–To continue to observe existing arms limitation agreements while seeking to negotiate broader and more effective agreements.

IV. Finally, we appeal:

1. To national leaders, to take the initiative in seeking steps to reduce the risk of nuclear war, looking beyond narrow concerns for national advantage; and to reject military conflict as a means of resolving disputes.

2. To scientists, to use their creativity for the betterment of human life and to apply their ingenuity in exploring means of avoiding nuclear war and developing practical methods of arms control.
3. To religious leaders and other custodians of moral principles, to proclaim forcefully and persistently the grave human issues at stake so that these are fully understood and appreciated by society.
4. To people everywhere, to reaffirm their faith in the destiny of humanity, to insist that the avoidance of war is a common responsibility, to combat the belief that nuclear conflict is unavoidable, and to labor unceasingly toward insuring the future of generations to come.

Participants in Conference on Nuclear Warfare
The Pontifical Academy of Sciences
Vatican City
23–24 September, 1982

E. Amaldi	Italy	M. Lora-Tamayo	Spain
I. Badran*	Egypt	T. Malone (SC)	USA
A. Balevski*	Bulgaria	G.B. Marini-Bet-tolo*	Italy
D.A. Bekoe (Ghana)*	International Council of Scientific Unions	M. Menon*(SC)	India
F. Benvenuti	Italy	G. Montalenti	Italy
O. Bikov	Russia	M. Peixoto	Brazil
B. Bilinski	Poland	J. Peters	Belgium
C. Chagas (Brazil)*	Vatican	G. Porter	England
B. Dinkov	Bulgaria	F. Press*	USA
G. Hambraeus*	Sweden	G. Puppi	Italy
T. Hesburgh (SC)	USA	B. Rifai	Indonesia
H. Hiatt (SC)	USA	W. Rosenblith	USA
D. Hodgkins (England)*	Pugwash Conference	P. Rossano	Italy
		P. Rudomin*	Mexico
S. Hsieh	Taipei	B. Rysavy	Czechoslovakia
A. Huxley*	England	I. Saavedra	Chile
S. Iijima	Japan	V. Sardi*	Venezuela
S. Isaev	Russia	T. Shin	Korea
P. Jacquinot*(SC)	France	E. Simpson*	South Africa
W. Kalweit	E. Germany	J. Sirotkovic*	Yugoslavia
M. Kazi	Pakistan	L. Sosnovski*	Poland
S. Keeny (SC)	USA	O. Stoppani*	Argentina
K. Komarek	Austria	J. Szentagothai*	Hungary
F. Konig (SC)	Austria	S. Tanneberger	E. Germany
J. Labarbe	Belgium	C. Townes	USA
J. Lejeune	France	E. Velikhov*(SC)	Russia
L. Leprince-Ringuet	France	W. Watts*	Ireland
R. Levi-Montalcini	Italy	V. Weisskopf (SC)	USA

*President of national academy of science (17), national academy of engineering (Hambraeus), or equivalent (Bekoe and Hodgkins). Total: 20.
(SC) Members of Steering Committee. In addition to those indicated here, there are three: C.F. Von Weizeacker, West Germany; K. Husimi, Japan; and M. Perutz, England.

APPENDIX 2

Statement by Religious Leaders

Vienna, 15 January 1983

Last September at a meeting called by the Pontifical Academy of Sciences in Rome, presidents or their representatives of 36 academies of science from around the world issued a statement entitled, "Declaration on Prevention of Nuclear War," in which they told us of the catastrophic consequences for humanity of a nuclear war. They warned us there is no real defense against the weapons now poised in the arsenals of nuclear powers. They pointed to the fact that the world is drifting toward a fatalistic acceptance of the inevitability of nuclear conflict. They said the issue is not one to be confronted only by reason. It is not simply a problem to be solved by factual analysis, but one which demands to be examined from the standpoint of faith and of moral values.

As persons from diverse religious traditions, we are impressed by the declaration of these eminent scientists; we speak as one to emphasize that humanity for the first time in history has the power to destroy itself. We believe that there is no cause that would morally justify the death and destruction caused by a nuclear conflagration. We deny the assertion that any side can "win" a nuclear war. As believers, our first duty is to praise our Creator and revere the life given us. Indeed, the longing for peace is deep in the breast of all peoples. But peace is both a gift of the Creator and a work of ours. Genuine peace cannot be based on mutually assured destruction; balanced nuclear terror mocks the message of love shared by all religions. Lasting peace can only be based upon global justice, respect for the dignity of each person, a conversion of mind and heart regarding war and peace, and, finally, the Creator's call for reconciliation between estranged peoples.

To the statement of the scientists we add our own declaration of moral and religious conviction. We must begin now to reduce the number of nuclear weapons stockpiled and deployed. We must stop an arms race that produces ever more sophisticated agents of annihilation at enormous cost, diverting resources that could be used to feed, clothe, house and cure millions of people in need. We must end the international proliferation of nuclear weapons. We must repudiate as a means of settling disputes between nation-states a destructive force that outstrips our ability to calculate its effects. We believe that nations must not threaten the existence and well-being of their opponents but must engage in dialogue and collaborative efforts to improve social and cultural conditions all over the world. We must press continually toward the ultimate goal of total elimination of nuclear weapons, remembering that what human beings have made, they can unmake. Fatalism must give way to hope.

What faith impels us to say here in Vienna must be fortified by the hope that it is possible to build a world which will reflect the love of the Creator and respect for the life given us, a life certainly not destined to destroy itself. Because of the deterioration of the international political atmosphere and the great danger posed by the rapid developments in military technology, humanity today is in a critical period of its history. We join the scientists in their call for urgent action to achieve verifiable disarmament agreements leading to the elimination of nuclear weapons. Nothing less is at stake than the future of humanity, with its rich and variegated cultures and religious traditions.

Signers of Statement of Religious Leaders

Franz Cardinal Koenig, Archbishop of Vienna
Rev. Theodore M. Hesburgh, President University of Notre Dame (USA)
Bishop James Armstrong, President National Council of Churches of Christ (USA)
Bishop Anba Gregorios, Cairo (Coptic)
Paulus Mar Gregorios, Metropolitan of Delhi, India (Orthodox)
Rev. J. Bryan Hehir, Director, Office of International Affairs, United States Catholic Conference
Archbishop Jean Jadot, Pro-President, Vatican Secretariat for Non-Christians
Dr. Hashim Mahdi (signed as observer), Muslim World League, London
Archbishop John R. Roach, President, National Council of Catholic Bishops (USA)
Professor and Rev. Keith Ward, University of London (Anglican)
Ahmed Zabara, Grand Mufti of United Yemen (Muslim)

Scientific Consultants to the Meeting (not signatories)

Professor André Guinier, French Academy of Sciences
Dr. Howard Hiatt, Harvard University School of Public Health (USA)
Dr. Spurgeon M. Keeny, National Academy of Sciences (USA)
Professor G.K. Skryabin, USSR Academy of Sciences
Professor Yerguenij Velikhov, USSR Academy of Sciences
Professor Victor F. Weisskopf, Massachusetts Institute of Technology (USA), Pontifical Academy of Sciences

Contributors

Charles E. Curran is ordinary professor of moral theology at Catholic University of America. His most recent book is *American Catholic Social Ethics*.

Harry A. Fagan is associate director of the National Pastoral Life Center. He is the former director of the Commission for Catholic Community Action of the Diocese of Cleveland and former chairman of the Catholic Committee on Urban Ministry. Mr. Fagan has published *Empowerment: Skills for Parish Social Ministry*.

James Finn is editor of *Freedom at Issue* published by Freedom House, an independent organization formed to support principles of democracy and human rights around the world. He has written on morality, politics, and modern war for many years.

John C. Haughey, S.J., is a research fellow of the Woodstock Theological Center. Father Haughey's interests and writings are in areas of political theology, the relationships between faith and justice, and spirituality for public servants among other areas. He has edited *The Faith That Does Justice* and *Personal Values and Public Policy*.

J. Bryan Hehir is director of the Office of International Affairs of the United States Catholic Conference and visiting lecturer at St. John's Seminary in Boston. Father Hehir served on the staff of the Bernardin Committee for the bishops' pastoral on war and peace.

Theodore M. Hesburgh, C.S.C., is president of the University of Notre Dame. He has also served in many public positions related to human rights and human development.

David Hollenbach, S.J., is associate professor of moral theology and program director of the Th.M. program at Weston School of Theology in Cambridge, Massachusetts. Father Hollenbach's writings include the book *Claims in Conflict: Retrieving and Renewing the Catholic Human Rights Tradition*.

George F. Kennan is a former ambassador to the Soviet Union and Yugoslavia and is a leading expert on Russian affairs. He is currently professor emeritus at the Institute for Advanced Study, at Princeton University. Mr. Kennan has published widely and has won two Pulitzer Prizes and two National Book Awards. His most recent book is *The Nuclear Delusion: Soviet-American Relations in the Atomic Age*.

Joseph A. Komonchak is associate professor of religion and religious education at Catholic University of America. His research and writing have been in the areas of ecclesiology, the development of theology, and the relationship between the church and the social order.

Richard A. McCormick, S.J., is Rose F. Kennedy Professor of Christian Ethics of the Kennedy Institute of Ethics, Georgetown University. His most recent book, co-authored with Charles Curran, is *Readings in Moral Theology III: Morality and Authority*.

Philip J. Murnion is director of the National Pastoral Life Center and director of clergy continuing education for the Archdiocese of New York. Father Murnion has written widely on questions of parish, ministry, and specifically on the social ministry of the church. He is former director of The Parish Project of the National Conference of Catholic Bishops.

William E. Murnion is associate professor of philosophy and religious studies at Ramapo College, New Jersey. His research is in the areas of philosophy of history and critical thinking.

David J. O'Brien is associate professor of history at Holy Cross College. His research and writing have been devoted to the American Catholic experience. He co-edited with Thomas Shannon *Renewing the Earth: Catholic Documents on Justice, Peace and Liberation* and is currently completing a biography of Isaac Hecker, founder of the Congregation of St. Paul (Paulist Fathers).

Bruce Martin Russett is professor of political science at Yale University and served on the staff of the Bernardin Committee for the pastoral. His most recent book is *Prisoners of Insecurity*.

Sandra M. Schneiders, I.H.M., is associate professor of New Testament and Spirituality at the Jesuit School of Theology at Berkeley and the Graduate Theological Union. She serves as associate editor of the *Catholic Biblical Quarterly* and the *Classics of Western Spirituality*. She has published many articles in journals such as *Theological Studies, Thought*, and *Biblical Theology Bulletin*.

Peter Steinfels is executive editor of *Commonweal* magazine. He has written widely on the history and philosophy of public policy and is the author of *The Neo-Conservatives*.

Lester C. Thurow is professor of management and economics at the Sloan School of Management, M.I.T. Professor Thurow has published widely on matters of economics and economic policy. His most recent book is *Dangerous Currents*.

Gordon C. Zahn is director of the Pax Chrisi USA Center on Conscience and War in Cambridge, Massachusetts, and professor emeritus of the University of Massachusetts in Boston. Dr. Zahn, a sociologist, has written widely on questions of war and peace and particularly on pacifism.